NOTE: Turn to *How to Use This Book* (page xiv) for further guidance in using this text. All grammar and usage lessons are based on a similar organization, and the model presented in this section walks you through a sample lesson.

FIFTH EDITION

A Commonsense Guide to Grammar and Usage

Larry Beason

University of South Alabama

Mark Lester

Eastern Washington University

Bedford/St. Martin's   Boston ◆ New York

FOR BEDFORD/ST. MARTIN'S

Developmental Editor: Anne Leung
Production Editor: Katherine Caruana
Production Supervisor: Jennifer Peterson
Marketing Manager: Casey Carroll
Editorial Assistant: Melissa Cook
Copyeditor: Lisa Wehrle
Indexer: Steve Csipke
Text Design: Claire Seng-Niemoeller
Cover Design: Donna Lee Dennison
Composition: TexTech International
Printing and Binding: RR Donnelley and Sons

President: Joan E. Feinberg
Editorial Director: Denise B. Wydra
Editor in Chief: Karen S. Henry
Director of Marketing: Karen Melton Soeltz
Director of Editing, Design, and Production: Marcia Cohen
Assistant Director of Editing, Design, and Production: Elise S. Kaiser
Managing Editor: Elizabeth M. Schaaf

Library of Congress Control Number: 2008923919

For information, write:
Bedford/St. Martin's, 75 Arlington Street, Boston, MA 02116
(617-399-4000)

ISBN-10: 0–312–54618–1
ISBN-13: 978–0–312–54618–2

Preface for Instructors

A Commonsense Guide to Grammar and Usage, Fifth Edition, helps students to write clear, error-free sentences by combining the easy access of a reference handbook with the practicality of a skills workbook. This book is intended for a range of students who need a firmer foundation in the grammar and usage of formal writing. These students might be enrolled in a beginning writing course, an ESL course, a first-year composition course, or a course in a field such as business, history, or science.

At the core of our approach is the firm belief that errors can be signs of risk taking, experimentation, and growth. Once students understand that errors are part of the learning process and do not necessarily reflect a lack of effort or ability, they can develop the confidence they need to recognize and correct sentence-level problems in their own writing—something they can do without an overwhelming amount of grammar terminology. We wrote this book, and agreed to revise it, because we believe students and teachers need a textbook largely devoted to commonsense ways to avoid common errors. Avoiding errors is not the most important aspect of writing effectively, but it is important enough to deserve writers' attention.

What Does This Book Offer—and Why?

The following combination of features makes this textbook a uniquely practical resource for instructors and students.

Emphasis on the most common errors keeps students focused on essential skills. Using a straightforward, practice-oriented approach, *A Commonsense Guide* helps students learn to identify and correct thirty-eight common problems in written English. On the basis of research, experience, and feedback from students and teachers, we concentrate on the grammar and usage problems that occur most frequently or are most distracting in the writing of first-year college students.

Easy-to-remember tips simplify grammar and usage. Each grammar lesson includes at least one handy tip—a commonsense way of identifying and correcting an error. These tips, located in easy-to-find boxes, rely not on complex rules but on intuitive, practical strategies that writers actually use. Presented as friendly pieces of advice, these tips are easier for students to remember and apply than hard-and-fast rules or intimidating technical explanations.

Accessible, everyday language builds students' confidence. The text's explanations and tips are written in clear, everyday language, so students will be confident about (rather than intimidated by) grammar and usage. We place special emphasis on learning how to identify and correct problems—not on learning terminology. We even include hand-edited example errors in the table of contents so students do not have to rely on grammar terms to find help for a specific problem.

The text shows students—rather than just telling them—how to avoid the most serious errors in their writing. Each lesson involves hands-on practice, so that students do not merely read about errors and how to correct them. Even before this practice, each lesson guides students through several examples so that they can "see" how to identify and correct problems. Along these lines, the lessons are designed to engage visual learners, with ample charts and diagrams.

Modular approach to grammar breaks complex topics into manageable lessons. To avoid overwhelming students, we focus each lesson on a single, essential skill and follow a consistent organization.

- Brief diagnostic exercises in each lesson show whether students need help with a particular topic.

- Each lesson opens with at least two sample errors and corrections. We then offer a straightforward explanation of the errors—we explain why even the most intelligent writer might be confused about formal English.

- Next, we offer correction strategies centered on each lesson's commonsense tips. We not only help students identify errors, we also equip them with practical strategies for revising their writing to make it error free.

How to Use This Book, on pages xiv–xviii, guides students through a sample lesson.

Abundant, carefully sequenced exercises build skills. Each lesson concludes with ample opportunities for students to practice what they learn, as they find and fix errors in sentences, paragraphs, and finally in their own writing.

A reference that students can use on their own. While lessons and exercises can be assigned as classwork or homework, several features allow the book to be used as a self-paced reference that students use on their own.

- The inside back cover offers a quick way to find major topics or grammatical issues (see Finding What You Need in This Book).

- The table of contents includes sample errors for each lesson so students do not have to rely on grammar terms to locate specific topics.

- A chart of common correction symbols directs students to the right lessons as well.

- In the back of the book, answers to some exercises allow for self-study.

- The spiral binding, two-color format, tabbed unit dividers, and boxed tips and checklists make the book quick and easy to navigate.

Practical coverage of reading, writing, and research. Unit Twelve: A Commonsense Writing Guide is a mini-rhetoric that balances two important issues. Students often want "bottom line" advice about what to do — and what not to do — as they write. However, many aspects of writing are too complex to reduce to fixed rules. Students need to understand that writers must react to their own writing situations — not to a formula or a set of rules. The following features help balance these two important concepts:

- A lesson on critical reading provides an overview of the connections between reading and writing and helps students understand how to respond to what they read. Student examples illustrate the critical reading and annotating process, and reading tips and checklists highlight practical strategies.

- The planning stage of the writing process receives special emphasis.

- Commonsense tips throughout offer practical advice for completing each stage of the writing process.

- Goal-oriented checklists and critical thinking questions guide students as they write expressive, informative, and persuasive paragraphs and essays.

- Sample student-written thesis statements, outlines, and drafts of student writing offer accessible models.

- A to-the-point documentation appendix features the latest MLA guidelines with plenty of examples.

Support for non-native speakers of English. ESL coverage is separated into two easy-to-locate units (Unit Ten ESL: Choosing the Right Article and Unit Eleven ESL: Using Verbs Correctly). Throughout the rest of the book, ESL icons 🌐 in the margins point out topics that may be especially challenging to non-native speakers of English.

New to This Edition

As we planned the fifth edition of *A Commonsense Guide*, students and teachers asked us to take our commonsense approach even further, to make the book even easier to use. We do so by simplifying our explanations and using even less technical grammatical terminology, offering more help for visual learners, and adding more reference features that help students use the book on their own.

More quick reference aids and an improved design help students find what they need. Unit Review charts succinctly explain problem areas, direct students to relevant tips, and now include sample errors and corrections. New diagrams, bulleted lists, and boxes make concepts easier to understand.

Up-to-date, real-life examples reflect topics students care about. Almost half of the Editing Practices have been revised to address fresh, engaging topics such as choosing a major, dealing with a difficult boss, and moving into an apartment.

More practice with sentences for the most frequently assigned lessons. Instructors asked for more exercises, and now almost half of the lessons have an expanded set of Sentence Practices with ten sentences. Many of these expanded sets ask students to combine sentences.

More thorough and practical coverage of commas. The text groups the lessons on commas together in one cohesive unit, clearly outlining when and where to use a comma.

New and strengthened commonsense tips offer clearer help. We revised tips for misplaced and squinting adverbs, pronouns, and apostrophes.

New Applying What You Know activities and Critical Questions in Unit Twelve. Each lesson in A Commonsense Writing Guide ends with a hands-on activity that reinforces a key skill and a list of questions to consider at each stage of the writing process.

More MLA documentation models. In addition to updating models, we have added more examples of how to properly document electronic sources.

New glossary of commonly misspelled words. This handy appendix warns students not to rely on spell-checkers and offers practical tips on how to actively learn these challenging words.

Practical Resources for Instructors and Students

The Book Companion Site, at **bedfordstmartins.com/commonsense**, offers helpful resources for both students and instructors. For students, we offer Exercise Central practices, links to ESL resources on the Web, and Bottom Line boxes from the text. For instructors, we provide the complete text of the instructor's resource manual, a Quiz Gradebook for monitoring students' progress on Exercise Central, and links to resources for teaching ESL.

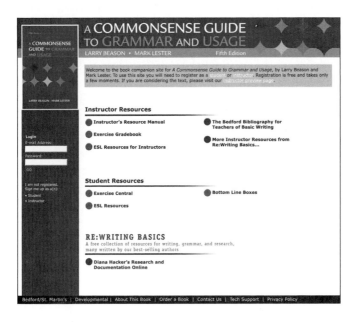

Re:Writing Basics, at **bedfordstmartins.com/rewritingbasics**, is an extensive collection of our most widely used online resources for the developmental writing course on a free, easy-to-access Web site. For students, there are helpful tutorials, exercises, research guides, bibliography tools, and more. For instructors, *Re:Writing Basics* offers such resources as *The Bedford Bibliography for Teachers of Basic Writing* and other free bibliographies, workshops, and online journals for professional development.

Exercise Central 3.0, at **bedfordstmartins.com/exercisecentral**, with over 8,000 items, is the largest online collection of grammar exercises available. Conveniently arranged by topic and level, *Exercise Central* is now a comprehensive resource for skill development as well as skill assessment. In addition to immediate feedback and reporting, *Exercise Central* can help identify students' strengths and weaknesses, recommend personalized study plans, and provide tutorials for common problems. The exercises are also available on a CD-ROM, *Exercise Central To Go.* (package ISBN-13: 978-0-312-55030-1, ISBN-10: 0-312-55030-8)

Make-a-Paragraph Kit **CD-ROM** gives students all the tools they need to write successful paragraphs, and the visuals, sound, and interactivity appeal to all types of learning styles. (package ISBN-13: 978-0-312-55027-1, ISBN-10: 0-312-55027-8)

The Bedford/St. Martin's ESL Workbook supports students that have varying English-language skills and cultural backgrounds. (package ISBN-13: 978-0-312-55028-8, ISBN-10: 0-312-55028-6)

Testing Tool Kit: A Writing and Grammar Test Bank allows instructors to test students' writing and grammar skills by creating secure, customized tests and quizzes from a pool of nearly 2,000 questions. (package ISBN-13: 978-0-312-43032-0, ISBN-10: 0-312-43032-9)

Instructor's Resource Manual to Accompany A Commonsense Guide to Grammar and Usage offers the following extensive support for instructors:

- Advice on teaching grammar and usage
- Four sample syllabi that pair *A Commonsense Guide* with Bedford/St. Martin's readers
- A full chapter on teaching ESL students
- Lesson-by-lesson teaching tips for using *A Commonsense Guide* in the classroom or as a reference that students use on their own
- Answers to the Unit Review tests and the final practices in each lesson
- Supplemental exercises for additional practice, along with answers
- Tips on how to use Exercise Central

Instructor's Resource Manual
to Accompany

A COMMONSENSE
GUIDE TO GRAMMAR
AND USAGE

LARRY BEASON · MARK LESTER

Acknowledgments

We would like to thank the following instructors who responded to a questionnaire that allowed us to develop the fifth edition of this book: Elisabeth Aiken, Saint Leo University; Bill Beverly, Trinity College; Vicki Byard, Northeastern Illinois University; Ja'net Daniels, Long Beach City College and Cerritos College; Leah Dilworth, Long Island University–Brooklyn; Kathleen Dorantes, Imperial Valley College; Jaclyn Geller, Central Connecticut State University; Karen George, Ashland Community and Technical College; Tom Ghering, Ivy Tech Community College of Indiana; Barbara Henry, West Virginia State University; Debbie Hlady, Camosun College; Cindy Hubble, Bakersfield College; Jill Hughes, Casper College; Steven Konopacki, Palm Beach Community College; Elisabeth Kuhn, Virginia Commonwealth University; Scott Nelson, Bellevue Community College; Teresa Roberts, University of Maine–Farmington; Delrita Rudnitski, St. Cloud Technical College; Mary Stewart, Reedley College; Elizabeth M. Sturgeon, Mount St. Mary's College; Bonita Sutliff, University of Wisconsin–Superior; Kerry L. Thomas, Rufus King International Baccalaureate High School; Beth VanRheenen, Lourdes College; Bradley Whitman, Community College of Southern Nevada; Marjorie Wikoff, St. Petersburg College; Monica Windley, Community College of Baltimore County; Elizabeth Winkler, Western Kentucky University; Rebecca Wolfe, Cornerstone University; and Steven Yarborough, Bellevue Community College.

We extend special thanks to the people at Bedford/St. Martin's for their significant contributions to this revision: Anne Leung, developmental editor; Karin Halbert, Shannon Leuma, Michelle Clark, and Amanda Bristow, for their work on previous editions of *A Commonsense Guide*; Melissa Cook, editorial assistant; Katherine Caruana, production editor; Lisa Wehrle, copyeditor; Chuck Christensen, former president; Joan Feinberg, president; Denise Wydra, editorial director; Karen Henry, editor in chief; Elizabeth Schaaf, managing editor; Casey Carroll, marketing manager; and Claire Seng-Niemoeller, text designer.

Finally, we wish to thank our wives, Colleen Beason and Mary Ann Lester, for their unwavering support and patience.

Larry Beason
Mark Lester

Why Use This Book—For Students

Why use this book? We believe you have a right to an answer. Not only are you paying for this book, but you will also be asked to commit time and energy to its material.

Some people enjoy the study of grammar and the formal rules that tell writers how to put words and sentences together. Most people, however, do not put such study at the top of their list of favorite things to do. So, we are not going to try to "sell" this book by claiming grammar is fun (though it can be for some people). Rather, we want readers to understand why the study of grammar and usage is worthwhile, despite the difficulties of studying language. In addition, we want you to know why this book takes a different approach than most grammar textbooks.

The most pressing reason why you should use this book is that it will help you in many college courses. Students are often surprised to learn how much writing is required outside the English department. Research has proven that history, business, computer science, education, and even math teachers—just to name a few—frequently ask students to write papers or documents. A physics teacher, for example, might ask you to write a detailed lab report so you will learn more about electricity. However, this teacher will not be able to tell if you have learned anything about physics unless your writing is clear. Errors such as fused sentences can make a report hard to follow.

Most teachers look to general rules and conventions that indicate how words, sentences, and punctuation are supposed to be used in formal writing situations. Unless you understand these rules and conventions, numerous teachers—not just English teachers—will be confused, distracted, and even annoyed. If you have ever thought that only English teachers care about "good grammar," now is the time to realize that this assumption is dangerous—dangerous because it can harm your chances for succeeding in college.

You should be aware that people in the workplace can be even more strict about grammar and usage than college teachers. A study conducted by one of the authors of this textbook indicates that businesspeople are greatly affected by writers' errors in formal English. Professionals in the study frequently noted the importance of clear writing in jobs as diverse as banking, health care, software development, and even laboratory work for gold mining companies. These people pointed out many instances when errors, such as comma splices and misspellings, confused readers. These businesspeople also made judgments, based on those errors, about the writers' workplace skills and attitudes. That is, businesspeople sometimes assume that errors reflect negatively on the writer's ability to think logically or to work effectively with other people. Such generalizations are not always valid, but it seems to be part of human nature to make large-scale judgments about people based on how well they use language in formal situations. We are not by any means saying such judgmental behavior is right, but it's what some people do.

In short, we believe this book can help you enable your teachers—and other readers—to concentrate on the more important parts of your writing (namely, the content itself and not the details of your language choices). Briefly, we want to point out why this book can help you in ways that other grammar books might not.

First, this textbook avoids, as much as possible, technical terms and jargon. By giving commonsense explanations and advice, we indicate how to avoid errors. For instance, each lesson focuses on a "tip" that is not really a rule but a piece of advice; this tip is easier to remember and understand than a drawn-out technical explanation. In addition, exercises in each lesson focus on applying these tips so you will remember them. Too many textbooks rely on asking you to find and fix errors, as if you were just a proofreader. In this book, the Sentence Practice exercises help you learn commonsense tips that draw on what you already know about language.

Second, we think you need more than just a quick explanation. Thus, each lesson gives other types of guidance. We think it helps clear up confusion if you understand *why* many people make a certain type of error, so each lesson covers major misconceptions about whatever the lesson focuses on. But most information in each lesson is devoted to how to correct an error—not to rules. We avoid elaborating needlessly about these correction strategies; in fact, we believe it's best to avoid a lengthy lecture. Still, we offer more than the typical one- to two-sentence explanation found in some handbooks.

Why use this book? We wrote it because we found that these strategies have helped students improve one important aspect of academic and workplace writing—grammar and usage. We believe the tools you take from this book will help you succeed in more than one classroom and in more than one stage of life.

Larry Beason
Mark Lester

How to Use This Book

A Commonsense Guide to Grammar and Usage is designed to offer you nuts-and-bolts strategies for improving your writing—especially for improving your sentences. Units One through Eleven, which focus on grammar and usage, help you to identify, understand, and correct errors in your sentences with commonsense advice and plenty of opportunities for practice. Unit Twelve, the writing guide, helps you to read, plan, draft, and revise a paragraph or an essay.

The grammar and usage lessons follow a consistent organization:

Example Errors and Corrections
Look at these examples to see whether you are making a similar error in your writing. (Note that throughout the text, ungrammatical phrases and sentences are indicated by an ✗.) These examples are discussed in greater detail in the *Fixing This Problem in Your Writing* section of each lesson.

EXAMPLE 1	*Renamer Fragment*
Error:	Blocking my driveway was a car. ✗ A huge SUV.
Correction:	Blocking my driveway was a car/ ‚ ᵃ A huge SUV.

EXAMPLE 2	*Adverb Fragment*
Error:	I was really upset. ✗ Because I knew I would be late for work.
Correction:	I was really upset/ because ~~Because~~ I knew I would be late for work.

EXAMPLE 3	*-ing Fragment*
Error:	I beeped my horn a couple of times. ✗ Letting the driver know I had to get out.
Correction:	I beeped my horn a couple of times/ , letting ~~Letting~~ the driver know I had to get out.

What's the Problem?
This section explains a rule or convention of English that causes difficulty for many writers. If English is not your first language, you may want to pay special attention to material marked by this symbol: 🌐 **ESL**

Boldface words are defined in Appendix B: Guide to Grammar Terminology.

What's the Problem?

A **run-on sentence** contains two **independent clauses** that have been incorrectly joined together. (An independent clause is a group of words that can stand alone as a complete sentence.) Run-on sentences fail to show the reader where one idea ends and the next one begins.

The examples above illustrate two types of run-on sentence errors. When two independent clauses are joined with no punctuation at all, the error is called a **fused sentence**. When two independent clauses are joined with just a comma (without a coordinating conjunction like *and*, *but*, *or*), the error is called a **comma splice**. In both cases, the writer confuses the reader by failing to correctly signal the separation between two complete ideas.

In the following examples, notice how the clauses are separated by nothing at all or by just a comma.

Diagnostic Exercise
To find out if you need help with the topic of the lesson, do this exercise. Then check your answers in the back of the book.

> ### Diagnostic Exercise
>
> CORRECTED SENTENCES APPEAR ON PAGE 457.
>
> Correct all errors in the following paragraph using the first correction as a model. The number in parentheses at the end of the paragraph indicates how many errors you should find.
>
> I wish I could change my worst bad habit. ~~Always~~ , *always* running late. I am always tempted to do just one more thing before heading out the door in the morning. I know I am going to be busy all day. Trying to balance schoolwork with my job. I have learned that it helps to make a schedule. Which I really do try to follow. However, I never seem to budget enough time for routine chores. Because I really hate doing things in a sloppy way. As a result, I am always tempted to take an extra minute or two to do things right. The problem is that those few extra minutes quickly add up. Before I know it, I am late. Again. Another problem is that I don't have enough time built in for unexpected delays. Which seem to happen with depressing regularity. You wouldn't believe what happened to me this morning. A huge SUV was parked in front of my driveway. Blocking me for a good fifteen minutes. (6)

Fixing This Problem in Your Writing
This section offers practical strategies for identifying and correcting the error.

Fixing This Problem in Your Writing

Identifying Run-ons

Run-ons are easy to correct once you have identified them. The problem is finding them to begin with. Here is a tip for spotting potential run-on sentences in your writing.

Commonsense Tip
Use this concrete strategy to identify or correct the error.

> **IMAGINARY PERIOD TIP** If a sentence contains two separate ideas, put an imaginary period between them. Now ask: Can BOTH parts now stand alone as complete sentences? If so, then the sentence might be a run-on.

Correction Sequence
This sequence shows you how to apply the commonsense tip to correct the example errors. Use this same step-by-step strategy to help you identify, understand, and correct errors in your writing.

A third way to punctuate two independent clauses is to combine them with a comma and a **coordinating conjunction** (*for, and, nor, but, or, yet, so*). We'll illustrate this method with Example 1 from the beginning of the lesson.

Example 1:   ✗ I have a test on Thursday it should not be difficult.

Tip applied: I have a test on Thursday. It should not be difficult.

An imaginary period works, so the clauses are independent.

Correction: I have a test on Thursday , *and* it should not be difficult.

Add a comma and conjunction where the imaginary period could go.

More Examples
Study the examples in this section as a further reminder of the concepts in the lesson. *Note:* Only some chapters include this box.

 **More Examples**

Error:	✗ Jamal is a physics major he plans to work for NASA.
Correction:	. He Jamal is a physics major ~~he~~ plans to work for NASA.
Error:	✗ Traffic today was horrible I am thirty minutes late.
Correction:	, so Traffic today was horrible I am thirty minutes late.

Putting It All Together
This checklist will help you identify and correct the error in your writing.

 **Putting It All Together**

Identify Fragments

____ Understand and look for the most common types of fragments: *renamers*, *adverbs*, and *-ing fragments*.

____ Proofread your paper starting at the last sentence and moving to the first, reading one sentence at a time.

____ Put *I realize* in front of each group of words that you think might be a fragment. The *I realize* sentence will not make sense if the word group is a fragment.

Correct Fragments

____ Attach each fragment to the previous sentence, or rewrite the fragment to make it a complete sentence if you want to emphasize it.

Sentence Practice
Do these exercises to practice applying the lesson's tips. You can check your answers to the first two sets against the answer key in the back of the book. A box after the first exercise set directs you to the Web for further practice.

Sentence Practice 1

CORRECTED SENTENCES APPEAR ON PAGE 458.

Find the independent clauses in the following run-on sentences by using the Imaginary Period Tip. Correct each run-on by inserting a semicolon between the two independent clauses, by adding a comma and a coordinating conjunction, or by turning the imaginary period into a real one. If a sentence does not contain a run-on, write *OK* above it.

Example:	My friend owns two pigs he keeps them as house pets.
Tip applied:	My friend owns two pigs. He keeps them as house pets.
Correction:	My friend owns two pigs; he keeps them as house pets.

 For more practice correcting run-ons, go to **Exercise Central** at
bedfordstmartins.com/commonsense

Editing Practice
Do these exercises to practice identifying and correcting the error in a paragraph or mini-essay similar to one you might write. You can check your answers to the first one or two editing practices against the answer key in the back of the book.

> ### Editing Practice 1
>
> CORRECTED SENTENCES APPEAR ON PAGE 458.
>
> Correct all run-ons in the following paragraph using the first correction as a model. The number in parentheses at the end of the paragraph indicates how many errors you should find.
>
> I was late to my first class; my car broke down on the side of the highway. This is the third time this fall that I have had to pull over because of an engine problem, I am not going to suffer through a fourth time. According to a mechanic, the problem has something to do with the fuel injector. I have replaced the fuse, and the mechanic has tried various other methods. Nothing has worked it does not make sense spending yet more money on something that cannot be fixed. I might need a whole new fuel injector, I am considering buying a new car. The one I have is only six years old, so I hate buying a new one already. It all depends on what I can afford. (3)

Applying What You Know
Do this activity to demonstrate your ability to avoid the error in your own writing.

> ### Applying What You Know
>
> Select fifteen sentences from one of your textbooks, and use the Imaginary Period Tip to determine how many are composed of two or more independent clauses — complete ideas that can stand alone as separate sentences. How many of the fifteen sentences use a comma and a coordinating conjunction to separate independent clauses? How many use a semicolon?

The Bottom Line
Here is a final reminder of the main point of the lesson. The sentence is written so that it both demonstrates and describes the concept of the lesson.

> **The Bottom Line**
>
> See if your sentence has two independent clauses, **and** make sure they are separated with a period, a semicolon, or a comma and coordinating conjunction.

Using the Tabs

You may have noticed that there are tabs in the outside margins of this book. These tabs are designed to help you find your way around. If you open to a unit overview or unit review, the tab will indicate the unit number and whether you are in the overview or the review. If you flip through the book from front to back, you will notice twelve sets of tabs. These correspond to the twelve units in *A Commonsense Guide.*

Unit One

overview

If you open to an individual lesson, the tab will indicate the lesson number and a symbol for the topic of the lesson. For example, frag is the symbol used for Lesson 1: Fragments. You may notice that your instructor uses a similar system of symbols to indicate errors in your writing.

Lesson 1

frag

The last page of *A Commonsense Guide to Grammar and Usage* lists other common correction symbols.

Contents

Unit One   *Understanding the Basic Sentence*   7

, a

Blocking my driveway was a car/ A huge SUV.
                              ^

, and

I have a test on Thursday it should not be difficult.
                         ^

Unit Two   *Making Subjects and Verbs Agree*   32

are

The advantages of this entertainment system is that it is
                                            ^
more compact and less expensive than others on the market.

are

There is a million stories in every big city.
      ^

Unit Three   *Using Correct Verb Tenses*   57

Unit Four   *Understanding Pronouns*   78

While I was taking my morning walk, a car almost
hit me.
    ^

Sally met a teacher, who will be teaching composition
this fall.

Shakespeare's play, *Macbeth,* was recently made into a
movie again.

wasn't
Henry Pym ~~wasnt~~ in class today.
    ^

judge's
The ~~judges~~ robe was torn and dirty.
    ^

Today's
~~Todays~~ high temperature set a new record.
    ^

commas
Your sentence has four ~~comma's~~ in it.
    ^

Unit Twelve	*A Commonsense Writing Guide*	*385*

Grammar without Tears

This brief overview of grammar basics will help you understand what a sentence is and how it is built. There are two requirements for sentences to be sentences: (1) Sentences must contain both a **subject** (the topic of the sentence) and a **predicate** (what the subject does). (2) Sentences must express a complete thought. Here are some examples of minimal sentences that express complete thoughts with just single-word subjects and predicates:

Subjects

The subjects of sentences are typically **nouns** (names of people, places, things, and ideas) or **pronouns**. The most common pronouns used as subjects are the **personal pronouns** (*I, you, he, she, it, we,* and *they*). Here are some sentences that use personal pronouns (underlined) as subjects:

I know the answer.   You are completely wrong.

In the examples we have looked at so far, the subject has consisted of a single word. If all sentences were that simple, finding the subject would not be much of a challenge. Usually, however, the subject, especially when it is a noun, is used with other words that modify the subject. The subject word together with all its modifiers is called the **complete subject**:

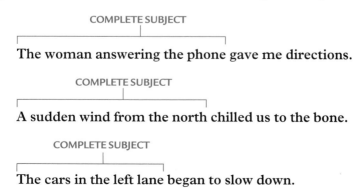

1

A very important part of knowing when a sentence is a sentence is identifying the subject part of the sentence and telling it apart from the rest of the sentence (the predicate). Here is a tip for doing just that.

> **PRONOUN REPLACEMENT TIP**   The subject of a sentence—whether it is a single-word noun or a long, complicated complete subject—can always be identified by replacing it with a subject pronoun: *he, she, it,* or *they.*

Let's apply the Pronoun Replacement Tip to the examples on page 1:

She
The woman answering the phone gave me directions.

It
A sudden wind from the north chilled us to the bone.

They
The cars in the left lane began to slow down.

Grammar Test 1

Underline the complete subjects in the sentences below. Confirm your answer by applying the Pronoun Replacement Tip.

Example: All the computers in the lab use Windows.

                         They
Answer: All the computers in the lab use Windows.

1.   The early spring weather was completely unpredictable.

2.   The new lamp in the den doesn't give me enough light.

3.   The guys in the back of the bus were hogging all the seats.

4.   The waitress behind the counter finally came out to get our orders.

5.   The telephone and the doorbell both began ringing at the same time.

Verbs

Identifying Verbs

Verbs have a distinctive grammatical feature that makes them easy to identify—**tense**. Verbs are unique in that only verbs have past tense, present tense, and future tense forms. A good test for verbs is to see if you can make the word into a future tense by putting *will* in front of it.

> **WILL TIP**   Put *will* in front of the word you want to test. If the result makes sense, then the word is a verb.

Compare the following two sentences that both use the word *chain,* but in different ways:

The <u>chain</u> is heavy.   The janitors <u>chain</u> the gate.

The *Will* Tip tells us that in the first sentence, *chain* is not a verb:

✗ The <u>will chain</u> is heavy.

However, *chain* is a verb in the second sentence; we can tell this by applying the *Will* Tip:

The janitors <u>will chain</u> the gate.

Identifying Predicates

Like subjects, verbs are generally used along with other words. The **predicate** consists of a verb together with its **complement** — whatever the verb requires for the sentence to make sense. The complement, in turn, may be followed by one or more optional **adverbs** that tell *when, where, why, how,* or *to what degree* about the verb. This is the fundamental pattern of all English sentences:

PREDICATE

Subject + Verb + Complement + (Optional adverb)

Here are three examples of verbs with different types of complements:

Example 1:   Harry calls Sally every afternoon.

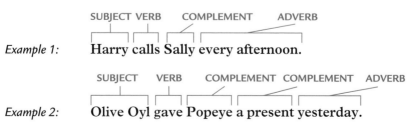

Example 2:   Olive Oyl gave Popeye a present yesterday.

SUBJECT   VERB   COMPLEMENT   COMPLEMENT

Example 3:   Thelma told Louise to be quiet.

Grammar Test 2

Below are pairs of related words. Use the *Will* Tip to identify which is the verb.

Example: **realize/realization**

Tip applied: *Will realize = grammatical = verb; will realization = ungrammatical = not a verb.*

1. large/enlarge

2. sale/sell

3. authority/authorize

4. choose/choice

5. publish/publication

Complete Thoughts

As you learned above, sentences must have **subjects** and **predicates**. The second requirement for a sentence is that it must be able to stand alone as a complete thought. The reason for this second requirement is that there are other structures besides sentences that have subjects and predicates.

Identifying Clauses

The term *clause* includes *all* groups of words that have subjects and predicates, not just sentences. Sentences are just one type of clause; though, of course, sentences are by far the most important type of clause.

Sentences are **independent clauses**. To be independent, clauses must be able to stand alone (make sense by themselves) without being dependent on some other sentence. Clauses that fail to stand alone are called **dependent clauses**. To see the difference between independent clauses (sentences) and dependent clauses, compare the following clauses.

Independent Clause (Sentence):   He gets upset.

Dependent Clause: Whenever he gets upset

The independent clause *He gets upset* stands by itself as a complete idea. The dependent clause *whenever he gets upset* cannot stand by itself as a complete idea. It needs to be attached to an independent clause, for example:

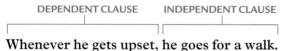

Whenever he gets upset, he goes for a walk.

or

He goes for a walk whenever he gets upset.

Distinguishing between Independent and Dependent Clauses

The following tip will help you distinguish between independent and dependent clauses.

> **I REALIZE TIP**   You can put *I realize* in front of independent clauses (sentences). However, when you put *I realize* in front of dependent clauses, the result will not make sense.

Here is the *I Realize* Tip applied to the two example clauses given above:

Independent Clause: <u>I realize</u> he gets upset.

Dependent Clause: ✗ <u>I realize</u> whenever he gets upset.

As you can see, when we add *I realize* to an independent clause, the result is a grammatical sentence. However, when we add *I realize* to a dependent clause, the result does not make sense.

Grammar Test 3

Label the following clauses as independent or dependent. Confirm your answer by using the *I Realize* Tip.

                            Dependent clause

Example: **Because he feels like it.**

Confirmation: ✗ *I realize because he feels like it.*

1. When I was your age.

2. After it started to rain.

3. Whatever you want.

4. The punishment fits the crime.

5. Which is exactly right.

UNIT ONE
Understanding the Basic Sentence

Terms That Can Help You Understand the Basic Sentence

If you are not familiar with any of the following terms, look them up in the Guide to Grammar Terminology beginning on page 435.

comma splice

complete sentence

coordinating conjunction

dependent clause

fragment

fused sentence

independent clause

run-on sentence

The Nuts and Bolts of Understanding the Basic Sentence

This unit will help you to understand the most basic concept in writing: the correct punctuation of complete sentences. A **complete sentence** has the following characteristics:

- It contains both a **subject** and a **verb**.

- It expresses a complete thought — a freestanding, self-contained idea.

The two lessons in this unit present the two ways that a sentence can be mispunctuated: as a **fragment** or as a **run-on**.

Lesson 1 shows you how to identify and correct fragments. In a sentence fragment, something less than a sentence has been punctuated as though it were a complete sentence. Here is an example of a fragment:

Fragment: Celeste found a cat. ✗ Which she promptly took home.

Correction: Celeste found a cat. ̷ W̶h̶i̶c̶h̶ she promptly took home.
                                          , which

7

The fragment *which she promptly took home* contains both a subject and a verb, but it cannot stand alone as a self-contained idea. Most fragments are continuations of the preceding sentence, so the easiest way to correct fragments is to attach them to the preceding sentence.

Lesson 2 shows you how to identify and correct run-ons. In a run-on, two complete sentences have been joined together incorrectly and punctuated as though they were a single sentence. Here is an example of a run-on:

Run-on:	✗ The boss liked my idea, she said she would take it to the board of directors.
Correction:	The boss liked my idea,/; she said she would take it to the board of directors. ^

This kind of run-on is called a **comma splice** because it incorrectly uses a comma to join two complete sentences. If the two sentences had been put together without any punctuation at all, it would be another kind of run-on called a **fused sentence**. Writers sometimes create run-ons when they try to keep closely related ideas together within the same sentence. Two good ways to achieve the same goal are to join the related sentences together with a comma and a **coordinating conjunction** (*and, but, or*) or with a semicolon (;).

Fragments

EXAMPLE 1	*Renamer Fragment*
Error:	Blocking my driveway was a car. ✗ <u>A huge SUV.</u>

Correction: Blocking my driveway was a car/ <s>A</s> huge SUV.
           , a

EXAMPLE 2	*Adverb Fragment*
Error:	I was really upset. ✗ <u>Because I knew I would be late for work.</u>

Correction: I was really upset/ <s>Because</s> I knew I would be late for work.
           because

EXAMPLE 3	*-ing Fragment*
Error:	I beeped my horn a couple of times. ✗ <u>Letting the driver know I had to get out.</u>

Correction: I beeped my horn a couple of times/ <s>Letting</s> the driver know I had to get out.
           , letting

What's the Problem?

A **fragment** is a group of words that cannot stand alone as a **complete sentence** but is mistakenly punctuated as though it were. In English, a subject, a verb, and a complete thought are needed for a complete sentence. Many fragments lack a verb, as in Example 1, or lack a subject, as in Example 3. Example 2 has a subject and a verb, but it does not express a complete thought.

Fragments are hard for writers to spot because they sound normal. In the quick give-and-take of conversation, fragments are a way of clarifying, elaborating on, or emphasizing what we have just said without having to stop and reformulate the previous sentence. In formal, written language, however, fragments are inappropriate. Readers expect formal writing to be carefully planned.

Diagnostic Exercise

CORRECTED SENTENCES APPEAR ON PAGE 457.

Correct all errors in the following paragraph using the first correction as a model. The number in parentheses at the end of the paragraph indicates how many errors you should find.

I wish I could change my worst bad habit. / ~~Always~~ *, always* running late. I am always tempted to do just one more thing before heading out the door in the morning. I know I am going to be busy all day. Trying to balance schoolwork with my job. I have learned that it helps to make a schedule. Which I really do try to follow. However, I never seem to budget enough time for routine chores. Because I really hate doing things in a sloppy way. As a result, I am always tempted to take an extra minute or two to do things right. The problem is that those few extra minutes quickly add up. Before I know it, I am late. Again. Another problem is that I don't have enough time built in for unexpected delays. Which seem to happen with depressing regularity. You wouldn't believe what happened to me this morning. A huge SUV was parked in front of my driveway. Blocking me for a good fifteen minutes. (6)

Fixing This Problem in Your Writing

Identifying Fragments

A fragment is almost always a continuation of the preceding sentence. To find and then fix a fragment, we need to separate it from the previous sentence. When a fragment is by itself, isolated from preceding sentences, we are much more likely to notice it doesn't make sense on its own. Here is one tip that will help you isolate fragments.

> **LIKELY FRAGMENTS TIP** Most fragments fall into one of three categories: *renamers, adverbs,* and *-ing fragments.* If you are aware of what the most common types of fragments are, you are more likely to spot them.

Renamers. These fragments rename or give further information about the last noun in the preceding sentence. Example 1 illustrates this type of fragment.

FRAGMENT

Example 1: Blocking my driveway was a <u>car</u>. ✗ <u>A huge SUV</u>.

The fragment renames the noun *car*.

Another common type of renamer begins with *which:*

FRAGMENT

Along the curb, there was a <u>car</u>. ✗ <u>Which was completely blocking my driveway</u>.

The fragment gives further information about the car.

Adverbs. In this category are adverb clauses that tell when, where, and especially why something happened. Example 2 illustrates this type of fragment.

FRAGMENT

Example 2: I was really <u>upset</u>. ✗ <u>Because I knew I would be late for work</u>.

The fragment expands on the entire previous sentence, explaining why the writer was upset.

-ing *Fragments.* These fragments begin with the *-ing* form of a verb. Example 3 illustrates this type of fragment.

FRAGMENT

Example 3: I beeped my horn a couple of <u>times</u>. ✗ <u>Letting the driver know I had to get out</u>.

Typically, *-ing* fragments explain something about the meaning of the preceding sentence. In this example, the *-ing* fragment explains why the writer beeped the horn.

Here is a tip to help you spot all three types of fragments.

> **BACKWARD PROOFREADING TIP**   Proofread your paper backward, one sentence at a time. Use one hand or a piece of paper to cover up all but the last sentence in each paragraph. See if that sentence can stand alone. If it can, then uncover the next-to-last sentence to see if it can stand alone, and so on.

Backward proofreading is a standard and quite effective way of identifying fragments because fragments generally don't make sense when they are separated from preceding sentences. Try this tip on the Diagnostic Exercise at the beginning of this lesson.

Here is a third tip to help you catch fragments.

> **I REALIZE TIP**   You can put *I realize* in front of most complete sentences and make a new grammatical sentence. However, when you put *I realize* in front of a fragment, the result will not make sense.

The *I Realize* Tip is a particularly handy way to test whether something is actually a fragment. Here is how it would be applied to each of the three sample fragments:

Tip applied:	✗ I realize a huge SUV.
Tip applied:	✗ I realize because I knew I would be late for work.
Tip applied:	✗ I realize letting the driver know I had to get out.

The *I Realize* Tip confirms that these examples are fragments: they do not make sense when you put *I realize* in front of them.

Correcting Fragments

Once you identify a fragment, the easiest way to correct it is to attach it to the preceding sentence. Use the following guidelines in deciding how to punctuate the new sentence.

- If the fragment is a renamer or an *-ing* fragment, you will probably need to add a comma.

- If it is an adverb fragment, you will usually need no punctuation to attach it to the previous sentence. A comma is required only if the fragment begins with a word such as *although* or *even though*, to show a strong contrast.

Alternatively, you could expand the fragment to a complete sentence in its own right. Decide if the material in the fragment is worth emphasizing. If it is, expand the fragment to a full sentence. If it is not that important (most of the time, this is the case), attach it to the preceding sentence.

Let's use the *I Realize* Tip to identify fragments in three new examples. We'll then correct each fragment using both methods: connecting the fragment to the preceding sentence and expanding the fragment to a complete sentence.

RENAMER FRAGMENT

Example: I have to commute on the beltway. ✗ The Highway from Hell.

Tip applied: ✗ I realize the Highway from Hell.

Connected: I have to commute on the beltway. **,** *the* ~~The~~ Highway from Hell.

Use a comma to connect a renamer fragment.

Expanded: I have to commute on the beltway. *It is called the* ~~The~~ Highway from Hell.

ADVERB FRAGMENT

Example: Yesterday's traffic was worse than usual. ✗ Because there was an accident.

Tip applied: ✗ I realize because there was an accident.

Connected: Yesterday's traffic was worse than usual. *because* ~~Because~~ there was an accident.

Don't use a comma to connect most adverb fragments.

Expanded: Yesterday's traffic was worse than usual. Because there was an accident. *, it took me over an hour to get to work.*

-*ING* FRAGMENT

Example: Today, I actually left home on schedule. ✗ Showing

that I can be on time if I try.

Tip applied: ✗ I realize showing that I can be on time if I try.

, showing

Connected: Today, I actually left home on schedule. / ~~Showing~~ that
I can be on time if I try.
^

Use a comma to connect an -*ing* fragment.

See,

Expanded: Today, I actually left home on schedule. ~~Showing~~
~~that~~ I can be on time if I try.
^

✳ *Putting It All Together*

Identify Fragments

____ Understand and look for the most common types of fragments: *renamers, adverbs,* and -*ing fragments.*

____ Proofread your paper starting at the last sentence and moving to the first, reading one sentence at a time.

____ Put *I realize* in front of each group of words that you think might be a fragment. The *I realize* sentence will not make sense if the word group is a fragment.

Correct Fragments

____ Attach each fragment to the previous sentence, or rewrite the fragment to make it a complete sentence if you want to emphasize it.

Sentence Practice 1

CORRECTED SENTENCES APPEAR ON PAGE 457.

Find the fragments by using the *I Realize* Tip. Write *OK* above each complete sentence. Write *frag* above each fragment and identify which of the three types it is—*renamer, adverb,* or -*ing fragment.* Correct the fragment by combining it with the complete sentence next to it.

Example: The Rocky Mountains form the largest mountain chain in North America. Running from New Mexico to northern Alaska.

       OK

Tip applied: *I realize* the Rocky Mountains form the largest

            frag, -ing fragment

     mountain chain in North America. *I realize* running from New Mexico to northern Alaska.

Correction: The Rocky Mountains form the largest mountain

          , running

     chain in North America./~~Running~~ from New

             ^

     Mexico to northern Alaska.

1. The Rockies are actually part of a larger chain. Which stretches to the Andes in South America.

2. The climate to the east of the Rockies is relatively dry. Because the mountains cut off moist winds from the Pacific.

3. To the west of the Rockies there is another, newer mountain range. The Sierra Nevadas.

4. The Rockies are called the Continental Divide. They separate the Pacific watershed from the Atlantic watershed.

5. To the east of the Rockies are the Great Plains. The remains of a gigantic inland sea.

 For more practice correcting fragments, go to **Exercise Central** at
bedfordstmartins.com/commonsense

Sentence Practice 2

CORRECTED SENTENCES APPEAR ON PAGE 457.

Find the fragments by using the *I Realize* Tip. Write *OK* above each complete sentence. Write *frag* above each fragment and identify which of the three types it is — *renamer, adverb,* or *-ing fragment*. Correct the fragment by combining it with the complete sentence next to it.

Example: We took a trip to Florida this winter. Using frequent flyer miles.

OK

Tip applied: *I realize* we took a trip to Florida this winter.

          frag, -ing fragment

          I realize using frequent flyer miles.

                                    , using

Correction: We took a trip to Florida this winter. / ~~Using~~ frequent flyer miles.

                                      ^

1. We had to go this winter. Because our miles were going to expire.

2. We decided to skip Orlando. It's somewhat isolated in the middle of the state.

3. We didn't want to spend half of our vacation on the road. Driving from Orlando to Key West and back.

4. After all, from Orlando to Key West is a 400-mile trip. A full day's journey.

5. We ended up flying to Miami. Which is much closer to where we wanted to go.

Sentence Practice 3

Combine the following pairs of sentences by turning the second sentence into a renamer, an adverb clause, or an *-ing* expression (as appropriate) and attaching it to the first sentence.

Example: The Florida Keys are actually hundreds of little islands. The islands run from the mainland to Key West.

Answer: The Florida Keys are actually hundreds of little

             , running

   islands. / ~~The islands run~~ from the mainland to

              ^

   Key West.

or

Answer: The Florida Keys are actually hundreds of little

             , which

   islands. / ~~The islands~~ run from the mainland to

             ^

   Key West.

1. The keys end at Key West. Key West is the westernmost of the bigger keys.

2. The road to Key West is on a causeway. The causeway jumps from key to key on short bridges.

3. The causeway follows the track of an old railway line. The railway line went bankrupt.

4. Building the railroad was a huge task. One problem was that many hurricanes strike the keys.

5. What doomed the railroad, though, was a different problem. The problem was the lack of docking facilities on Key West.

6. Portions of the railroad were destroyed in the Labor Day Hurricane of 1935. A major storm that killed hundreds of people in the Keys.

7. The railroad was abandoned after the storm. Since rebuilding it would be prohibitively expensive.

8. Today, Key West is connected to the mainland by a highway. Much of it running on filled land originally built up for the old railroad.

9. The highway is an amazing construction. A series of bridges that goes from key to key for 127 miles.

10. In 2005 the highway easily survived Hurricane Wilma. Which flooded 60% of the homes in Key West.

Editing Practice 1

CORRECTED SENTENCES APPEAR ON PAGE 457.

Correct all fragment errors in the following paragraph using the first correction as a model. The number in parentheses at the end of the paragraph indicates how many errors you should find.

Key West is a great place to visit. /For a lot of reasons. First of all,
for

the physical setting is magnificent. Blue sky and beautiful ocean views.

Being on an island makes you much more aware of the water and the sky. Unlike the often cloudless skies on the Pacific coast, the skies in the keys often have small puffy clouds. Giving a sense of space and depth to the sky. The color of the water is always changing. Because the coral reefs reflect the continually changing play of sun and cloud. The fact that the ocean around Key West is so shallow and so varied gives the water vibrant colors. With dozens of shades of green and blue everywhere you look. The beaches in California are quite drab by comparison. Because they are mostly made up of uniform, gray sandy bottoms. (5)

Editing Practice 2

CORRECTED SENTENCES APPEAR ON PAGE 457.

Correct all fragment errors in the following paragraph using the first correction as a model. The number in parentheses at the end of the paragraph indicates how many errors you should find.

It is interesting to compare Key West with a similar ocean-side destination in California/, Santa Barbara, for instance. Besides being beach destinations, they share another important feature. A lengthy Spanish heritage. Key West today doesn't feel Spanish at all. Even though it (and the rest of Florida) was part of the Spanish empire for nearly three hundred years. There was never any permanent Spanish settlement there. Because there was no source of fresh water on the island. Key West was a temporary home for fishermen and pirates. A source of much humor today. Santa Barbara, on the other hand, is overflowing with its Spanish heritage. Especially in its architecture. Santa Barbara today looks classically Spanish. With its white buildings and red tile roofs. (6)

Editing Practice 3

Correct all fragment errors in the following paragraph using the first correction as a model. The number in parentheses at the end of the paragraph indicates how many errors you should find.

, the

There is one huge difference between Key West and Santa Barbara./~~The~~

climate. Key West is in the Caribbean. A shallow, warm tropical sea.

As a result, Key West is uniformly warm. And excessively humid. The

sun and humidity generate a lot of clouds. Resulting in almost daily rain

showers. Lots of sun and rain support luxurious tropical vegetation. And

plenty of bugs. Santa Barbara is almost the exact opposite. Southern

California is essentially a desert. Resulting in distinctly un-lush,

drought-tolerant vegetation. Even though the beaches in Santa Barbara

are beautiful, very few people actually go in the water. Because it

is bone-numbingly cold. On the other hand, there are very few bugs. (6)

Applying What You Know

On your own paper, write a paragraph or two comparing the advantages and disadvantages of two places you have been on vacation. Use the Putting It All Together checklist on page 14 to make sure that there are no fragments.

The Bottom Line	I realize you can use *I realize* to spot fragments.

Run-ons: Fused Sentences and Comma Splices

EXAMPLE 1   *Fused Sentence*

Error: ✗ I have a test on Thursday it should not be difficult.

Correction: I have a test on Thursday **, and** it should not be difficult.

EXAMPLE 2   *Comma Splice*

Error: ✗ The student government election is this week, I have no idea who is running.

Correction: The student government election is this week, **but** I have no idea who is running.

What's the Problem?

A **run-on sentence** contains two **independent clauses** that have been incorrectly joined together. (An independent clause is a group of words that can stand alone as a complete sentence.) Run-on sentences fail to show the reader where one idea ends and the next one begins.

The examples above illustrate two types of run-on sentence errors. When two independent clauses are joined with no punctuation at all, the error is called a **fused sentence**. When two independent clauses are joined with just a comma (without a coordinating conjunction like *and, but, or*), the error is called a **comma splice**. In both cases, the writer confuses the reader by failing to correctly signal the separation between two complete ideas.

In the following examples, notice how the clauses are separated by nothing at all or by just a comma.

INDEPENDENT CLAUSE   INDEPENDENT CLAUSE

Fused Sentence: ✗ I went to the store it was closed.

Problem: Nothing separates the two clauses.

INDEPENDENT CLAUSE   INDEPENDENT CLAUSE

Comma Splice: ✗ I went to the store, it was closed.

Problem: Only a comma separates the two clauses.

Diagnostic Exercise

CORRECTED SENTENCES APPEAR ON PAGE 458.

Correct all run-on errors in the following paragraph using the first correction as a model. The number in parentheses at the end of the paragraph indicates how many errors you should correct.

, and

My friend Miranda is a junior majoring in government she plans to

go to law school. Most law schools accept applicants from all majors, she

thinks that majoring in government would help her prepare for law.

All law schools do require good grades and a high score on the LSAT.

Her grades are high she has about a 3.8 GPA currently. She works very

hard, she studies more than any person I know. She plans to take the

LSAT this fall she will be studying for it on top of everything else. I admire

her energy, I'm sure she has what it takes to be a good law student. (5)

Fixing This Problem in Your Writing

Identifying Run-ons

Run-ons are easy to correct once you have identified them. The problem is finding them to begin with. Here is a tip for spotting potential run-on sentences in your writing.

run-on

> **IMAGINARY PERIOD TIP** If a sentence contains two separate ideas, put an imaginary period between them. Now ask: Can BOTH parts now stand alone as complete sentences? If so, then the sentence might be a run-on.

Here is the Imaginary Period Tip applied to the fused sentence and the comma splice from the beginning of the lesson:

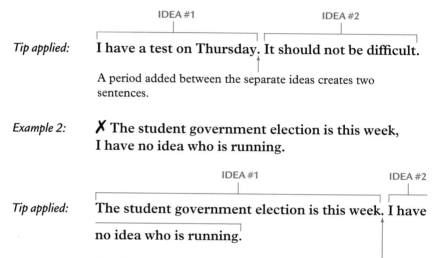

Example 1: ✗ I have a test on Thursday it should not be difficult.

IDEA #1   IDEA #2

Tip applied: I have a test on Thursday. It should not be difficult.

A period added between the separate ideas creates two sentences.

Example 2: ✗ The student government election is this week, I have no idea who is running.

IDEA #1   IDEA #2

Tip applied: The student government election is this week. I have no idea who is running.

A period added between the separate ideas creates two sentences.

In both cases, the two new sentences created by the Imaginary Period Tip can stand alone. In other words, each part of the Tip Applied sentence is a complete sentence, not a fragment. (See Lesson 1 if you need help recognizing a complete sentence.)

Correcting Run-ons

The Imaginary Period Tip does not prove that a sentence is a run-on. It only helps you determine whether a sentence contains two independent clauses and *might* be a run-on. Now you must determine if the two independent clauses are correctly separated. The easiest way to correctly separate two independent clauses is with a period. The Tip Applied step in the examples above illustrates this method.

Another way to separate two independent clauses is with a semicolon (;). A semicolon allows you to keep two closely related ideas together within the same sentence. (See Lesson 27 for more on semicolons.) Here is an example of how to correct a run-on with a semicolon.

Example: ✗ I did pretty well on the last test I got an 82.

Tip applied: I did pretty well on the last test. I got an 82.

An imaginary period works, so the clauses are independent.

Correction: I did pretty well on the last test; I got an 82.

Add a semicolon where the imaginary period could go.

A third way to punctuate two independent clauses is to combine them with a comma and a **coordinating conjunction** (*for, and, nor, but, or, yet, so*). We'll illustrate this method with Example 1 from the beginning of the lesson.

Example 1:   ✗ I have a test on Thursday it should not be difficult.

Tip applied: I have a test on Thursday. It should not be difficult.

An imaginary period works, so the clauses are independent.

Correction: *, and*
                I have a test on Thursday it should not be difficult.

Add a comma and conjunction where the imaginary period could go.

Example 2 (the comma splice) has only half of what we need: a comma but no coordinating conjunction. A comma alone should not separate two independent clauses.

Example 2:   ✗ The student government election is this week, I have no idea who is running.

Tip applied: The student government election is this week. I have no idea who is running.

An imaginary period works, so the clauses are independent.

Correction: *but*
                The student government election is this week, I have no idea who is running.

Use a comma and conjunction where the imaginary period could go.

✳ *More Examples*

Error: ✗ Jamal is a physics major he plans to work for NASA.

Correction: Jamal is a physics major ~~he~~ plans to work for NASA.
                    . He

Error: ✗ Traffic today was horrible I am thirty minutes late.

Correction: Traffic today was horrible I am thirty minutes late.
                    , so

Error: ✗ On a cold day in December, my car broke down on the highway, it is parked there.

Correction: On a cold day in December, my car broke down on the highway, ; it is parked there.

Error: ✗ George has two sons, they are both in elementary school.

Correction: George has two sons, they are both in elementary school.
                    and

✳ *Putting It All Together*

Identify Run-ons

____ Insert an imaginary period between two ideas in a sentence. If both ideas can stand alone as complete sentences, the original sentence might be a run-on.

____ Check to see whether the two ideas are correctly separated. A semicolon or a comma plus a coordinating conjunction (such as *and* or *but*) should come between the two ideas.

Correct Run-ons

____ Join two independent clauses with a semicolon or with a comma and a coordinating conjunction in the spot where you placed the imaginary period.

____ Or, turn the imaginary period into a real one, making each idea into a separate sentence.

Sentence Practice 1

CORRECTED SENTENCES APPEAR ON PAGE 458.

Find the independent clauses in the following run-on sentences by using the Imaginary Period Tip. Correct each run-on by inserting a semicolon between the two independent clauses, by adding a comma and a coordinating conjunction, or by turning the imaginary period into a real one. If a sentence does not contain a run-on, write *OK* above it.

Example:	My friend owns two pigs he keeps them as house pets.
Tip applied:	My friend owns two pigs. He keeps them as house pets.
Correction:	My friend owns two pigs; he keeps them as house pets.

1. Colleen called, she wants me to help her with her homework.

2. London was the first city to have a population of over one million, it reached that milestone in 1811.

3. My son wants to buy a snake, his mother is not happy about the idea.

4. The mascot for Yale is now a bulldog, its mascot over a hundred years ago was a cat.

5. Colombia was once considered part of South America, its government decided in 1903 to proclaim Colombia was part of North America.

 For more practice correcting run-ons, go to **Exercise Central** at bedfordstmartins.com/commonsense

Sentence Practice 2

CORRECTED SENTENCES APPEAR ON PAGE 458.

Find the independent clauses in the following run-on sentences by using the Imaginary Period Tip. Correct each run-on by inserting a semicolon between the two independent clauses, by adding a comma and a coordinating conjunction, or by turning the imaginary period into a real one. If a sentence does not contain a run-on, write *OK* above it.

> *Example:* Susan has a portrait above her desk, it is her daughter.
>
> *Tip applied:* Susan has a portrait above her desk. It is her daughter.
>
> *Correction:* Susan has a portrait above her desk./; it is her daughter.

1. When Benita first decided to go to college, her parents wanted her to stay near home.

2. The first home TV set was demonstrated in 1928, it measured only 3 inches by 4 inches.

3. The street lights in the city of Hershey, Pennsylvania, look strange, they resemble Hershey's chocolate kisses.

4. I liked the early *Harry Potter* books better, the later ones got too dark for me.

5. I thought the actors in the *Harry Potter* movies were terrific even the minor characters were wonderful.

Sentence Practice 3

Combine each pair of sentences by attaching the second sentence to the first with a comma and an appropriate coordinating conjunction (*for, and, nor, but, or, yet, so*).

> *Example:* My sister plans to go to college next year. She is sending out dozens of applications now.
>
> , so she
> *Answer:* My sister plans to go to college next year./She is sending out dozens of applications now.

1. We are going to San Diego in September. Then we are going to Los Angeles in October.

2. My iPod isn't working. Maybe it just needs to be recharged.

3. She had to stay up late last night. This morning she is sleeping in.

4. I am coming down with a cold. My allergies are really acting up.

5. I am coming down with a cold. Unfortunately, I still have to go to work.

6. It looked like rain. I decided to take my umbrella.

7. It looked like rain. I decided not to take my umbrella because I had no place to keep it if it got wet.

8. It looked like it would rain at any minute. Not surprisingly, it began to pour a few minutes later.

9. I hate having lunch alone. I always look for a friend to eat with.

10. I hate having lunch alone. Sometimes I have to, though.

Editing Practice 1

CORRECTED SENTENCES APPEAR ON PAGE 458.

Correct all run-ons in the following paragraph using the first correction as a model. The number in parentheses at the end of the paragraph indicates how many errors you should find.

I was late to my first class ; my car broke down on the side of the highway. This is the third time this fall that I have had to pull over because of an engine problem, I am not going to suffer through a fourth time. According to a mechanic, the problem has something to do with the fuel injector. I have replaced the fuse, and the mechanic has tried various other methods. Nothing has worked it does not make sense spending yet more money on something that cannot be fixed. I might need a whole new fuel injector, I am considering buying a new car. The one I have is only six years old, so I hate buying a new one already. It all depends on what I can afford. (3)

Editing Practice 2

CORRECTED SENTENCES APPEAR ON PAGE 458.

Correct all run-ons in the following paragraph using the first correction as a model. The number in parentheses at the end of the paragraph indicates how many errors you should find.

              , and

At my college, on-campus parking can be extremely difficult ^ the situation will soon be worse. Currently, the college has eight parking lots for students, two of them hold only about a dozen cars. During the summer, construction will begin on a new library, which we certainly need. The construction will last a year, two parking lots will be closed during the construction phase. When the library opens up next year, only one of the two lots will be reopened the other will have vanished because the library will cover it. Almost everyone believes we need a new library, it is too bad that the administration has not made plans about what to do about the parking problem, which is only going to get worse. (4)

Editing Practice 3

Correct all run-ons in the following paragraphs using the first correction as a model. The number in parentheses at the end of each paragraph indicates how many errors you should find.

            is. It or *is; it*

Most people do not really know what an infinitive ~~is, it~~ is *to* + the ^ dictionary form of a verb, for example: *to work, to sleep, to laugh.* However, there is one thing that everybody can tell you about infinitives, it is bad grammar to split them. Here is an example of a sentence with a split infinitive: "He promised to *always* use good grammar." This is a split infinitive because the adverb *always* come in between (i.e., splits) the infinitive *to use.* So, why is it considered bad grammar to split an infinitive? (1)

To answer this question we must go back in time. People have been happily splitting infinitives since at least the fourteenth century nobody noticed or cared. Splitting infinitives was never an issue until the early grammar books for English were written in the eighteenth century. These grammar books based their analysis of English on Latin grammars they were the only model of grammar that eighteenth-century grammarians had. In Latin grammar, the infinitive is a single-word construction, unlike English there is no *to*. Since it is literally impossible to split the one-word infinitive in Latin, these grammarians decreed that it was therefore improper to split an infinitive in English. (3)

Modern grammarians know that there is no valid reason to condemn split infinitives after all, English and Latin are totally different languages. However, since so many people are absolutely convinced that it is wrong to split infinitives, grammarians advise writers to avoid them, not because there is anything actually wrong with split infinitives, but because they bother some people why upset people needlessly? (2)

Applying What You Know

Select fifteen sentences from one of your textbooks, and use the Imaginary Period Tip to determine how many are composed of two or more independent clauses — complete ideas that can stand alone as separate sentences. How many of the fifteen sentences use a comma and a coordinating conjunction to separate independent clauses? How many use a semicolon?

The Bottom Line	See if your sentence has two independent clauses, **and** make sure they are separated with a period, a semicolon, or a comma and coordinating conjunction.

To write effectively, you must be able to recognize and correctly punctuate basic sentences. Every basic sentence has these components:

- a subject and a verb
- a self-contained, complete idea

Another term for a basic sentence is an independent clause. The following chart points you to the tips that will help you avoid errors when punctuating basic sentences.

TIP(S)	QUICK FIX AND EXAMPLE
Lesson 1. Fragments	
The Likely Fragments Tip (p. 11) helps you remember the most common types of fragments. The Backward Proofreading Tip (p. 12) and the *I Realize* Tip (p. 12) help you spot fragments in your writing.	Attach a fragment to the previous sentence, or rewrite the fragment to make it a complete sentence if you want to emphasize it. *Error:* Laura has been exhausted. ✗ Since she has been working on the weekends. *Correction:* Laura has been exhausted./ ~~Since~~ *since* she has been working on the ˄ weekends.
Lesson 2. Run-ons	
The Imaginary Period Tip (p. 22) helps you determine whether a sentence contains two independent clauses so you can make sure they are punctuated correctly.	Separate the two independent clauses of a run-on with a period, a semicolon, or a comma and a coordinating conjunction (such as *and, but, or*). *Error:* ✗ Laura is exhausted she has been working weekends. *Correction:* Laura is exhausted ~~she~~ . *She* has been working weekends. ˄

Review Test

Correct fragment and run-on errors in the following paragraphs using the first correction as a model. The number in parentheses at the end of each paragraph indicates how many errors you should find.

after

I read an article on washing clothes. ~~After~~ I shrank an expensive sweater. I thought I could just toss everything in the washer. Without checking the color or type of fabric. I learned a valuable lesson I just wish it hadn't been such an expensive lesson, though. (2)

Most items made of heavy cotton can be washed in very hot water, they won't shrink. It is best if white cotton items are washed by themselves. Because they can pick up colors from other things being washed. Lightweight cottons do best in warm water. Unless they are dark colors. Which always require cold water. (4)

Badly soiled laundry needs to be washed in very hot water. Unless the garment label says otherwise. That is how I ruined my sweater, I simply didn't know to look at its label. (2)

Making Subjects and Verbs Agree

Terms That Can Help You Understand Subject-Verb Agreement

If you are not familiar with any of the following terms, look them up in the Guide to Grammar Terminology beginning on page 435.

compound subject	**subject**
plural	**subject-verb agreement**
singular	**verb**

The Nuts and Bolts of Subject-Verb Agreement

This unit will help you to make your subjects and verbs agree in your writing. By "agree," we mean that the **subject** of any sentence must match the **verb** in number. For example, a singular subject (one person, place, or object) should be paired with the singular form of a verb. A plural subject (more than one person, place, or object) should be paired with the plural form of a verb.

Singular: The <u>student</u> <u>uses</u> the Internet for research.

Plural: The <u>students</u> <u>use</u> the Internet for research.

One basic rule to follow in making subjects and verbs agree is to add an *-s* to the **present tense** form of the verb if the subject is *he, she,* or *it* or if the subject can be replaced by one of these **personal pronouns**. The lessons in this unit deal with three common errors writers make in **subject-verb agreement**.

Lesson 3 shows you how to make the subject and verb agree when the subject phrase is so long or complicated that the actual subject gets lost. Here is an example of an error involving a lost subject.

Example: ✗ The cost of all the repairs we needed to make were more than we could afford.

                                                                    was
Correction: The cost of all the repairs we needed to make ~~were~~
                more than we could afford.   ^

The verb in this sentence must agree with the subject *cost,* not the nearby noun *repairs.*

Lesson 4 shows you how to make the subject and verb agree when the subject follows the verb, as in sentences that begin with *there is* or *there was.* Here is an example of this type of error.

Example: ✗ There is usually some leftovers in the refrigerator.

                      are
Correction: There ~~is~~ usually some leftovers in the refrigerator.
                      ^

The verb in this sentence must agree with the subject *leftovers.*

Lesson 5 shows you how to make the subject and verb agree when the sentence includes a **compound subject** (two or more subjects joined by *and*). Here is an example of an error involving a compound subject.

Example: ✗ Good planning and careful follow-through is necessary for success in any field.

                                                          are
Correction: Good planning and careful follow-through ~~is~~ necessary
                for success in any field.   ^

The verb in this sentence must agree with the compound subject *planning and follow-through.*

LESSON 3

Nearest-Noun Agreement Errors

EXAMPLE 1	*Plural Subject with a Singular Verb*

Error: ✗ The <u>advantages</u> of this entertainment system <u>is</u> that it is more compact and less expensive than others on the market.

Correction: The <u>advantages</u> of this entertainment system ~~is~~ *are* that it is more compact and less expensive than others on the market.

EXAMPLE 2	*Singular Subject with a Plural Verb*

Error: ✗ Last night, <u>one</u> of the new cottages <u>were</u> damaged in the storm.

Correction: Last night, <u>one</u> of the new cottages ~~were~~ *was* damaged in the storm.

What's the Problem?

When a sentence contains a **subject-verb agreement** error, most often the problem is caused because the **verb** in the sentence is agreeing with a word that is not the actual **subject**—usually it is agreeing with a noun that is closer to the verb than the actual subject. We call this error the "nearest-noun" agreement error.

Let's look once again at the two examples of nearest-noun agreement errors that started the lesson. In Example 1, the verb *is* mistakenly agrees with the nearest noun, *entertainment system*, rather than the actual subject of the sentence, *advantages*.

ACTUAL SUBJECT   NEAREST NOUN

Example 1:   ✗ The <u>advantages</u> of this <u>entertainment system</u> <u>is</u> that . . .

34

In Example 2, the problem is that the verb *were* mistakenly agrees with the nearest noun, *cottages*, rather than the actual subject of the sentence, *one*.

ACTUAL SUBJECT   NEAREST NOUN
                ↓   ↓

Example 2:   ✗ Last night, <u>one</u> of the new <u>cottages</u> <u><u>were</u></u> damaged in the storm.

It is easy to make nearest-noun agreement errors when many words separate the subject of the sentence from the verb or when another noun comes between the subject of the sentence and the verb.

Diagnostic Exercise

CORRECTED SENTENCES APPEAR ON PAGE 459.

Correct all subject-verb agreement errors in the following paragraph using the first correction as a model. The number in parentheses at the end of the paragraph indicates how many errors you should find.

                                                                         dates

The beginning of the first public schools in the United States ~~date~~
                                                                           ^

from the early 1800's. The pressure to create public schools open to children of working-class parents were a direct result of the union movements in large cities. In response, state legislatures gave communities the legal right to levy local property taxes to pay for free schools open to the public. By the middle of the nineteenth century, control of the school policies and curriculum were in the hands of the state government. As school populations outgrew one-room schoolhouses, the design of school buildings on the East Coast were completely changed to accommodate separate rooms for children of different ages. Before this time, all children in a schoolhouse, regardless of age, was taught together in the same room by the same teacher. (4)

Fixing This Problem in Your Writing

Lesson 3

s-v
agr

To avoid making nearest-noun agreement errors, your first job is to find the correct subject of the sentence. The subject is *usually* the first noun (or pronoun) in the sentence. When you look for the subject, remember not to be fooled by nouns that are nearer to the verb than the actual subject is.

One exception to the rule that the subject is the first noun in a sentence is when a sentence begins with an introductory element that contains a noun, as in the following example:

<pre>
FIRST   ACTUAL
NOUN   SUBJECT   VERB
  ↓   ↓   ↓
Last night, <u>one</u> of the new cottages <u>was</u> damaged in the storm.
</pre>

Here the first noun in the sentence is *night*. However, *night* is not the subject of the sentence because it is part of an introductory element and does not make sense as the subject (the *night* was not damaged in the storm). To find the subject, you therefore need to find the first plausible noun *after* any introductory phrase. In this case, the word *one* is the subject.

Use the following tip to find the correct subject in a sentence.

> **FINDING THE SUBJECT TIP**   To find the correct subject of a sentence, jump back to the beginning of the sentence and find the *first* noun (or pronoun) that makes sense as the subject and is not part of an introductory element. Once you find the correct subject, make sure that the verb agrees with that subject.

In the following examples, see how jumping back to the beginning of the sentence and finding the first plausible noun correctly identifies the subject:

Example 1:   ✗ The advantages of this entertainment system is that it is more compact and less expensive than others on the market.

Tip applied: The (advantages) of this entertainment system is that it is . . .

Correction: The advantages of this entertainment system ~~is~~ that
                                                                          are
                 it is . . .
                                                                    ^

In this example, the first noun in the sentence (*advantages*) is the subject, not the noun closest to the verb (*entertainment system*). The subject is plural, so the verb should also be plural.

Example 2:   ✗ Last night, one of the new cottages were damaged in the storm.

SUBJECT   ✗

Tip applied: Last night, (one) of the new cottages <u>were</u> damaged in the storm.

was

Correction: Last night, one of the new cottages ~~were~~ damaged in the storm.
                                                                    ^

In this example, the subject (*one*) is the first noun after the introductory phrase, not the first noun in the sentence (*night*) or the noun closest to the verb (*cottages*). The subject is singular, so the verb should also be singular.

✱ Putting It All Together

Identify the Subject

____ Jump back to the beginning of the sentence to find the *first* noun or pronoun that makes sense as the subject and that is not part of an introductory element.

Correct Nearest-Noun Agreement Errors

____ Use a singular verb form for a singular subject and a plural verb form for a plural subject.

Sentence Practice 1

CORRECTED SENTENCES APPEAR ON PAGE 459.

In the following sentences, the verb is in **boldface** type. Jump to the beginning of the sentence and find the first word that makes sense as the subject. Underline this subject and then make the verb agree with it. If the form of the verb is correct, write *OK* above it.

seems

Example: Uncle Ted's <u>investment</u> in several emu farms **seem** to have failed.
                                                                          ^

1. The newest schedule for fall classes **are** ready.

Lesson 3

*s-v
agr*

2. The federal government's proposal for the pricing of prescription drugs **were** just published in the Federal Register.

3. The problems with his idea about the contest **is** what we expected.

4. In the first place, access to the computers in all campus buildings **require** a student ID.

5. I understand that the problem with the faucets **has** been fixed.

 For more practice correcting nearest-noun agreement errors, go to **Exercise Central** at **bedfordstmartins.com/commonsense**

Sentence Practice 2

CORRECTED SENTENCES APPEAR ON PAGE 459.

In the following sentences, the verb is in **boldface** type. Jump to the beginning of the sentence and find the first word that makes sense as the subject. Underline this subject and then make the verb agree with it. If the form of the verb is correct, write *OK* above it.

Example: The <u>carpets</u> we got for the new house **need** to be professionally cleaned.   *OK*

1. The characteristics of the early hominid found in Java by an archaeologist **is** still under debate.

2. Uncertainty about the terms of the agreement **have** thrown the issue into the courts.

3. As a result of the election, the public awareness of the many environmental issues surrounding the wetlands **have** been heightened.

4. The motion by the student council president and the two members **were** rejected.

5. Anne told me that one of those MP3 players that can play over five thousand songs **were** sold last week on eBay for just $50.

Sentence Practice 3

Check each of the following sentences for nearest-noun agreement errors and then correct the errors. Write *OK* in front of the sentences that do not contain a subject-verb agreement error. Then confirm your answer by rewriting each sentence to eliminate all words between the subject and the verb so that the subject and verb are next to each other. In the new sentence, underline the subject once and the verb twice.

Example: Most programs on the History Channel i̶s̶ quite $\overset{are}{}$ informative.

Rewrite: *Most programs are quite informative.*

1. The reporters covering the story for the local station has already left.

2. A movie based on a collection of the author's short stories are being filmed.

3. The hearings chaired by Senator Blather was a complete waste of time.

4. The files kept in the locked cabinet in the main office is never to leave the office.

5. The family involved in the fire at the warehouse deserves some privacy.

Editing Practice 1

CORRECTED SENTENCES APPEAR ON PAGE 459.

Correct all nearest-noun agreement errors in the following paragraph using the first correction as a model. The number in parentheses at the end of the paragraph indicates how many errors you should find.

Owning a pet, even the least demanding of creatures, a̶r̶e̶ never $\overset{is}{}$ easy. Over the years, we have had a number of cats, each of which have had a unique personality. Sometimes people seek out cats, and sometimes cats, instinctively knowing the house with the most defenseless owner, chooses where to live. One of the cats that fall into the latter category is a big, yellow tomcat we call Ferdinand. If cats could belong to political parties, Ferdinand would be a pacifist. Absolutely nothing that happens around him seem to upset him. For example, every one of the cats that we had before as pets were terrified of the vacuum cleaner. Ferdinand, however, completely ignores it. When he is sleeping on the rug, I have to vacuum around him. (5)

Editing Practice 2

CORRECTED SENTENCES APPEAR ON PAGE 459.

Correct all nearest-noun agreement errors in the following paragraph using the first correction as a model. The number in parentheses at the end of the paragraph indicates how many errors you should find.

               believes

A researcher who has studied the history of cats ~~believe~~ that

the ancestor of today's domestic cats were a species of small wildcats

native to northern Africa and southern Europe. The first evidence of cats

being domesticated animals kept by humans were found in Egypt. An

Egyptian official who oversaw large government grain storehouses were

apparently the first to use cats to control rats and mice. In fact, in Egypt,

the pet cats of an important official was considered sacred. When a

favored cat died, it was not uncommon to mummify the cat and to

give it tiny mummified mice to play with throughout eternity. (4)

Editing Practice 3

Correct all nearest-noun agreement errors in the following paragraph using the first correction as a model. The number in parentheses at the end of the paragraph indicates how many errors you should find.

is

The universe of pet owners ~~are~~ divided into two groups: cat

owners and dog owners. Of course, there are a few who actually keeps

both cats and dogs, but they do not count because they are the kind of

universal animal lovers who also end up with pet rabbits, gerbils, goldfish,

and nasty things that creep and crawl. The choice of animals, to a

certain degree, reflect the personality of the owner. Typically, the cat

lover, like cats, have a tendency to be an introvert who needs a lot of quiet

time alone. Many dog lovers, on the other hand, are like their pets. They

are both extroverts, social beings, who dislike being alone. (3)

Applying What You Know

On your own paper, write a paragraph or two about your experience with
pets. Draw an arrow from each subject to its verb. How many of the subjects
are the first noun or pronoun in the sentence?

The Bottom Line	If the verb is far away from the beginning of the sentence, **jump back** to the beginning and find the first subject that makes sense with the verb.

Agreement with
There is and *There was*

| EXAMPLE 1 | *Plural Subject Follows a Singular Verb* |

Error: ✗ There <u>is</u> a million <u>stories</u> in every big city.

                            are
Correction: There ~~is~~ a million <u>stories</u> in every big city.
                        ^

| EXAMPLE 2 | *Plural Subject Follows a Singular Verb* |

Error: ✗ There <u>was</u> <u>dozens</u> of books piled on the couch.

                            were
Correction: There ~~was~~ <u>dozens</u> of books piled on the couch.
                        ^

What's the Problem?

English, like most languages, has a special construction used to point out the existence of something. This type of sentence is constructed using *there* plus some form of the verb *be* (or a similar verb like *seem* or *appear*). For example, you might call your server's attention to a fly floating in your soup by saying, "Waiter! *There is* a fly in my soup!"

In sentences that begin with *There is* or *There was*, the subject is not in its normal position. Instead, it *follows* the verb. In our sentence about the soup, for example, the verb (*is*) agrees with the subject that follows it (*fly*):

There <u>is</u> a fly in my soup.

Subject-verb agreement errors occur in this type of sentence when the **subject** is **plural** but the preceding **verb** is **singular**, as in the two example sentences that started the lesson. Why do such errors occur? The problem is a conflict between casual spoken English and the more formal requirements

ESL

of the written language. When speaking English, we tend to use a singular verb, *there is* (present tense) or *there was* (past tense), even when the subject following it may be plural. Look at the two example sentences at the beginning of the lesson. If you heard those two sentences in a casual conversation, odds are you might not have noticed that they were actually ungrammatical.

Diagnostic Exercise

CORRECTED SENTENCES APPEAR ON PAGE 459.

Correct all errors in the following paragraph using the first correction as a model. The number in parentheses at the end of the paragraph indicates how many errors you should find.

> *are*
> Each year there ~~is~~ many new movies coming out of Hollywood.
> ^
>
> Each is designed for a certain segment of the moviegoing audience. There
>
> is car-crash films aimed at males under thirty. There is heart-warming
>
> romantic comedies for women over twenty. There is even the dreadful
>
> "slasher" movies for an audience that it is better not to think about. (3)

Fixing This Problem in Your Writing

Because subject-verb agreement errors with *there is* and *there was* are common in everyday speech, you may not be able to trust your ear to tell you when a sentence beginning with these words is ungrammatical. When you begin a sentence with *There is* or *There was*, check that it is grammatically correct with the following tip.

> **THERE IS/THERE WAS TIP**   When a sentence begins with *There is* or *There was*, the subject is the first noun (or pronoun) AFTER the verb that makes sense as the subject. Make sure the verb agrees with this subject.

Let's apply the tip to our two example sentences to find the correct subject and make sure the verb agrees with it:

Example 1:   ✗ There is a million stories in every big city.

SUBJECT

Tip applied: **✗** There is a million stories in every big city.

The plural subject *stories* does not agree with the singular verb *is*.

Correction:
are
There is a million stories in every big city.
^

Example 2: **✗** There was dozens of books piled on the couch.

SUBJECT

Tip applied: **✗** There was dozens of books piled on the couch.

The plural subject *dozens* does not agree with the singular verb *was*.

Correction:
were
There was dozens of books piled on the couch.
^

✱ Putting It All Together

Identify There is/There was Errors

_____ When you use a sentence that begins with *There is* or *There was*, check to make sure that the verb agrees with the actual subject — the first noun (or pronoun) that follows the verb and makes sense as the subject.

Correct There is/There was Errors

_____ If the subject and verb do not agree, change the form of the verb to match the subject. Use a singular verb form for a singular subject and a plural verb form for a plural subject.

Sentence Practice 1

CORRECTED SENTENCES APPEAR ON PAGE 460.

Using the *There is/There was* Tip, underline the first word or words following the verb that make sense as the subject. If there is an error in subject-verb agreement, write the correct form of the verb above the incorrect verb. If there is no error, write *OK* above the verb.

Example: There <u>is</u> never enough <u>hours</u> in the day to get
                 everything done.

(above "is": are; with caret under "is")

1. There was still dozens of presents to wrap.

2. Recently, there has been complaints about the noise in the dorms.

3. In the past, there was many more independently owned grocery stores.

4. There is still five shopping days until Christmas.

5. I didn't like the ending because there was too many loose ends that
    were not tied up.

 For more practice with subject-verb agreement, go to **Exercise Central** at
bedfordstmartins.com/commonsense

Sentence Practice 2

CORRECTED SENTENCES APPEAR ON PAGE 460.

Using the *There is/There was* Tip, underline the first word or words following the verb that make sense as a subject. If there is an error in subject-verb
agreement, write the correct form of the verb above the incorrect verb. If
there is no error, write *OK* above the verb.

Example: There <u>is</u> a <u>book store and a coffee shop</u> in the
                 building.

(above "is": are; with caret under "is")

1. There was an old woman who lived in a shoe.

2. Since it had snowed all night, there was only some trucks on the road.

3. There is some cookies and pastries to go with the coffee.

4. Fortunately, there was a flashlight and some candles in the closet.

5. There is lots of things for the kids to do there.

Sentence Practice 3

Rewrite the following sentences as *There is/There was* sentences.

Example: **An opener is in the drawer.**

Answer: *There is an opener in the drawer.*

1. A tavern is in the town.

2. A really nasty flu is going around.

3. A light golden haze is on the meadow.

4. Some good movies are playing this weekend.

5. Lots of fish are in the ocean.

6. Several fountains were spraying water in the courtyard.

7. People were waiting to be served.

8. A suite is available if you want to stay there.

9. Paint and masking tape were all over the floor where he had been working.

10. Is an airport in Coeur d'Alene?

Editing Practice 1

CORRECTED SENTENCES APPEAR ON PAGE 460.

Correct all the *there is/there was* errors in the following paragraph using the first correction as a model. The number in parentheses at the end of the paragraph indicates how many errors you should find.

           are

There is lots of reasons to visit Spain. First of all, there is all

those wonderful, long, sunny afternoons. Even though Spain is west of

England, Spain uses the same time zone as France and Italy, essentially

giving Spain year-round daylight savings time. Moreover, when Spain

goes on daylight savings time in the summer with the rest of Europe, there is actually two extra hours of daylight in Spain. The extra daylight in the

afternoon means that when the stores reopen after the siesta at 6 P.M.,

there is still plenty of daylight when people are out and about. Most

businesses and offices open at 8 or 9 in the morning to take advantage

of the fact that there is many hours of relative coolness in the morning

before the sun gets high enough to make it unbearable. (3)

Lesson 4

s-v agr

Editing Practice 2

CORRECTED SENTENCES APPEAR ON PAGE 460.

Correct all the *there is/there was* errors in the following paragraph using the first correction as a model. The number in parentheses at the end of the paragraph indicates how many errors you should find.

      Another reason to visit Spain is to explore the art and architecture.

        are

There is some of the world's greatest museums, art galleries, and

churches in Spain. In Madrid, there is half a dozen great art collections,

the most famous being the Prado. The Prado has the world's greatest

collection of Spanish paintings: there is innumerable paintings by Goya,

Velazquez, and El Greco. The enormous wealth Spain acquired from its

conquests in the New World allowed Spanish kings to purchase numerous

collections of great art masterpieces from the rest of Europe. In the Prado

there is fantastic collections of Dutch and Flemish paintings. For example,

there is nearly one hundred paintings by Rubens alone. (4)

Editing Practice 3

Correct all the *there is/there was* errors in the following paragraph using the first correction as a model. The number in parentheses at the end of the paragraph indicates how many errors you should find.

Another reason to visit Spain is that it is a lot of fun. There ~~is~~ *are*
wonderful local dishes and wines. A great way to sample local food is to
order *tapas*—small snacks or appetizers. There is a huge variety of tapas.
Every bar and restaurant has its tapas menu. Tapas are usually eaten
standing up at a counter with a glass of wine or beer. There is usually two
or three seafood dishes, several kinds of dried hams, and, of course, a
Spanish omelet. The dried hams, more or less like Italian prosciutto, are
really quite special. There is literally dozens of types of dried hams with
a wide range of prices. The upscale ones are quite expensive. With your
tapas, you might want a glass of local wine. Spain has become one of the
world's major wine producers. There is deep, earthy reds and surprisingly
good sparkling white wines—all at quite reasonable prices. Enjoy. (3)

Applying What You Know

Skim through a magazine or newspaper article and find five examples of sentences beginning with *There* plus some form of the verb *be*. Draw an arrow from the subject that follows the verb back to the verb. Do you find any mistakes?

The Bottom Line	There **is** always a **subject** after the verb in a *there is* or *there was* construction.

Agreement with Compound Subjects

Compound Subject with a Singular Verb

Error: ✗ The <u>pencils</u> and some <u>paper</u> <u>is</u> on the desk.

Correction: The <u>pencils</u> and some <u>paper</u> i̶s̶ on the desk.
                                      are

Compound Subject with a Singular Verb

Error: ✗ Our genetic <u>makeup</u> and our personal <u>experience</u> <u>defines</u> us.

Correction: Our genetic <u>makeup</u> and our personal <u>experience</u> d̶e̶f̶i̶n̶e̶s̶ us.
                          define

What's the Problem?

When two (or more) subjects are joined by *and,* they are called a **compound subject**. Compound subjects can cause **subject-verb agreement** errors when writers incorrectly think of the compound subject as a single unit and therefore use a singular verb. Compound subjects, however, are always plural and therefore must use plural verbs.

Diagnostic Exercise

CORRECTED SENTENCES APPEAR ON PAGE 460.

Correct all errors in the following paragraph using the first correction as a model. The number in parentheses at the end of the paragraph indicates how many errors you should find.

I work in a busy law office. Even though we now have voice mail,

take

answering the phone and writing down messages ~~takes~~ up a lot of

my time. I am also responsible for maintaining the law library, although

most of the time I do nothing more glamorous than shelving. The law

books and reference material is always left scattered around the library,

and some of the lawyers even leave their dirty coffee cups on the tables.

I used to have a relatively comfortable working area, but the new

computer terminal and modem has now taken up most of my personal

space; that's progress, I guess. Despite all the stress, meeting the needs

of clients and keeping track of all the information required in a modern

law office makes it a fascinating job. (3)

Fixing This Problem in Your Writing

Whenever your sentence contains *and,* check to see whether the *and* has joined two subjects to create a compound subject. If so, then the subject is plural, and you must use a plural verb. Use the following tip to help you identify compound subjects and get the right form of the verb.

> **THEY TIP**   Whenever *and* is used in the subject part of a sentence, see whether you can replace the entire subject portion of the sentence with the pronoun *they*. If you can, then the subject is a compound, and the verb must be made plural to agree with *they*.

Here is how the *They* Tip identifies the compound subject and the right form of the verb in the two example sentences:

Example 1:   ✗ The pencils and some paper is on the desk.

Tip applied: ✗ <u>They</u> <u>is</u> on the desk.

They does not agree with *is*. It requires a plural verb.

are

Correction: The pencils and some paper ~~is~~ on the desk.

Example 2:   ✗ Our genetic makeup and our personal experience defines us.

/ ✗ \

Tip applied: ✗ They <u>defines</u> us.

They does not agree with *defines*. It requires a plural verb.

Correction: Our genetic makeup and our personal experience
define
~~defines~~ us.
^

✳ Putting It All Together

Identify Compound-Subject Errors in Your Writing

____ When you see *and* in the subject part of your sentence, use the *They* Tip to determine whether you have a compound subject.

____ If *they* makes sense when it replaces the subject, the subject is compound and requires a plural verb.

Correct Compound-Subject Errors in Your Writing

____ If the verb in a sentence with a compound subject does not agree with *they*, change the verb to the plural form.

Sentence Practice 1

CORRECTED SENTENCES APPEAR ON PAGE 460.

Underline the compound subjects in the following sentences. If there is an error in subject-verb agreement, make the necessary correction.

were

Example: Two <u>dollars</u> and some <u>loose change</u> ~~was~~ not going to
^
be enough.

1. The milk and the eggs was still in the car.

2. The causes and treatments of chronic disease is becoming much better understood.

3. You don't have to be a health nut to believe that vegetables and fruit is the basis of a good diet.

4. Weekends and holidays lasts forever when you're not busy.

5. The advantages and disadvantages always seems to balance out.

 For more practice with subject-verb agreement, go to **Exercise Central** at **bedfordstmartins.com/commonsense**

Sentence Practice 2

CORRECTED SENTENCES APPEAR ON PAGE 461.

Underline the compound subjects in the following sentences. If there is an error in subject-verb agreement, make the necessary correction.

Example: *scare*
Thunder and lightning always ~~scares~~ my dog.

1. A rifle and a shotgun is used for very different kinds of hunting.

2. French, Latin, and German is the main source of English vocabulary.

3. The heat and humidity makes it very uncomfortable in the summer.

4. A cup of coffee and a cigarette doesn't make a complete meal.

5. What we see and what we get is not always the same thing.

Sentence Practice 3

Combine the following sentences by making a compound subject. Make the verb agree with the new subject. Underline the subject once and the verb twice in your new sentence.

Example: The dishpan is under the sink. The soap is under the sink.

Answer: *The dishpan and the soap are under the sink.*

1. Time waits for no man. Tide waits for no man.

2. Communism was a powerful force in the middle of the century. Fascism was a powerful force in the middle of the century.

3. The captain was reviewing the troops. The major was reviewing the troops.

4. What we say is important. What we do is important.

5. The advancing storm was enough to make us turn back. The gathering darkness was enough to make us turn back.

6. A hammer is in the garage. A chisel is in the garage.

7. The kitchen is in pretty bad shape. The bathroom is in pretty bad shape.

8. Her imagination makes her one of the best new novelists. Her strong sense of place makes her one of the best new novelists.

9. An officer was manning the checkpoint. A group of enlisted men was manning the checkpoint.

10. The ship's constant rocking was making us feel queasy. The smell of diesel fuel was making us feel queasy.

Editing Practice 1

CORRECTED SENTENCES APPEAR ON PAGE 461.

Correct all the compound-subject errors in the following paragraph using the first correction as a model. The number in parentheses at the end of the paragraph indicates how many errors you should find.

Many stories, plays, and even a famous opera ~~is~~ *are* based on the

legend of Don Juan. Don Juan's charm and wit supposedly makes him

utterly irresistible to women. The most famous treatment of the Don

Juan legend is in Mozart's opera, *Don Giovanni* (*Giovanni* is the Italian

form of the Spanish name *Juan,* or *John* in English). Mozart's opera is

highly unusual in that comedy and villainy is mixed together in almost

equal parts. For example, the actions and behavior of the Don constantly

keeps the audience off balance. His charm and bravery makes him almost

a hero at times. However, at other times, his aristocratic arrogance and deliberate cruelty to women reveals he is far from a true hero. The

delicate seduction of a willing woman and a violent rape is all the same

to him. (6)

Editing Practice 2

Correct all the compound-subject errors in the following paragraph using
the first correction as a model. The number in parentheses at the end of the
paragraph indicates how many errors you should find.

           The role and character of Don Giovanni's servant Leporello *are* ~~is~~

also quite unusual. Leporello and Don Giovanni often works together to

carry out a seduction. At first, his constant complaining and caustic asides

to the audience makes Leporello seem to be just a conventional comic

sidekick. Yet in some ways, Leporello's comments on and reactions to his

master's behavior becomes the focus of the opera. Leporello's grudging

admiration for the Don's charm and his repulsion at the Don's behavior

reflects the audience's equally mixed feelings. (4)

Applying What You Know

Using the Editing Practice essays in this lesson as models, write a paragraph
or two about a fictional character from a movie, play, or book. What are the
personality features that make this person interesting? Try to use as many
examples of compound subjects as you can. Then, use the *They* Tip to show
that the verbs you have used with compound subjects are correct.

The Bottom Line	A noun/pronoun and another noun/pronoun joined by *and* make a compound subject and **require** a plural verb.

REVIEW

Writers make errors in subject-verb agreement when they make the verb agree with a word that is not the actual subject of the sentence. The following chart points you to the tips that will help you avoid these kinds of errors.

TIP(S)	QUICK FIX AND EXAMPLE
Lesson 3. Nearest-Noun Agreement Errors	
The Finding the Subject Tip (p. 36) helps you find the real subject of a sentence so you can check for subject-verb agreement.	Find the real subject of long sentences by jumping back to the beginning of the sentence. *Error:* ✗ The <u>plan</u> that we have developed for city roads <u>are</u> ready for approval. *Correction:* The <u>plan</u> that we have developed for city roads *is* <s>are</s> ready for approval.
Lesson 4. Agreement with *There is* and *There was*	
The *There is/There was* Tip (p. 43) helps you find the subject of a sentence that begins with *There is* or *There was* so you can check for subject-verb agreement.	Make sure the verb agrees with the first noun (or pronoun) *after* the verb that makes sense as the subject. *Error:* ✗ There <u>is</u> a dozen <u>things</u> that could go wrong with your plan. *Correction:* There *are* <s>is</s> a dozen <u>things</u> that could go wrong with your plan.
Lesson 5. Agreement with Compound Subjects	
The *They* Tip (p. 50) helps you identify compound subjects (*diet and exercise*) so you know to use a plural verb.	If you can replace the subject portion of the sentence with *they*, use a plural verb. *Error:* ✗ The <u>sun</u> and the <u>wind</u> <u>was</u> chapping my lips. *Correction:* The <u>sun</u> and the <u>wind</u> *were* <s>was</s> chapping my lips.

Review Test

Underline the subjects in every sentence. Then, correct all errors using the first correction as a model. The number in parentheses at the end of each paragraph indicates how many errors you should find.

Although European explorers came to the New World in search

of gold, the new <u>fruits</u> and <u>vegetables</u> of the New World w̶a̶s̶ *were* much

more important to the Old World than all the gold they ever found. Before

contact with the New World, there was no tomatoes, corn, or potatoes in

the Old World. However, for many of us, the greatest gift of all the New

World's many agricultural products were the food and beverage that we

call *chocolate.* All products containing chocolate in any form comes from

the seeds of the cacao tree. The Mayas in Central America was the first to

discover how to produce chocolate from cacao seeds. (4)

A number of large, melon-shaped pods grow directly on the trunk

and larger branches of the cacao tree. Each of these pods contain up to

forty almond-shaped seeds. The seeds, after being removed from the pod,

fermented, and dried, is transformed into the commercial cocoa bean. (2)

The first step in producing chocolate from the cacao beans are to

remove the outer shells. What remains after the shells have been removed

are called *nibs.* Nibs contain a high percentage of a natural fat called *cocoa*

butter. When nibs are heated and ground, the cocoa butter is released. The

mixture of cocoa butter and finely ground nibs form a liquid called *chocolate*

liquor. The chocolate liquor, after being cooled and molded into little cakes,

are what we know as baking chocolate. Baking chocolate and sugar is at the

heart of all those wonderful chocolate goodies that we would all die for. (5)

Using Correct Verb Tenses

Terms That Can Help You Understand Verb Tenses

If you are not familiar with any of the following terms, look them up in the Guide to Grammar Terminology beginning on page 435.

helping verb	perfect tense
participle	present tense
past participle	tense
past tense	verb

The Nuts and Bolts of Verb Tenses

Verb *tense* indicates when the action in a sentence occurred. The lessons in Unit Three show you how to use the past tense, the present tense, and the perfect tense correctly.

Lesson 6 shows you how to avoid improper *tense shifting* between the present and past tenses. Knowing when to shift from one to the other requires an understanding of the fundamentally different roles of the two tenses. The **present tense** is used to state facts or make generalizations. The **past tense** is used to narrate events completed in the past.

> *Example:* ✗ Michelle took the bus whenever she has to work.
>
> *takes*
> *Correction:* Michelle ~~took~~ the bus whenever she has to work.

Lesson 7 shows you how to use the **perfect tenses**, which are made with the **helping verb** *have* (in some form) followed by a verb in the **past participle** form. If you use a present tense form of *have*, you create a *present perfect* verb (*Jesse has seen that movie dozens of times*). If you use the past tense *had*, you create a *past perfect* verb (*Aisha had seen the movie before she read the book*). Sometimes writers mistakenly use the past tense when they should use either the present perfect or the past perfect.

Example: ✗ I felt much more secure ever since we installed a home alarm system.

Correction: I *have* felt much more secure ever since we installed a home
                 alarm system.

Present, Past, and Tense Shifting

EXAMPLE 1	*Verbs Shift Tenses*

Error: ✗ Whenever we <u>went</u> to a restaurant, Robert always <u>makes</u> a fuss about ordering the best wine.

Correction 1:   Whenever we went to a restaurant, Robert always
made
~~makes~~ a fuss about ordering the best wine.
          ^
[*Both verbs are in past tense.*]

Correction 2:   Whenever we ~~went~~ to a restaurant, Robert always
          go
makes a fuss about ordering the best wine.
[*Both verbs are in present tense.*]

EXAMPLE 2	*Verbs Don't Shift Tense*

Error: ✗ She <u>went</u> to Trident Technical College, which <u>was</u> in South Carolina.

Correction: She went to Trident Technical College, which ~~was~~ in
          is
South Carolina.
          ^

What's the Problem?

Readers usually expect a piece of writing to maintain a consistent use of verb **tense** from beginning to end. For instance, in Example 1, the writer starts in the **past tense** and then inappropriately shifts to the **present tense**:

PAST TENSE
Example 1:   ✗ Whenever we <u>went</u> to a restaurant, Robert always
PRESENT TENSE
<u>makes</u> a fuss about ordering the best wine.

However, sometimes the opposite is true: the sentence is wrong if we don't shift verb tenses. For instance, in Example 2, the writer needs to shift the past tense *was* to the present tense *is* because, as the sentence is written, it implies something that the writer does not mean: that Trident Technical College is no longer in South Carolina.

Lesson 6

shift

Diagnostic Exercise

CORRECTED SENTENCES APPEAR ON PAGE 461.

Correct all verb tense errors in the following paragraph using the first correction as a model. The number in parentheses at the end of the paragraph indicates how many errors you should find.

Last summer we took a trip to Provence, a region in the southeast
                                    borders
corner of France, which ~~bordered~~ Italy. The name *Provence* referred
                                    ^
to the fact that it was the first province created by the ancient Romans

outside the Italian peninsula. Today, Provence still contained an amazing

number of well-preserved Roman ruins. While there were a few big towns

on the coast, Provence was famous for its wild country and beautiful

scenery. Provence was especially known for its abundance of wildflowers

in the spring. These flowers were used to make some of the world's most

expensive perfumes. (6)

Fixing This Problem in Your Writing

To shift or not to shift? Past tense and present tense have different uses, and we shift between the two tenses as we have need for those uses.

The past tense is used to describe events that happened in the past. Most stories and novels use the past tense as the basic vehicle of narration, for example:

My mother <u>called</u> us during dinner last night.

She <u>wanted</u> my sister's new phone number.

Fortunately, I <u>had</u> it in my Palm Pilot.

The present tense is used to make "timeless" statements or generalizations that are not only true for the time of the story but will continue to be true indefinitely. For example:

> **My mother always <u>seems</u> to call at the most inconvenient moment.**

> **She <u>lives</u> in a different time zone.**

> **She never <u>remembers</u> to take the time change into account.**

Here are two tips that will help you decide which tense to use.

PAST TENSE TIP   Use the past tense when telling a story about something that was completed in the past.

PRESENT TENSE TIP   Use the present tense to make "timeless" statements of fact or generalizations that are true now and will continue to be true indefinitely unless something happens to change the situation.

Let's return to the two examples that started the lesson:

PAST TENSE NARRATION

Example 1:   ✗ Whenever we <u>went</u> to a restaurant, Robert always
PRESENT TENSE GENERALIZATION
<u>makes</u> a fuss . . .

In this example, the writer couldn't decide whether he or she was telling a story (past tense) or making a generalization about Robert's wine ordering practices (present tense). The writer's jumping from past tense to present tense is an example of improper tense shifting. The solution is to be consistent: either tell a story in the past tense (following the Past Tense Tip) or make a generalization in the present tense (following the Present Tense Tip):

- **Tell a story.** Use the past tense to describe a specific event or events that happened in the past.

  PAST TENSE
  Tip applied: Whenever we <u>went</u> to a restaurant, Robert always
  PAST TENSE
  <u>made</u> a fuss about ordering the best wine.

- **Make a generalization.** Use the present tense to generalize about something that will continue to be true indefinitely unless something happens to change the situation.

PRESENT TENSE

Tip applied: Whenever we <u>go</u> to a restaurant, Robert always

PRESENT TENSE

<u>makes</u> a fuss about ordering the best wine.

Let's look at the other example.

Lesson 6

shift

| PAST TENSE | PAST TENSE |
| NARRATION | NARRATION |

Example 2:   ✗ She <u>went</u> to Trident Technical College, which <u>was</u> in South Carolina.

In this sentence, a shift in tense is necessary. *She* has finished attending Trident Technical College, so the use of the past tense in this part of the sentence is correct. However, the college is still, and probably always will be, in South Carolina. So, in the second part of the sentence, the verb must shift to the present tense:

| PAST TENSE | PRESENT TENSE |
| NARRATION | STATEMENT OF FACT |

Tip applied: She <u>went</u> to Trident Technical College, which <u>is</u> in South Carolina.

✳ *Putting It All Together*

Identify Problems with Verb Tense and Tense Shifting

_____ Identify every present and past tense verb in your sentence.

_____ Ask yourself whether the verb is used in a narrative that deals with past events or whether the verb is used to make a statement of fact or a generalization.

Correct Problems with Verb Tense and Tense Shifting

_____ Use the past tense when describing or discussing events that happened or were completed in the past.

_____ Use the present tense to make statements of fact or generalizations.

_____ If your sentence combines narratives of past events with statements of fact or generalizations, shift tenses accordingly.

Sentence Practice 1

CORRECTED SENTENCES APPEAR ON PAGE 461.

Correct the present and past tense errors in the following sentences by drawing a line through each error and writing the correct tense above it. If the sentence is correct, write *OK* above it.

Lesson 6

shift

seem

Example: I always ~~seemed~~ to be running late on Mondays.

1. Key West was the southernmost point in the continental United States.

2. Whenever the weather changes, my joints started to ache.

3. We visited one ancient site after another until they all run together.

4. Shakespeare is idolized in the nineteenth century.

5. Interstate Highway 405 went around downtown Seattle, allowing drivers to miss the worst of urban traffic.

 For more practice with past and present tense shifting, go to **Exercise Central** at **bedfordstmartins.com/commonsense**

Sentence Practice 2

CORRECTED SENTENCES APPEAR ON PAGE 461.

Correct the present and past tense errors in the following sentences by drawing a line through each error and writing the correct tense above it. If the sentence is correct, write *OK* above it.

go

Example: It always seems to rain whenever we ~~went~~ to the beach.

1. Telephone marketers always call when we were eating.

2. According to the style sheet, scientific papers were rarely written in the first person.

3. I always try to return messages before I left the office.

4.   She broke her ankle skiing down the trail that led to the ranger cabin.

5.   When it rains, it poured.

Sentence Practice 3

Circle the correct form of the verb in the following sentences.

Example: **We all know that Boxing Day (is / was) the day after Christmas.**

1.   I think that a matinee performance typically (started / starts) at two.

2.   I got a shock when I (plug / plugged) that old lamp in.

3.   She always calls her kids when she (is / was) going to be late.

4.   Artists today are still influenced by the art styles that (originate / originated) in prewar Germany.

5.   After all our work, we discovered that the answer (is / was) in the back of the book.

6.   He makes it sound like every little problem (is / was) a major crisis.

7.   My parents always traveled first class, which (seems / seemed) ostentatious today.

8.   The guide informed us that the trains for Rome (leave / left) from Platform 3.

9.   It is amusing that the governor (pretends / pretended) that he was a simple man of the people.

10. It is really true; the French (do / did) go on vacation all of August.

Editing Practice 1

CORRECTED SENTENCES APPEAR ON PAGE 461.

Correct all the verb tense errors in the following paragraphs using the first correction as a model. The number in parentheses at the end of each paragraph indicates how many errors you should find.

Even though Shakespeare died in 1616, performances of his plays
have
~~had~~ continued without interruption right up to today. I recently attend
^
the Oregon Shakespeare Festival in Ashland, Oregon. In planning the

performances, the director has to make some big decisions about how to

stage plays that were more than 350 years old. The biggest problem for

all directors today was whether to present Shakespearian plays in period

costume or in more modern dress. (4)

Lesson 6

shift

Staging the plays in modern dress made the plays more interesting

and often a lot more fun. For example, in a performance of *Henry IV,*

Part I at Ashland a few years ago, Falstaff comes on stage for the first time

on a motor scooter with a case of beer strapped on behind. Sometimes,

staging plays in different time periods allowed the director to make

political or social comments. An outstanding example of this was the 1995

movie version of *Richard III* with Ian McKellen in an imaginary Fascist

England in the 1930's. McKellen's performance as an all-powerful, sadistic

ruler in an authoritarian state chilled the viewers' blood. Nobody could see

this film and not be terrified of unrestrained government power. (5)

Editing Practice 2

CORRECTED SENTENCES APPEAR ON PAGE 462.

Correct all the verb tense errors in the following paragraph using the first correction as a model. The number in parentheses at the end of the paragraph
indicates how many errors you should find.

began
Ashland's Shakespeare Festival ~~begins~~ almost by accident as
^
an outgrowth of the old Chautauqua circuit. Chautauqua provides

entertainment to rural America before the days of radio and movies.

Chautauqua is a mix of popular lecturers, music, and vaudeville acts —

something that seems strange today. After the collapse of Chautauqua,

Ashland finds itself with a good-sized summer theater facility. After

unsuccessfully trying a variety of entertainments, including boxing

matches, the faculty from the local college decides to stage a few

Shakespearian plays. The plays proved to be so successful that the

Oregon Shakespeare Festival is born and has grown to become a highly

successful theatrical company today. (5)

Lesson 6

shift

Editing Practice 3

Correct all the verb tense errors in the following paragraph using the first correction as a model. The number in parentheses at the end of the paragraph indicates how many errors you should find.

> *is*
> Shakespeare ~~was~~ certainly the most influential playwright in the
>   ^
> history of drama. Given the fact that his plays are written about four
>
> hundred years ago in a language that is now quite hard to follow, it was
>
> a testament to his importance that so many of his plays were still staged
>
> today. Another measure of Shakespeare's importance was the number of
>
> his plays that appeared as operas, ballets, and movies. Three movies based
>
> on Shakespeare's plays had won Oscars for best picture. They are *Hamlet*
>
> in 1948; *West Side Story* (based on *Romeo and Juliet*) in 1961; and
>
> *Shakespeare in Love* (about the writing of *Romeo and Juliet*) in 1998. (6)

Applying What You Know

On a separate sheet of paper, write about a play or movie you have seen recently. Try to mix past tense descriptions of the action and present tense generalizations about the meaning or effectiveness of the play or movie.

The Bottom Line	**Keep** the verbs in a sentence in the same tense unless you **have** a reason for mixing past tense narration with present tense generalizations or statements of fact.

LESSON 7

The Past and the Perfect Tenses

| EXAMPLE 1 | *Past Tense Used Instead of Present Perfect Tense* |

Error: ✗ We <u>regretted</u> our choice ever since we bought that car.

Correction: We regretted our choice ever since we bought that car.
              have
              ^

| EXAMPLE 2 | *Past Tense Used Instead of Past Perfect Tense* |

Error: ✗ When we bought the house last year, it <u>was</u> empty for ten years.

Correction: When we bought the house last year, it ~~was~~ empty for ten years.
                                        had been
                                        ^

What's the Problem?

The **perfect tenses** are formed with the helping verb *have* in some form followed by the **past participle** form of a second verb. When the present tense forms of *have* (*has* or *have*) are used, the **present perfect tense** is formed. When the past tense *had* is used, the **past perfect tense** is formed. Here are some examples:

Present Perfect Tense	*Past Perfect Tense*
has walked, have walked	had walked
has sung, have sung	had sung
has been, have been	had been

The present perfect and past perfect tenses allow us to express subtle differences in the time relationship of past events. The *present perfect tense* is used to indicate an action that began in the past and continues to the present. The *past perfect tense* is used to indicate an action that took place in the past before another past action. Many writers mistakenly use the past tense

68

when they should use either the present perfect tense (Example 1) or the past perfect tense (Example 2). We'll discuss these examples in detail below.

Diagnostic Exercise

CORRECTED SENTENCES APPEAR ON PAGE 462.

Correct all verb tense errors in the following paragraph using the first correction as a model. The number in parentheses at the end of the paragraph indicates how many errors you should find.

have been

Unfortunately, most people ~~were~~ involved in an automobile
^

accident at some time. I was involved in several, but my luckiest

accident was one that never happened. Just after I got my driver's

license, I borrowed the family car to go to a party. Although it was

a very tame party, I left feeling a little hyper and silly. It was night, and

there were no street lights nearby. I parked a little distance from the

house, so my car was by itself. I got into the car and decided to show

off a little bit by throwing the car into reverse and flooring it. I went

about twenty yards backward before I thought to myself that I was

doing something pretty dangerous. I slammed on the brakes in a panic.

I got out of the car and found that my back bumper was about four inches

from a parked car that I never saw. Whenever I feel an urge to push my

luck driving, I remind myself of the accident that almost happened. (6)

Fixing This Problem in Your Writing

Understanding the Perfect Tenses

The key to using the perfect tenses correctly is understanding the difference in meaning between the past tense and the two perfect tenses. The following are brief descriptions of these three tenses.

- The **past tense** is used to refer to an event that is over and done with. The event could have happened at a single moment in time or lasted for years. In either case, the event is now history.

Past Tense: Elliot <u>lived</u> in Chicago for ten years. [He no longer lives there.]

- The **present perfect tense** is used to refer to an event that began at some point in the past and that continues in the present.

Present Perfect Tense: Elliot <u>has lived</u> in Chicago for ten years. [He still lives there.]

- The **past perfect tense** is used to indicate that a particular event in the past was completed *before* some more recent past event took place. Here is an example:

Past Perfect Tense: Elliot <u>had lived</u> in Chicago ten years before we met.
[Elliot had lived in Chicago ten years before he met the writer, and he may or may not still live there today.]

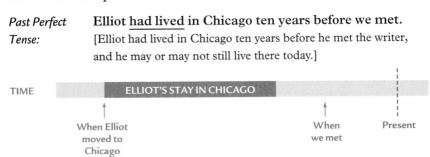

Choosing between Past Tense and Present Perfect Tense

The basic distinction between the past tense and the present perfect tense is whether the past event is over and done with (past tense) or whether it continues up to the present (present perfect). Here is a tip to help you know when to use the present perfect tense.

> **PRESENT PERFECT TIP** Use the present perfect tense to emphasize that a past action has continued over a span of time up to the present moment.

Let's apply this tip to the first example sentence:

	PAST TENSE
Example 1:	✗ We <u>regretted</u> our choice ever since we bought that car.
Tip applied:	✗ Past tense = *regretted* = We no longer regret the choice.
	✓ Present perfect tense = *have regretted* = We still regret the choice.
Correction:	We _∧ regretted our choice ever since we bought that car. (*have*)

In this example, the use of the past tense *regretted* is incorrect because the writer still regrets the choice of car, even today. Therefore, the present perfect tense should be used instead.

Choosing between Past Tense and Past Perfect Tense

As noted above, the past tense is used to describe an event that happened in the past. The past perfect tense emphasizes the before-and-after sequence of *two* past events. Here is a tip to help you know when to use the past perfect tense.

> **PAST PERFECT TIP** Use the past perfect tense to show that one event in the past was completed *before a* more recent past event took place.

Let's apply the tip to the second example sentence:

	PAST TENSE
Example 2:	✗ When we bought the house last year, it <u>was</u> empty for ten years.
Tip applied:	✗ Past tense = *was* = The house was empty (but when?).
	✓ Past perfect tip = *had been* = The house was empty before we bought it.

Correction: had been
When we bought the house last year, it ~~was~~ empty for
ten years.
                                                    ^

There are two past events here: (1) a ten-year period before last year during which time the house had stood empty and (2) the moment last year when the writer bought the house. The sentence is much clearer if we use the past perfect tense to emphasize the time sequence between the two different past events.

Writers often use the past perfect tense to imply that one past event *caused* a later past event. For example, the sentence *They had gotten into a big fight just before they broke up* implies that they broke up *because* of their big fight.

Lesson 7

vt

✳ *Putting It All Together*

Identify Errors in Using the Past and the Perfect Tenses

_____ Identify past tense verbs in your sentence.

_____ Ask yourself whether you are describing an event that began and ended entirely in the past or one that began in the past and continues into the present.

_____ Check to see whether you are describing two past events in a definite sequence or with a cause-and-effect relationship.

Correct Errors in Using the Past and the Perfect Tenses

_____ If you are describing an event that began and ended entirely in the past, use the past tense (usually the *-ed* form of the verb).

_____ If you are describing an event that began in the past and continues into the present, use the present perfect tense (*has* or *have* + past participle).

_____ If you are connecting two past events in a single sentence, use the past perfect tense (*had* + past participle).

Sentence Practice 1

CORRECTED SENTENCES APPEAR ON PAGE 462.

The following sentences contain mistakes involving the use of the past, the present perfect, and the past perfect tenses. Correct each error as shown in the following example.

had closed

Example: The storm ~~closed~~ the runways before we got clearance
to take off. ^

Lesson 7

vt

1. We had a test every week this semester.

2. It has rained last week during the parade.

3. When we returned from vacation, we found that our house was
broken into.

4. I was interested in Egyptology for years.

5. After Holmes solved a case, Watson wrote it up for posterity.

 For more practice using the past and perfect tenses, go to **Exercise Central** at
bedfordstmartins.com/commonsense

Sentence Practice 2

CORRECTED SENTENCES APPEAR ON PAGE 462.

The following sentences contain mistakes involving the use of the past, the
present perfect, and the past perfect tenses. Correct each error as shown in
the following example.

have seen

Example: Ever since I got my DVD player, I ~~saw~~ dozens of
movies. ^

1. He has wrecked his knee making a tackle on the first play of the game.

2. I already noticed the problem before you told me about it.

3. He worked overtime for the past six months.

4. We had to forfeit the game after we used an ineligible player.

5. It snowed every day since Christmas.

Sentence Practice 3

Combine the following sentences by adding the underlined information in
the second sentence to the first sentence. Change the past tense of the first
sentence to the present perfect or past perfect tense as appropriate.

Example: The board met. They met <u>every Monday this past year.</u>

has met

Answer: The board ~~met~~ every Monday this past year.
                                    ^

1. The whistle already sounded. This was <u>before the ball went into the net.</u>

2. We worked on our car. We worked <u>since early this morning.</u>

3. I just stepped into the shower. I did that <u>when the phone rang.</u>

4. Our team played together. They did that <u>for three seasons now.</u>

5. Fortunately, Elvis already left the building. He left <u>before the reporters arrived.</u>

Editing Practice 1

CORRECTED SENTENCES APPEAR ON PAGE 462.

Correct all the tense errors in the following paragraph using the first correction as a model. The number in parentheses at the end of the paragraph indicates how many errors you should find.

has

The number of deaths resulting from traffic accidents declined
                                                                          ^
steadily over the past decade. In recent years, researchers cited a number

of different reasons: improved safety of vehicles, increased use of seat

belts and airbags, and fewer drunk drivers. Automobile manufacturers

were reluctant to even talk about safety until the federal government

began mandating standards in the 1980's. Over the years, manufacturers

continued to resist installing even inexpensive safety features. For example,

manufacturers were very slow to produce cars with daytime headlights,

even though in recent years many Canadian researchers demonstrated

that this no-cost item results in significantly fewer accidents. (5)

Editing Practice 2

Correct all tense errors in the following paragraph using the first correction as a model. The number in parentheses at the end of the paragraph indicates how many errors you should find.

Actually, two large factors in reducing automobile accident
deaths over the last decade ~~were~~ *have been* changes in driver behavior. First,

we became much more consistent in routinely using seat belts for

ourselves, and car seats for our children. Now, most of us would never

start the car until we first fastened the seat belts and buckled the kids in.

It is appalling to think how common it was even a few years ago to see kids

standing up on the seats of cars. How quickly that sight became a rarity.

Second, in recent years there was a general decline in the use of alcohol.

As a result, alcohol-related accidents, although still too common, became

a lot less frequent than they used to be. In the last few years, there was

a real change in society's tolerance of drinking and driving. (6)

Applying What You Know

On your own paper, write a short essay about some aspect of automobile safety. Try to use a mixture of the past tense and the two perfect tenses. Use the Putting It All Together checklist on page 72 to make sure that the tenses in your essay are correct.

The Bottom Line	Use the present perfect tense for an action that **has continued** up to the present. Use the past perfect tense to emphasize that an earlier event **had ended** before a more recent event started.

UNIT THREE: Using Correct Verb Tenses

Unit Three discussed how to use verb tenses correctly. The following chart points you to the tips that will help you avoid verb-tense errors.

TIP(S)	QUICK FIX AND EXAMPLES
Lesson 6. Present, Past, and Tense Shifting	
The Past Tense Tip (p. 61) and Present Tense Tip (p. 61) help you remember the difference between the two tenses so you know when it is appropriate to shift tenses and when it is not.	Use the past tense when telling a story and the present tense to make "timeless" statements of fact or generalizations. *Error:* ✗ Denver was on the eastern slopes of the Rockies. *Correction:* Denver ~~was~~ *is* on the eastern slopes of the Rockies.
Lesson 7. The Past and the Perfect Tenses	
The Present Perfect Tip (p. 71) and Past Perfect Tip (p. 71) help you understand the difference between the two perfect tenses.	Use the present perfect (*has* or *have* + *walked*) when a past action continues up to the present moment. Use the past perfect (*had* + *walked*) to show that one event in the past (in this case, the walking) was completed before another event. *Error:* ✗ I saw the memo before the announcement was made public. *Correction:* I ~~saw~~ *had seen* the memo before the announcement was made public.

Review Test

Correct the verb errors in the following paragraphs using the first correction as a model. The number in parentheses at the end of each paragraph indicates how many errors you should find.

Thanks to federal regulations, industrial pollution ~~was~~ *has been* significantly reduced over the past several decades. However, we begin to realize that there is another form of water pollution that was completely outside state

76

and federal regulation: "nonpoint-source" pollution. Existing regulations dealt with pollution that has a distinct point of origin — a particular factory or plant, for example, whose unregulated discharge can be directly measured. "Point-of-origin" pollution consists of relatively high levels of pollutants in a small area. The effects that a particular point-of-origin had on the immediate area are easy to identify, and we can cost them out. (4)

Nonpoint-source pollution is a different matter altogether. Every time we get into our car and start it up, we release a relatively small amount of various pollutants into the atmosphere. These pollutants are dispersed over such a wide area that nobody can tell where they came from or even when they are put into the air. The problem that defeated environmental agencies for years is how to deal with such overwhelming numbers of little polluters. A similar problem existed for years with runoff. Every time it rains, water dissolves the grease and oil on our driveways and washes it off into nearby streams. The amount of pollution per square foot of paved surface is not very great, but the cumulative effect from millions of square feet of pavement can be devastating. (3)

UNIT FOUR
Understanding Pronouns

Terms That Can Help You Understand Pronouns

If you are not familiar with any of the following terms, look them up in the Guide to Grammar Terminology beginning on page 435.

adjective
agreement
direct object
noun
object
personal pronoun
preposition

pronoun
pronoun antecedent
relative pronoun
sexist language
subject
verb

The Nuts and Bolts of Understanding Pronouns

Pronouns are an important part of many languages. As noun replacers, they help us avoid having to use the same words over and over (as in *Ms. Ramone stopped by yesterday, and Ms. Ramone took us for a ride in Ms. Ramone's new car*). Pronouns are useful because they can fit into almost any sentence.

But the adaptability of pronouns also creates problems. Because they can refer to so many things, writers must take care to make the reference of each pronoun clear. The lessons in this unit address some common difficulties involving pronouns.

Lesson 8 shows you how to make a pronoun and the word it refers to either both singular *or* both plural.

Example: ✗ The person who called didn't leave their phone number.

Correction: The person who called didn't leave ~~their~~ *her* phone number.

78

Lesson 9 shows you how to make clear what a pronoun refers to.

Example: ✗ Our dog gets so mad at the cat that it chases its tail.

Correction: Our cat gets the dog so mad it chases its own tail.

Lessons 10 and 11 help you to choose between similar pronouns: *I* or *me?*
she or *her? he* or *him?* (see Lesson 10); *who, whom,* or *that?* (see Lesson 11).

Example: ✗ Dolly and me went skiing.

                                  I
Correction: Dolly and ~~me~~ went skiing.
                                  ^

Example: ✗ Our group decided whom would type our paper.

                                        who
Correction: Our group decided ~~whom~~ would type our paper.
                                        ^

Lesson 12 helps you to use nonsexist language to ensure that nouns and
pronouns refer, as appropriate, to both males and females.

Example: ✗ Everyone should have completed his assignment.

                                              the
Correction: Everyone should have completed ~~his~~ assignment.
                                              ^

Pronoun Agreement

EXAMPLE 1

Error: ✗ A <u>teacher</u> should explain <u>their</u> assignments carefully.

Teachers

Correction: ~~A teacher~~ should explain their assignments carefully.
            ^

EXAMPLE 2

Error: ✗ Did <u>everybody</u> cast <u>their</u> vote in the last election?

Correction: Did everybody ~~cast their~~ vote in the last election?

What's the Problem?

Personal pronouns include *I, he, she, it, they, we,* and all their varied forms, such as *me, him, his, her, its, their,* and *them.* A personal pronoun often refers back to a person, place, or thing (called a **pronoun antecedent**). This pronoun and antecedent should be in **agreement**; that is, they should match in number, person, and gender. In the following example, the pronoun *they* refers back to its antecedent, *voters.* Both *they* and *voters* are plural, so they agree.

Example: The <u>voters</u> turned out even in pouring rain, and <u>they</u> reelected the mayor.

This lesson focuses on the most common problem with pronoun agreement: making sure a personal pronoun agrees in number with its antecedent. Let's look at the two example sentences from the beginning of the lesson, which illustrate this problem.

Example 1: ✗ A <u>teacher</u> should explain <u>their</u> assignments carefully.

The pronoun *their* is plural, but *teacher* is singular.

Example 2:   ✗ Did everybody cast their vote in the last election?

The pronoun *their* is plural, but *everybody* is singular.

It is easy to see why these errors occur. Words such as *everybody, everyone, anybody,* and *someone* seem plural; *everybody* in particular appears to refer to many people. In Example 1, *teacher* similarly refers to an entire category of people, not just one particular teacher. Nonetheless, these words are always grammatically singular. Another reason this error occurs is that writers do not want to be sexist. If Examples 1 and 2 used *his* instead of *their*, the writer would avoid an agreement error but might be considered sexist for excluding females. Writers should learn ways to avoid both kinds of problems—agreement errors and sexist language. (See Lesson 12 for more on sexist language.)

Lesson 8

pron agr

Diagnostic Exercise

CORRECTED SENTENCES APPEAR ON PAGE 463.

Correct all the pronoun agreement errors in the following paragraph using the first correction as a model. The number in parentheses at the end of the paragraph indicates how many errors you should find.

Soldiers commit
~~A soldier commits~~ a war crime when they violate norms of acceptable behavior in times of war. Few people want war, but most want their rights and those of others to be respected as much as possible when war occurs. For instance, almost everybody agrees that a prisoner should have their physical needs attended to and should not be physically or mentally tortured. An officer who orders their troops to massacre civilians is also considered to be committing a war crime; the My Lai massacre during the Vietnam war is an example. (2)

Fixing This Problem in Your Writing

Identifying Pronoun Agreement Errors

Most pronoun agreement errors involve one particular pronoun (*they*) and its various forms (*their, them*). *They, their,* and *them* are always plural. This first tip helps you determine if an antecedent is singular or plural.

> **ARE TIP**   When using *they*, *their*, or *them*, make sure the antecedent is also plural. If you can use the plural verb *are* after the antecedent, it is indeed plural and in agreement with *they*, *their*, or *them*. If *are* does not seem to fit, there is an agreement error.

In Example 1, the *Are* Tip shows us that there is a problem with pronoun agreement.

ANTECEDENT   PRONOUN
↓   ↓

Lesson 8

pron
agr

Example 1:   ✗ A <u>teacher</u> should explain <u>their</u> assignments carefully.

Tip applied: ✗ A teacher *are*?

The test sentence sounds strange because *are* is not a verb you would use with *teacher*: *teacher* is singular while *are* is plural. Thus, the *Are* Tip shows us that the singular noun *teacher* cannot agree with the plural pronoun *their*.

Correcting Pronoun Agreement Errors

In the following tip, we explain one of the easiest ways to correct pronoun agreement errors involving *they*, *their*, and *them*.

> **PLURAL TIP**   To correct most agreement errors involving forms of the pronoun *their*, replace the singular antecedent with a plural one.

In Example 1, we corrected the agreement error by making the antecedent plural.

Teachers

Correction: ~~A teacher~~ should explain their assignments carefully.

The plural pronoun *their* now agrees with the plural antecedent *teachers*.

Example 2 is trickier because *everybody* has a plural "feel" to it. But would you ever say *Everybody are*?

ANTECEDENT   PRONOUN
↓   ↓

Example 2:   ✗ Did <u>everybody</u> cast <u>their</u> vote in the last election?

Tip applied: ✗ Everybody *are*?

Because *everybody* fails the *Are* Tip test, we know that it is singular and does not agree with the plural *their*. Using the Plural Tip, we could change *everybody* to a plural term:

Correction: Did ~~everybody~~ cast their ~~vote~~ in the last election?
    all members ^   *votes* ^

> The plural pronoun *their* now agrees with the plural antecedent *all members*. Because *all members* is plural, *vote* must change to *votes*.

A second strategy is to revise so you don't need the pronoun *their*. Eliminating the pronoun eliminates the problem with pronoun agreement. (Notice also that the revised sentence is more concise.)

Correction: Did everybody ~~cast their~~ vote in the last election?

A third way to correct pronoun agreement errors is to use *his or her* instead of *their* with a singular subject.

Correction: Did everybody cast ~~their~~ vote in the last election?
        his or her   ^

> The singular pronoun combination *his or her* now agrees with the singular antecedent *everybody*.

✳ More Examples

Error: ✗ <u>Everyone</u> in my dorm parks <u>their</u> car in Lot B.

Correction: ~~Everyone~~ in my dorm ~~parks~~ their ~~car~~ in Lot B.
        All residents ^   *park* ^   *cars* ^

Error: ✗ <u>Somebody</u> at the airport forgot to bring <u>their</u> ID card.

Correction: Somebody at the airport forgot to bring ~~their~~ ID card.
            an ^

Error: ✗ Almost every <u>woman</u> who has dated Ralph did not let him meet <u>their</u> parents.

Correction: Almost every woman who has dated Ralph did not let him meet ~~their~~ parents.
            her ^

✱ *Putting It All Together*

Identify Pronoun Agreement Errors

_____ Most pronoun agreement errors involve *they, their,* or *them,* so look for these pronouns, which are always plural.

_____ Does each of these pronouns have an antecedent—a word that the pronoun refers back to? If so, the antecedent should also be plural.

_____ To make sure the antecedent is plural, use the *Are* Tip. If *are* sounds odd after the antecedent, the antecedent is singular, meaning it does not agree with *they, their,* or *them.*

Correct Pronoun Agreement Errors

_____ The Plural Tip is one easy way to correct most agreement errors. Revise the antecedent so that it is plural.

_____ Other correction strategies are to reword the sentence so that you do not need a pronoun at all, or to use *his, her,* or *his or her* instead of *their* with a singular subject.

Lesson 8

*pron
agr*

Sentence Practice 1

CORRECTED SENTENCES APPEAR ON PAGE 463.

In each sentence, underline the pronoun once and the antecedent twice. Write *plural* or *singular* above the pronoun and its antecedent. Correct any agreement problems. If a sentence has no such error(s), write *OK* above it.

> *singular*   *plural*
> *Example:*   **Everybody** in my composition class had **their** first essay returned.

> *Correction:*   **Everybody** in my composition class had ~~their~~ first essay
>   *his or her*
>   returned.
>   ^

1. A doctor must have insurance covering them against malpractice liability.

2. Everyone must bring their calculator on Friday.

3. College students have to pick majors that interest him.

4. I asked my roommates whether they wanted to go out to eat, but they had already eaten.

5. Anybody who hasn't turned in their test should do so now.

 For more practice with pronoun agreement, go to **Exercise Central** at **bedfordstmartins.com/commonsense**

Sentence Practice 2

CORRECTED SENTENCES APPEAR ON PAGE 463.

In each sentence, underline the pronoun once and the antecedent twice. Write *plural* or *singular* above the pronoun and antecedent. Correct any agreement problems. If a sentence has no such error(s), write *OK* above it.

Example:
          singular   *plural*
Every <u>teacher</u> is giving <u>their</u> final exam on the same day!

Correction:
     All teachers are   *exams*
~~Every teacher is~~ giving their final ~~exam~~ on the same day!

1. Someone parked their car in a place where it will be towed.

2. Almost everyone brought his or her book to class today.

3. Most people who can recall the assassination of John F. Kennedy seem able to remember exactly what they were doing when they heard the news.

4. Did somebody take my pen instead of theirs?

5. Out of thirty people in their class, nobody knew that Becca and Alyssa are sisters.

Sentence Practice 3

Combine the following sentences with *and, but,* or *or.* Make whatever changes are necessary to eliminate errors in pronoun agreement.

> *Example:*　　Sometimes, a teacher has to act like a drill sergeant.
> They also need the patience of a saint.

> *Answer:*　　*Sometimes, teachers have to act like drill sergeants, but they also need the patience of a saint.*

Lesson 8

pron agr

1. A driver needs to be careful. They might have a wreck.

2. Everyone here needs to be quiet for a moment. They can continue talking after I finish adding these numbers.

3. A mall is a convenient place to shop. They all seem the same.

4. Someone ate at this table before us. They were sloppy.

5. Each book in this room is old. These are part of a valuable collection.

6. A lab assistant is available. They will come to you if you raise your hand.

7. Replace worn out fan belts. It might break when you are on the road.

8. Final course examinations are normally given in the morning. Not if it is for a lab course.

9. Get their names. Help get him seated as soon as possible.

10. The restaurant is nearby. They aren't very good.

Editing Practice 1

CORRECTED SENTENCES APPEAR ON PAGE 463.

Correct all the pronoun agreement errors in the following paragraphs using the first correction as a model. The number in parentheses at the end of each paragraph indicates how many errors you should find.

My brother has been collecting certain cards that have been
popular in the last few years. ~~Someone~~ *People* might merely collect these
cards, or they might actually play games with them. Many years ago,
a card collector would have likely collected sports cards, but nowadays
they collect cards based on strange creatures or superhuman characters
from comics and TV shows. Many of these cards are based on Japanese
popular culture, and they are especially likely to deal with magical beings
that engage in duels. (1)

At one time, Pokémon was the most popular card game. The person
who created these cards must have made a great deal of money from their
creations. Another Japanese-inspired game is called Yu Gi Oh, and it is
still popular. In Yu Gi Oh, a player selects a card from their hand to play.
The opponent likewise picks a card they will duel with. I thought this was
a mindless game until I saw how much math and strategy are involved
in the dueling stage. The game is so complex that somebody learning
the game needs all the help they can get from an experienced player.
I doubt I will collect or play this game, but I won't make fun of it anymore
either. (4)

Editing Practice 2

Correct all the pronoun agreement errors in the following paragraph using
the first correction as a model. The number in parentheses at the end of the
paragraph indicates how many errors you should find.

When I was young, sports were only available through the schools.
That meant that during the summer, ~~a kid~~ *kids* had absolutely no access to
organized sports when they actually had free time to engage in them.

The situation is completely different for kids today. The big problem for them is having so many options that he doesn't know what to pick. Should kids play Little League baseball, should he do tennis at Parks and Recreation, or should they take swimming lessons at the "Y"? Should they take karate or should he take tae kwon do? It sometimes seems to me that kids today are absolutely lost in a sea of options, making it easy for him to flit from one sport to another without ever getting very good at any one of them. Maybe it is not so critical with individual sports or martial arts because it can be started up again without too much loss of skills. A team sport is a totally different matter because they take a long time to build team spirit or a sense of group cohesiveness. (6)

Lesson 8

pron agr

Applying What You Know

Using *they, their,* or *them* at least five times, write a paragraph or two on how you would help a child decide on what activities he or she should engage in during the summer. Help him or her weigh the pros and cons of different kinds of activities.

The Bottom Line	Pronouns should agree with **their** antecedents.

LESSON 9

Vague Pronouns:
This, That, and *It*

EXAMPLE 1 *Two Possible Antecedents*

Error: Two of Ryland's hobbies are fishing and skiing.
✗ <u>It</u> requires a lot of money for good equipment.

Correction: Two of Ryland's hobbies are fishing and skiing.
Skiing
I̶t̶ requires a lot of money for good equipment.
‸

EXAMPLE 2 *Missing Antecedent*

Error: Contrary to her campaign promises, the governor announced cutbacks in welfare and an increase in education spending. ✗ <u>That</u> is sure to anger voters.

Correction: Contrary to her campaign promises, the governor announced cutbacks in welfare and an increase in
announcement
education spending. That is sure to anger voters.
‸

What's the Problem?

Many pronouns refer back to a previous noun or pronoun: the **pronoun antecedent**. A problem occurs when the antecedent is unclear or missing. In Example 1, it is not clear *which* of Ryland's hobbies is expensive. In Example 2, the writer is vague about *what* "is sure to anger voters." The following guidelines will help you avoid vague pronouns.

- The antecedent should be a specific person, place, or thing that the pronoun refers to.

- The antecedent should be in the same sentence as the pronoun or in the previous sentence.

- Avoid using other nouns between the pronoun and its antecedent.

- If you must include an "interrupting" noun between the pronoun and antecedent, make sure readers could not logically mistake this noun for the antecedent.

The following example satisfies all four guidelines.

My <u>car</u> has not been running well, so Paul took <u>it</u> to a mechanic.

    ↑   ↑

ANTECEDENT   PRONOUN

Lesson 9

pron ref

The pronoun (*it*) refers clearly to a specific antecedent (*car*). Although an "interrupting" noun (*Paul*) comes between the pronoun and the antecedent, *it* cannot logically refer to *Paul*.

A speaker can use pronouns such as *this, that,* or *it* without clear antecedents because physical gestures (such as pointing) can clarify what *this* or *that* refers to. Unfortunately, people often carry over their uses of vague pronouns into their writing.

This lesson focuses on *this, that,* and *it,* which account for most problems involving vague pronouns. However, the concepts in this lesson apply to all pronouns that require an antecedent (*many, few,* and *they,* for example).

Diagnostic Exercise

CORRECTED SENTENCES APPEAR ON PAGE 463.

Correct all vague uses of *this, that,* and *it* in the following paragraph using the first correction as a model. The number in parentheses at the end of the paragraph indicates how many changes you should make.

"Star Wars" was the name of a military program as well as a
The program
movie. ~~It~~ was a large research program calling for military defense in
    ^

outer space. This was initiated by President Reagan in the 1980's, and it

had the official title of "Strategic Defense Initiative." The public never

embraced that as much as the catchier title "Star Wars." This project was

heavily funded for years, but it underwent major cutbacks once the cold

war ended. (2)

Fixing This Problem in Your Writing

To avoid vague pronouns, see if you can easily locate the antecedent by using the following tip.

> **ANTECEDENT TIP**   Locate what you think the pronoun refers to, and make sure this antecedent is a *noun*—a person, place, or thing. Next, make sure there is no "want-to-be antecedent"—another noun that the pronoun could possibly refer to.

In Example 1, *it* seems to refer to either *fishing* or *skiing*. Both are nouns, so the sentence passes the first part of the Antecedent Tip.

NOUN   NOUN

Tip applied: Two of Ryland's hobbies are (fishing) and (skiing). It requires a lot of money for good equipment.

The sentence does not, however, pass the second part of the tip. If the writer assumes that only one of these hobbies (fishing or skiing) is expensive, then the other hobby is a "want-to-be antecedent." In other words, one noun is the real antecedent; the other is in a position that could make readers think it is the real antecedent.

The simplest way to correct this sentence is to replace *It* with the word being renamed. We'll assume the author had *skiing* in mind.

Skiing

Correction: Two of Ryland's hobbies are fishing and skiing. ~~It~~ requires a lot of money for good equipment.   ^

Now look at Example 2, which does not pass the first part of the Antecedent Tip. The pronoun *That* seems to refer to the entire idea of the first sentence, not to a specific noun.

Tip applied: Contrary to her campaign promises, the governor

announced cutbacks in welfare and an increase in

?

education spending. ✗ That is sure to anger voters.

That does not refer to any specific noun in the first sentence.

Keep in mind where the word *pronoun* comes from—*for a noun* (as in *pronoun*). The origin of the word will help you remember that a pronoun should stand only for a noun (or another pronoun). In Example 2, we're guessing that the writer was trying to refer to the entire group of words in the first sentence.

One way to correct this error is to revise the sentence before the pronoun to provide a specific antecedent, the noun *reversal*.

The

Correction: ~~Contrary to her campaign promises, the~~ governor

announced cutbacks in welfare and an increase in

, a reversal of her campaign promises.

education spending. That is sure to anger voters.

Lesson 9

Another way to correct the error in Example 2 is to apply this next tip.

*pron
ref*

> **THIS/THAT TIP**   Add a noun after *this* or *that* to clarify your meaning.

Adding a noun after *this* or *that* turns these pronouns into **adjectives**, eliminating the need to worry about antecedents.

Correction: Contrary to her campaign promises, the governor

announced cutbacks in welfare and an increase in

ADJECTIVE   NOUN

announcement

education spending. That is sure to anger voters.

Because *That* is now an adjective describing *announcement*, it does not require an antecedent. Although *this* and *that* can correctly be used as pronouns, your writing will often be clearer if you use these words as adjectives instead.

✳ *More Examples*

This, That, *and* It *Used as Pronouns with Clear Antecedents*

Do you know how to make <u>tortilla soup</u>? I'm craving <u>that</u> for dinner.

My weekend <u>plan</u> was ruined because <u>it</u> depended on our having good weather.

This *and* That *Used as Adjectives to Avoid Vague Pronouns*

The college president decided tuition would be increased to give teachers a raise. <u>This decision</u> was appreciated by teachers but not by students.

You need a haircut, a shave, and a bath because you have been camping for a week. I cannot help you with <u>that problem</u>.

✱ *Putting It All Together*

Identify Vague Pronouns

____ The most common vague pronouns are *this, that,* and *it,* so look for these pronouns in your writing.

____ Each of these pronouns should have a clear antecedent—a previous, nearby noun (or pronoun) that means the same thing.

____ If readers see more than one logical choice for the antecedent, the pronoun is vague.

Lesson 9

Correct Vague Pronouns

pron ref

____ Make sure the antecedent is close to its pronoun, either in the same sentence or in the previous sentence. Often, you can correct a vague pronoun by moving either it or the antecedent so that they are closer.

____ Replace the vague pronoun with the noun that it refers to, or revise the sentence to provide a specific antecedent (a noun or a pronoun).

____ Alternatively, add a noun after *this* or *that* to turn the pronoun into an adjective.

Sentence Practice 1

CORRECTED SENTENCES APPEAR ON PAGE 463.

If the underlined pronoun is vague, correct the sentence using one of the methods described in this lesson. If the pronoun is not vague, write *OK* above it and underline the antecedent.

mad rush

Example: I hurried to answer the phone, and <u>this</u> caused me to fall.

1. In 1920, the largest known meteorite was found. <u>It</u> weighed 65 tons.

2. The printer for the computer is not working, and I have a paper due in an hour. I knew <u>this</u> was going to happen!

3. There are approximately 320,000 icebergs in the world. <u>This</u> could change, however.

4.   So far, the election results indicate the governor will be reelected. <u>That</u> is not a surprise.

5.   A deer poked its head up from the grass where a fawn was resting, and then I saw <u>it</u> run away.

 For more practice correcting vague pronouns, go to **Exercise Central** at **bedfordstmartins.com/commonsense**

Lesson 9

pron ref

Sentence Practice 2

CORRECTED SENTENCES APPEAR ON PAGE 463.

If the underlined pronoun is vague, correct the sentence using one of the methods described in this lesson. If the pronoun is not vague, write *OK* above it and underline the antecedent.

> *Example:*   My boyfriend told me his teacher lectured
>   *The lecture*
>   on the Industrial Revolution. ~~It~~ lasted two hours.
>   ^

1.   Alena called today to talk about the antismoking law passed by the city government. <u>This</u> took almost an hour of my time.

2.   We need a new governor, but <u>that</u> won't happen anytime soon.

3.   Cincinnati was a boomtown because of its strategic location. In the early 1800's, <u>it</u> was built on the busy Ohio River.

4.   A car swerved in between the truck that was close behind me. <u>It</u> seemed to want to pass me.

5.   World War I was ended by the Versailles Treaty; <u>this</u> also led to the formation of the League of Nations.

Sentence Practice 3

The second sentence in each pair contains a vague pronoun that is underlined. Rewrite the second sentence so that it makes a clear reference.

> *Example:*   My roommate met an old friend recently. <u>She</u> is going to graduate school now.

> *Answer:*   *Her friend is going to graduate school now.*

1. A squirrel appeared outside the window of my bedroom. <u>It</u> is not pretty.

2. My algebra teacher kept us ten minutes after we were supposed to leave. <u>This</u> made me mad.

3. The crack in my windshield is getting bigger. I knew <u>that</u> might happen.

4. Besides bringing a shovel, Dalit brought food for us to eat on our camping trip. We might not need <u>it</u>, but the food will come in handy.

5. In his speech, Louis argued that the best way to increase involvement in student government is to give a tuition break to members of the student senate. <u>That</u> happened last week.

Lesson 9

pron ref

Editing Practice 1

CORRECTED SENTENCES APPEAR ON PAGE 464.

Correct all errors in the following paragraphs using the first correction as a model. The number in parentheses at the end of each paragraph indicates how many errors you should find.

Some credit card companies are taking advantage of students. ~~It~~ is
        This practice
becoming increasingly common. I see salespeople from the card

companies almost every week on my campus, and it seems even more

common in the spring semester when students are graduating. Most

students have little experience with credit companies, and the

representatives know that. (2)

The companies give away T-shirts or candy bars to get students'

attention. This gimmick sparks students' interest, and then the salespeople

tell students that they are "preapproved" and can get a card immediately.

It seems to work because I always see students signing up for these cards.

The salespeople often forget a small detail: that little card is going to cost an annual fee plus 21 percent interest on all charges. Most students seem

to think it is still great, but they will change their minds when they see the

bills adding up. Believe me, it happened to me. (3)

Editing Practice 2

CORRECTED SENTENCES APPEAR ON PAGE 464.

Lesson 9

*pron
ref*

Correct all errors in the following paragraphs using the first correction as a
model. The number in parentheses at the end of each paragraph indicates
how many errors you should find.

My college finally decided to invest in a new system for allowing

students to register online without having to come to campus during

          The new system
registration. I̶t is a good idea. In fact, I am surprised this has taken
        ^

so long to implement here. This has been used at other colleges in the

region. That is not unusual, however. I like my school, but it often seems

behind the times in terms of technology. (3)

Under the new system, students will be given passwords allowing

them to access their student accounts. Initially, it will be automatically

assigned to each student, but the password can be changed later. By

following the onscreen directions, students can pick and choose which

classes they want to take, and this can be changed anytime up to the first

day of the semester. Students can now pay tuition online as well by using

their credit cards. That is good, even though I live across the street from

our campus. This new procedure is especially convenient for people who

commute a long distance to school. (3)

Editing Practice 3

Correct all errors in the following paragraph using the first correction as a model. The number in parentheses at the end of the paragraph indicates how many errors you should find.

This past summer, the National Spelling Bee was televised on two
telecast
major networks. This is not exactly new. ESPN began showing the final
^

rounds of the contest during the early 1990's. It is not really an

athletic contest, but the network decided to broadcast the event because

of the competitive nature of spelling bees. This has apparently paid off for

ESPN, considering the high ratings the broadcast usually receives. The

popularity of the bees has greatly increased in the last few years. That can

be seen by the release of two major films and a Broadway musical that

focus on spelling bees. (3)

Lesson 9

*pron
ref*

Applying What You Know

Write a paragraph or two describing your first efforts to learn a new sport, game, or hobby. Use *this, that,* and *it* (any combination and any use) at least five times. Use the two tips discussed in this lesson to make sure you use these three terms correctly.

The Bottom Line	When using a **pronoun**, be sure **it** has a clear antecedent.

Choosing the Correct
Pronoun Form

EXAMPLE 1	*Pronoun as Subject*

Error: ✗ Jennifer Wong and <u>me</u> both took the same art class.

Correction: Jennifer Wong and ~~me~~ *I* both took the same art class.

EXAMPLE 2	*Pronoun as Object*

Error: ✗ They sang a song just for <u>she</u>.

Correction: They sang a song just for ~~she~~ *her*.

What's the Problem?

Most personal pronouns have one form when they are used as subjects and a second form when they are used as objects. Here is a complete list of the subject and object forms of all personal pronouns:

SINGULAR

Subject:	**I**	you	**he**	**she**	it
Object:	**me**	you	**him**	**her**	it

PLURAL

Subject:	**we**	you	**they**	**they**	**they**
Object:	**us**	you	**them**	**them**	**them**

The pronoun forms in bold show a difference between subject and object forms.

As the names indicate, subject pronouns play the role of subjects of verbs; object pronouns play the role of objects of verbs or objects of prepositions.

In Example 1, the object form *me* is incorrectly used where a subject pronoun is needed. In Example 2, the subject form *she* is incorrectly used as the object of a proposition.

The examples illustrate the two places where the large majority of subject/object pronoun errors occur: in compounds and in the use of subject pronouns where we should use object pronouns. Let's look at these two situations in more detail.

Pronouns in compounds. Compounds are two grammatical elements of the same kind joined by coordinating conjunctions. Here are some examples of pronouns (in bold) in compounds: *Sally and **I**; **you** and Fred; the Smiths and **us**; **you** and **me**.* Whether the pronoun is in the subject form or the object form depends entirely on how the compound is used. If the compound is used as a subject, then the pronoun is in the subject form; if the compound is used as an object, then the pronoun is in the object form, for example:

Lesson 10

pron case

Subject:	Lois and <u>I</u> are going out tonight.
Object:	They left a note for <u>Lois and me</u>.

For some reason, people find the pronouns in compounds (especially if the pronoun is in the second position within the compound) extremely difficult to monitor for correctness. Errors involving pronouns in compounds are the only grammatical errors that commonly occur in the speech of sophisticated people such as news broadcasters and educators.

Subject pronouns in object positions. The most common place for this error is following prepositions, for example:

✗ They went shopping with <u>we</u>.

✗ The paint store matched the sample for <u>he</u>.

✗ The girls sat down next to <u>I</u>.

It is not so easy to understand why this mistake is so common. There is some evidence that people assume that subject forms of pronouns are somehow more formal or proper than object forms. In other words, we have a kind of unconscious bias against object pronoun forms. This would explain why the reverse error of incorrectly using object pronouns in subject positions is quite rare. For example, nobody would make the following mistake unless they were trying (not very successfully) to be funny:

✗ <u>Him</u> went to the beach.

Diagnostic Exercise

CORRECTED SENTENCES APPEAR ON PAGE 464.

Correct all pronoun errors in the following paragraph using the first correction as a model. The number in parentheses at the end of the paragraph indicates how many errors you should find.

Lesson 10

pron case

A friend and ~~me~~ $\overset{I}{}$ visited her cousin Jim, who lives in a cabin he built from scratch. My friend asked Jim if he would mind if her and me could stay in the cabin with he for a few days this summer. He said that was fine if we would work with he building a new storeroom he wanted to add onto his cabin. My friend told him that neither her nor me had any real experience building things. Jim said that it was OK. He would work with we. Both my friend and me learned how to measure and cut lumber, pound nails, and paint without getting it all over ourselves. Jim was very good-natured about the whole thing, even though my friend and me were probably more trouble than we were worth. (9)

Fixing This Problem in Your Writing

Here is a very useful tip for checking to see if the pronouns in a compound are correct.

> **PLURAL PRONOUN TIP**   Replace compounds with a plural pronoun and test for grammatical correctness. If a plural subject pronoun such as *they* is correct, use a subject pronoun in the compound. If a plural object pronoun such as *them* is correct, use an object pronoun in the compound.

This tip works because by replacing the compound with a plural pronoun, we get around the problem of monitoring compounds. In other words, we are much less likely to make a mistake with a pronoun that appears by itself than we are to make a mistake with a pronoun that appears in a compound. Here is the tip applied to Example 1:

> *Example 1:*   ✗ Jennifer Wong and <u>me</u> both took the same art class.
>
> *Tip applied:*   <u>We</u> both took the same art class.
>
> *Tip applied:*   ✗ <u>Us</u> both took the same art class.
>
> The Plural Pronoun Tip shows us that we must use a subject pronoun in the compound.
>
> *I*
> *Correction:*   Jennifer Wong and ~~me~~ both took the same art class.
>   ^

Here is a tip to help you tell if you are using subject form pronouns incorrectly in positions where you should be using object form pronouns.

> **NO VERB, NO SUBJECT TIP**   Use the object form for every pronoun UNLESS there is a verb right after it that enters into a subject-verb relationship with that pronoun.

The implication of this tip is that you should use object forms for pronouns unless you know for a fact that the pronoun is playing the role of a subject. Here is the No Verb, No Subject Tip applied to Example 2:

> *Error:*   ✗ They sang a song just for <u>she</u>.

Since the subject pronoun *she* is not followed by a verb, we must change *she* to the corresponding object form, *her*:

> *her*
> *Correction:*   They sang a song just for ~~she~~.
>   ^

Note that the No Verb, No Subject Tip requires that the subject form pronoun be followed by a verb that enters into a subject-verb relationship with the pronoun. The reason for the subject-verb relationship provision is that often object pronouns are followed by present and past participle verb forms. These participle forms cannot enter into subject-verb relations with pronouns; only present and past tense verbs can do that. Here are some examples of object pronouns followed by participles:

> *Present Participle:* We heard <u>her</u> singing in the next room.
>
> *Past Participle:*   The kids found <u>them</u> hidden in the attic.

We cannot use subject pronouns in these positions because there is no true subject-verb relationship:

Present Participle: ✗ We heard <u>she</u> singing in the next room.

Past Participle: ✗ The kids found <u>they</u> hidden in the attic.

✳ *More Examples*

Subject Pronoun Followed by a Verb

Nicole and <u>he</u> traveled by plane to El Paso.

Next spring, Rahim and <u>they</u> are driving all the way to Denver.

Object Pronoun Not Followed by a Verb

The decision is not up to Sue and <u>him</u>.

Our only hope is <u>them</u> coming up with the necessary funding.

Note that *them* is followed by a verb (*coming up*), but not a verb form that can enter into a subject-verb relationship.

✳ *Putting It All Together*

Identify Errors in Pronoun Forms

____ Identify the five personal pronouns in your own writing that have different subject and object forms: *I/me; he/him; she/her; we/us; they/them.*

____ When using a pronoun in a compound phrase, replace the compound phrase with a single plural pronoun.

____ Check to see whether the pronoun is followed by a verb.

Correct Errors in Pronoun Forms

____ If a pronoun is followed by a verb that can enter into a subject-verb relationship, use the subject form: *I, he, she, we, they.*

____ Otherwise, use the object form: *me, him, her, us, them.*

Lesson 10

pron
case

Sentence Practice 1

CORRECTED SENTENCES APPEAR ON PAGE 464.

Underline all personal pronouns and correct all pronoun errors in the following sentences. Write *OK* above pronouns that are used correctly.

> *Example:*   I thought the cat was missing, but Marsha said
>
>   *her*
> <u>it</u> was with ~~she~~.
>   ^

Lesson 10

*pron
case*

1. The pharaoh visited the burial tomb intended for just he.

2. Janet and me are going out this Friday.

3. This cake is for me—not you.

4. Her and the dog were rescued by firefighters.

5. Mom promised to write, and today I received a card from she.

 For more practice using pronouns, go to **Exercise Central** at
bedfordstmartins.com/commonsense

Sentence Practice 2

CORRECTED SENTENCES APPEAR ON PAGE 464.

Underline all personal pronouns and correct all pronoun errors in the following sentences. Write *OK* above pronouns that are used correctly.

>   *me*
> *Example:*   That table was reserved for Velda and <u>I</u>.
>   ^

1. Just between you and I, we are having an unannounced quiz on Monday.

2. Dwayne and me are studying on Sunday.

3. Are you ready to meet with them?

4. If not for I, you would not be having a birthday at all today.

5. Elian and him left on Thursday for a vacation.

Sentence Practice 3

Replace the underlined noun with the appropriate pronoun.

he

Example: I assumed that Shirley and ~~Ray~~ were engaged.
                                                    ^

1. The landlord and <u>Ms. Gray</u> are meeting with us today about the security problem.

2. That pie is for <u>Mark</u>.

3. Carl and <u>Stacy</u> will be leaving soon.

4. The request was made by <u>Kim</u>, not <u>Hank</u>.

5. Dr. Wang asked her students to write a letter to <u>the dean</u> describing their concerns over the tuition increase.

6. <u>Wilbur</u> asked <u>Orville</u> to gas up the plane.

7. <u>A team of scientists</u> were reviewing the report.

8. Jayne was thinking of moving to Austin so that she could be near <u>her children</u>.

9. <u>Lord Banbury and Lady Agatha</u> were expecting <u>guests</u> for tea that afternoon.

10. We noticed <u>the horse</u> grazing in the pasture behind the barn.

Editing Practice 1

CORRECTED SENTENCES APPEAR ON PAGE 464.

Correct all errors in the following paragraphs using the first correction as a model. The number in parentheses at the end of each paragraph indicates how many errors you should find.

I

    When I was in high school, my father and ~~me~~ would build a new
                                                                    ^

house every other summer. My father and mother were both teachers so them always had summers off. During the first summer, my father and me would pour the foundation and do the framing and roofing. During the school year, a contractor would supervise the plumbing, wiring, and other specialties. The following summer, my father and me would finish the interior work. During the next school year, my mother would take charge of all the interior decoration, and then her would put the house on the market. (4)

The key to making this scheme work was having the contractor; without he, we could never have done it. When we first started building houses, we needed he for his expertise. Later on that was not the case. We needed he because he could control the subcontractors. (3)

Lesson 10

pron case

Editing Practice 2

Correct all errors in the following paragraph using the first correction as a model. The number in parentheses at the end of the paragraph indicates how many errors you should find.

When you build a house, most of the work is actually done by specialized subcontractors: plumbing, wiring, drywall, cabinetry, tile work, and so on. If my father built a house by himself, without a

he

contractor, ~~him~~ would be unable to get the subcontractors to do the work. The problem is not hiring they — they are delighted to sign contracts. The problem is getting they to actually show up and do the work. Typically, contractors are working three or four jobs at once. The subcontractors would know that them would never work for my father again. Thus, my father would be the lowest priority; the contractors would work on our house only when them had time available, which could be once a week or once a month. Since these specialized jobs are sequenced (electrical and plumbing, for example, have to be done before the drywall contractor can close up the walls), delays in one subcontractor's work snowball and cause huge delays for the other subcontractors. Our contractor, on the other hand, could call up a subcontractor and say to he, "Listen, if you ever want to work for I again, you will finish the job by next Wednesday." Guess what? Them would show up and finish the job by next Wednesday. (7)

Lesson 10

pron
case

Applying What You Know

Write a paragraph or two describing how you and another person worked together on some project. Use as many of the following pronouns as you can: *I/me, he/him, she/her, we/us, they/them.*

The Bottom Line	Subject forms of personal pronouns are fairly predictable. Usually, <u>**they are followed**</u> by verbs.

LESSON 11

Who, Whom, and *That*

EXAMPLE 1	**That** *Used Instead of* **Who/Whom**
Error:	✗ The student <u>that</u> read my draft said it was clear.
Correction:	The student ~~that~~ ^{who} read my draft said it was clear.

EXAMPLE 2	**Who** *Used Instead of* **Whom**
Error:	✗ Bobbie met a person <u>who</u> you might know.
Correction:	Bobbie met a person ~~who~~ ^{whom} you might know.

What's the Problem?

Who, whom, and *that* usually function as pronouns, and writers are often confused about which one of them to use in a given sentence. Many times, writers use *that* when they should use either *who* or *whom* (as with Example 1). But even if writers know that *that* is the wrong choice, they might not know whether *who* or *whom* is correct (as with Example 2).

You can avoid these two errors by first understanding how *who, whom,* and *that* often refer back to a previous noun (or another pronoun), as seen in the following correct examples.

I once had a <u>crack</u> in my windshield <u>that</u> prevented me from driving.

I had it fixed by <u>someone</u> <u>whom</u> I could trust.

The previous word that the pronoun refers back to is called a **pronoun antecedent** — a noun or pronoun that essentially means the same thing as *who, whom,* or *that* in the sentence. *Crack* and *someone* are the antecedents in the example sentences above.

In general, do not use *that* when the antecedent is a person. Example 1 is incorrect because *that* refers back to a person (a *student*). Writers often incorrectly use *that* because they hope to avoid having to choose between *who* or *whom*, which indeed is a more difficult decision.

To decide whether to use *who* or *whom,* you need to determine how the pronoun functions in the sentence.

- If the pronoun functions as a subject, use *who* (the subject form):

I have a friend <u>who</u> wears a red hat every Valentine's Day.

Who functions as a subject: it performs the action (*wears*).

- If the pronoun is a direct object or an object of a preposition, use *whom* (the object form):

She got the hat from someone <u>whom</u> she once loved.

Whom functions as an object. Here, it is receiving the action of the verb (*loved*).

Lesson 11

*pron
case*

Diagnostic Exercise

CORRECTED SENTENCES APPEAR ON PAGE 465.

In the following paragraph, every *that* is underlined. Using the first correction as a model, change each inappropriate *that* to *who* or *whom*. The number in parentheses at the end of the paragraph indicates how many errors you should find.

An experience <u>that</u> we all have had is working for a bad boss. One
whom
boss ~~that~~ we have all had is the petty tyrant, a person <u>that</u> loves to find
^

fault with every employee <u>that</u> works in the building. It seems like the

petty tyrant is more interested in finding employees <u>that</u> he or she can

belittle than in getting the job done. Even worse than the petty tyrant is

a supervisor <u>that</u> is inconsistent. An inconsistent boss is a person <u>that</u> the

employees can never trust. A game <u>that</u> this kind of boss loves is playing

favorites. One day, this boss is your best buddy; the next day, the boss acts

as if he or she doesn't know the name of a person <u>that</u> has worked with the

company for ten years. (6)

Fixing This Problem in Your Writing

Knowing When to Use *That*

The following tip simplifies the guidelines on when to use *that*.

> **THAT THING TIP**   Use *that* only if it refers back to a nonhuman thing (such as an object, idea, place, animal, or thing).

The *That Thing* Tip reveals the problem with Example 1. The antecedent is a human, not a thing. Thus, we should not use *that*.

Example 1:   ✗ The student that read my draft said it was clear.

NOT A THING
~✗~

Tip applied: ✗ The <u>student</u> <u>that</u> read my draft said it was clear.

Student is not a thing, so *that* is wrong.

At this point, we have determined only that it is incorrect to use *that* in the sentence. We still need to decide whether to use *who* or *whom,* which takes us to the next step.

Exception: Some people believe it is fine to use *that* if it refers to a type of person — not to a real person (as in *I need a lawyer <u>that</u> I can trust*). Not everyone agrees with this exception, and you are never wrong to use *who/ whom* to refer to a person or type of person. Thus, we suggest always avoiding *that* to refer to people.

Choosing between *Who* and *Whom*

As noted earlier, use *who* when the pronoun is the subject of a verb. Use *whom* when the pronoun serves as an object (a direct object or object of a preposition). The following tip will help you make the right choice between *who* and *whom.*

> **WHO + VERB TIP**   Look at the word following (usually immediately following) *who* or *whom.* If this word is a verb, use *who.*

The *Who* + Verb Tip works because the subject form (*who*) is used when the pronoun is a subject of a verb, and verbs normally appear very soon after a subject. Now we know how to correct Example 1. There is a verb right after the pronoun, so *who* is the right choice:

Example 1:   ✗ The student that read my draft said it was clear.

WHO   +   VERB

Tip applied: The student [who/whom] read my draft said it was clear.

A verb comes after the pronoun, so *who* is the correct choice.

who

Correction: The student ~~whom~~ read my draft said it was clear.

Compare this example with Example 2, however. In this second example, the pronoun is followed by a pronoun, not a verb. Thus, our correction changes *who* to *whom*.

Example 2:   ✗ Bobbie met a person who you might know.

WHOM + PRONOUN

Tip applied: Bobbie met a person [who/whom] you might know.

The pronoun is *not* followed by a verb, so we use *whom*.

whom

Correction: Bobbie met a person ~~who~~ you might know.

It is possible for adverbs to come between *who* and its verb (as in *I know a man who always wears hats.*). Still, the *Who* + Verb Tip provides an easy way to remember the basic rules: use *who* as the subject of a verb.

✳ More Examples

Sentences Using That Correctly

My cousin bought a computer <u>that</u> burns CDs and DVDs.

Dr. Zeikowitz has a parrot <u>that</u> he has taught over two dozen words.

Sentences Using Who Correctly

I need a spouse <u>who</u> will be supportive of my emotional needs.

<u>Who</u> brought the cheesecake?

Sentences Using Whom *Correctly*

Mayor Beach is a leader <u>whom</u> the people trust and admire.

Adair is a person in <u>whom</u> you should place little trust.

✱ *Putting It All Together*

Lesson 11

*pron
case*

Identify Errors in Using Who, Whom, *and* That

_____ Look for the words *who*, *whom*, and *that* in your writing. These words are normally pronouns that require an antecedent. An antecedent is a previous noun (or pronoun) that the pronoun is referring to.

Correct Errors in Using Who, Whom, *and* That

_____ Use *that* only when referring to nonhuman things (such as an object, idea, place, animal, or thing). Do not use *that* to refer to people.

_____ Use *who* when the pronoun is the subject of a verb. Normally, a verb should follow *who* almost immediately.

_____ Use *whom* when the pronoun is the object of the sentence. There should NOT be a verb immediately following *whom*.

Sentence Practice 1

CORRECTED SENTENCES APPEAR ON PAGE 465.

Underline the word that *that* refers to in each sentence. If *that* is used correctly, write *OK* above it. Otherwise, replace it with the correct pronoun.

Example: The <u>teacher</u> t̶h̶a̶t̶ taught me English in high school
                              ^who

teaches part-time at my college.

1. The woman that answered the phone was chewing gum loudly.

2. Senator Blather ignored the reporters that had been waiting outside.

3. I called the couple that had answered the ad.

4. The information that Jim gave me was incorrect.

5. A friend that I have known for years loaned me her truck.

 For more practice using pronouns, go to **Exercise Central** at
bedfordstmartins.com/commonsense

Sentence Practice 2

CORRECTED SENTENCES APPEAR ON PAGE 465.

Lesson 11

pron

case

Underline the word that *that* refers to in each sentence. If *that* is used correctly, write *OK* above it. Otherwise, replace it with the correct pronoun.

Example: The <u>person</u> ~~that~~ was late distracted the speaker.
                             who

1. Here is the magazine that you wanted me to bring.

2. I want to know the name of the mechanic that fixed your car.

3. A guy that I knew in high school sits next to me in my art class.

4. Who was the president that succeeded Ronald Reagan?

5. The first person that makes fun of my hair color is going to be sorry.

Sentence Practice 3

Change the capitalized word(s) in the second sentence into *who* or *whom* and combine the sentences so that the second part modifies the underlined word in the first part.

Example: I found <u>someone</u>. SOMEONE will help me study.

Answer: *I found someone who will help me study.*

1. Yogi Berra is the baseball <u>player</u>. THE PLAYER holds the World Series record for most times on a winning team.

2. He is also a cultural <u>icon</u>. AN ICON is known for his humorous sayings.

3. We need to call <u>the person</u>. You spoke to THE PERSON.

4. Over there is <u>the man</u>. You want to avoid THE MAN.

5. A student angered <u>the teacher</u>. THE TEACHER asked the class to stop talking.

Editing Practice 1

CORRECTED SENTENCES APPEAR ON PAGE 465.

Correct all errors in the following paragraph using the first correction as a model. The number in parentheses at the end of the paragraph indicates how many errors you should find.

                  whom

My boss is someone ~~who~~ you might consider strange. I work

part-time at a convenience store that is located outside the city. My boss,

Ms. McDonald, is someone who wants everything exactly her way. If you

ever disagree with her, she tells you to hush and then covers her ears. She

is married to a man that sells exotic goats for a living, and he occasionally

brings them to the store. Last weekend, one goat bit a customer who was

buying tomatoes that the goat wanted. Ms. McDonald, who the goat also

tried to bite, called the police. By the time they arrived, both the goat

and my boss's husband had escaped. The customer whom was bitten

said he would sue the store; Ms. McDonald simply told him to hush and

covered her ears. The officers, whom were all too familiar with her strange

behavior, said she could no longer have goats in the store. It's not exactly

a funny situation, but she certainly makes my job interesting. (4)

Editing Practice 2

CORRECTED SENTENCES APPEAR ON PAGE 465.

Correct all errors in the following paragraphs using the first correction as a model. The number in parentheses at the end of each paragraph indicates how many errors you should find.

                                    who
Many Americans, even those ~~that~~ are knowledgeable about differ-
                              ^
ent cultures, know little about many religions. One example is Buddhism.

This religion was founded in India by Siddhartha Gautama, whom

is known as Buddha, and it has over 300 million followers worldwide.

Another example is Confucianism. This religion is based on the teachings

of Confucius, a Chinese philosopher that stressed the importance of

relationships among people, families, and members of society. (2)

   Some lesser-known religions were actually founded by people that

migrated to America. The Amish Mennonites can be traced back to the

birth of the Mennonite religion in Switzerland during the 1500's. In 1693,

however, the followers of Jacob Ammann broke from other Mennonites,

but a great many rejoined the main group in the eighteenth century.

The remainder, whom stayed loyal to Jacob Ammann's views, migrated

to Pennsylvania. These are the followers that became known as Amish

Mennonites. Today, there are some 40,000 Amish Mennonites in the

world. (3)

Editing Practice 3

Correct all errors in the following paragraph using the first correction as a
model. The number in parentheses at the end of the paragraph indicates how
many errors you should find.

                               who
   Several students ~~that~~ are in my calculus class have taken the course
                          ^
more than once. Paul, whom has taken the course three times, said many

students fail because they do not complete all the homework. He said that

not attending class also poses a problem for students that struggle with math. I also spoke with my friend Inez, who passed the course with an A. She formed a study group with three students that were in her class, and they all passed. Inez also received help from her teacher, who she frequently consulted during his office hours. Math does not come easily to me, so I'll need to plan ahead on finding additional help with the course. (4)

Applying What You Know

In groups of three, investigate the varied uses of *who, whom,* and *that.* These three words are not always pronouns having antecedents. See if you can identify the different uses of *who, whom,* and *that* covered in this lesson. Each member of your group should be assigned one of these words.

All group members should find their own magazine article; it must have at least three uses of the word the member was assigned. Each member does one of the following tasks:

1. Circle every *that* and put a check by each one that is a pronoun. Put a check also by the antecedent, if there is one.

2. Circle every *who.* If *who* is the subject of a verb, put a check by the verb.

3. Circle every *whom.* One function of *whom* is to serve as the object of a verb (see **direct object** in the Guide to Grammar Terminology on page 438). Place a check by the verb that is affecting each *whom* you circled.

This task is more difficult than it might seem, so go through your findings with your group.

The Bottom Line	The word *that* is a pronoun **that** should refer to ideas and things — not to people.

LESSON 12

Eliminating Sexist Pronouns

Error: **✗** Everybody should bring <u>his</u> book to class tomorrow.

Correction: Everybody should bring ~~his~~ book to class tomorrow.
                                 his or her
                                      ^

Error: **✗** A kindergarten teacher helps <u>her</u> students gain social as well as academic skills.

Correction: *Kindergarten teachers help their*
      ~~A kindergarten teacher helps her~~ students gain social as well as academic skills.

What's the Problem?

Sexist language, even when unintentional, is unacceptable in college and professional communication. Such language excludes one gender or the other, and it is demeaning. A writer who uses sexist language is likely to offend readers, who in turn will be less likely to respect the point that the writer is trying to make.

Sexist language takes many forms, but this lesson focuses on one of the most common forms: pronouns used in ways that exclude or ignore one gender. That is, sexist language occurs when certain **personal pronouns —** *he, his, him, she,* and *her* — are used in ways that indicate *only* males or *only* females are being discussed.

For instance, Example 1 suggests that only males should bring their books, while Example 2 indicates that all kindergarten teachers are female. Of course, you can use pronouns such as *he* or *her* when the pronouns logically refer only to males (a father or a member of an all-male class) or only to females (a bride or a pitcher on a women's softball team), but make such generalizations *only* if there is no chance of excluding people that are in the category.

At one time, it seemed acceptable to use the so-called generic *he* to refer to all people, meaning that sentences such as Example 1 would have been acceptable to some readers. It also seemed appropriate at one time to associate one gender with particular roles or professions (such as nurses = female; doctors = male). Thus, Example 2 might have once seemed acceptable. Today, however, people are aware of the subtle discrimination involved in using such language, and therefore it is no longer acceptable, even if the writer or speaker is not intentionally being sexist.

Diagnostic Exercise

CORRECTED SENTENCES APPEAR ON PAGE 466.

Correct all instances of sexist language in the following paragraph using the first correction as a model. The number in parentheses at the end of the paragraph indicates how many problems you should find.

My psychology teacher, Ms. Crystal, had each member of the class complete a questionnaire that would help him *or her* choose an appropriate career. I had already decided on a profession, but she said the questionnaire would offer me other options. I've always wanted to be an electrical engineer because I like to design things; an engineer spends much of his time drawing designs and writing specifications. Ms. Crystal said my survey results indicated I should consider being an accountant. She also told me, however, that the survey was just one resource for choosing a career. I agree. Each person has to consider what he knows better than anyone else: his own interests. (3)

Fixing This Problem in Your Writing

Identifying Sexist Pronouns

Many writers do not check their sentences for sexist language because few people consider themselves sexist. However, the following tip provides a way for you to check your writing for even unintentional problems.

Lesson 12

*sexist
pron*

ABSTRACT-REFERENCE TIP   First, look for *abstract* references to people (words that deal with a type of person or to people in general, not to specific individuals). Second, check to see whether you use personal pronouns to refer back to these abstract references later in your writing. If these pronouns exclude one gender, the language is probably sexist.

Let's apply the Abstract-Reference Tip to Example 1. In this example, *everybody* is an abstract reference because *everybody* could refer to anyone, not to a specific individual. However, the writer uses the personal pronoun *his*, which excludes females. Unless no females are in the class, the sentence contains sexist language.

Example 1:   ✗ Everybody should bring his book to class tomorrow.

ABSTRACT   "ONE GENDER"
REFERENCE   PRONOUN

Tip applied: ✗ Everybody should bring <u>his</u> book to class tomorrow.

As the above example illustrates, sexist pronouns tend to follow a predictable pattern:

Abstract Reference + "One Gender" Pronoun = Sexist Language

Example 2 has the same pattern. *A kindergarten teacher* is a general reference to a type of person; it could again be almost anyone. This time, the pronoun after this reference excludes males:

Example 2:   ✗ A kindergarten teacher helps her students gain social as well as academic skills.

ABSTRACT   "ONE GENDER"   SEXIST
REFERENCE   +   PRONOUN   =   LANGUAGE

Tip applied: ✗ A <u>kindergarten teacher</u> helps <u>her</u> students gain social as well as academic skills.

Correcting Sexist Pronouns

Here are two ways to revise these sentences to avoid sexist language:

1. Reword the sentence so that any abstract reference to people is in the plural form. Do the same with personal pronouns (such as *they* or *their*; see Lesson 8 on pronoun agreement).

> PLURAL   PLURAL
> Abstract Reference + Pronoun = Nonsexist Language

Our correction of Example 2 follows this correction pattern:

Correction: *Kindergarten teachers help their*
A kindergarten teacher helps her students gain social
as ˄well as academic skills.

PLURAL Abstract Reference (*teachers*) + PLURAL Pronoun
(*their*) = Nonsexist Language

2.   If for some reason you want to keep the singular form, you can include both genders by using some form of all three words *he or she* instead of using just *he* or just *she*:

> SINGULAR
> Abstract Reference + *He or She* = Nonsexist Language

We corrected Example 1 by keeping the singular *everybody* but changing *his* to *his or her*:

Correction: *or her*
Everybody should bring his˄ book to class tomorrow.

SINGULAR Abstract Reference (*Everybody*) + *his or her* = Nonsexist Language

✱ *More Examples*

Error: ✗ A supervisor who values his employees' rights is greatly needed here.

Correction: *Supervisors who value their*   *are*
A supervisor who values his employees' rights is˄
˄greatly needed here.

Error: ✗ If you see a professor, tell her to go to Room 264.

Correction: *him or*
If you see a professor, tell her˄ to go to Room 264.

✳ *Putting It All Together*

Identifying Sexist Pronouns

_____ Look for abstract references to people — very general nouns or pronouns that do not deal with particular people or individuals.

_____ Are there singular personal pronouns such as *he, his, she,* or *her* soon after these references? If so, these pronouns are sexist if they inappropriately exclude or ignore one gender.

Correcting Sexist Pronouns

_____ Use plural references and plural pronouns so that you can use inclusive pronouns such as *they, them,* and *their.*

_____ Another option is to use terms such as *he or she* to include both genders.

Lesson 12

*sexist
pron*

Sentence Practice 1

CORRECTED SENTENCES APPEAR ON PAGE 466.

If a sentence contains sexist language, identify it by underlining the noun and the sexist pronoun. Correct the problem. If a sentence avoids sexist language, write *OK* above it.

Example: <u>Someone</u> left <s>his</s> cell phone on the couch.

1. A leader has to be responsible to his constituents.

2. Boxer Vic Towell once knocked down his opponent fourteen times within ten rounds of their championship fight.

3. We must hire a secretary, and she must be organized and efficient.

4. I prefer a teacher who knows his subject material but who allows students to solve problems for themselves.

5. Every voter should cast his ballot in the upcoming school bond election.

For more practice eliminating sexist pronouns, go to **Exercise Central** at **bedfordstmartins.com/commonsense**

Lesson 12

sexist pron

Sentence Practice 2

CORRECTED SENTENCES APPEAR ON PAGE 466.

If a sentence contains sexist language, identify it by underlining the noun and the sexist pronoun. Correct the problem. If a sentence avoids sexist language, write *OK* above it.

                          Parents   *their*

Example: ~~A parent~~ should enable ~~her~~ child to be independent.

1. My neighbor thinks my car needs a new carburetor, but I told him I cannot afford one.

2. If you ever put your children into day care, meet with the person who will watch your children and see if she is patient.

3. Has everyone done his homework?

4. A writer must choose his words carefully.

5. I have never met anyone who brushes his teeth as often as you!

Sentence Practice 3

In the spaces provided, add an appropriate personal pronoun. You might also need to change the subject of some sentences and make other revisions.

    Example: Nobody in class did _____ homework correctly.

    Answer: Nobody in class did *his or her* homework correctly.

1. Everybody watching the movie got _____ money's worth.

2. Each employee who uses the restroom must wash _____ hands before returning to work.

3. A good spouse knows when to keep _____ mouth shut.

4. If you see someone breaking curfew, report _____ immediately.

5. When you meet a superior officer, _____ must be saluted.

Editing Practice 1

CORRECTED SENTENCES APPEAR ON PAGE 466.

Correct all instances of sexist language in the following paragraph using the first correction as a model. The number in parentheses at the end of the paragraph indicates how many problems you should find.

Lesson 12

sexist
pron

  In American high schools and colleges, a ~~student~~ can avail ~~himself~~ of

  students   *themselves*
a number of free activities open to him. This is completely different from
European schools where a student has virtually no extracurricular
activities available to him. In Europe, a school-aged athlete must find
(and pay for) a private, after-school sports club that he can join. When
a European student comes to the United States, he is astonished
at the extracurricular activities routinely available to him. Often an
exchange student will single out the extracurricular activities that he
participated in as the most enjoyable part of his experience in the United
States. Europeans point out that one reason why test scores for the
average American are so low (by international standards) is that the
American student spends too much of his school day in nonacademic
activities. Whether or not the American student is well served by his
extracurricular experience is obviously a matter of debate. (8)

Editing Practice 2

Correct all sexist language in the following paragraphs using the first correction as a model. The number in parentheses at the end of each paragraph indicates how many problems you should find.

young people　　　*have*
It seems to me that ~~a young person~~ today ~~has~~ fewer opportunities for
　^ *they*
part-time and summer work than ~~he~~ did a generation ago. For example,
it used to be that a high school student could find as much work as he
wanted. He could even find work in his neighborhood doing yard work or
child care. If the teenager had a car, there were lots of jobs within his
driving range. Virtually every labor-intensive business in town could
find a use for him doing low-skilled jobs. (5)

A teenager today lives in a world where he has very different needs
than he did a generation ago. Today, a teenager needs to work on getting
into the college of his choice. He needs to build up his resume. Rather than
working for money to help out his family or to pay for his own expenses,
a kid today is more likely working to pull up his grades in school or to try
to prepare for his SATs. If he does work, it may well be in a nonprofit
humanitarian organization, either because he believes in its mission or
because it will look good on his college application (or both). (12)

Applying What You Know

People sometimes use sexist pronouns because they incorrectly assume only
women do a certain type of work, only men are a certain way, all men do certain things, and so on. On a piece of paper, write three common generalizations about men or women that you believe are or are not valid. Share these
in groups of three or four. Decide whether the generalizations other group
members develop are valid, and explain your reasoning.

The Bottom Line	Writers can avoid sexist pronouns if **they** use plural nouns for references to people.

UNIT FOUR: Understanding Pronouns

Pronouns replace nouns (and sometimes other pronouns) in a sentence. The following chart points you to the tips that will help you avoid common pronoun problems.

TIP(S)	QUICK FIX AND EXAMPLE
Lesson 8. Pronoun Agreement	
The *Are* Tip (p. 82) helps you check whether an antecedent agrees with the plural pronouns *they, their,* or *them.* The Plural Tip (p. 82) helps you correct errors involving these pronouns.	To correct an agreement error with *they, their,* or *them,* revise the antecedent so that it is plural. For other strategies, see page 83. *Error:* ✗ Everyone should turn off their cell phone. *Correction:* ~~Everyone~~ All students should turn off their cells phone.
Lesson 9. Vague Pronouns: *This, That,* and *It*	
The Antecedent Tip (p. 91) helps you make sure that a pronoun has a clear antecedent. The *This/That* Tip (p. 92) also helps you clarify the meaning of a pronoun.	Move the pronoun closer to its antecedent, or revise the sentence to provide a specific antecedent. You could also add a noun after *this* or *that.* *Error:* I slipped and fell on the ice while walking to class. ✗ That made me late. *Correction:* I slipped and fell on the ice while walking to class. That accident made me late.
Lesson 10. Choosing the Correct Pronoun Form	
The Plural Pronoun Tip (p. 100) helps you use the correct pronoun in a compound structure. The No Verb, No Subject Tip (p. 101) helps you choose between the subject and object form of pronouns.	If a pronoun is followed by a verb, use the subject form: *I, he, she, we, they.* Otherwise, use *me, him, her, us, them.* *Error:* ✗ Jay and me went for a walk. *Correction:* Jay and ~~me~~ I went for a walk.

Lesson 11. *Who, Whom, and That*	
The *That Thing* Tip (p. 109) tells you when to use *that*. The *Who* + Verb Tip (p. 109) helps you choose between *who* and *whom*.	Use *that* only when referring to nonhuman things. Use *who* when a verb immediately follows the pronoun; otherwise, use *whom*. *Error:* ✗ We called a friend that is good at math. *Correction:* We called a friend ~~that~~ *who* is good at math.
Lesson 12. Eliminating Sexist Pronouns	
The Abstract-Reference Tip (p. 118) will help you check your writing for sexist language.	Make the pronoun reference plural and change the gender-exclusive pronoun to *they, them,* or *their.* Other strategies are replacing the pronoun with *his or her* or revising the sentence to avoid personal pronouns altogether. *Error:* ✗ I asked everyone to bring his own lunch to the meeting. *Correction:* I asked everyone to bring his *or her* own lunch to the meeting.

Unit Four

review

Review Test

Correct all errors in the following paragraph using the first correction as a model. The number in parentheses at the end of the paragraph indicates how many errors you should find.

     Yesterday, I received a call from my neighbor Elena, ~~whom~~ *who* wanted me to meet her friend Janie. She has just arrived in town and is staying with Elena for a short time. Elena and me have been friends a long time, so I was glad to meet a friend of hers. Janie, who is an electrician, is looking for a job, and I know a number of contractors that work in the area. An electrician can get a job if he is really experienced and willing to work his way up the pay scale. Typically, an electrician is experienced because their skills are so technical that they do a lot of hands-on learning to acquire these skills. (6)

UNIT FIVE
Placing and Punctuating Modifiers

OVERVIEW

Terms That Can Help You Understand Modifiers

If you are not familiar with any of the following terms, look them up in the Guide to Grammar Terminology beginning on page 435.

adverb	**misplaced modifier**
dangling modifier	**modifier**
introductory element	**squinting adverb**

The Nuts and Bolts of Placing and Punctuating Modifiers

Modifiers are adjectives and adverbs that describe or qualify other words in a sentence. This unit deals with two types of modifiers that are often misplaced or mispunctuated.

Lesson 13 will help you to identify and correct **dangling modifiers**. Certain modifiers can be moved outside the main sentence to provide background information for understanding the main sentence. If these modifiers are not clearly connected to the words they describe, the meaning may be misunderstood. These modifiers are called "dangling" modifiers because they are not properly attached to the main sentence.

Example: ✗ **While still a student, Microsoft recruited my sister for a job as a programmer.**

The dangling modifier *while still a student* makes it sound like Microsoft is a student.

Correction: **While** ^*my sister was* **still a student, Microsoft recruited** ~~**my sister**~~ ^*her* **for a job as a programmer.**

Lesson 14 will help you recognize and correct two different types of adverbs that say something completely different from what the writer intends to say. One type of adverb, called a **misplaced adverb**, modifies a word different from the word the writer intends to modify. A second type of adverb, called a **squinting adverb**, is totally ambiguous: the adverb can equally well modify two different things, with, of course, two quite different meanings.

Example: ✗ We almost needed another gallon of paint to finish.

The adverb *almost* is misplaced.

Correction: We ~~almost~~ needed *almost* another gallon of paint to finish.

Example: ✗ The man who fixed my car recently took a new job.

The adverb *recently* is a squinting adverb.

Correction 1:   The man who *recently* fixed my car ~~recently~~ took a new job.

Correction 2:   The man who fixed my car ~~recently~~ took a new job *recently*.

LESSON 13

Dangling Modifiers

EXAMPLE 1	*Introductory Modifier Not Followed by Word It Describes*

Error: ✗ <u>Damaged beyond repair</u>, <u>Nina</u> threw her watch away.

Correction: Damaged beyond repair, ~~Nina threw her watch away~~.
Nina's watch had to be thrown away.

EXAMPLE 2	*No Word in Sentence for Introductory Modifier to Describe*

Error: ✗ <u>While waiting for my bus</u>, it began to snow.

Correction: While waiting for my bus, ~~it began to snow~~.
I noticed that it had begun to snow.

What's the Problem?

Modifiers are words that describe other words. Some modifiers are simple. For example, *big* is a modifier (or an **adjective**) describing *house* in *big house*. Other modifiers are complex and involve several words that together function as a modifier. Consider this sentence: *Suddenly feeling sick, Barry went home.* In this example, *Suddenly feeling sick* is a modifier that describes *Barry*.

Sometimes, these complex modifiers are not placed close enough to the words they describe (Example 1), or there is *nothing* in the sentence they can correctly modify (Example 2). Such errors are called **dangling modifiers**. Dangling modifiers tend to occur because on first glance they might seem to be correctly modifying a word in the sentence, but in fact they are not.

We will discuss the problem in more detail, but first let's consider a correct example of a complex modifier. Here, the modifier *Working all day* is indeed right next to the word it modifies (*Jody*):

MODIFIER   NOUN

Working all day, Jody finished her essay on time.

Introductory modifier describes a nearby noun.

This example is correct because there is no confusion about what the modifier is modifying. In contrast, dangling modifiers either lack something to modify or are not sufficiently close to what they are supposed to describe.

The most common errors with modifiers occur when the modifier is at the beginning of a sentence, so this lesson focuses on these types of dangling modifiers.

Diagnostic Exercise

CORRECTED SENTENCES APPEAR ON PAGE 466.

Correct all errors using the first correction as a model. The number in parentheses at the end of the paragraph indicates how many dangling modifier errors you should find.

I felt my eyes grow tired.
Studying for hours, ~~my eyes grew tired~~. I walked to the snack bar

for a cup of coffee. Upon arriving, the place was closed. Deciding against

walking a mile to another place, the thought crossed my mind that maybe

I should quit for a while and get some sleep. I returned to my room and

tried to decide what to do. Torn between the need to sleep and the need to

study, the alarm clock went off and made me realize it was time for class.

After struggling to stay awake in class, my decision was to get some sleep

and then get back to work. (4)

Fixing This Problem in Your Writing

As we mentioned above, most dangling modifiers occur at the beginning of a sentence, right before the main subject and verb. Not all introductory elements contain dangling modifiers, however, so how do you know which ones do? Here is a tip that will help you identify dangling modifiers.

> **ILLOGICAL ACTION TIP**   Look for introductory elements that involve an *action* and check to see whether these elements are making illogical claims about the noun or pronoun that directly follows them. If so, the introductory element is a dangling modifier.

Lesson 13

dm

Let's apply this tip to a sentence that uses a complex modifier correctly:

After leaving the theater, Makayla stopped by my apartment.

The introductory modifier includes an action, and the noun immediately follows the action.

As you can see, this introductory element contains an action that is making a *logical* claim about the noun right after it. Essentially, the following claim is being made:

After leaving the theater, Makayla . . . = Makayla left the theater = Logical action

The sentence is correct because it implies that Makayla left the theater, and that is a logical action.

Consider Example 1 that began the lesson, however. Here, too, the introductory element includes an action, but the claim made about the noun is not logical.

Lesson 13

dm

Example 1: ✗ **Damaged beyond repair, Nina threw her watch away.**

The introductory element includes an action, and the noun immediately follows the introduction.

Tip applied: ✗ **Damaged beyond repair, Nina . . . = Nina was damaged beyond repair = Illogical action**

Actually, Nina's *watch* was damaged beyond repair — not Nina. You can correct such an error in many ways. In the correction below, we leave the introductory element as it was but change the noun that follows it to the correct one (*watch*). Below the correction you see the logical claim the revised sentence makes.

Correction: *Nina's watch had to be thrown away.*

Damaged beyond repair, ~~Nina threw her watch away~~.

Verification: **Damaged beyond repair, Nina's watch . . . = Nina's watch was damaged beyond repair = Logical action**

Now let's look at Example 2:

Example 2: ✗ **While waiting for my bus, it began to snow.**

The introductory element includes an action, and the pronoun immediately follows the introduction.

Tip applied: ✗ While waiting for my bus, it . . . = it waited for my
                  bus = **Illogical action**

To correct this error, we can add an appropriate word (*I*) for the introductory modifier to describe.

Correction: *I noticed that it had begun to snow.*
                  While waiting for my bus, ~~it began to snow~~.

We can also revise the modifier itself to correct the sentence.

Correction: *I was*
                  While waiting for my bus, it began to snow.

Because we added *I was,* the introduction is no longer making a claim about *it,* meaning there is no chance of a dangling modifier:

Verification: While I was waiting for my bus, it began . . . = No claim
                    made about *it* = No problem

✳ *More Examples*

Error: ✗ Pulling as hard as he could, the rope broke in
            Rodney's hand.

Correction: *Rodney felt the rope break in his hand.*
                  Pulling as hard as he could, ~~the rope broke in
                  Rodney's hand~~.

Error: ✗ When hearing the cars collide, my heart
            skipped a beat.

Correction: *When I heard the cars collide,*
                  ~~When hearing the cars collide~~, my heart skipped a beat.

*Error: ✗ After eating at a restaurant, Haley's stomach
              became upset.

Correction: *After she ate at that restaurant,*
                  ~~After eating at a restaurant~~, Haley's stomach
                  became upset.

*This example illustrates a common misunderstanding. The sentence might *seem* fine because readers can figure out that Haley is at a restaurant. Grammatically, though, there is an error because the word *Haley's* is an adjective (modifying *stomach*). An adjective cannot eat at a restaurant — only nouns or pronouns can perform an action. The nearest noun is *stomach*, but a stomach cannot eat out either.

✳ *Putting It All Together*

Identify Dangling Modifiers

____ Look for groups of words that describe something else in a sentence. Dangling modifiers occur when the group of words is not close enough to what it describes OR when there is nothing in the sentence for it to describe.

____ In particular, look for introductory elements that involve an action and check to see whether these elements are making illogical claims about the noun (or pronoun) that directly follows them. If the action implies something illogical about the noun (or pronoun) right after the introduction, you have identified a dangling modifier.

Correct Dangling Modifiers

____ You can correct many dangling modifiers by adding a subject to the introductory element. For example, you would change *While waiting for my bus, it began to snow* to *While I was waiting for my bus, it began to snow*.

____ To correct other dangling modifiers, leave the introductory element alone and instead revise the *rest* of the sentence so the noun (or pronoun) immediately following the introductory element is the subject actually performing the action described. For example, you would change *Damaged beyond repair, Nina threw her watch away* to *Damaged beyond repair, Nina's watch had to be thrown away*.

Lesson 13

dm

Sentence Practice 1

CORRECTED SENTENCES APPEAR ON PAGE 467.

In each sentence, underline the dangling modifier using the example below as a model. Then confirm the error by using the Illogical Action Tip and correct the sentence.

Example: ✗ <u>Surprised by the gunfire</u>, panic spread through the elephant herd.

Tip applied: Panic was surprised by the gunfire . . . = Illogical action

Correction: Surprised by the gunfire, ~~panic spread through the elephant herd.~~
                                                    the elephant herd panicked.
                                                              ^

1. Realizing that it was time to eat, lunch was served to the hungry students.

2. Hoping there was plenty of air in her tank, the sunken wreck was explored a bit longer by the scuba diver.

3. After seeing the wreck, Sharon's day was ruined.

4. While reading my e-mail, somebody knocked at the door.

5. Running up the stairs, Vajra's nose broke as she fell.

 For more practice with dangling modifiers, go to **Exercise Central** at **bedfordstmartins.com/commonsense**

Lesson 13

dm ## Sentence Practice 2

CORRECTED SENTENCES APPEAR ON PAGE 467.

In each sentence, underline the dangling modifier using the example below as a model. Then confirm the error by using the Illogical Action Tip and correct the sentence.

Example: ✗ When traveling overseas, hepatitis A shots are a good idea.

Tip applied: Hepatitis A shots travel overseas = Illogical action

Correction: When traveling overseas, hepatitis A shots are a good idea.
(you are inserted above)

1. Reading the contract carefully, it was decided to wait a few days before both parties would sign.

2. While relaxing in the sun, dark clouds suddenly appeared.

3. Enraged by his pitiful score, Ted's tennis racket was hurled across the court.

4. Breaking the pencil in anger, Ted's bad temper again revealed itself.

5. Feeling hungry because I skipped lunch, eating supper seemed a really good idea.

Sentence Practice 3

Combine the two short sentences by making the second sentence into a phrase or clause that can be moved in front of the underlined subject. Punctuate appropriately, and avoid dangling modifiers.

> *Example:*   The <u>chicken</u> was injured by a speeding truck. The chicken was crossing the road.
>
> *Answer:*   *While crossing the road, the chicken was injured by a speeding truck.*

1.   The <u>cat</u> seemed nervous. The cat heard the panting of a dog.

2.   <u>We</u> left the party early. We were disgusted by the obnoxious behavior of the host.

3.   <u>Carlos</u> easily jumped over the barricade. Carlos was in excellent shape.

4.   The <u>chicken</u> looked both ways. The chicken was concerned about the heavy traffic.

5.   The <u>chicken</u> decided never to cross the road again. The chicken was frightened by her near-death experience.

Lesson 13

dm

Editing Practice 1

CORRECTED SENTENCES APPEAR ON PAGE 467.

Correct all errors in the following paragraphs using the first correction as a model. The number in parentheses at the end of each paragraph indicates how many errors you should find.

Last summer I flew from Seattle to New York. Not having flown for a while, ~~the trip was quite an eye-opener~~. I had an eye-opening experience On the positive side, it really is much easier than it used to be to compare rates and schedules. Spending a few minutes (well, quite a few minutes actually) on the computer, the best choice was obvious. That's it for the good news. Everything else was downhill from there. Knowing that I needed to get to the airport in plenty of time, my plan was to get there an hour and a half before departure time. Even then, I very nearly missed my flight. What I hadn't bargained on was how much longer it would take to get through security. Taking off my coat, jacket, and shoes and unpacking my laptop was awkward enough. The real problem was trying to get my shoes back on while juggling all my clothes and my computer. Balancing on one foot and then the other, my shoes proved almost impossible to wedge onto my feet one-handed. (3)

The flight itself was uneventful, though not very pleasant. Seated in the middle seat, it seemed like the flight lasted forever. One thing that had changed since the last time I have flown was the lack of leg room. Even being of only average height, my legs did not fit into the space. I thought that was pretty bad; then the person in front of me reclined his seat to the maximum. The top of his seat was about 12 inches from my face. I quickly discovered that I could not read. Holding my book so close to my face, my eyes could not focus on the page. Nevertheless, I lived to tell the tale and even survived the return flight. (3)

Editing Practice 2

Correct all errors in the following paragraphs using the first correction as a model. The number in parentheses at the end of each paragraph indicates how many errors you should find.

Annoyed by the swarm of students trying to buy textbooks, *Jacquita was not having a good day* ~~it was not a good day for Jacquita~~. While trying to register for classes earlier in the week, a computer glitch occurred. As a result, she had to register for new classes. Unable to take the classes she had originally wanted, replacements were necessary, and Jacquita had to return her old books to buy new ones. (2)

Now, she was back in the bookstore along with dozens of other students. Searching for used textbooks, Jacquita had to compete with other students wanting the same books. Her new classes also required more books. After finding all of the books she needed, a long line of students waiting at the register confronted Jacquita. Frustrated by the slow pace, another register opened up, but a dozen students stepped in front of her as she moved to the new line. Jacquita decided that next semester she would register earlier in case another computer glitch occurred. (2)

Applying What You Know

Introductory elements can always be deleted because they are not grammatically necessary. However, they are commonly used because they add useful information. Write a paragraph describing an awkward or embarrassing classroom experience. Try to write it without using introductory elements. Now, go back and add useful information in the form of introductory elements. Add at least three, and put a comma after each one. Use the Illogical Action Tip to make sure you avoid dangling modifiers.

The Bottom Line	Using a little caution, you can avoid dangling modifiers.

LESSON 14

Misplaced and Squinting Adverbs

Misplaced Adverb

Error: ✗ The kids <u>almost</u> ate a dozen donuts.

                                almost
Correction: The kids ~~almost~~ ate a dozen donuts.
                                        ^

Squinting Adverb

Error: ✗ A friend whom I e-mail <u>frequently</u> has computer viruses.

                                   frequently
Correction 1:   A friend whom I e-mail ~~frequently~~ has computer viruses.
                                     ^

Correction 2:   A friend whom I e-mail ~~frequently~~ has computer
                              frequently
         viruses.
           ^

What's the Problem?

Adverbs are words that modify other words. Adverbs are doubly unusual in that (1) they can modify more than one part of speech, and (2) they can move around. The placement of adverbs can make a big difference in meaning. For example, see how much difference the placement of *only* makes in the following sentence:

<u>Only</u> I love you.

Nobody else loves you.

I love <u>only</u> you.

You are the only person I love.

There are two types of mistakes that writers commonly make with adverbs. The mistakes are so common that they even have special names: **misplaced adverbs** and **squinting adverbs**.

Example 1 shows us a typical misplaced adverb. Ask yourself this question about the sentence in Example 1: How many donuts did the kids actually eat (if we take the sentence literally)? The answer is NONE. They didn't actually eat any, though they *nearly* ate a dozen. It is not that the sentence in Example 1 is ungrammatical. It isn't. The problem is that the sentence says something the writer didn't mean to say at all (namely, that the kids didn't eat any donuts at all).

Example 2 shows us a typical squinting adverb. The problem in this example is where the writer placed the adverb *frequently*. The writer put it in an ambiguous position where it can modify either the verb in front of it (*e-mail*) or the verb after it (*has*). We call it a "squinting adverb" because it looks two different directions at once — both to the verb in front of it and to the verb behind it. The example isn't really ungrammatical either; in fact, it has *two* perfectly grammatical meanings. The problem is that the reader has absolutely no way of knowing *which* of the two meanings the writer intended.

Lesson 14

m-s
adv

Diagnostic Exercise

CORRECTED SENTENCES APPEAR ON PAGE 467.

Correct all errors in the following paragraph using the first correction as a model. The number in parentheses at the end of the paragraph indicates how many errors you should find.

today
My brother informed me ~~today~~ he would travel to Europe. He plans

to go as soon as school is out this summer. A travel agent told him it

would only cost $400 for a round-trip ticket to London. The agent he spoke

with enthusiastically said that he should take advantage of this price.

My brother asked whether I wanted to go with him, but I have already

committed myself to a summer job. He almost talked for an hour before

I convinced him I couldn't go with him. (3)

Fixing This Problem in Your Writing

Misplaced Adverbs

Fortunately, the number of adverbs that are commonly misplaced is limited. All of them are single-word adverbs. The most common ones are *almost, barely, hardly, merely, nearly, often, only, quickly,* and *recently.*

Here is a tip to help you determine whether you have a misplaced adverb.

> **LITERAL ADVERB TIP** Double-check that single-word adverbs literally modify the words that follow them.

Here are some more examples of misplaced modifiers:

Error:	✗ I <u>nearly</u> took fifteen minutes to find my notes.
Tip applied:	If you nearly took fifteen minutes, then you literally didn't take any minutes at all.

Nearly does not modify *took*. *Nearly* modifies *fifteen minutes*.

Correction:	nearly I ~~nearly~~ took fifteen minutes to find my notes. ^
Error:	✗ We <u>barely</u> packed enough clothes for the trip.
Tip applied:	You can't barely pack. Either you packed or you didn't pack.

Barely does not modify *packed*. *Barely* modifies *enough*.

Correction:	barely We ~~barely~~ packed enough clothes for the trip. ^

Squinting Adverbs

Squinting adverbs are adverbs (either single-word adverbs or short adverb phrases) that are placed at the boundary between two major sentence parts so that the reader can't tell which sentence part the adverb goes with. One (somewhat unrealistic) solution is to never put adverbs at these boundaries. A more practical solution is to use the next tip to see which part of the sentence the adverb goes with, and then move the adverb to a less ambiguous position.

> **SAY-IT-BOTH-WAYS-TEST TIP** Whenever you use an adverb in the middle of a sentence, say it to yourself both ways: once with a pause in front of the adverb and then a second time with a pause after the adverb.

If both pronunciations make sense when you use the Say-It-Both-Ways-Test Tip, then you have a squinting adverb. Move the adverb away from the boundary between the two clauses to an unambiguous position elsewhere in that part of the sentence (or even change the adverb to an adjective). Here is the Say-It-Both-Ways-Test Tip applied to the sample error:

Error:　　　✗ A friend whom I e-mail <u>frequently</u> has computer viruses.

When we say the sentence aloud, we can say it this way:

A friend whom I e-mail <u>frequently</u> // has computer viruses.

Frequently modifies *e-mail.*

or the writer will say it this way:

A friend whom I e-mail // <u>frequently</u> has computer viruses.

Frequently modifies *has.*

> Once you have identified a squinting adverb, it is easy to move the adverb so that its placement is unambiguous. In this case, we also have a third option: if *frequently* goes with *has computer viruses,* change the adverb *frequently* to the adjective *frequent*:

has frequent

Correction 3:　　A friend whom I e-mail ~~frequently has~~ computer viruses.

Here are two more examples of the Say-It-Both-Ways-Test Tip:

Error:　　　✗ I decided <u>the next day</u> to look for a new job.

Tip applied:　　I decided <u>the next day</u> // to look for a new job.

The next day modifies *decided.*

I decided // <u>the next day</u> to look for a new job.

The next day modifies *to look.*

Once you recognize that *the next day* is in an ambiguous position, it is easy to move the adverb away from the clause boundary so that it modifies the part of the sentence that you intend it to modify:

The next day,

Correction 1:　　I decided ~~the next day~~ to look for a new job.
　　　　　　　　　　^

the next day

Correction 2:　　I decided ~~the next day~~ to look for a new job.
　　　　　　　　　　　　　　　　　　　　　　　　　　　^

Lesson 14

m-s adv

Here is another sentence with a squinting adverb error:

Error:	✗ The manager told me <u>yesterday</u> my rent was due.
Tip applied:	The manager told me <u>yesterday</u> // my rent was due.
	The manager told me // <u>yesterday</u> my rent was due.

> We can say the sentence with the adverb *yesterday* on either side of the pause point.

We would move the adverb depending on the meaning we intend:

Correction 1:   ^{Yesterday, the}
    ~~The~~ manager told me ~~yesterday~~ my rent was due.
    ^

Correction 2:   The manager told me ~~yesterday~~ my rent was due. ^{yesterday}
                                                                        ^

Lesson 14

m-s
adv

✳ *Putting It All Together*

Identify Misplaced Adverbs

____ Identify all short adverbs that you use in the middle of a sentence (especially the adverbs *almost, barely, hardly, merely, nearly, often, only, quickly,* and *recently*).

Correct Misplaced Adverbs

____ Carefully check that the adverb *literally* modifies the following word. If it does not, look for another word that the adverb does modify.

Identify Squinting Adverbs

____ Identify all adverbs (single-word and short phrases) that are used in the middle of sentences.

____ See if you can use the adverb or adverb phrase on both sides of a clause boundary. If you can, then you have a squinting adverb.

Correct Squinting Adverbs

____ Move the adverb or adverb phrase away from the clause boundary so that it is clear to the reader which part of the sentence the adverb goes with. Sometimes you also have the possibility of changing the adverb to an adjective.

Sentence Practice 1

CORRECTED SENTENCES APPEAR ON PAGE 468.

Underline misplaced and squinting adverbs. Then, correct the error by moving the adverb to a more appropriate position. If there is no error, write *OK* above the sentence.

> *Example:*   The man who was dancing <u>slowly</u> began laughing.
>
> *Correction:*   The man who was dancing ~~slowly~~ began laughing.
> *slowly*

1. Professor Washington almost gave us a quiz over the homework.

2. Hamsters are only pregnant for sixteen days.

3. We almost read forty short stories in my American literature class.

4. My biology teacher said that there are 138,000 varieties of butterflies and moths yesterday.

5. She nearly hit the ball out of the park.

 For more practice correcting misplaced and squinting adverbs, go to **Exercise Central** at **bedfordstmartins.com/commonsense**

Lesson 14

m-s
adv

Sentence Practice 2

CORRECTED SENTENCES APPEAR ON PAGE 468.

Underline misplaced and squinting adverbs. Then, correct the error by moving the adverb to a more appropriate position. If there is no error, write *OK* above the sentence.

> *Example:*   Jean <u>nearly</u> talked for two hours on the phone.
>
> *Correction:*   Jean ~~nearly~~ talked for two hours on the phone.
> *nearly*

1. The man reading slowly asked me to turn off my radio.

2. Iva said yesterday she found my keys.

3. He only bought that DVD for $6.

4. We located only three sources for our group paper.

5. Gardening often gives me both relaxation and time alone.

Sentence Practice 3

For each of the following sentences, place the word in parentheses into the sentence so that it is clear what the word modifies.

> *Example:*   **I was a vegetarian for five years. (almost)**
>
>   *almost*
> *Answer:*   **I was a vegetarian for five years.**
>   ^

1. José lost his hearing last month as a result of an accident at the factory. (nearly)

2. On my income tax statement, I can deduct half of my travel expenses. (only)

3. His study group met to discuss the goals of the project. (quickly)

4. She goes to the gym after class. (often)

5. WebTech Corporation did not lose revenue once in the past fiscal year. (even)

Editing Practice 1

CORRECTED SENTENCES APPEAR ON PAGE 468.

Correct all errors in the following paragraphs using the first correction as a model. The number in parentheses at the end of each paragraph indicates how many errors you should find.

>   *hardly*
>
>   I don't watch a lot of TV. I suppose that I ~~hardly~~ watch three
>   ^
>
> programs a week. It's not that I don't like television; the problem is that
>
> I never seem to find programs that I really want to watch when I have

a little down time. I suppose that if I had TiVo, I would watch more often since I could watch my favorites whenever I wanted to. As it is now, I flick through the program guide quickly losing interest. Besides, I tell myself, watching TV too often is a complete waste of time. (2)

Another problem is that many TV programs seem actually to have become serials. That is, they have a storyline that continues from week to week. Each new episode builds on what has happened before. I suppose this soap opera-like construction is attractive to the producers since they can build in layers of complicated relations that bring the audience back week after week. The trouble with this approach for casual viewers like me is that tuning into an ongoing program is like starting to read a long book by starting in the middle — I have no idea what is going on. This kind of program almost accounts for half the shows on TV today. (2)

Editing Practice 2

Correct all errors in the following paragraph using the first correction as a model. The number in parentheses at the end of the paragraph indicates how many errors you should find.

        recently

I went to a mall ~~recently~~ voted one of the best in the state. The vote was conducted by a national marketing firm and almost involved eight thousand shoppers. I learned there are twenty-four major malls in this state yesterday. The mall I went to was proud of highly being ranked, so its management posted the results on signs in the mall. To be honest, I am not sure what makes this mall special. The same stores you find at other malls usually are at the one I went to yesterday. I saw a few special shops that I had not seen before, but most of the shops were standard.

The people who worked there happily greeted me and were more helpful than I expected. Also, the mall was particularly clean, and it had plenty of space for walking. On the whole, however, it seemed like every other mall I have been to. (5)

Applying What You Know

Misplaced modifiers can lead to confusion for readers, and even experienced writers make mistakes. Find a short article written by a professional writer or journalist. Circle every word that could be replaced by *often*. Put a question mark next to any modifier that might be misplaced, and discuss with either a classmate or your teacher whether these modifiers are correct or misplaced.

Lesson 14

*m-s
adv*

The Bottom Line	Modifiers are **normally** placed close to the words they **best** describe.

UNIT FIVE: Placing and Punctuating Modifiers

REVIEW

Using modifiers is a key step in writing clearly. When writers misplace or mispunctuate modifiers, they may confuse readers, who will not understand their intended meaning. The following chart points you to the tips that will help you avoid errors when placing and punctuating modifiers.

TIP(S)	QUICK FIX AND EXAMPLES
Lesson 13. Dangling Modifiers	
The Illogical Action Tip (p. 130) helps you identify dangling modifiers.	If an introductory element makes an illogical claim about the noun or pronoun that follows it, the sentence probably needs to be revised. *Error:* ✗ Confused by the question, my answer was wildly off the mark. *Correction:* Confused by the question, *I gave an answer that* ~~my answer~~ was wildly off the mark.
Lesson 14. Misplaced and Squinting Adverbs	
The Literal Adverb Tip (p. 140) reminds us to double-check that single-word adverbs literally modify the words that follow them. The Say-It-Both-Ways-Test Tip (p. 140) helps identify squinting adverbs in the middle of sentences. Say the adverb both ways: once with a pause in front of the adverb and then with the pause after the adverb. If both pronunciations make sense, then you have a squinting adverb.	Move a misplaced adverb closer to the word it describes. *Error:* ✗ I almost read a dozen essays that week. *Correction:* I ~~almost~~ read a *almost* dozen essays that week. *Error:* ✗ Sometimes I surf through the television channels rapidly becoming bored with what I see. *Correction 1:* Sometimes I *rapidly* surf through the television channels ~~rapidly~~ becoming bored with what I see. *Correction 2:* Sometimes I surf through the television channels ~~rapidly~~ *rapidly* becoming bored with what I see.

Correct all dangling modifiers, misplaced adverbs, and squinting adverbs using the first correction as a model. The number in parentheses at the end of the paragraph indicates how many errors you should find.

All of us spend more time in meetings than we would like.

we can easily

Discouraged by poorly run meetings, ~~it is easy to~~ conclude that all
meetings are a waste of time. However, the only thing worse than an
organization that almost meets every day is an organization that does
not hold meetings at all. In this kind of organization usually the staff feels
that they have no input into decision making at all, or even that they don't
know what is going on. If nothing else, meetings ensure that a certain
amount of face-to-face interaction takes place. Without sitting down and
talking to one another, the office quickly becomes distant and impersonal.
The best meetings make us all feel connected to each other and to the
organization. Of course, it would be nice once in a while to have agendas
and minutes. By doing things the right way, meetings can be worth the
time we spend on them. (5)

UNIT SIX
Using Commas Correctly

OVERVIEW

Terms That Can Help You Use Commas Correctly

If you are not familiar with any of the following terms, look them up in the Guide to Grammar Terminology beginning on page 435.

adjective clause	introductory element
adverb	nonessential adjective clause
adverb clause	participial phrase
appositive	prepositional phrase
compound verb	proper noun
coordinating conjunction	relative pronoun
dependent clause	subordinate clause
essential adjective clause	subordinating conjunction
independent clause	transitional term
infinitive	

The Nuts and Bolts of Using Commas Correctly

This unit will help you with one of the most challenging aspects of written English: when to use (or not to use) commas. These six lessons cover the most common or most bothersome types of errors involving commas (see Lessons 2 and 26 as well). Some of these "comma lessons" are clearly inter-related, as with Lessons 17 and 18. Others, however, have their own distinct rules and guidelines on commas.

Lesson 15 shows you how to combine two independent clauses with a comma and a coordinating conjunction. This lesson also explains when you do not use a comma before a coordinating conjunction that separates two parts of a sentence.

Example: ✗ Thelma ran away from the charging lion but she was unable to run fast enough.

Correction: Thelma ran away from the charging lion, but she was unable to run fast enough.

149

Lesson 16 shows you how to punctuate transitional terms. A transitional term (often called a conjunctive adverb) clarifies the relationship between two ideas. Below is a correction involving two ideas that are separated by a semicolon. The transitional term (*however*) helps readers understand just how closely connected these two ideas are. A comma is usually placed after the transitional term in this sort of sentence.

Example: ✗ My toast was badly burnt, however, I decided to eat it.

Correction: My toast was badly burnt,/; however, I decided to eat it.

Lesson 17 shows you how to combine two clauses when one clause begins with a subordinating conjunction. Here is an example:

Example: ✗ Because I was in a hurry I had no time to call you.

Correction: Because I was in a hurry, I had no time to call you.

Lesson 18 shows you how to punctuate introductory elements. Some introductory elements require a comma, while for others a comma is optional. Failure to use a comma with introductory elements is one of the most common errors in the writing of college students.

Example: ✗ While I was revising my paper my hard drive crashed.

Correction: While I was revising my paper, my hard drive crashed.

Lesson 19 shows you how to punctuate adjective clauses. If the adjective clause does not significantly alter the meaning of the noun it modifies, it is said to be nonessential to the meaning of the sentence. A nonessential adjective clause should be set off from the rest of the sentence with commas. If the adjective clause does significantly alter the meaning of the noun, it is said to be essential to the meaning of the sentence. Essential adjective clauses do not require commas.

Example: ✗ I wanted to go to a place, where I could relax.

Correction: I wanted to go to a place,/ where I could relax.

Lesson 20 shows you how to punctuate appositives. Appositives are nouns or pronouns that rename or modify the nouns they follow. If the appositive does not significantly alter the meaning of the noun it renames, it is said to be nonessential to the meaning of the sentence. A nonessential appositive should be set off from the rest of the sentence with commas. If the appositive

(margin) Unit Six

overview

does significantly alter the meaning of the noun, it is said to be essential to the meaning of the sentence and does not require the use of commas.

Example: ✗ I recently visited Julia my aunt.

Correction: I recently visited Julia, my aunt.
                                    ^

LESSON 15

Commas with
And, But, Or, and Other
Coordinating Conjunctions

EXAMPLE 1   *Missing Comma*

Error: ✗ Derek finally finished writing his book of poems <u>but</u> his publisher was not satisfied.

Correction: Derek finally finished writing his book of poems, but his publisher was not satisfied.

EXAMPLE 2   *Unnecessary Comma*

Error: ✗ A moose wandered into town, <u>and</u> scared several kids.

Correction: A moose wandered into town, and scared several kids.

What's the Problem?

Coordinating conjunctions are the most common way of joining **independent clauses** (see Lesson 1 for tips on identifying an independent clause, a group of words that can stand alone as a complete sentence). This lesson focuses on the most common coordinating conjunctions: *and, but,* and *or.* The easiest way to remember all seven coordinating conjunctions is by the term FANBOYS, formed from the first letter of each conjunction:

FANBOYS = <u>F</u>or, <u>A</u>nd, <u>N</u>or, <u>B</u>ut, <u>O</u>r, <u>Y</u>et, <u>S</u>o

Coordinating conjunctions, or FANBOYS, are punctuated in two different ways depending on what the conjunctions join. As you can see in Example 1, a comma must go in front of the FANBOYS when the FANBOYS joins two independent clauses.

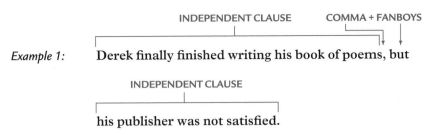

Example 1:   Derek finally finished writing his book of poems, but

INDEPENDENT CLAUSE

his publisher was not satisfied.

When one of the FANBOYS joins just parts of sentences, you should not use a comma. In Example 2, no comma is needed because *and* does not join two independent clauses.

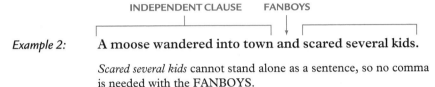

Example 2:   A moose wandered into town and scared several kids.

Scared several kids cannot stand alone as a sentence, so no comma is needed with the FANBOYS.

It is easy to understand why punctuation errors occur with coordinating conjunctions. Both examples above *seem* similar because each conjunction joins a group of words. The key to knowing when to use a comma with a coordinating conjunction is to determine what the FANBOYS joins together — word groups that could be complete sentences or just parts of sentences. You can avoid punctuation problems by looking at what comes before and after the coordinating conjunction.

Lesson 15

coord

Diagnostic Exercise

CORRECTED SENTENCES APPEAR ON PAGE 468.

Correct all comma errors in the following paragraph using the first correction as a model. The number in parentheses at the end of the paragraph indicates how many errors you should find.

When he reached the Americas, Christopher Columbus believed he had reached the East Indies, so he called the people whom he found *Indians*. That term is still used but many indigenous people prefer the term *Native Americans*. Some people think of Native Americans as a group but that is really a mistake because there are vast differences in their cultures and languages. People also tend to think of the tribes from the plains as being typical Native Americans for those are the tribes most often represented in movies, and on TV. The plains tribes hunted buffalo, and lived in tepees but few coastal tribes ever saw a buffalo or a tepee. Instead, coastal tribes hunted whales, and lived in wooden homes. (7)

Fixing This Problem in Your Writing

The following tip helps determine whether you should use a comma with FANBOYS.

> **IMAGINARY PERIOD TIP**   Pretend there is a period right before the FAN-BOYS. If *both* parts divided by the imaginary period can stand alone as complete sentences, use a comma before the FANBOYS in the original sentence. Otherwise, leave out the comma.

In other words, if an imaginary period works in the sentence, you should use a comma before the FANBOYS. Like a period, a comma before a coordinating conjunction lets readers know that you are moving on to a new idea — to a new subject and a new verb.

Here is how the Imaginary Period Tip can be applied to the two example sentences.

Example 1:	✗ Derek finally finished his book of poems but his publisher was not satisfied.
Tip applied:	Derek finally finished his book of poems. But his publisher was not satisfied.
	Imaginary period works, confirming that *but* is used with two independent clauses. A comma must be added.
Correction:	Derek finally finished his book of poems, but his publisher was not satisfied.

Usually, it is what comes *after* the imaginary period that tells you if you should use a comma. In Example 2, a comma is unnecessary because the phrase after the imaginary period — *scared several kids* — cannot stand alone.

Example 2:	✗ A moose wandered into town, and scared several kids.

Lesson 15

coord

Tip applied:	A moose wandered into town. ✗ And scared several kids.

Imaginary period does not work, so no comma is needed.

Correction:	A moose wandered into town⁄ and scared several kids.

This example contains a **compound verb**, two lengthy verbs combined with a conjunction (*wandered into town and scared several kids*). Because the two verbs are being combined, a comma should not separate them. The following diagram will help you remember this rule.

No Comma before a FANBOYS

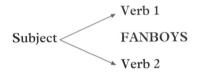

Verb 1

Subject   FANBOYS

Verb 2

Let's look at an example that correctly follows this formula for leaving out a comma before a FANBOYS:

threw four interceptions

The quarterback   but

somehow managed to win the game.

Also, avoid using a comma immediately *after* any FANBOYS. Some people mistakenly do so because they pause when reading the sentence aloud, but only very rarely is a comma needed right after a coordinating conjunction.

✳ *More Examples*

Error:	✗ You must return my car by Thursday or I will not allow you to borrow it again.
Correction:	You must return my car by Thursday, or I will not allow you to borrow it again.
Error:	✗ We ate at a nearby restaurant, but could not get back to campus on time.
Correction:	We ate at a nearby restaurant⁄ but could not get back to campus on time.

✳ *Putting It All Together*

Identify Errors in Using Coordinating Conjunctions

____ Put an imaginary period before each coordinating conjunction (the FANBOYS).

____ Check to see if what comes before and after the imaginary period can stand alone as two complete sentences.

Correct Errors in Using Coordinating Conjunctions

____ If both parts can stand alone, use a comma in front of the coordinating conjunction.

____ If one or both parts cannot stand alone, do not use a comma.

Lesson 15

coord

Sentence Practice 1

CORRECTED SENTENCES APPEAR ON PAGE 468.

Correct the comma errors in the following sentences. If there is no error, write *OK* above the sentence. Confirm your corrections by applying the Imaginary Period Tip.

> *Example:*   This paper is torn,/ but can still be used for scratch paper.
>
> *Confirmation:*   *This paper is torn. But can still be used for scratch paper.* [*Imaginary period does not work, so no comma is needed.*]

1. Pig iron is refined in a blast furnace, and contains iron along with small amounts of manganese and other minerals.

2. Piero di Cosimo was a Florentine painter, and is remembered for his scenes depicting mythology.

3. Tom decided he would walk to class, but changed his mind when it started raining.

4. You should return this book to the library, or you can renew it by phone.

5. The Norman Conquest of England took place in 1066, and brought many changes in English life.

For more practice using commas, go to **Exercise Central** at
bedfordstmartins.com/commonsense

Sentence Practice 2

CORRECTED SENTENCES APPEAR ON PAGE 469.

Correct the comma errors in the following sentences. If there is no error, write *OK* above the sentence. Confirm your corrections by applying the Imaginary Period Tip.

> *Example:*   **My friend Al didn't need a car, nor could he afford one.**
>   ^
>
> *Confirmation:*   *My friend Al didn't need a car. Nor could he afford one.*
>   [*Imaginary period works, so a comma is needed.*]

ESL

Non-native speakers of English will notice the odd fact that after the coordinating conjunction *nor* the subject and verb are reversed — *could he* rather than *he could*. This is grammatically correct. Be sure, however, to use a comma before *nor* when *nor* joins two independent clauses.

Lesson 15

coord

1. Jeremy did not arrive on time today, nor was he on time yesterday.

2. My roommate was ill this morning, so she missed class.

3. My father bought an old sword in England but the old relic is not worth much.

4. After class, Jan asked me if I would loan her my notes, and I was more than happy to do so.

5. Bahir is dropping by my place later so I suppose I should try to clean up a bit.

Sentence Practice 3

Combine each pair of sentences using a coordinating conjunction of your choice. If you want to keep both as independent clauses, you must use a comma with the coordinating conjunction. If you reduce one of the sentences to less than an independent clause, do not use a comma with the coordinating conjunction. When possible, combine them both ways.

Example: My hat doesn't fit very well. It keeps falling off when I ride my bike.

Answer: My hat doesn't fit very well. ~~It~~ *, so it* keeps falling off when I ride my bike.

My hat doesn't fit very well. ~~It~~ *and* keeps falling off when I ride my bike.

1. The water at the beach is cold today. It will be even colder tomorrow.

2. This desk is too big. That one is too small.

3. My coach told us not to be late. He comes in late often.

4. I downloaded software from the Internet. I am supposed to send money to the author of the software.

5. Ellen wrote you a check. She will put it in the mail tomorrow.

6. The giant armadillo has almost one hundred teeth. They are very small.

7. The giant anteater has no teeth. It uses a long tongue to catch its food.

8. A cell phone rang during the middle of my math class. The teacher was really annoyed.

9. My roommate said it would rain today. It rained 2 inches in less than an hour.

10. The Anglo-Zanzibar War occurred in 1896. The conflict ended after some forty-five minutes.

Lesson 15

coord

Editing Practice 1

CORRECTED SENTENCES APPEAR ON PAGE 469.

Correct all errors involving commas and coordinating conjunctions in the following paragraph using the first correction as a model. The number in parentheses at the end of the paragraph indicates how many errors you should find.

Writing is a form of visible language, but there is a form of writing
that is not meant to be seen. Braille is written as a series of dots or bumps
so visually impaired people can "read" it with their fingers. It is written as
a series of cells and each cell contains dots that can be variously arranged.
Each particular arrangement of dots has its own meaning but what the
dots represent depends on the style of Braille. There are two forms of
Braille: Grade 1, and Grade 2. Grade 1 Braille is a system in which the
dots represent letters, and some very short words. Grade 2 Braille is not
a completely different system but it is a shorthand version of Grade 1 that
is much harder to read. (6)

Editing Practice 2

CORRECTED SENTENCES APPEAR ON PAGE 469.

Correct all errors involving commas and coordinating conjunctions in the
following paragraph using the first correction as a model. The number in
parentheses at the end of the paragraph indicates how many errors you
should find.

The wedding ring has been around for many centuries, and its
history is more complex than people might think. Ancient Greeks are
often credited with inventing this tradition but many historians believe it
started with the Egyptians or Hebrews. We do know the first rings were
not made of precious metals. Many of the earliest rings were made of iron,
and did not have a gemstone. The ring was usually placed on the woman's
fourth finger for it was believed a nerve behind this finger led directly
to the heart. In the United States, the ring is placed on the left hand but
it is traditionally placed on the right hand in many other countries, such

as Russia and Germany. In many areas of the world, the ring is an important part of the wedding ceremony, yet this is often not the case in some countries. In Eastern Orthodox religions, the ring is part of the formal engagement ceremony, but its role in the actual wedding is small. Around the world, the wedding ring has become part of a multimillion dollar industry. (4)

Editing Practice 3

Correct all errors involving commas and coordinating conjunctions in the following paragraph using the first correction as a model. The number in parentheses at the end of the paragraph indicates how many errors you should find.

Lesson 15

coord

Liechtenstein is one of the smallest countries in the world,/ but was once one of the 343 states that made up the enormous Holy Roman Empire. In 1806, Napoleon invaded this empire, and it soon began to fall apart. Liechtenstein was forced to become a "protectorate" of France but this arrangement ended a few years later. The country then became part of the German Confederation yet this alliance also failed to last. In 1868, Liechtenstein declared itself independent and neutral. However, it remained closely allied with varying countries, such as Switzerland and the Austrian Empire. Liechtenstein might be small, and its history might be turbulent. Nonetheless, it is now a prosperous country and its royal head of state is one of the richest in the world. (3)

Applying What You Know

Write seven sentences about your past week, but do not put periods at the end of these sentences. Next, use each of the seven FANBOYS to connect each of your sentences to a new thought (for example, *My girlfriend cut her hair this week, yet I could not see any difference*). Use a different coordinating conjunction for each sentence.

Trade your sentences with a classmate and use the Imaginary Period Tip to see if your partner's sentences are correctly punctuated.

The Bottom Line	See whether what comes before and after *and*, *but*, or *or* can stand alone, **and** use a comma if they both can.

Commas with Transitional Terms

EXAMPLE 1   *Comma Splice*

Error: ✗ The Hope diamond is the best-known diamond, <u>however</u>, the Cullinan diamond, before being cut, was larger.

Correction: The Hope diamond is the best-known diamond,⁄; however, the Cullinan diamond, before being cut, was larger.

EXAMPLE 2   *Missing Comma*

Error: Ancient Egyptians used various substances to brush their teeth. ✗ For instance they used a powder made from the ashes of burnt ox hooves.

Correction: Ancient Egyptians used various substances to brush their teeth. For instance, they used a powder made from the ashes of burnt ox hooves.

What's the Problem?

Transitional terms (sometimes called **conjunctive adverbs**) are words such as *furthermore* and *however*. Usually, transitional terms are just one word, although they can consist of two or more words (as with *in fact* and *for example*).

These terms have little meaning by themselves, but they are important "signpost" words that allow readers to see a connection between two ideas. A transitional term might connect two ideas within the same sentence or show how an entire sentence relates to a previous sentence.

Transitional terms can lead to two types of punctuation errors. Example 1 illustrates the most significant error: a **comma splice**, the use of just a comma to separate what could be two separate sentences, or **independent**

clauses (see Lesson 2). As Example 1 shows, a transitional term *cannot* be used with just commas to join two independent clauses. A semicolon (or even a period) must be used before the transitional term.

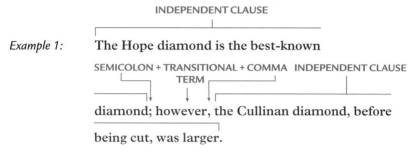

Example 1: The Hope diamond is the best-known

diamond; however, the Cullinan diamond, before being cut, was larger.

The second type of error is far less severe: the omission of commas around transitional terms that do not separate independent clauses. When a transitional term begins a sentence, as in Example 2, you should usually follow the term with a comma. The following examples show other cases in which a transitional term does not separate two independent clauses and, therefore, is set off with just commas.

> **I saw several classmates at the movie last night. Kate and Trisha, for example, were sitting right behind me.**
>
> *Kate and Trisha* and *were sitting right behind me* cannot stand alone as complete sentences, so for example is set off with commas.
>
> **Jay looked very tired when he arrived at baseball practice. He played better than usual, however.**

Handbooks and teachers do not always agree on whether it is necessary to set off transitional terms with commas. In fact, some readers might not consider Example 2 from the beginning of the lesson to be an error at all. It is this sort of inconsistency that makes the "rule" confusing. We suggest using commas because they draw attention to the transitional terms, helping readers make clearer connections between ideas. Most teachers seem to prefer the more formal guideline of using commas to set off transitional terms, so this is the safest approach in college-level writing.

Lesson 16

trans

Diagnostic Exercise

CORRECTED SENTENCES APPEAR ON PAGE 469.

Correct all errors involving transitional terms in the following paragraph using the first correction as a model. The number in parentheses at the end of the paragraph indicates how many errors you should find. (Only one error is counted per transitional term — semicolon and comma errors are not counted separately.)

Many places around the globe have universal appeal. They are, however, not necessarily accessible to the general public. An international committee has designated some sites as World Heritage Sites, which are sites having international value and responsibility. In the United States for example the committee has chosen Yosemite Park and the Statue of Liberty, both of which are part of our national parks system. We tend to take our parks system for granted, however, it is really quite unusual. Very few developed countries have extensive public land, consequently their important public sites are little more than individual buildings. The vast size of some national parks in the American West makes them unique, therefore they attract visitors from every country. (4)

Lesson 16

trans

Fixing This Problem in Your Writing

Identifying Transitional Terms

The first step in punctuating transitional terms is recognizing them. This chart lists common transitional terms grouped into categories according to their meaning.

TRANSITIONAL TERMS

In Addition	*For Example*	*On the Other Hand*	*As a Result*
again	for instance	however	accordingly
also	in fact	instead	consequently
besides	in particular	nevertheless	subsequently
further(more)	namely	nonetheless	therefore
likewise	specifically	on the contrary	thus
moreover		otherwise	
similarly		still	

Look for such words that establish a relationship between two ideas. Then, use the following tip to determine if indeed there is a transitional term.

> **TRANSITIONAL TERM MOVEMENT TIP**   A transitional term can be moved around in a sentence (or even deleted). Move *only* the term you are testing—not any other word or group of words.

If a word or group of words establishing a relationship between ideas can be moved, it is probably a transitional term. Coordinating conjunctions such as *and* or *but* cannot be moved. Words such as *because* and *while* also cannot be moved, despite seeming similar to transitional terms.

ESL

How do you know *where* a transitional term can be moved in a sentence? The Movement Tip relies on a person's intuition about whether a word sounds right when it is moved around. A non-native speaker of English might need to consult a native speaker on this matter.

Example 1 still makes sense when we use the Movement Tip to shift *however* to the end of the sentence:

Example 1: ✗ The Hope diamond is the best-known diamond, however, the Cullinan diamond, before being cut, was larger.

Tip applied: . . . the Cullinan diamond, before being cut, was larger, however.

Because *however* provides transition and can be moved around, it is a transitional term.

In Example 2, we can move *for instance*. This time, the transitional term works in the middle of a sentence:

Example 2: ✗ For instance they used a powder made from the ashes of burnt ox hooves.

Tip applied: They used, for instance, a powder made from the ashes of burnt ox hooves.

Punctuating Transitional Terms

Once you find a transitional term in your writing, first make sure you do not create a comma splice in using it. That is, use a semicolon before the term *if* it joins what could be two separate sentences. Do not leave out commas completely, though. Normally, a comma goes after a transitional term used with a semicolon.

Because the transitional term in Example 1 separates what could be two separate sentences, we know that it cannot be used with just commas.

Lesson 16

trans

Correction: The Hope diamond is the best-known
diamond,/; however, the Cullinan diamond, before
being cut, was larger.

A semicolon corrects the comma splice, and a comma is still
needed after the transitional term.

In Example 2, the transitional term does *not* separate two independent
clauses, so the original sentence needs only a comma after the transitional
term.

Correction: For instance, they used a powder made from the
ashes of burnt ox hooves.

The transitional term is set off with a comma.

If the transitional term is in the middle of a sentence and does *not* separate
two independent clauses, a comma should come before and after the term.

They used, for instance, a powder made from the ashes
of burnt ox hooves.

Lesson 16

trans ✳ *More Examples*

Error: ✗ My parents warned me about credit cards,
nonetheless, I have six of them.

Correction: My parents warned me about credit cards,/;
nonetheless, I have six of them.

Error: My boyfriend recently became a vegetarian.
✗ I consequently have been eating less meat.

Correction: I, consequently, have been eating less meat.

✳ *Putting It All Together*

Identify Transitional Terms

____ Look for words that establish a clear connection between two
ideas.

____ See if you can move the word (or words) around in the sentence.
If so, it is probably a transitional term.

> ## Correct Errors in Punctuating Transitional Terms
>
> ____ To avoid a comma splice, use a semicolon before the transitional term if what comes before and what comes after the term could each be separate sentences. Then, be sure to use a comma right after the transitional term.
>
> ____ Otherwise, set off a transitional term with at least one comma.

Sentence Practice 1

CORRECTED SENTENCES APPEAR ON PAGE 469.

Underline the transitional terms in the following sentences, and punctuate each sentence correctly. Confirm your answer by moving the transitional term to another position in the sentence. If the sentence contains no transitional terms, write *none* above the sentence.

Example: *none*
In the early 1800's, Tecumseh roused most tribes east of the Mississippi in an attempt to drive out the whites. His forces, <u>however,</u> were defeated by General Harrison.

Confirmation: <u>However,</u> his forces were defeated by General Harrison.

Lesson 16

trans

1. Bill said he might be late. Indeed he was four hours late.

2. Little is known about the Pilgrim ship *Mayflower*; we do know however that it weighed about 180 tons.

3. English is the predominant language in the United States, nevertheless, over three hundred languages are spoken within its borders.

4. The oldest known weapon is a broken spear found in Great Britain; it is estimated to have been made around 200,000 B.C.

5. A serious accident has caused major delays. In fact some commuters have decided to stay home.

 For more practice using transitional terms, go to **Exercise Central** at bedfordstmartins.com/commonsense

Sentence Practice 2

CORRECTED SENTENCES APPEAR ON PAGE 469.

Underline the transitional terms in the following sentences, and punctuate each sentence correctly. Confirm your answer by moving the transitional term to another position in the sentence. If the sentence contains no transitional terms, write *none* above the sentence.

> *Example:*   Most fans believe a football team must have a coach,/; nonetheless, the Chicago Bears won the 1943 championship without a head coach.
>
> *Confirmation:*   *The Chicago Bears, nonetheless, won the 1943 championship without a head coach.*

1. Sean Connery is remembered most for his James Bond movies. However he won an Oscar for a different role in *The Untouchables*.

2. Scott Joplin wrote over sixty musical compositions. He wrote for instance an opera entitled *Treemonisha*.

3. Some people consider Scotland part of England, but both are part of the United Kingdom.

4. The top position in the British army is field marshal. The top position in its navy in contrast is admiral of the fleet.

5. The singer Prince has gone by more than one name, for example, his birth name is Prince Rogers Nelson.

Sentence Practice 3

Combine the two short sentences with a semicolon and an appropriate transitional term (see the list on page 164). Underline the transitional term.

> *Example:*   My parents want me to major in accounting,/ I want to major in drama.   ; however,

1. The doctors diagnosed the problem. They were able to recommend a treatment.

2. There has been a 20 percent increase in fertilizer use. Food production has increased substantially.

3. The legislature has set new limits on enrollments. Each school must reassess its admission policies.

4. The experiment had failed. It had damaged the equipment badly.

5. The witch had frightened Dorothy and her friends. They decided to continue their trip.

6. Many people believe that nothing rhymes with *orange*. The term *sporange* is one word that does.

7. The water in our city tastes awful. The citizens are planning to complain to the mayor.

8. Most cucumbers are 95 percent water. They have few calories.

9. Alfred Butts invented Scrabble, an enormously successful game. He invented a game called "Alfred's Other Game," which did not do so well.

10. I like card games. Solitaire is one of my favorites.

Lesson 16

trans

Editing Practice 1

CORRECTED SENTENCES APPEAR ON PAGE 469.

Correctly punctuate all transitional terms in the following paragraphs using the first correction as a model. The number in parentheses at the end of each paragraph indicates how many errors you should find.

I am facing a difficult decision,/; however, it is one I have to make soon. My family would like me to help with our family business after I graduate from college. My parents own a construction company, and my major is in accounting. Consequently I believe that I would have a lot to offer my parents' company once I finish my degree. I could for example

help them develop more precise estimates for construction projects.
My plans seemed so clear and logical at one time. (2)

I enjoy talking with my parents about different accounting methods, nevertheless, I have lately been considering moving to a different part of the country and working in a different type of business. New England would be a great place to live for example. Additionally I am considering working as an accountant for a company that manufactures computer parts. Even though I want the family business to do well, I want to try something very different. My parents have always supported my choices, still, I know they will be disappointed if I do not work for them. (4)

Lesson 16

trans

Editing Practice 2

Correctly punctuate all transitional terms in the following paragraphs using the first correction as a model. The number in parentheses at the end of each paragraph indicates how many errors you should find.

My best friend and I enjoy watching professional football*. Thus,* ~~thus~~ we talk a great deal about the sport. The problem is that we have strong feelings about different teams. His favorite team is the Chicago Bears, in contrast, mine is the Dallas Cowboys. Consequently we argue frequently and loudly. (2)

Neither of our teams has done particularly well in the last few years. Nevertheless we are diehard fans. Even though our teams rarely play one another, he and I still argue about which team is better. Last week in fact we were almost shouting at each other over the simple matter of which team has a tougher schedule this year. If our teams played better, maybe we would not be so defensive, furthermore, maybe we would not argue so much if we were not both so competitive. (3)

Applying What You Know

Write down five transitional terms and switch lists with someone in the class. Using each of the transitional terms on your partner's list, write five sentences. Punctuate these sentences correctly, using a semicolon at least twice. The ideas you connect within each sentence should be logically related, but the sentences can be on different topics. When you have finished, switch papers and check your partner's sentences for correct punctuation.

The Bottom Line	Transitional terms clarify how ideas connect; **however,** you must punctuate these terms correctly.

Lesson 16

trans

LESSON 17

Commas with Adverb Clauses

EXAMPLE 1	*Missing Comma*

Error: ✗ When Paula and I go to a movie I always have to buy the popcorn.

Correction: When Paula and I go to a movie **,** I always have to buy the popcorn.

EXAMPLE 2	*Unnecessary Comma*

Error: ✗ Steven was late for class, because the bus was unusually slow.

Correction: Steven was late for class **,** because the bus was unusually slow.

What's the Problem?

An **adverb clause** is a group of words that answers the question *when, where, why, how,* or *to what degree* about the verb in the sentence. Adverb clauses are **dependent clauses**: they always have a subject and a verb, but they cannot stand alone.

Some writers become confused about when to use a comma with an adverb clause. What's important is the *position* of the adverb clause in the sentence. A comma is needed in Example 1 because the adverb clause is lengthy and appears at the beginning of the sentence; the comma signals to readers where the introductory adverb clause ends and the main clause begins. When an adverb clause appears at the end of a sentence, as in Example 2, a comma is rarely needed.

Here are more examples:

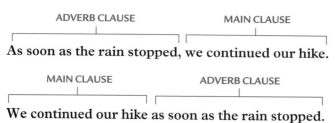

ADVERB CLAUSE   MAIN CLAUSE

As soon as the rain stopped, we continued our hike.

MAIN CLAUSE   ADVERB CLAUSE

We continued our hike as soon as the rain stopped.

Diagnostic Exercise

CORRECTED SENTENCES APPEAR ON PAGE 470.

Correct all errors involving adverb clauses in the following paragraph using the first correction as a model. The number in parentheses at the end of the paragraph indicates how many errors you should find.

After everybody was asleep Monday night, there was a fire in the

dorm next door. Fortunately, a smoke detector went off, when smoke

got into the staircase. While the fire department was fighting the fire six

rooms were totally destroyed. A friend of mine in another part of the

building lost her computer, because of the smoke and water damage. If

school officials close down the dorm for repairs she will have to find a new

place to stay. I heard they will make a decision today, as soon as they get a

report from the fire inspectors. (5)

Lesson 17

adv
cl

Fixing This Problem in Your Writing

Identifying Adverb Clauses

The first step in correcting problems with adverb clauses is to locate them in your writing. Adverb clauses begin with **subordinating conjunctions,** flag words that tell readers an adverb clause will follow. Here is a list of the most common ones grouped according to meaning.

SUBORDINATING CONJUNCTIONS

Cause	*Condition*	*Contrast*	*Place*	*Time*
as	as if	although	where	after
because	assuming that	even though	wherever	as soon as
since	if	though		before
so that	in case			since
	unless			until
	when			when
	whether			whenever

In an adverb clause, a subject and verb follow the flag word. Note that an adverb clause must always be part of a complete sentence; it can never stand alone.

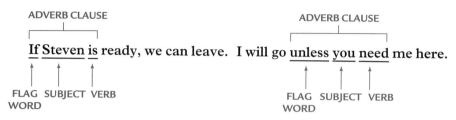

Here is an easy way to identify an adverb clause.

> **ADVERB CLAUSE MOVEMENT TIP**   An adverb clause is the only type of dependent clause that can be moved around in a sentence.

We know that the sentences above contain adverb clauses because we can move them to another part of the sentence.

Tip applied: If Steven is ready, we can leave. [*We can leave if Steven is ready.*]

Tip applied: I will go unless you need me here. [*Unless you need me here, I will go.*]

Punctuating Adverb Clauses

Once you have identified an adverb clause in your writing, check to make sure it is punctuated correctly. In Example 1, the adverb clause is at the beginning of the sentence, so a comma should come after the clause to let readers know where it stops:

Example 1:   ✗ When Paula wants to go to a movie I always have to buy the popcorn.

Tip applied: When Paula wants to go to a movie I always have to buy the popcorn. [*I always have to buy the popcorn when Paula wants to go to a movie.*]

The clause can be moved around, so it is an adverb clause.

Correction: When Paula wants to go to a movie, I always have to buy the popcorn.

Use a comma after an introductory adverb clause.

In some cases, particularly in business writing, it is acceptable to omit a comma after a very short introductory clause. In college writing, however, it is best to use the comma. Most instructors prefer that you use one to

---

Lesson 17

adv cl

show where the introductory clause ends and the main part of the sentence begins.

In Example 2, no comma is needed because the adverb clause comes at the end of the sentence.

Example 2:	✗ Steven was late for class, because the bus was unusually slow.

Tip applied: Steven was late for class, (because the bus was unusually slow). [*Because the bus was unusually slow, Steven was late for class.*]

The clause can be moved around, so it is an adverb clause.

Correction: Steven was late for class,/ because the bus was unusually slow.

Omit a comma before a sentence-ending adverb clause.

Sometimes rules have exceptions. If an adverb clause conveys a strong sense of contrast by using a flag word such as *although*, *even though*, or *though*, the clause must always be set off with a comma even if it is at the end of the sentence.

I didn't like the movie, <u>even though it received excellent reviews</u>.

 More Examples

Introductory Adverb Clauses

<u>Whenever I go to the mall</u>, I seem to forget my checkbook.

<u>Unless it rains</u>, class will be held under the oak tree.

Sentence-Ending Adverb Clauses

Someone shut the door on my foot <u>as I was leaving the building</u>.

You need to study hard <u>because the next test will cover the entire textbook</u>.

 Putting It All Together

Identify Adverb Clauses

____ Look for groups of words in your writing that answer the question *when, where, why, how,* or *to what degree* about the verb in a sentence.

→

_____ Ask yourself whether the clause follows this formula: *Flag Word + Subject + Verb.*

_____ Try moving the clause around in the sentence. If it can be moved around, it is an adverb clause.

Correct Errors in Punctuating Adverb Clauses

_____ Use a comma after an adverb clause that begins a sentence.

_____ Use no comma before an adverb clause that ends a sentence, unless the clause strongly contrasts with the first part of the sentence. Contrasting adverb clauses usually begin with *although, even though,* or *though.*

Sentence Practice 1

Lesson 17

adv cl

CORRECTED SENTENCES APPEAR ON PAGE 470.

In each of the following sentences, underline the adverb clause and correct the comma error. Confirm your answer by moving the adverb clause to another position in the sentence.

Example: <u>When we got the tests back,</u> we all went out for coffee.

Confirmation: We all went out for coffee <u>when we got the tests back.</u>

1. When I visit my parents in New Mexico I always bring them something from my part of the country.

2. I will go with you, after I finish eating.

3. After Omar competed in the third basketball tournament of the season he was not eager to travel again.

4. Because the test included over a hundred questions I could not finish it in just fifteen minutes.

5. Stephanie wants to leave, because she smells a strange odor in the room.

 For more practice using adverb clauses, go to **Exercise Central** at **bedfordstmartins.com/commonsense**

Sentence Practice 2

CORRECTED SENTENCES APPEAR ON PAGE 470.

In each of the following sentences, underline the adverb clause and correct the comma error. Confirm your answer by moving the adverb clause to another position in the sentence.

>   *Example:*   I was upset,/ because I should have known better.

>   *Confirmation:*   *Because I should have known better, I was upset.*

1. While we were watching some children playing in the park Luis and I talked about our own childhoods.

2. Although sharks are normally found in salt water some freshwater sharks exist in Lake Nicaragua.

3. We need to stop at the next gas station even though we stopped at one just an hour ago.

4. Because I tend to work forty hours each week I have to spend most of my weekends studying.

5. Whenever you are ready to leave I will be happy to go.

Lesson 17

adv cl

Sentence Practice 3

Combine each pair of sentences by turning the second sentence into an adverb clause. Choose an appropriate subordinating conjunction, or flag word, from the list on page 173. Underline the adverb clause, and show that it can be used both at the beginning and at the end of the sentence. Punctuate each version correctly.

>   *Example:*   I need to hang up. I have to go to class now.

>   *Answer:*   *I need to hang up because I have to go to class now.*
>   *Because I have to go to class now, I need to hang up.*

1. I cannot study. You are beating those drums.

2. Our party was cancelled with little notice. The person hosting it had to leave town.

3. You made a strange comment about Ray. Everyone was offended.

4. The test will be in two weeks. The teacher decides to postpone it.

5. Keisha should not come to class. She gets better.

6. The car will not start. You put some gas in it.

7. Napoleon Bonaparte was a famous military leader. He was afraid of cats.

8. You called me. I was in the shower.

9. I used ketchup to clean the candleholder. Ketchup is good for cleaning brass.

10. Sharon bought a new keyboard. Her old one was not working correctly.

Editing Practice 1

CORRECTED SENTENCES APPEAR ON PAGE 470.

In the following paragraphs, correctly punctuate each sentence that contains an adverb clause. The number in parentheses at the end of each paragraph indicates how many errors you should find.

Because I am a full-time student, my income is limited. I don't want to borrow money from my family, unless no other option is available. Twice, I have used a government loan to pay for my tuition, fees, and books. Without those loans, I would not have been able to attend college. Although I would prefer not to take out any more student loans I will likely have to do so again. (2)

My part-time job does not pay well, since it is a minimum-wage position. Although I can't afford any luxuries living on this meager income is manageable. In a few years, I will likely be able to improve my standard of living greatly, so my situation is not depressing. When I graduate from college I should be able to find a job, because my field is very much in demand. Until then, I will be able to get by on an occasional student loan. (4)

Editing Practice 2

In the following paragraphs, correctly punctuate each sentence that contains an adverb clause. The number in parentheses at the end of each paragraph indicates how many errors you should find.

Although many people may not be aware of it, Pearl Buck was the first American woman to win a Nobel Prize in literature. After her parents had spent years as missionaries in China they returned to the United States for a short time in the early 1890's, during which time Pearl was born. When she was just three months old Pearl returned to China with her parents. She grew up speaking Chinese, because her family lived among the Chinese rather than in a Western compound. (3)

Lesson 17

*adv
cl*

While they were living in China there were many protests against the Western governments that had controlled China's economy for years. Since she had lived among ordinary people Pearl was aware of their daily struggles for bare survival. Because she had such a depth of personal experience in China her most famous novel, *The Good Earth*, reflected her compassion for the Chinese and their culture. When Pearl Buck died President Nixon said that she had served as a "human bridge between the civilizations of the East and West." (4)

Applying What You Know

Write a paragraph describing the field you are concentrating in and why it interests you. In a second paragraph, imagine what you might be doing in that field ten years from now. Try to use as many adverb clauses as possible, punctuating them as discussed in this lesson.

The Bottom Line	If you use an introductory adverb clause, set it off with a comma.

Lesson 17

adv cl

LESSON 18

Commas with Introductory Elements

EXAMPLE 1	*Long Introductory Element*
Error:	✗ <u>While I was taking my morning walk</u> a car almost hit me.
Correction:	While I was taking my morning walk, a car almost hit me.

EXAMPLE 2	*Short but Confusing Introductory Element*
Error:	✗ <u>When you called</u> Sam was in the backyard.
Correction:	When you called, Sam was in the backyard.

What's the Problem?

In formal writing, an **introductory element** is usually set off with a comma. This comma tells the reader where the introductory element ends and the "real" sentence begins. Inserting a comma after an introductory element is especially important when the introductory element is long. Example 1 above is easier to read when a comma is used, telling the reader where to "take a breath" before proceeding.

However, even short introductory elements might need commas. In Example 2, *When you called* is short, but if the comma is left out, the reader might think the introductory element is *When you called Sam* and read the sentence incorrectly. Thus, even a short introductory element might need a comma to prevent confusion.

Punctuation errors involving introductory elements often occur because writers are confused about when they should use commas. Some introductory elements *must* be followed by a comma, while other types do not require one. In addition, some people have strong feelings about when commas should be used with introductory elements, no matter what the "rules" are. Many

181

teachers prefer commas even when the commas are optional, whereas many people in the business world prefer not to use commas after most introductory elements.

Diagnostic Exercise

CORRECTED SENTENCES APPEAR ON PAGE 470.

Correct all the comma errors in the following paragraph using the first correction as a model. The number in parentheses at the end of the paragraph indicates how many problems you should find.

Last Tuesday, there was a fire in one of the dorms. According to the school newspaper no one was hurt. When the fire department finally arrived several rooms were engulfed in flames. A friend of mine had her room filled with smoke. However her room suffered no major damage. Tomorrow school officials will tour the dorm and make recommendations. I have heard they plan to move everybody out within the next week. (4)

Lesson 18

intro

Fixing This Problem in Your Writing

Identifying Introductory Elements

Here are several examples of types of introductory elements that *always* require a comma:

- **Transitional terms always require commas** (see Lesson 16).

    <u>However</u>, there is no reason to vote against him.

- **Long adverb clauses always require commas** (see Lesson 17).

    <u>When you leave to go to the library</u>, lock the front door.

- **Infinitive phrases always require commas.**

    <u>To finish on time</u>, we had to write quickly.

- **Participial phrases always require commas.**

    <u>Seeing that the game was almost over</u>, the crowd started to leave.

Commas with other types of introductory elements are optional. We show some examples of these cases in the More Examples section on page 184. With all these types of introductory elements, knowing when a comma is optional can be confusing. We recommend a simple approach for most college writing: identify introductory elements in your writing, and — in most cases — punctuate them with a comma.

Here is a tip that will help you identify introductory elements.

> **DELETION TIP**   To make sure you have found an introductory element, see if you can delete it. If what remains is a complete sentence, what you deleted is an introductory element.

Unlike most parts of a sentence, an introductory element can always be deleted without creating an ungrammatical sentence. The Deletion Tip confirms that Example 1 has an introductory element:

Error:	✗ While I was taking my morning walk a car almost hit me.
Tip applied:	~~While I was taking my morning walk~~ A car almost hit me.

Using the tip, we can delete the introductory element (*While I was taking my morning walk*) and still have a grammatical sentence (*A car almost hit me*).

Punctuating Introductory Elements

Once you have determined that a sentence contains an introductory element, use this next tip to help you decide whether you should insert a comma after the introductory element.

> **COMMA TIP**   Unless you know readers prefer otherwise, use a comma after *all* introductory elements.

Although some readers might *prefer* that you not use a comma in cases when the comma is optional, using a comma after an introductory element is never a grammatical error. In contrast, leaving out the comma after certain introductory elements is always a grammatical mistake. Thus, we suggest using the comma *unless you know your reader believes in the "don't use it unless you have to" philosophy of commas.*

Using the Comma Tip, we can correct the errors in Examples 1 and 2:

Correction:	While I was taking my morning walk, a car almost hit me.
Correction:	When you called, Sam was in the backyard.

Lesson 18

intro

✳ *More Examples*

Long Prepositional Phrases   Commas are required:

In a state of rage over the drastic increase in taxes, the voters elected a new governor.

At a bookstore in the Bronx, Chuck found a karate manual.

Short Prepositional Phrases   Commas are optional if the omission of a comma does not cause confusion:

In my day, we used typewriters for our college papers.

After lunch Bijan went to the library.

Long Adverb Clauses   Commas are required:

Even though the teacher gave everyone two more days to study, the test was still difficult.

Because the employee parking lot is being painted, you must park elsewhere.

Short Adverb Clauses   Commas are optional:

When the storm ended we jogged for an hour.

If it's sunny we'll go to the lake.

Lesson 18

intro

✳ *Putting It All Together*

Identify Introductory Elements

_____ Use the Deletion Tip to identify introductory elements. Introductory elements come in many types, but all can be deleted without creating an error.

Correctly Punctuate Introductory Elements

_____ Whether a comma is required or is optional after an introductory element depends on the type of element and your readers' preferences. If you know that your readers do not like optional commas, leave out commas after short introductory elements unless the omission causes confusion.

_____ If you do not know what your readers prefer, use a comma after all introductory elements.

Sentence Practice 1

CORRECTED SENTENCES APPEAR ON PAGE 471.

Correct the following sentences. Confirm your answer by applying the Deletion Tip.

Example: **When we got the test back, nobody even thought about sleeping.**

Confirmation: *Nobody even thought about sleeping.*

1. Although Wally Amos is best known for his brand of cookies he was also the first African American talent agent for the William Morris Agency.

2. In France shepherds once carried small sundials as pocket watches.

3. Even though he was best known as an actor Jimmy Stewart was a brigadier general in the U.S. Air Force Reserve.

4. After eating our cat likes to nap.

5. Whenever I walk our dog likes to go with me.

 For more practice using introductory elements, go to **Exercise Central** at **bedfordstmartins.com/commonsense**

Lesson 18

intro

Sentence Practice 2

CORRECTED SENTENCES APPEAR ON PAGE 471.

Correct the following sentences. Confirm your answer by applying the Deletion Tip.

Example: **According to a recent study, more women than men take Oreo cookies apart to eat the middle.**

Confirmation: *More women than men take Oreo cookies apart to eat the middle.*

1. To keep people from sneaking up on him Wild Bill Hickok placed crumpled newspapers around his bed.

2. Before his career was suddenly ended Jesse James robbed twelve banks and seven trains.

3. Therefore he was a successful criminal for a time.

4. Believe it or not the state "gem" of Washington is petrified wood.

5. When she was in a high school band singer Dolly Parton played the snare drum.

Sentence Practice 3

Combine the following sentences by changing one sentence in each pair into an introductory element. Attach the introductory element to the other sentence, and punctuate correctly. You may have to add another word or two, as in the example.

Lesson 18

intro

> *Example:*   **I put on a sweater. I was getting cold.**
>
> *Answer:*   *Because I was getting cold, I put on a sweater.*

1. The house is too hot. The air conditioner is broken.

2. Claire must leave early. Claire has to go get a haircut.

3. I crept into the house. I moved slowly and cautiously.

4. We have to eat. We must eat as soon as class is over.

5. The vultures circled overhead. They were waiting for a wounded animal to die.

6. Bolivia has no coastline. This country has a navy.

7. A fire devastated almost half of London in 1666. Only six people were reported injured.

8. I am hungry. We can eat now.

9. The cat was sleeping soundly. Three mice scurried into the kitchen.

10. Dinosaurs are extinct now. They survived seventy-five times longer than humans have existed.

Editing Practice 1

CORRECTED SENTENCES APPEAR ON PAGE 471.

Correct the errors in the following paragraph using the first correction as a model. The number in parentheses at the end of the paragraph indicates how many errors you should find.

When I tried to start a student organization on campus last semester,
I was surprised by the difficulties and hurdles. I wanted to establish a club
for students who enjoy science fiction. After being encouraged by several
friends I contacted the school official who oversees campus organizations.
She informed me I would need a faculty sponsor and had to go through an
approval process that could take several weeks. Upon reading some twelve
pages of forms and directions I almost gave up. Fortunately a couple of
friends agreed to help me fill out the forms and gather signatures from
students interested in the club. However the work was still not finished.
We had to arrange a schedule of events and apply for funding. It took three
months before the science fiction club was approved by various committees and school administrators. Now that the club has had three successful
meetings I feel that all the work was worthwhile. (5)

Lesson 18

intro

Editing Practice 2

CORRECTED SENTENCES APPEAR ON PAGE 471.

Correct the errors in the following paragraph using the first correction as a model. The number in parentheses at the end of the paragraph indicates how many errors you should find.

As you might expect, there are heavy physical demands on
marathon runners. In addition to the common problem of fatigue the
greatest problem marathon runners have is with their feet. Among all

marathon runners the universal topic of conversation is shoes. Every brand is minutely compared in terms of weight, support, and cost. Because most runners train on asphalt running shoes wear out amazingly quickly. Replacing an expensive pair of shoes every few months can be pretty costly; nevertheless every runner has learned that running in worn shoes is asking for foot and ankle problems. Despite the fact that running shoes are tremendously expensive there is no doubt that they are getting better. The improved design of modern running shoes has eliminated many of the nagging foot and ankle problems that used to plague runners. For most runners the main issue in shoes is the trade-off between weight and support — the more weight, the more support; the less weight, the less support. (6)

Lesson 18

intro

Editing Practice 3

Correct the errors in the following paragraph using the first correction as a model. The number in parentheses at the end of the paragraph indicates how many errors you should find.

When I have time for recreation, sometimes I like to play video games. I have other interests, but playing video games is fun as well. Contrary to what many people believe there is a social aspect to playing many games. Obviously some games are meant to be played solo. However a game such as Halo 3 can be played alone or with multiple players. When you play a multiplayer game you can be in the same room as other people or you can play them online. Either way you do more than just simply fight these other people on the screen. With many multiplayer games that are played online you can converse with teammates by using a headset to discuss strategy. By playing such games over the last couple of years I have been able to meet new people and make friends. To me playing games is one aspect of socializing, so I disagree with those people who say that playing video games means a person lacks a social life. (8)

Applying What You Know

Knowing how to punctuate introductory elements might seem confusing, but introductory elements are useful because they help to clarify your ideas and add variety to your writing style. Write five sentences without introductory elements. The sentences need not be related to one another. Trade sentences with someone else and add an introductory element to each sentence. Notice how these elements add new ideas or clarify the writing in some way. Work with your partner to make sure each introductory element uses a comma correctly.

Lesson 18

intro

The Bottom Line	**When you use an introductory element,** set it off with a comma.

LESSON 19

Commas with Adjective Clauses

Unnecessary Comma

Error: ✗ Sally met a teacher, <u>who will be teaching composition this fall</u>.

Correction: Sally met a teacher,/ who will be teaching composition this fall.

Missing Comma

Error: ✗ I called Ms. Watson <u>who lives in Atlanta</u>.

Correction: I called Ms. Watson, who lives in Atlanta.

What's the Problem?

An **adjective clause** is a group of words that describes a person, place, thing, or idea. Adjective clauses usually begin with a **relative pronoun**, such as *who, whom, whose, which,* or *that,* or relative adverbs, such as *when* and *where.* Unlike a one-word adjective such as *big* or *red,* an adjective clause appears right *after* the noun it modifies, not before. In Example 1, the adjective clause *who will be teaching composition this fall* describes the noun *teacher.* In Example 2, *who lives in Atlanta* describes the noun *Ms. Watson.*

Writers often make punctuation errors with adjective clauses because some clauses *must* be set off from the rest of the sentence with a comma(s), whereas others *must not.* To punctuate adjective clauses correctly, you must first understand that there are two types of adjective clauses: *essential* (or **restrictive**) **clauses** and *nonessential* (or **nonrestrictive**) **clauses.** The following chart explains their functions and correct punctuation.

Adjective clause	Function	Punctuation
Essential	Provides important identifying information about the noun it describes	Do NOT set off with a comma (see Example 1).

Adjective clause	Function	Punctuation
Nonessential	Provides extra information about the noun, but the meaning of the noun would not significantly change if the clause were deleted	Set off with a comma (see Example 2).

The following is a summary of what to remember about adjective clauses:

Essential Clause = Essential Information = No Comma

Nonessential Clause = "Extra" Information = Comma

Unfortunately, there is no simple grammatical rule you can use to determine whether an adjective clause is essential or nonessential. Instead, you must think carefully about how the meaning of the adjective clause affects the noun it modifies. The following examples illustrate how meaning determines the distinction between essential and nonessential clauses.

Essential: **All my roommates who went to the party were late for class.**

Nonessential: **All my roommates, who went to the party, were late for class.**

In the first sentence, some roommates went to the party and some did not. The ones who were late for class were the ones who went to the party (not the ones who stayed home). In the second sentence, *all* the roommates went to the party, and thus *all* the roommates were late for class.

Diagnostic Exercise

CORRECTED SENTENCES APPEAR ON PAGE 471.

Correct all the comma errors in the following paragraph using the first correction as a model. The number in parentheses at the end of the paragraph indicates how many commas you should either add or delete.

It was strange going back to my high school reunion‸ which was held this summer. Allison who was my best friend once didn't recognize me. I guess she didn't expect to see me bald. I also saw a friend, whom I have stayed in touch with through e-mail but have not seen in years.

He told me he moved to Oregon where he found a job. Since I now live in Idaho, we agreed to get together. After the reunion was over, I had dinner with him and Allison at a restaurant, that we enjoyed when we were in high school. (5)

Fixing This Problem in Your Writing

Essential adjective clauses change the meaning of the nouns they modify by providing specific, identifying information. Because they contain information necessary to understanding the intended meaning of the sentence, essential clauses should *not* be set off from the rest of the sentence with a comma(s). Here is a tip that will help you determine whether an adjective clause is essential.

Lesson 19

adj
cl

> **DELETION TIP** Delete the adjective clause and look again at the noun it modified. If the noun is still clear, the clause is not essential. If deleting the clause creates confusion, the clause is essential.

When we apply the Deletion Tip to Example 1, a vague sentence results.

Example 1:   ✗ Sally met a teacher, <u>who will be teaching composition this fall.</u>

?

Tip applied: Sally met a teacher, ~~who will be teaching composition this fall~~.

By deleting the underlined clause, we have removed crucial information about *which* teacher Sally met. The clause identifies the teacher as someone who will teach composition this fall. That information is important to understanding the sentence, so the clause is essential. To punctuate the sentence correctly, we apply the guideline described earlier.

Correction: Sally met a teacher͵ who will be teaching composition this fall.

Essential Clause = Essential Information = No Comma

If we apply the tip to Example 2, however, we find that the sentence still makes sense even after the adjective clause is deleted.

Example 2:   ✗ I called Ms. Watson <u>who lives in Atlanta.</u>

✓

Tip applied: I called Ms. Watson ~~who lives in Atlanta~~.

This adjective clause is considered a nonessential clause because it just adds extra information — "gravy" that provides detail that might be useful but is not crucial in terms of identifying *Ms. Watson*. This does not mean we should permanently delete the adjective clause. In fact, effective writers frequently use nonessential clauses to provide further clarification and specifics. To punctuate the sentence correctly, we apply the guideline described earlier.

Correction: **I called Ms. Watson, who lives in Atlanta.**

Nonessential Clause = "Extra" Information = Comma

It is not unusual for one sentence to have both types of adjective clauses, but you should follow the same guidelines discussed so far. In this final example, the first clause is a nonessential clause, so it is set off with commas, but the second clause is not set off with commas because it is an essential clause:

NONESSENTIAL CLAUSE (COMMAS)

Mr. Gordon, who is my math teacher, owns the house

ESSENTIAL CLAUSE (NO COMMA)

that is across from mine.

✳ *More Examples*

Essential Clauses   *Do not set off with a comma(s):*

Jonathan lives next to a woman <u>who is from Denmark</u>.

Somebody <u>who was in a hurry</u> asked me to give you this note.

Nonessential Clauses   *Set off with a comma(s):*

I am leaving for San Diego, <u>where I was born and raised</u>.

My car, <u>which is fifteen years old</u>, has never needed a repair.

✳ *Putting It All Together*

Identify Adjective Clauses

_____ Find the adjective clauses in your writing. An adjective clause is a group of words that functions as an adjective. Adjective clauses usually begin with relative pronouns (*who, whom, that, which*) or relative adverbs (*when, where*). →

Lesson 19

adj
cl

_____ Determine whether the adjective clause is essential or nonessential. If you can delete the clause without confusing readers or changing the meaning of the sentence, the clause is nonessential. If the clause is necessary for readers to understand the sentence, then the clause is essential.

Correctly Punctuate Adjective Clauses

_____ If the adjective clause is essential, do NOT set it off with a comma(s).

_____ If the adjective clause is nonessential, set it off with a comma(s).

Sentence Practice 1

Lesson 19

adj
cl

CORRECTED SENTENCES APPEAR ON PAGE 472.

Label the underlined adjective clauses in the following sentences as *essential* or *nonessential* and punctuate accordingly. If a sentence is already punctuated correctly, write *OK* next to it.

> *essential*
>
> *Example:*   Houses,/ that are made of wood,/ often survive major earthquakes.

1. Bo is reading a novel <u>that was written by J. R. R. Tolkien</u>.

2. Bo is reading *The Silmarillion* <u>which was written by J. R. R. Tolkien</u>.

3. She wanted to go to a place <u>where she could be alone</u>.

4. This neighborhood cafe <u>which first opened in 1939</u> is one of my favorite places to drink coffee.

5. My parents were married in the Middle Eastern country of Yemen <u>where a wedding feast can last three weeks</u>.

 For more practice using adjective clauses, go to **Exercise Central** at bedfordstmartins.com/commonsense

Sentence Practice 2

CORRECTED SENTENCES APPEAR ON PAGE 472.

Label the underlined adjective clauses in the following sentences as *essential* or *nonessential* and punctuate accordingly. If a sentence is already punctuated correctly, write *OK* next to it.

Example: I bumped into my second-grade teacher, <u>whom I hadn't seen in years.</u>

1. My dentist is from Seattle <u>which is over 600 miles from here.</u>

2. Queen Latifah <u>who is best known as a rap artist</u> has also been a television host and an actress.

3. Do you know a lawyer <u>who can help you with your legal problem?</u>

4. Meet me at the place <u>where you and I first met.</u>

5. The only river, <u>that flows north and south of the equator,</u> is the Congo River <u>which crosses the equator twice.</u>

Sentence Practice 3

Combine the two short sentences by making the second sentence into an adjective clause that modifies the underlined word in the first sentence. Correctly punctuate each modifier.

Example: The <u>truck</u> is mine. The truck is parked in the driveway.

Answer: *The truck that is parked in the driveway is mine.*

1. My roommate and I like to watch <u>the New Orleans Saints.</u> The New Orleans Saints play near us this Sunday.

2. <u>People</u> often do not like dogs. People like cats.

3. <u>I</u> hope I do well on this biology test. I did not know we were having this test.

Lesson 19

adj
cl

4. My friend from England likes to play <u>checkers</u>. Checkers is usually called "draughts" in Britain.

5. I know <u>someone</u>. Someone wants you to work for her.

6. The <u>saguaro</u> does not have branches until it is about seventy-five years old. The saguaro is a type of cactus.

7. Candice had to replace the carpet in her <u>home</u>. Her home was flooded in the recent hurricane.

8. At midnight, Desirat called her <u>boyfriend</u>. Her boyfriend said he was playing basketball.

9. <u>Louis Armstrong</u> died on his birthday. Louis Armstrong was a famous jazz musician.

10. <u>Hans Christian Andersen</u> carried a rope when he traveled in case he needed to escape a burning building. Hans Christian Andersen was a famous writer from Denmark.

Lesson 19

adj
cl

Editing Practice 1

CORRECTED SENTENCES APPEAR ON PAGE 472.

Correct all errors in the following paragraph using the first correction as a model. The number in parentheses at the end of the paragraph indicates how many commas you should add or delete.

I recently purchased a green-cheeked conure, which is a type of small parrot. It is an intelligent bird, that is becoming increasingly popular as an exotic pet. *Pyrrhura molinae* which is the bird's scientific name is mostly green. The green-cheeked conure obtains its name from the bright green feathers on its cheeks. It is a very playful and active bird. My father who generally dislikes all birds even likes my bird, which I named "Pepper" because she likes to eat raw peppers. Most of the time, Pepper eats a blend of colored pellets that I buy at the pet store. Like many conures, Pepper is capable of mimicking speech but is not a great talker. She mainly whistles

and makes a variety of odd noises, that often wake me early in the

morning. (6)

Editing Practice 2

CORRECTED SENTENCES APPEAR ON PAGE 472.

Correct all errors in the following paragraph using the first correction as a model. The number in parentheses at the end of the paragraph indicates how many commas you should add or delete.

I am rooming with Harold Lee, who is very practical. We couldn't

afford to spend much for Christmas gifts this year, so we decided to can

some vegetables. First, we made a relish, that was primarily composed

of tomatoes, onions, and cabbage. The tomatoes which we bought at the

local market had to be completely green. The jars had to be carefully

sterilized, and the directions confused us. Luckily, we received advice

from my mom whom I called in a panic. Once we understood the process

better, we went on to asparagus which has always been my favorite. I'm

not sure we saved much time or money, but the experience was fun. (5)

Lesson 19

adj
cl

Editing Practice 3

Correct all errors in the following paragraph using the first correction as a model. The number in parentheses at the end of the paragraph indicates how many commas you should add or delete.

I live in a small town, that is on the Gulf of Mexico. Gulf Shores,

which is the name of this Alabama town, is a tourist attraction for people,

who want to sunbathe or enjoy the ocean. Gulf Shores has more than one

beach, but the beach, where most people go, is practically in the middle of town. Traffic can be really bad in summer which of course is the best time to go to the beach. Unfortunately, there is only one road that can take you to the main beach. Noon is the time, when you probably do not want to travel to the beach. Anyone who really wants to avoid the congestion can do so by arriving at the beach no later than 9:00 A.M., when relatively few people are coming or going. You might not think such a small town could have significant traffic problems, but I promise that you will change your mind if you visit this beach in summer. (5)

Applying What You Know

Even though nonessential adjective clauses are not truly essential to a sentence's meaning, they can add details and information that help readers better understand what the writer is trying to say. To illustrate this point, write five sentences that state a fact but that do not use any nonessential clauses. Trade your sentences with someone else and add a nonessential adjective clause to each of your partner's sentences so that each sentence is even clearer. Each nonessential clause should be set off with a comma (or two). Start each nonessential clause with one of the following relative pronouns: *who, whom, whose, which,* or *that.*

Lesson 19

adj
cl

| The Bottom Line | Nonessential clauses, **which can always be deleted,** should be set off with commas. |

Commas with Appositives

EXAMPLE 1	*Unnecessary Commas*
Error:	✗Shakespeare's play, <u>Macbeth</u>, was recently made into a movie again.
Correction:	Shakespeare's play／ *Macbeth*／ was recently made into a movie again.

EXAMPLE 2	*Missing Commas*
Error:	✗ Our governor <u>Seth Nodar</u> is making an important speech at my campus.
Correction:	Our governor‚ Seth Nodar‚ is making an important speech at my campus.

What's the Problem?

An **appositive** is a noun (or pronoun) that renames a previous noun (or pronoun). In Example 1 above, *Macbeth* is an appositive renaming the noun *play*. An appositive and the word it renames mean the same thing. For instance, you could think of Example 2 above as making the following claim:

our governor = Seth Nodar

Writers often make punctuation errors with appositives because some appositives *must* be set off from the rest of the sentence with a comma(s), whereas others *must not*. Whether a comma is necessary depends on whether the appositive is *essential* or *nonessential*. In this way, appositives are similar to adjective clauses (see Lesson 19). Let's look at the definition of each type of appositive and how each type is punctuated.

Appositive	Function	Punctuation
Essential	Provides important identifying information about the noun it renames	Do NOT set off with a comma (see Example 1).

Appositive	Function	Punctuation
Nonessential	Provides extra information about the noun being renamed; removing the appositive doesn't make the noun any less clear	Set off with a comma (see Example 2).

Without essential appositives, readers might not be able to identify the person, place, or thing that the appositive renames. In the following example, the appositive (*Adam*) is essential because the writer likely has several friends. The appositive indicates which friend is being referred to:

WORD BEING
RENAMED   APPOSITIVE

My friend Adam is thirty years old.

Which friend? The appositive is essential because it provides necessary information about the noun.

In contrast, the appositive in this next example is nonessential because the word being renamed (*Fort Worth*) is already specific:

WORD BEING
RENAMED   APPOSITIVE

I am flying to Fort Worth, a large city near Dallas.

The word being renamed is specific, so the appositive is nonessential.

The rules for commas with appositives can be summarized this way:

Essential Appositive = Essential Information = No Comma

Nonessential Appositive = "Extra" Information = Comma

Diagnostic Exercise

CORRECTED SENTENCES APPEAR ON PAGE 472.

Correct all the comma errors in the following paragraph using the first correction as a model. The number in parentheses at the end of the paragraph indicates how many appositive errors you should find. (Each error involves a pair of commas unless the appositive is at the end of a sentence.)

Every summer, I visit my Aunt Carol, a vigorous woman of

sixty-five. Aunt Carol lives in a small town in Minnesota a state in the

northern part of the American Midwest. Even though I love her, we argue

Lesson 20

appos

about one thing coffee. Like many midwesterners, she drinks coffee all day, and her coffee is very weak. The problem is that I am from Seattle the home of Starbucks. Starbucks one of the fastest growing companies in the United States has made espresso into a lifestyle choice. My favorite drink a double mocha has the caffeine equivalent of a dozen cups of Aunt Carol's coffee. The first time I made coffee at her house, she had a fit. She not only threw out all the coffee I made, but also made me wash the pot. From then on, she made the coffee the kind you can see through. (6)

Fixing This Problem in Your Writing

Identifying Appositives

Lesson 20

appos

The first step in correcting appositive errors is identifying appositives in general. Knowing that appositives are nouns or pronouns that rename a previous noun or pronoun helps, but here is another tip.

> **FINDING THE APPOSITIVE TIP**   Try using *only* what you think is the appositive in the sentence, deleting the previous noun it renames. If the sentence still makes sense and is grammatically correct, you have identified the appositive.

Remember the "equation" noted earlier regarding Example 2. Because the appositive = the word being renamed, you should be able to use *just* the appositive in the sentence, letting it replace the word it renames. Let's apply this tip to our example sentences. Don't worry about commas yet; just note how it is possible to delete the word being renamed.

Example 1:	✗ Shakespeare's play, *Macbeth*, was recently made into a movie again.
Tip applied:	~~Shakespeare's play,~~ *Macbeth* was recently made into a movie again.
Example 2:	✗ Our governor Seth Nodar is making an important speech at my campus.
Tip applied:	~~Our governor~~ Seth Nodar is making an important speech at my campus.

As you can see, these sentences still make sense when we delete the words the appositives rename. The tip confirms that *Macbeth* and *Seth Nodar* are indeed appositives.

Punctuating Appositives

Once you have identified appositives in your writing, you need to determine whether they are *essential* appositives (which don't use commas) or *nonessential* appositives (which require commas). Use the following tip to determine whether an appositive is essential or nonessential.

> **GENERAL-NOUN TIP**   Identify the word(s) that the appositive renames. The more general this noun phrase is, the more likely that its appositive is essential.

In this tip, *noun phrase* refers not just to the noun being renamed but to its modifiers as well. It's the whole phrase that determines whether the idea is vague. Vague noun phrases tend to pair with essential appositives. Noun phrases that are already specific do not.

In Example 1, the appositive *Macbeth* renames *Shakespeare's play*. At first, *Shakespeare's play* seems specific, but Shakespeare wrote many plays, so the noun phrase is general after all. Thus, the appositive *Macbeth* is essential and should not be set off with commas.

GENERAL NOUN PHRASE

Tip applied: ✗ (Shakespeare's play), *Macbeth,* was recently made into a movie again.

The appositive is essential because it renames a general, vague noun phrase.

Correction: Shakespeare's play⁄ *Macbeth⁄* was recently made into a movie again.

Essential Appositive = Essential Information = No Comma(s)

In contrast, the noun renamed in Example 2 is specific. *Our governor* could mean only one person, so the appositive is not necessary and should be set off with commas.

SPECIFIC NOUN PHRASE

Tip applied: ✗ (Our governor) Seth Nodar is making an important speech at my campus.

Lesson 20

appos

The noun phrase is specific, so the appositive is nonessential.

Correction: **Our governor, Seth Nodar, is making an important speech at my campus.**

Nonessential Appositive = "Extra" Information = Comma(s)

More Examples

Essential Appositives   *Do not set off with a comma(s):*

My neighbor <u>Cindy</u> works part-time in a lawyer's office.

I need to read the story "<u>Snow</u>" by Friday.

Nonessential Appositives   *Set off with a comma(s):*

I was taught to respect fire by my father, <u>a retired firefighter</u>.

My brother, <u>Gary</u>, lives in Boston.*

*This last example could be either essential or nonessential. If the writer has only one brother, the sentence is fine. But if the writer has *more* than one brother, the appositive is essential and we must remove the commas.

Lesson 20

appos

Putting It All Together

Identify Appositives in Your Writing

____ Look for appositives—nouns or pronouns that rename a previous noun or pronoun. To confirm that a word or group of words is an appositive, delete the previous noun it renames. If the sentence still makes sense and is grammatically correct, you have identified an appositive.

____ Next, determine whether the appositive is essential or nonessential. Essential appositives tend to rename noun phrases that are general and vague. Nonessential appositives rename noun phrases that are already specific and clear to readers.

Correctly Punctuate Appositives in Your Writing

____ If the appositive is essential, do NOT set it off with a comma(s).

____ If the appositive is nonessential, set it off with a comma(s).

Sentence Practice 1

CORRECTED SENTENCES APPEAR ON PAGE 472.

All the appositives in the following sentences are nonessential. Underline each appositive, and add the necessary commas. Confirm your answer by applying the Finding the Appositive Tip.

> *Example:* The university is in the capital of Thailand, <u>Bangkok</u>.
>
> *Confirmation:* *The university is in Bangkok.*

1. Ian Fleming the creator of 007 named James Bond after the author of a book about birds.

2. Ian Fleming also wrote *Chitty Chitty Bang Bang* a children's book.

3. Tim's mother a registered nurse thinks I have a virus.

4. Richard a guy in my geology class fell asleep during the lecture.

5. Spanish Fort a town in south Alabama was the site of one of the last battles of the Civil War.

> For more practice using appositives, go to **Exercise Central** at
> **bedfordstmartins.com/commonsense**

Sentence Practice 2

CORRECTED SENTENCES APPEAR ON PAGE 473.

Underline the appositives. Label them *essential* or *nonessential*, and punctuate them correctly. If a sentence is already punctuated correctly, write *OK* next to it. Using the General-Noun Tip, circle the noun phrases that the appositives rename and write *general* or *specific* above them.

> *Example:*   (My English assignment), a ten-page essay, is due next week.
> *[specific]*   *[nonessential]*

1. My roommate a political science major plans to run for public office.

2. He has a date this Friday with Janet Spain the woman who sits next to you in History 101.

Lesson 20

appos

3. This note is for your friend Natalie.

4. Matthew Henson an African American codiscovered the North Pole with Robert Peary in 1909.

5. I had to take Junior one of my cats to get his shots.

Sentence Practice 3

Combine the two short sentences by making the second sentence into an appositive that renames the underlined words in the first sentence. Punctuate correctly.

> *Example:*   **My grandparents still recall "Black Thursday." "Black Thursday" is the day the stock market crashed in 1929.**
>
> *Answer:*   *My grandparents still recall "Black Thursday," the day the stock market crashed in 1929.*

Lesson 20

appos

1. His mother has a revolver. His mother is a police officer.

2. Victoria Woodhull and Tennessee Cook were the first female stockbrokers in New York. Victoria Woodhull and Tennessee Cook were sisters.

3. This summer, I will be in Detroit. Detroit is a city that I have never visited.

4. Janis Joplin left $2,500 in her will to pay for a party for her friends. Janis Joplin was a female rock singer.

5. I went to see my favorite musical. My favorite musical is *Rent*.

6. You need to talk to Dr. Olfason. Dr. Olfason is the chair of the history department.

7. Shouldn't we have a day off on August 24? August 24 is the day the waffle iron was patented.

8. Jo Ann called for you early this morning. Jo Ann is a woman in your physics class.

9. The city zoo has a bumblebee bat. A bumblebee bat is the world's smallest mammal.

10. Caesar ran away but returned after two days. Caesar is my neighbor's dog.

Editing Practice 1

CORRECTED SENTENCES APPEAR ON PAGE 473.

Correct all errors in the following paragraphs using the first correction as a model. The number in parentheses at the end of each paragraph indicates how many commas you should add or delete.

World War II, one of the best-known wars of all time, was followed a few years later by a conflict that still is not well understood. The Korean War, a conflict between the United Nations and North Korea, was never officially a war. Harry Truman the U.S. president at the time of the conflict never asked Congress to declare war. The U.S. troops fought as part of the U.N. forces. The conflict was therefore called a "police action." (2)

This war caused many problems for the United States, possibly because its status and purpose were not clear. General Douglas MacArthur the commander of the U.N. forces was removed from office for insubordination to President Truman the commander in chief. After the landings at Inchon a major turning point the North Koreans were pushed back. Neither side completely achieved its goals, and a truce was signed in 1953. (5)

Editing Practice 2

Correct all errors in the following paragraphs using the first correction as a model. The number in parentheses at the end of each paragraph indicates how many commas you should add or delete.

I received an unusual gift on July 1, my nineteenth birthday. My oldest brother, Gary, gave me a gift certificate for a free ride on a biplane at an airstrip outside Foley, our hometown. The pilot was a young man who had rebuilt the old plane so he could sell rides lasting thirty minutes. The plane was a Travelair an open cockpit biplane built in the late 1920's. I was nervous about riding in an old plane, but when I arrived at the airstrip, I was impressed by how sturdy and well kept the plane appeared. (3)

Jerry Burns the pilot gave me a set of goggles to wear as he escorted me to the passenger's seat. It was located right behind his seat in the *Bird of Paradise* the name he gave his plane. The motor was incredibly loud, and the plane vibrated greatly when we finally took off. Before long, the ride became much smoother, and I could see all of Gulf Shores the nearest city. I have ridden many times in a commercial plane, yet this was a totally different experience I will always remember. (4)

Lesson 20

appos

Applying What You Know

Write a paragraph or two describing places in your hometown that you enjoy, but do not use appositives yet. Then, to show how nonessential appositives still play a useful role in providing extra detail, go back and insert at least three nonessential appositives. Underline these appositives.

Trade your paper with a partner so that you can have someone see if (1) you used appositives, (2) these are nonessential appositives, and (3) you used commas correctly with these appositives. Use the Finding the Appositive Tip and General-Noun Tip to check your work.

The Bottom Line	A nonessential appositive, **the optional "gravy,"** is always set off with a comma or commas.

UNIT SIX: Using Commas Correctly

Commas are used in so many ways that knowing when to use (and not use) a comma can be particularly challenging. This chart helps you avoid the most common problems involving commas.

TIP(S)	QUICK FIX AND EXAMPLE
Lesson 15. Commas with *And, But, Or,* and Other Coordinating Conjunctions	
The Imaginary Period Tip (p. 154) helps you determine whether a sentence contains two independent clauses so you can join them with correct punctuation.	If the FANBOYS is connecting two independent clauses, use a comma before the FANBOYS. Otherwise, do not use a comma. *Error:* ✗ My physics instructor was not in class today but another teacher took her place. *Correction:* My physics instructor was not in class today, but another teacher took her place.
Lesson 16. Commas with Transitional Terms	
The Transitional Term Movement Tip (p. 165) helps you identify transitional terms so you can punctuate them correctly.	If the transitional term separates two independent clauses, use a semicolon before it and a comma after it. If it comes at the beginning or end of a sentence, set it off with just a comma. *Error:* ✗ My bus was late, therefore, I could not make it to class on time. *Correction:* My bus was late; therefore, I could not make it to class on time.
Lesson 17. Commas with Adverb Clauses	
The Adverb Clause Movement Tip (p. 174) helps you identify adverb clauses so you can punctuate them correctly.	Set off most introductory adverb clauses with a comma. Use no comma with a sentence-ending clause unless it conveys a strong sense of contrast. *Error:* ✗ While we were taking a test in my astronomy class a fire alarm went off. *Correction:* While we were taking a test in my astronomy class, a fire alarm went off.

208

Lesson 18. Commas with Introductory Elements	
The Deletion Tip (p. 183) helps you identify introductory elements, and the Comma Tip (p. 183) helps you remember when to use a comma with them.	Use a comma after all introductory elements unless your readers prefer otherwise. *Error:* ✗ In the middle of the movie someone began snoring. *Correction:* In the middle of the movie, someone began snoring. ∧

Lesson 19. Commas with Adjective Clauses	
The Deletion Tip (p. 192) helps you determine whether an adjective clause is essential or nonessential so you can punctuate it correctly.	Do not use commas with essential clauses. Use commas with nonessential clauses. *Error:* ✗ I called Dr. Perez who referred me to another doctor. *Correction:* I called Dr. Perez, who referred me to another doctor. ∧

Lesson 20. Commas with Appositives	
The Finding the Appositive Tip (p. 201) helps you identify appositives. The General-Noun Tip (p. 202) tells you whether an appositive is essential or nonessential.	Do not use commas with essential appositives. Use commas with nonessential appositives. *Error:* ✗ My old friend, Rusty, called me last night. *Correction:* My old friend / Rusty / called me last night. ∧ ∧

Review Test

Correct the comma problems in the following paragraphs using the first correction as a model. The number in parentheses at the end of each paragraph indicates how many commas you should add or delete.

My English teacher, Ms. Gonzales, asked us to find three magazine
                   ∧   ∧
articles for our next essay assignment. My paper which will deal with solar

energy is a fairly easy one to research. I found fourteen articles in less than

an hour and almost all of these appear to be credible and useful. (3)

Some of these articles were online, but most can be found only in a hard copy of the magazine. However it did not take long for me to go to the library, and find the ones I needed. Even though Ms. Gonzales asked for only three articles I decided to find several more and choose the best for my paper. I needed some advice picking the best sources, so I asked for help from my roommate, who is an English major. She did not read them thoroughly, but gave me advice on how to determine what magazines were most credible. I am confident, therefore, that I have chosen effective sources for my next paper. (4)

Unit Six

review

Using Apostrophes Correctly

Terms That Can Help You Understand Apostrophes

If you are not familiar with any of the following terms, look them up in the Guide to Grammar Terminology beginning on page 435.

> **contraction**
> **gerund**
> **possessive apostrophe**

The Nuts and Bolts of Using Apostrophes Correctly

An apostrophe (') is a mark of punctuation used to indicate that letters are missing in a contraction and to show possession or ownership. Your writing may be unclear to your readers if you misplace or misuse apostrophes.

Lesson 21 shows you the proper way to build contractions with apostrophes. Contractions are shortened forms of words. For example, *I'll* is short for *I will*; *didn't* is short for *did not*; and *what's* is short for *what is*. Writers use an apostrophe to take the place of the letters dropped from a contracted word.

Example:　　✗ Wasnt that course canceled last semester?

Correction:　　Wasn't that course canceled last semester?

Lesson 22 covers the use of possessive apostrophes. Writers use an apostrophe to show that someone possesses something. The placement of the apostrophe depends upon whether the "owner" is singular (the *girl's books* = the books of one girl) or plural (the *girls' books* = the books of two or more girls). This lesson covers the use of apostrophes and spelling of contractions.

> *Example:*   ✗ Five students cars were towed from the parking lot.
>
> *Correction:*   Five students᾽ cars were towed from the parking lot.

Lesson 23 covers other uses of the apostrophe, the most common of which involves expressions of time or measure.

> *Example:*   ✗ I can carry over a weeks worth of vacation at the end of the year.
>
> *Correction:*   I can carry over a week᾽s worth of vacation at the end of the year.

Lesson 24 shows you when *not* to use an apostrophe. Sometimes writers use an apostrophe when there is no need for one.

> *Example:*   ✗ Your sentence has too many apostrophe's.
>
> *Correction:*   Your sentence has too many apostrophe⁄s.

Unit Seven

overview

Apostrophes in Contractions

EXAMPLE 1

Error: ✗ Henry Pym wasnt in class today.

Correction: Henry Pym ~~wasnt~~ in class today.
                            wasn't

EXAMPLE 2

Error: ✗ I heard its going to rain this weekend.

Correction: I heard ~~its~~ going to rain this weekend.
                         it's

What's the Problem?

Contractions are shortened forms of words, and—for better or worse—they add an informal tone, as well as some conciseness. Many readers prefer that writers not use contractions in formal writing, so one way to avoid contraction errors is to avoid using contractions. However, many writers want to use contractions, so here we describe how they can be correctly "assembled."

An error occurs when a contraction lacks an apostrophe or when the apostrophe appears in the wrong place. We focus on the "missing apostrophe" error because it is more frequent. Example 1 has a contraction error because *wasnt* (*was not*) lacks an apostrophe between *n* and *t*. Example 2 requires an apostrophe to show that *its* stands for *it is*.

Contractions are common in speech. In fact, many writers use contractions to provide the relaxed, natural tone found in conversation. Thus, it is easy to overlook the apostrophe since we do not worry about it in speech. In addition, there is widespread confusion about the contraction *it's* (meaning *it is*) and the possessive *its* (as in *The fish ate its neighbor*). Many computerized spell-checkers and grammar-checkers are unable to catch the error that results when writers confuse these two words. Shortly, we will offer strategies for avoiding contraction errors.

Diagnostic Exercise

CORRECTED SENTENCES APPEAR ON PAGE 473.

Correct all errors in the following paragraph using the first correction as a model. The number in parentheses at the end of the paragraph indicates how many errors you should find.

    The student government announced today the election results for

representation in the student senate. Almost half the students ~~didnt~~ *didn't* vote

at all, and there werent many candidates running. Im not sure why, but

apathy was widespread. My guess is that many students dont think the

senators have much real power, or perhaps the candidates' qualifications

and goals were unclear. Its clear that students arent enthusiastic about

our student government, so perhaps we should consider large-scale

changes to the system. (5)

Lesson 21

Fixing This Problem in Your Writing

This editing tip will help you avoid contraction errors.

> **EXPANSION TIP** Reread any word that might possibly be a contraction to see if you can "expand" that word by filling in missing letters. If you can, make sure that there is an apostrophe in the spot where the missing letters would appear.

Here are some examples of contractions showing first the contracted form and then the expanded form that fills in the missing letters. The filled-in letters in the expanded form are underlined:

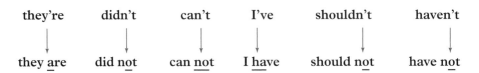

they're	didn't	can't	I've	shouldn't	haven't
↓	↓	↓	↓	↓	↓
they a̱re	did no̱t	can no̱t	I ha̱ve	should no̱t	have no̱t

Notice that the missing letters are vowels, sometimes both a vowel and a consonant (for example, *ha* in *I have*). For complicated historical reasons, there is one contraction that does not fit the normal pattern: the contracted form of *will not* is *won't*.

The Expansion Tip shows that Examples 1 and 2 each contain a word that can be expanded:

Example 1: ✗ Henry Pym <u>wasnt</u> in class today.

Tip applied: Henry Pym <u>was not</u> in class today.

Correction 1: Henry Pym <u>wasn't</u> in class today.

Correction 2: Henry Pym <u>was not</u> in class today.

The Expansion Tip shows that *wasnt* is really an incorrectly formed contraction of *was not*. We can correct the error in one of two ways: (1) use an apostrophe to show the place where the letters are missing—*wasn't*, or (2) use the uncontracted form *was not*. Both choices are perfectly grammatical. If you want what you are writing to have a conversational tone, then you will probably want to use the contracted form *wasn't*. On the other hand, if you want what you are writing to be more formal, then you will probably want to use the uncontracted, expanded form *was not*.

Example 2: ✗ I heard <u>its</u> going to rain this weekend.

Tip applied: I heard <u>it is</u> going to rain this weekend.

Correction 1: I heard <u>it's</u> going to rain this weekend.

Correction 2: I heard <u>it is</u> going to rain this weekend.

Lesson 21

The Expansion Tip shows that *its* is really an incorrectly formed contraction of *it is*. Again, we can correct the error either by using an apostrophe to show the missing letters in the contracted form or by using the full, uncontracted form.

It's is by far the most troublesome contraction because there are actually two *its* that are easily confused: the contraction of *it is* and the possessive pronoun *its* as in *The dog bit **its** tail.* The Expansion Tip is very useful for helping you tell the two *its* apart. We can always expand the contracted *it's* to *it is*. We can never expand the possessive pronoun *its* to *it is*. Here is the Expansion Tip applied to both uses of *its*:

Contraction: ✗ <u>Its</u> a nice day.

Tip applied: <u>It is</u> a nice day.

Correction: <u>It's</u> a nice day.

The fact that we can expand *its* to *it is* tells us that *its* is a contraction that must be spelled with an apostrophe.

Possessive: **The car had been parked with <u>its</u> headlights still on.**

Tip applied: **✗ The car had been parked with <u>it is</u> headlights still on.**

The fact that the Expansion Tip gives us an incorrect answer tells us that this *its* is not a contraction of *it is*. Therefore, *its* must be the possessive pronoun, which is never used with an apostrophe because there are no missing letters.

✳ Putting It All Together

Identify Contraction Errors

_____ Proofread to see if any word can be "expanded" into two words. If so, that word is a contraction.

_____ Look at every use of *its* and *it's*. If *its* can be expanded to *it is*, it is the contraction *it's*; if *its* cannot be expanded, it is the possessive pronoun *its*.

Correct Contraction Errors

_____ Make sure all contractions have apostrophes in the spots where letters were omitted.

_____ In formal writing, consider using the full, uncontracted forms rather than the contracted ones.

Lesson 21

Sentence Practice 1

CORRECTED SENTENCES APPEAR ON PAGE 473.

If a sentence does not have a contraction error, write *OK* above it. If there is an error, cross it out. Then, write out the full form of the words. In addition, supply the correct form of the contraction.

Example: *it is (it's)*
    I think ~~its~~ time to leave.
              ^

1. Lets get one thing straight.

2. It wont be a problem.

3. Im afraid that we werent ready for the test.

4. Theyre ready for you now.

5. Even if it's raining, we still have to go.

 For more practice using contractions, go to **Exercise Central** at **bedfordstmartins.com/commonsense**

Sentence Practice 2

CORRECTED SENTENCES APPEAR ON PAGE 473.

If a sentence does not have a contraction error, write *OK* above it. If there is an error, cross it out. Then, write out the full form of the words. In addition, supply the correct form of the contraction.

Example: *There is (There's)*
          ~~Theres~~ no business like show business.
                ^

1. I think that's OK.

2. Youre really in trouble now.

3. Do you want to come; were going to the early show.

4. Ive had enough of you for one day.

5. Its six of one and half a dozen of the other. (traditional saying)

Lesson 21

Sentence Practice 3

Rewrite the sentences below using at least one contraction in each sentence.

Example: **I do not see the problem.**

Answer: *I don't see the problem.*

1. I could not agree with you more.

2. Here is another fine mess you have gotten me into!

3. I am sorry; there is nothing I can do about it.

4. They will not do that, will they?

5. They are sure that they are acting in her best interests.

Editing Practice 1

CORRECTED SENTENCES APPEAR ON PAGE 473.

Correct all errors in the following paragraphs using the first correction as a model. The number in parentheses at the end of each paragraph indicates how many errors you should find.

Rice might seem to be a common (and perhaps dull) subject to

it's

Americans. However, ~~its~~ such an important part of life in other parts

of the world that rice has an honored place in many cultures. Youve

probably long known about the tradition of throwing rice at newlyweds

when theyre leaving a church. But you probably did not know that in India

rice is traditionally the first food a bride offers her husband. In Indonesia,

tradition has it that a woman cant be considered for marriage until she

can skillfully prepare rice. (3)

Rice isnt associated with just marriage. Even the word itself is special.

Ive been to one region in China where the word for rice is also the word for

food. In Japan, the word for cooked rice is also the word for meal. Its also

common for rice fields in Japan to be given names as if they were people. (3)

Editing Practice 2

Correct all errors in the following paragraphs using the first correction as a model. The number in parentheses at the end of each paragraph indicates how many errors you should find.

I've

Like a lot of people, ~~Ive~~ been trying to lose some weight lately. I think

that part of the problem that were all facing is that our lifestyles are working against us. Most of us work in an office or behind a desk, places where its impossible to engage in any physical activity at all. When we go to work, we have to commute such long distances that we cant possibly walk or bicycle. I dont know about you, but my job is pretty stressful. For me, one of the worst consequences of stress is that I tend to compulsively snack on things that are quick and convenient (and loaded with calories). Lets not kid ourselves; no one snacks on apple slices. (5)

A friend of mine just got back from a trip to Italy. She said that she pretty much ate her way across northern Italy. She and her friends had three-course lunches and dinners with plenty of local wine. She thought that when she got back that she wouldve gained ten pounds. In fact, she didnt gain a pound—she actually lost five pounds. "Ive been thinking about it," she said. "I think therere two things I did differently: I didnt snack at all, and I walked all day long." (5)

Lesson 21

Applying What You Know

Formal writing tends to use few contractions, but sometimes they can be effective. Find at least three examples of published writing that uses contractions, and be ready to explain whether you think the contractions are useful or not. For at least one of your examples, find something that is not from the Internet and not taken from a short story or novel.

The Bottom Line	If you use a contraction, **you'll** need to use an apostrophe.

Apostrophes
Showing Possession

EXAMPLE 1	*Missing Apostrophe*

Error: ✗ The judges robe was torn and dirty.

judge's

Correction: The ~~judges~~ robe was torn and dirty.
            ^

EXAMPLE 2	*Misplaced Apostrophe*

Error: ✗ Those student's cars are illegally parked.

students'

Correction: Those ~~student's~~ cars are illegally parked.
            ^

What's the Problem?

Writers normally add an apostrophe and an *s* to indicate that somebody (or something) possesses something, as seen in this correct example:

This person owns this.

I paid for Randy's ticket.

The apostrophe lets readers know the *s* is added to show *possession*, not plurality. In Example 1, the apostrophe has been incorrectly left out, so at first it seems the sentence is referring to more than one judge. The apostrophe in the corrected version lets readers know that possession is involved.

A different problem occurs when the apostrophe is *misplaced*. This error is most likely to occur when the noun needing an apostrophe is plural (see Example 2). The solution is usually simple: If a noun ends in *s* because it is plural, you just add an apostrophe after this *s* to indicate possession.

Diagnostic Exercise

CORRECTED SENTENCES APPEAR ON PAGE 473.

Correct all errors in the following paragraph using the first correction as a model. The number in parentheses at the end of the paragraph indicates how many errors you should find.

family's

Paul Ortega has been one of my ~~familys~~ best friends over the years.

Although he was born in Mexico, he speaks English like a native because

his fathers employer relocated his family to Arizona when Paul was

six. In a few years, Pauls English was as good as anyones. Nearly every

summer, however, Paul and his sisters went back to Mexico City, where

they stayed at a relatives' house. As a result, he is completely at home in

either countrys culture. He and my father have been business partners for

many years. The companys success has been due largely to Paul's ability

to conduct business in both Mexico and the United States. (6)

Lesson 22

Fixing This Problem in Your Writing

Identifying Possession

An apostrophe is used to show possession, but you should be able to reword the sentence to show possession another way. Here is a tip to help you identify possessive forms.

> **OF TIP**   If a pair of words involves possession, you can usually reword the phrase using *of*.

If a pair of words passes the *Of* Tip, possession is involved, and an apostrophe is normally required. Example 1 passes the *Of* Tip, proving the sentence indicates possession.

Example 1:   ✗ The judges robe was torn and dirty.

Tip applied: The robe <u>of</u> the judge . . .

Example 2 also passes the *Of* Tip, proving it is possessive.

> *Example 2:*   ✗ Those student's cars are illegally parked.
>
> *Tip applied:*   Cars <u>of</u> those students . . .

Sometimes, the *Of* Tip produces a "double possessive." This occurs when possession is shown in two ways: with *of* AND an apostrophe. A double possessive is grammatical, as seen in this correct example:

> *Example:*   We were angered by Maria's statement.
>
> *Tip applied:*   . . . statement <u>of</u> Maria's.
>
> Double possessive is OK.

Using the Apostrophe

The *Of* Tip can help you find possessive words, but next you must make sure the apostrophe is in the correct place. The good news is there is a standard guideline. The bad news is there are some exceptions and options that seem to confuse people more than help them. Let's start with the standard guideline, which works most of the time.

Lesson 22

> **STANDARD TIP** For most singular possessive nouns, use an *'s* at the end of the word.

The *Of* Tip showed us that Example 1 involves possession. Because the sentence is referring to only one judge, we use the Standard Tip to show possession, adding the apostrophe before the *s* that is already present in our example:

> *Example 1:*   ✗ The <u>judges</u> robe was torn and dirty.
>
> Singular possession: One judge owns the robe.
>
>   *judge's*
> *Correction:*   The ~~judges~~ robe was torn and dirty.
>   ^
> Singular possessive nouns need an *'s*, so put an apostrophe before the final *s*.

The tip works with these correct examples as well: Each is a singular noun ending in *'s*.

> My <u>mother's</u> car is red.   I saw <u>Jin's</u> dog.
>
> <u>Sue's</u> house is big.   My <u>boss's</u> tie is ugly.

The last example (*boss's*) involves a singular word already ending in *s*, but we followed the Standard Tip and made sure there was a final *'s* at the end of the word.

Rare Exception: Most readers prefer you add *'s* to words that already end in *s*, unless the result is a tongue twister that is difficult to say aloud. For example, *Sarah Connors' son* is easier to say than *Sarah Connors's son*.

The Standard Tip is for singular nouns. This next tip helps with most plural nouns.

> **PLURAL POSSESSION TIP** If the possessive noun is plural, begin with the plural form. Then add JUST the apostrophe if the plural form ends in *s*.

Let's look at Example 2. The *Of* Tip proved that this sentence involves possession. Because the possession clearly deals with more than one student, we know that we should use the Plural Possession Tip to correctly place the apostrophe. Plural possessives show two separate things: plurality and possession. Thus, this tip involves two separate steps to construct the right form:

Example 2:	✗ Those student's cars are illegally parked.
Tip applied, Step 1:	students<u> </u>
	Start with the plural form.
Tip applied, Step 2:	students'
	Add an apostrophe to show possession.
Correction:	Those ~~student's~~ cars are illegally parked.
	students'

Lesson 22

Most plural nouns in English end in *s*, so usually you just add an apostrophe to show possession:

My <u>parents'</u> house is tiny.

These <u>cats'</u> bowls are empty.

The <u>students'</u> votes were counted.

Add just an apostrophe because plural forms already end in *s*.

Some plurals do not end in *s*, so add *'s* to make them possessive. The Plural Possession Tip still works, but you must now use *'s* at the end of the plural form:

Example:	✗ The <u>childrens</u> toys are broken.
Tip applied, Step 1:	children
	Start with the plural form.

Tip applied, Step 2:   children's

Plural form does not end in *s*, so use *'s* to show possession.

children's
Correction: The ~~childrens~~ toys are broken.

✳ More Examples

Possessive Singular Nouns   Add *'s*:

The man's arm was fractured in two places.

Tess's boyfriend lives in England.

Possessive Plural Nouns Ending in s   Add just an apostrophe:

All of my teachers' offices are in the Humanities Building.

The Smiths' house was vandalized this weekend.

Possessive Plural Nouns Not Ending in s   Add *'s*:

The men's score was considerably higher than usual.

My teeth's enamel is badly worn.

Lesson 22

✳ Putting It All Together

Identify Possessives

____ Look for possessive forms in your writing: nouns that "own" something right afterward.

____ To confirm that possession is involved, reword the phrase using *of* to show possession (*the cat's tail* becomes *tail of the cat*)

Show Possession Using an Apostrophe

____ Use an apostrophe to show possession.

____ If a noun is singular, form the possessive by adding *'s* (as in *mouse's tail*). Most singular nouns that end in *s* still need *'s* added at the end (as in *Gus's store*).

_____ If a noun is plural and already ends in *s*, add JUST an apostrophe (as in *neighbors' cars*).

_____ If a noun is plural and does not already end in *s*, add *'s* (as in *mice's cage*).

Sentence Practice 1

CORRECTED SENTENCES APPEAR ON PAGE 474.

Correct the possession error in each of the following sentences. Confirm your correction by applying the *Of* Tip.

> *Example:*   They put all the ~~visitors~~ suitcases in the hall.
>   *visitors'*
>
> *Confirmation:*   They put the suitcases of all the visitors in the hall.

1. It's nobodys business.

2. I really like that guitars sound.

3. The ladders rungs were covered with paint.

4. Platos dialogues are still an important part of philosophy.

5. The team met to discuss the tumors treatment.

 For more practice using apostrophes, go to **Exercise Central** at **bedfordstmartins.com/commonsense**

Sentence Practice 2

CORRECTED SENTENCES APPEAR ON PAGE 474.

Correct the possession error in each of the following sentences. Confirm your correction by applying the *Of* Tip.

> *Example:*   The ~~couples~~ car was parked in the driveway.
>   *couple's*
>
> *Confirmation:*   The car of the couple was parked in the driveway.

Lesson 22

1. The whole community was opposed to the bridges destruction.

2. Some of Wagners operas are the longest ever written.

3. I hastily scribbled my notes on the envelopes back.

4. We were met by the hospitals administrator.

5. Mikes' feelings were hurt by what you said.

Sentence Practice 3

Turn the *of* structures in the following sentences into possessive structures.

Example: *Enron's collapse*
The collapse of Enron sent shock waves throughout the
energy sector.

Lesson 22

1. Black Bart took the advice of the sheriff seriously.

2. The waterfront of Brooklyn used to be one of the busiest in the country.

3. The last episode of the soap opera was a complete waste of time.

4. The tempo of the conductor was really too fast for the orchestra.

5. The strength of the euro is directly tied to the value of the dollar.

6. The friend of Dr. Franklin was somebody I went to school with.

7. Economists are getting worried about the decline of the dollar against the euro.

8. The failure of the crop could be disastrous for the little village.

9. The tales were drawn from the many journeys of Sinbad.

10. The belongings of the travelers were locked up in the office.

Editing Practice 1

CORRECTED SENTENCES APPEAR ON PAGE 474.

Correct all possession errors in the following paragraph using the first correction as a model. The number in parentheses at the end of the paragraph indicates how many errors you should find.

     You have probably never heard Alfred ~~Wegeners~~ *Wegener's* name. Wegener was born in Berlin in 1880. He got a PhD in astronomy, but his lifes work was the new field of meteorology (the study of weather). As a young man, he became interested in ballooning and, for a time, held the worlds record for altitude. As a balloonist he was well aware of the fact the winds direction and speed on the earths surface did not correspond at all with the winds movement high above the surface. He was the first person to exploit the balloons ability to carry weather instruments high into the atmosphere and to track wind movement at various altitudes. He was one of a group of early researchers who studied a remarkable current of air that circulated around the North Pole. The researchers had discovered what we now call the jet stream. In 1930, he and a colleague disappeared in an expedition to Greenland. His and his colleagues frozen bodies were found a year later. (7)

Lesson 22

Editing Practice 2

Correct all possession errors in the following paragraphs using the first correction as a model. The number in parentheses at the end of each paragraph indicates how many errors you should find.

     Today, ~~Wegeners~~ *Wegener's* name is associated with his highly original theory of continental drift. If you have ever looked at a globe, you couldn't help noticing that the huge bulge on South Americas eastern coastline exactly matches the equally huge indentation on Africas western coastline. Wegener became fascinated with the idea that at some distant time in the past, South Americas and Africas coastlines were joined together in a single continent. If that were indeed the case, then the ancient land formations and fossils of eastern South America should be identical with the ancient land formations and fossils of western Africa. Once Wegener started looking, scientists work in many fields showed the connections. For example, fossils of highly unusual land lizards on South Americas eastern coast were also found on Africas western coast, and nowhere else. Since the lizards couldn't swim, Wegener argued, they must have originated in a single spot that was later split apart by the continents separation. (8)

Wegeners 1915 book *The Origin of Continents and Oceans* argued that all of the different continents today had once been part of a single giant supercontinent that he called *Pangaea*. Needless to say, the scientific communitys reaction was overwhelmingly negative. The books great weakness was its inability to show any mechanism that could split the continents apart and then drive them thousands of miles away from each other. Research in the mid-Atlantic Ocean in the 1950's and 1960's supplied Wegeners missing explanation: plate tectonics. We now know that all the continents are rafts floating on deep, liquid magma and that the continents are driven around by the magmas currents. (5)

Lesson 22

Applying What You Know

Write a paragraph or two describing someone's innovative idea. It could be the work of a scientist or the novel approach of a writer or musician. Try to use at least three possessive forms. Use the *Of* Tip and the Plural Possession Tip to show that your possessives are formed correctly.

<table>
<tr>
<td>**The Bottom Line**</td>
<td>A **writer's use** of the apostrophe can be checked by using the *Of* Tip.</td>
</tr>
</table>

Lesson 22

LESSON 23

Other Uses of the Apostrophe

<table>
<tr><td>EXAMPLE 1</td><td>Expressions of Time or Measure</td></tr>
</table>

Error: ✗ Todays high temperature set a new record.

Correction: ~~Todays~~ high temperature set a new record.
Today's

<table>
<tr><td>EXAMPLE 2</td><td>Plurality of Special Terms</td></tr>
</table>

Error: ✗ I made three As and two Bs last semester.

Correction: I made three ~~As~~ and two ~~Bs~~ last semester.
A's   B's

What's the Problem?

The apostrophe has two other functions besides indicating a *contraction* (Lesson 21) and showing *possession* (Lesson 22). One of these other uses involves an expression of time or measure, as seen in Example 1 and the following:

today's news   **last year's report**
arm's length   **your money's worth**

The other use is much different, less common, and sometimes confusing. You almost never use an apostrophe to indicate plurality. However, certain "special terms" can be turned into a plural form ending with *'s*. In Example 2, the apostrophe is correctly used to make a reference to several *A*'s and *B*'s. Special terms include numbers, letters, abbreviations, and "words used as words":

Numbers or Dates: In the 1990's, I lived overseas.

Letters and Symbols: The L's and &'s on this page are unusually large.

Abbreviations: The MRE's (Meals Ready to Eat) were loaded onto the truck.

Words as Words: Why do you have four *of*'s in this one sentence?

Note: There is a trend toward *not* using the apostrophe to indicate plurality of special terms, but many readers still prefer them. We suggest using an apostrophe with special terms unless your readers prefer otherwise.

Diagnostic Exercise

CORRECTED SENTENCES APPEAR ON PAGE 474.

Correct all errors in the following paragraph. The number in parentheses at the end of the paragraph indicates how many errors you should find.

       semester's
This ~~semesters~~ schedule is hectic for me. I seem to have only a moments ^ peace before I have to go to work or school. I am working and

attending school full time, and I want to do something about all the C's

I made last year. I cannot afford to work fewer hours because I lost two

months pay over the summer because of an accident. Even a few minutes

delay in getting to school or work seems to make me late. Next semesters

schedule is looking just as bad. (4)

Lesson 23

Fixing This Problem in Your Writing

Expressions of Time and Measure

Even though you might not detect "possession" in the time/measure ex-amples such as those discussed above, the *Of* Tip presented in Lesson 22 works with these expressions.

> **OF TIP**   If the expression of time or measure can be reworded using *of*, an apostrophe is needed.

Here is the *Of* Tip applied to Example 1.

    Example 1:   **✗** Todays high temperature set a new record.

    Tip applied: High temperature <u>of</u> today . . .

The rewording works, so we know the original sentence needs an apostrophe.

Correction: ~~Todays~~ high temperature set a new record.

Today's ^

See Lesson 22 for help with how and when to use *s* with the apostrophe. The *Of* Tip is not 100 percent accurate — a few expressions of time and measure might sound awkward when reworded (*a moment's notice*, for example, seems unnatural when reworded as *notice of a moment*). However, the tip works so often it is worth remembering.

Plurality of Special Terms

Special terms, such as dates or letters, are the *only* case in which you should use an apostrophe to indicate plurality. Even in these instances many readers consider it fine to leave out the apostrophe (or they might even insist you leave it out). Try to determine your readers' preferences, and be consistent within a given paper or document.

Some people mistakenly use the apostrophe to indicate plurality of ordinary words, which is a serious mistake (see Lesson 24). Thus, you must learn to recognize the true "special terms" that can be used with an apostrophe to indicate plurality. As noted earlier, there are various types of special terms, but this next tip will help you remember the most common ones.

Lesson 23

NUMBERS AND LETTERS TIP   The most common special terms that can use an apostrophe to indicate plurality are numbers and letters.

Numbers (including dates) and letters are by far the most common special terms you will likely encounter, so focus on remembering that numbers and letters can (or, with some readers, must) be used with *'s* to indicate plurality.

✳ *More Examples*

Expressions of Time and Measure

Dr. West gave us only a day's notice that there would be a test.

We could not get five minutes' worth of work from the new employee.

She lost a week's pay because of the hurricane.

Plurality of Special Terms

The X's indicate the sentences are incorrect.

Back in the 1970's, we actually had to get out of the chair to turn the TV channel.

The 1's need to be more clearly written on your next math test.

Spell out the %'s in your paper by writing the word *percent.*

✳ *Putting It All Together*

Identify Expressions of Time and Measure and Special Terms

_____ Look for expressions of time or measure in your writing. These expressions involve a noun that ends in *s* (such as *a month's pay*).

_____ Try rewording such expressions using *of* (as in *pay of a month*). If *of* works in the sentence, an apostrophe is needed. These expressions might not seem to involve possession, but an apostrophe is needed anyway.

_____ Look for special terms in your writing: numbers, letters, symbols, words used as words, and abbreviations. The most common special terms are numbers and letters.

Punctuate Expressions of Time and Measure and Special Terms

_____ An apostrophe *must* be used with expressions of time and measure (as in *yesterday's news*). See Lesson 22 on how and when to use *s* with the apostrophe.

_____ There are mixed opinions about using the apostrophe to indicate the plural form of special terms, so try to determine your readers' preferences. Most grammar handbooks indicate either option is fine as long as you are consistent.

_____ The most common special terms are numbers and letters, so at the very least remember that the plural forms of these terms might (or must, if your readers prefer) be used with an apostrophe.

Lesson 23

Sentence Practice 1

CORRECTED SENTENCES APPEAR ON PAGE 474.

Correct the possessive apostrophe errors in the following sentences. Confirm your corrections by applying the *Of* Tip.

Example: It is a problem in ~~todays~~ today's society.

Confirmation: *society of today*

1.   The attacks of September 11 were this centurys first major U.S. crisis.

2.   I don't know if this vacation was worth two weeks wages.

3.   That is tomorrows problem.

4.   Rafael bought five dollars worth of fabric.

5.   I can do it with just a minutes notice.

 For more practice using apostrophes, go to **Exercise Central** at **bedfordstmartins.com/commonsense**

Sentence Practice 2

CORRECTED SENTENCES APPEAR ON PAGE 474.

Correct the possessive apostrophe errors in the following sentences. Confirm your corrections by applying the *Of* Tip.

Example: *Yesterday's*
              ~~Yesterdays~~ big news was that the governor resigned.
                     ^

Confirmation: *big news of yesterday*

1.   Last winters snowfall was so bad that I missed school five times.

2.   An hours notice is not sufficient.

3.   I try to keep a weeks worth of food in the pantry.

4.   You are not giving me a moments peace about that little mistake I made.

5.   You will need a months pay to afford that wide-screen television.

Sentence Practice 3

For each special term, write a sentence in which you use the term in the plural form. For this exercise, use an apostrophe to show plurality.

Example: 8

Answer: *The 8's on this package look like B's.*

1. MIA [*Hint:* This is an abbreviation for soldiers who are missing in action.]

2. 1990

3. A

4. 10

5. T

Editing Practice 1

CORRECTED SENTENCES APPEAR ON PAGE 475.

Correct all errors in the following paragraph using the first correction as a model. The number in parentheses at the end of the paragraph indicates how many errors you should find.

Last week, a major hurricane hit the city where I live. Luckily,
we had two ~~days~~ *days'* notice that Hurricane Candice would almost certainly
come our way. Candice was a Category 4 hurricane, which is about as high
as they can get. To make matters worse, three other Category 4's have
affected our town in the last two years. The force of this one was so bad
that its effects are already being called this years biggest local story. I was
lucky. The house I am renting suffered no structural damage; a few trees
were blown over, and a few roof shingles were blown off. It would cost me
a weeks pay to cover these losses, but I don't have to pay for them since
I only rent the house. Despite the horrible weather a week ago, this weeks
weather is perfect, which makes cleaning up a lot easier. (3)

Lesson 23

Editing Practice 2

Correct all errors in the following paragraph using the first correction as a model. The number in parentheses at the end of the paragraph indicates how many errors you should find.

week's
This ~~weeks~~ excitement at my campus involves what is called
⌄
a "forgiveness policy." This policy, first proposed at last months

student government meeting, would be for students who retake classes

to earn a better grade; the policy would allow the old grade to completely

disappear from the transcripts. Thus, someone who has D's and F's could

eliminate all history of these low grades. College administrators discussed

the proposal this week, and several deans spoke strongly against the policy.

They said that, according to last years analysis of grades, relatively few

students made many D's and F's. Thus, they argued that the policy would

benefit few people but might actually harm students by giving them a false

sense of security. The debate was long; there were three hours worth of

back-and-forth arguments. Another meeting will be called next week with

students allowed to attend. I think that meeting will be next weeks big

controversy. (4)

Lesson 23

Applying What You Know

As mentioned, some people prefer apostrophes to be used with the plural
form of special words, while other readers do not. Write down at least two
reasons *for* using the apostrophe to show plurality with special terms, and
then write down at least two reasons *against* using it. Discuss your reasons
with other students in the class.

The Bottom Line	A few **minutes' worth** of work is all that is needed to help you remember the lesser-known functions of apostrophes.

Unnecessary Apostrophes

EXAMPLE 1	*Ordinary Nouns with Unnecessary Apostrophes*

Error: ✗ Your sentence has four comma's in it.

Correction: Your sentence has four ~~comma's~~ in it.
commas (correction above)

EXAMPLE 2	*Last Names with Unnecessary Apostrophes*

Error: ✗ Two of the Bush's have been elected president.

Correction: Two of the ~~Bush's~~ have been elected president.
Bushes (correction above)

What's the Problem?

The apostrophe (') is commonly used to show that letters have been left out of a word to form a *contraction* (Lesson 21) or to show *possession* (Lesson 22). In a few rare cases, an apostrophe is used to indicate *plurality* (see Lesson 23 for more on these rare occasions). For most words, however, it is incorrect to use an apostrophe to show that there is more than one of something. Example 1 illustrates this serious error.

Example 2 shows a similar error: Many people mistakenly add an apostrophe and an *s* to form the plural of a last name. An apostrophe should *not* be used to pluralize last names. Even if a last name already ends in *s* (or *sh*), the plural is formed by adding *es*, not an apostrophe. For example, when you are writing about more than one Clinton or Bush, the correct plural forms are *Clintons* and *Bushes*.

Diagnostic Exercise

CORRECTED SENTENCES APPEAR ON PAGE 475.

Correct all errors in the following paragraph using the first correction as a model. The number in parentheses at the end of the paragraph indicates how many errors you should find.

friends
Some old ~~friend's~~ of mine stopped by my apartment for coffee. My
      ^

roommate's coffee pot was broken, so I made them some instant coffee.

I'm not good at making coffee, but everybody had two cup's apiece. The

coffee was pretty old, yet nobody seemed to care. We talked about our

schedule's for next semester, and we decided we should try to leave some

time open for getting together every now and then. (2)

Fixing This Problem in Your Writing

Suppose you use an apostrophe, and you want to determine whether you
actually need one. Here are three tips you can use. You should apply all three
tips to determine if an apostrophe is needed, but we will go through each tip
one at a time.

> **OF TIP** Possessive words can usually be reworded using *of.* Possessive
> nouns need an apostrophe.

Lesson 24

no ?

The following example passes the *Of* Tip, showing us that *driver's* is possessive and does indeed require an apostrophe:

    Example: Our driver's eyesight was poor.
                       ✓

    Tip applied: The eyesight <u>of</u> our driver . . .

However, try applying this tip to Example 1:

    Example 1:   ✗ Your sentence has four comma's in it.

    Tip applied: ✗ ? <u>of</u> the comma's

                What does the comma possess? Cannot reword using *of.*

In Example 1, *comma* possesses nothing, so it is impossible to use the *Of* Tip
to rearrange the sentence. Thus, there is no need for a possessive apostrophe. The word *comma* is merely plural. To correct the sentence, delete the
apostrophe:

                              commas
    Correction: Your sentence has four ~~comma's~~ in it.
                              ^

EXPANSION TIP If you can expand a word containing an apostrophe to make up two different words without the apostrophe, then the apostrophe is used as a legitimate contraction of two words. However, if you cannot expand the word with an apostrophe to make two different words, then the apostrophe is not used as a legitimate contraction.

For example, the apostrophe in the following sentence is correctly signaling a legitimate contraction:

Example: We're about ready to leave.

Tip applied: We are (or we were) about ready to leave.

The Expansion Tip shows that the apostrophe in *we're* is a valid use of the apostrophe for making a contraction.

Compare the example above with the following:

Example: I knew that we we're about ready to leave.

Tip applied: ✗ I knew that we we are (or we were) about ready to leave.

                                              were

Correction: I knew that we we're about ready to leave.
                                           ^

Here the Expansion Tip shows that *we're* contains an unnecessary (and invalid) use of an apostrophe because the two words formed are nonsensical.

Here is the Expansion Tip applied to Example 2:

Example 2:   ✗ Two of the Bush's have been elected president.

Bush's cannot be expanded to form two new, uncontracted words, so the apostrophe does not correctly indicate a contraction.

                              Bushes

Correction: Two of the Bush's have been elected president.
                              ^

Lesson 24

no **'**

✳ *Putting It All Together*

Identify Unnecessary Apostrophes

_____ Use apostrophes only to show ownership (*the captain's hat*) or to indicate there is a contraction (*I'll go*).   →

Correct Apostrophe Errors

—— Remove apostrophes that do not fit one of the two situations described above. Most likely, your word should simply end in *s* or *es* rather than *'s*.

Sentence Practice 1

CORRECTED SENTENCES APPEAR ON PAGE 475.

Refer to the two tips in this lesson and write *OK* above each correct apostrophe. Then label each correct apostrophe as *contraction* or *possession*. If there is an error, make the necessary change by deleting the apostrophe.

              students   *OK — possession*

Example: The ~~students'~~ laughed at the teacher's shirt.

1. I can't wait to turn my essay's in.

2. We bought some maple bar's at the store.

3. We finally took out memberships' in a health club.

4. Please revise the schedule's as soon as possible.

5. Gary's excuses were the lamest reason's I've ever heard.

 For more practice using apostrophes, go to **Exercise Central** at **bedfordstmartins.com/commonsense**

Sentence Practice 2

CORRECTED SENTENCES APPEAR ON PAGE 475.

Refer to the two tips and write *OK* above each correct apostrophe. Then label each correct apostrophe as *contraction* or *possession*. If there is an error, make the necessary change by deleting the apostrophe.

                                                        wrappings

Example: The toys were still inside the plastic ~~wrapping's~~.

Lesson 24

no **?**

1. I can't believe that classes' were canceled today.

2. The president's remarks certainly raised some eyebrow's around the table.

3. Now that I have everyone's attention, I'd like to begin.

4. There is an amazing variety of red's in his photographs of desert sunsets.

5. Do you want to ask the Adamses' to give us a ride to Paolo's party this weekend?

Sentence Practice 3

Rewrite the underlined *of* expression to produce a correct possessive apostrophe.

Example: The ~~outcome of the election~~ was in doubt.
              election's outcome
                         ^

1. The <u>success of the team</u> was completely unexpected.

2. The <u>coastline of Canada</u> is absolutely immense.

3. An accident was averted thanks to the <u>vigilance of the crew</u>.

4. We got caught up in the <u>excitement of the children</u>.

5. The <u>worth of the stamps</u> was difficult to establish.

Lesson 24

no ?✓

Editing Practice 1

CORRECTED SENTENCES APPEAR ON PAGE 475.

Correct all errors in the following paragraph using the first correction as a model. The number in parentheses at the end of the paragraph indicates how many errors you should find.

The word *parasite* comes from a Greek word meaning a flunky who does no honest work but depends entirely on ~~handout's~~ from wealthy and
                                  handouts
                                    ^

powerful patrons. In biology, the term was adopted to describe a huge variety of creature's that steal their nourishment from hosts, often causing their hosts' death. The behavior of parasites' strikes all of us as profoundly vicious and ugly. One of the best fictional depiction's of parasites is in the 1979 science fiction movie *Alien*. In that movie, the crew of a spaceship investigates a clutch of egg's left on an otherwise lifeless planet. As one of the crewmen examines an egg, a crablike thing bursts out of the shell and wraps a tail around the crewman's neck. By the next day, the crablike thing has disappeared and the crewman seems normal. Later, the crewman clutches his stomach in terrible pain, and a little knobby-headed alien pierces through his skin and leaps out. The alien has laid an egg in the crewman's guts; the egg has hatched and has been devouring his intestines. This horrible scenario is in fact based on the real behavior of parasitic wasps' that lay their eggs' in living caterpillars. As the eggs' mature, they devour the internal organs of the caterpillar, sparing only the organs' necessary to keep the caterpillar alive. When the eggs are fully mature, they erupt through the skin of the caterpillar, leaving behind their hollowed-out host to die. (8)

Lesson 24

no ⸮

Editing Practice 2

Correct all errors in the following paragraphs using the first correction as a model. The number in parentheses at the end of each paragraph indicates how many errors you should find.

By far the worst parasite from the perspective of ~~human's~~ *humans* is malaria. Malaria experts' estimate that as many as half of all the human's who have ever lived on Earth died of malaria. One reason that malaria is such a terribly effective killer is that it has been evolving for a very long time. A substantial number of dinosaur's probably died of malaria. (3)

As you may know, malaria is spread by only one particular type of mosquito, the female *anopheles.* When a female anopheles mosquito bites an animal that is infected with malaria, thousands of malaria parasites' are sucked up in the victim's blood. The parasites travel to the mosquito's gut, where the parasites' mate with parasites from other bites. The parasites' offspring migrate up to the mosquito's salivary gland, where they are ready to be injected into any and all other creatures' that the mosquito bites. And thus the cycle starts all over again. (3)

Applying What You Know

Write a paragraph describing what you like to do when you have spare time. Skip lines so that you can revise later.

    When you are done, see if you can use the apostrophe at least three times (you might have already done so). Trade your paragraph with a partner who can proofread to determine if all your apostrophes are needed.

Lesson 24

no ﹐

| The Bottom Line | Writers sometimes add unnecessary apostrophes to plural words. However, only numbers, letters, or abbreviations use apostrophes to form plurals. |

UNIT SEVEN: Using Apostrophes Correctly

Apostrophes (') are used for several quite different purposes. This unit presented situations in which apostrophes are required and those in which apostrophes are unnecessary. The following chart points you to the tips that will help you avoid four problems writers encounter in using apostrophes.

TIP(S)	QUICK FIX AND EXAMPLES
Lesson 21. Apostrophes in Contractions	
The Expansion Tip (p. 214) helps you place an apostrophe in the correct place in a contraction.	Use an apostrophe in the spot where letters were omitted in a contraction. *Error:* ✗ You cant believe everything you hear. *Correction:* You ~~cant~~ *can't* believe everything you hear.
Lesson 22. Apostrophes Showing Possession	
The *Of* Tip (p. 221) helps you identify possessive forms so you know that an apostrophe is needed. The Standard Tip (p. 222) tells you how to make most singular nouns possessive. The Plural Possession Tip (p. 223) helps you make plural nouns possessive.	Add *'s* to make most singular nouns possessive. For plural nouns that already end in *s*, add just an apostrophe; for those that do not, add *'s.* *Error:* ✗ We looked for Jaynes pet turtle everywhere. *Correction:* We looked for ~~Jaynes~~ *Jayne's* pet turtle everywhere.
Lesson 23. Other Uses of the Apostrophe	
The *Of* Tip (p. 231) shows you when an apostrophe should be used with expressions of time or measure (*a moment's notice*). The Numbers and Letters Tip (p. 232) reminds you of the most common terms that can use an apostrophe to indicate plurality.	Use an apostrophe with expressions of time and measure that can be reworded using *of.* The plural forms of numbers and letters might use an apostrophe, depending on your readers' preferences. *Error:* ✗ The authors first draft had a completely different ending for the novel. *Correction:* The ~~authors~~ *author's* first draft had a completely different ending for the novel.

Lesson 24. Unnecessary Apostrophes	
The tips in Lessons 21–24 help you remember the *only* instances in which apostrophes should be used.	Use apostrophes only to show possession, to mark expressions of time or measure, or to show plurality of numbers and letters. Do not use an apostrophe to form the plural of a last name. *Error:* ✗ I'm sorry, but your essay had too many error's in it. *Correction:* I'm sorry, but your essay had too many ~~error's~~ *errors* in it.

Review Test

Correct all errors in the following paragraphs using the first correction as a model. The number in parentheses at the end of each paragraph indicates how many errors you should find.

~~American's~~ *Americans'* attitude toward flying has changed since the industry was deregulated. In the day's when fares and routes were strictly regulated, airlines could compete with each other only in terms of each airlines service and convenience. Customers preference for airlines was often decided by the quality of meal service. I can remember their serving three-course meals with free wine on linen tablecloths to coach customer's. Coach passengers meals on international flights were often rather elegant, more like first-class passengers meals today. Many airplanes on international flights had a passengers lounge with armchairs, couches, and an open bar for everyones use. (8)

In the world of todays deregulated industry, things are very different. Deregulations main effect was to force airlines into direct, open competition. Since airlines revenue is highly sensitive to passenger load (the average percentage of seats' occupied on each flight), airlines began cutting prices to ensure that every planes seating capacity was maximized. The more people on a flight, the more profitable it was. Airlines concerns about passengers leg room quickly became a thing of the past. Attracting passengers by offering the lowest fare means that airlines have to cut costs at every turn. One of the fare wars first casualties was meal service. Southwest Airlines even jokes about it's "two-course" meals — peanuts and pretzels. (9)

Using Other Punctuation and Capitalizing Words

Terms That Can Help You Understand Other Punctuation and Capitalization

If you are not familiar with any of the following terms, look them up in the Guide to Grammar Terminology beginning on page 435.

colon	paraphrase
common noun	proper adjective
complete sentence	proper noun
direct quotation	quotation
independent clause	semicolon
indirect quotation	transitional term

The Nuts and Bolts of Other Punctuation and Capitalization

This unit covers capitalization and the remaining marks of punctuation most likely to cause problems for writers.

Lesson 25 shows you how to use quotation marks with direct quotations and paraphrases. Using someone's words exactly as he or she said or wrote them is called **direct quotation**. Direct quotation requires the use of quotation marks. Summarizing or otherwise altering someone's words is called **paraphrase** (or **indirect quotation**). Paraphrase does not require the use of quotation marks.

Example:	✗ Camryn said that "she wanted to buy a laptop computer."
Correction 1:	Camryn said that ⁄she wanted to buy a laptop computer.⁄
	Correct this way if you are paraphrasing Camryn's words.

Correction 2:   Camryn said, ~~that~~ "*I want* ~~she wanted~~ to buy a laptop computer." ^

Correct this way if those were Camryn's exact words.

Lesson 26 shows you how to use periods, commas, semicolons, and other punctuation with quotation marks.

Example: ✗ The instructor warned, "This next test will be harder than the last one".

Correction: The instructor warned, "This next test will be harder than the last ~~one".~~ *one."*

Lesson 27 shows you how to use semicolons correctly in your writing. Semicolons have the same function as periods. They are both used to signal the end of a complete sentence. Semicolons are sometimes confused with colons.

Example: ✗ Soy sauce contains the following ingredients; water, extract of soya beans, wheat flour, and salt.

Correction: Soy sauce contains the following ingredients: water, extract of soya beans, wheat flour, and salt.

Lesson 28 shows you how to use colons correctly in your writing. The most common use of a colon is to introduce a list. It is not surprising that a common mistake is to use a colon to introduce a list that is actually a required part of the sentence. In this case, the colon is incorrect.

Example: ✗ To remove this wallpaper, I will need: a sponge, a bucket of warm water, a commercial stripping solution, and a 4-inch putty knife.

Correction: To remove this wallpaper, I will need a sponge, a bucket of warm water, a commercial stripping solution, and a 4-inch putty knife.

Lesson 29 gives you some guidelines for capitalizing certain words. **Proper nouns** and **proper adjectives** are capitalized to show that they are the "official" names of specific, individual persons, places, or institutions. Other special capitalization rules govern, for example, names of ethnic groups, languages, and certain academic courses.

Unit Eight

overview

Example: ✗ Gustavo barra, my Professor, has taught english and french in brazil, bolivia, and los Angeles.

Correction:

           Barra   *professor*   *English*

Gustavo ~~barra~~, my ~~Professor~~, has taught ~~english~~

    French   *Brazil*   *Bolivia*   *Los*

and ~~french~~ in ~~brazil~~, ~~bolivia~~, and ~~los~~ Angeles.

LESSON 25

Quotation Marks
with Direct Quotations
and Paraphrases

EXAMPLE 1   *Direct Quotation Missing Quotation Marks*

Error: ✗ In 1854, Chief Joseph of the Nez Percé tribe met with white leaders and said every part of this soil is sacred to my people.

Correction: In 1854, Chief Joseph of the Nez Percé tribe met with , "Every white leaders and said ~~every~~ part of this soil is sacred to my people. "

EXAMPLE 2   *Paraphrase with Unnecessary Quotation Marks*

Error: ✗ Iva said that "it was cold now in her part of the world."

Correction: Iva said that ⁄it was cold now in her part of the world.⁄

What's the Problem?

A primary function of quotation marks (" ") is to indicate exactly what a person has said or written. This kind of quotation is called a **direct quotation**.

An alternative to quoting someone exactly is to use a **paraphrase** (or **indirect quotation**). When you paraphrase someone, you put their ideas into your own words. A paraphrase does not use quotation marks because the paraphrase changes the words and/or the sentence structure of the original material. Note, however, that a paraphrase should not change the *meaning* of the original. Both direct quotations and paraphrases need to give credit to the source of the ideas you are using.

When you use someone else's material, you must decide whether to quote it directly or to paraphrase it. Once you have decided, use quotation marks with a direct quotation, but do not use them with a paraphrase. In Example 1, the writer seems to be quoting the exact words of Chief Joseph but incorrectly left out the quotation marks. In Example 2, the writer is trying to paraphrase what Iva said but incorrectly used quotation marks with a paraphrase.

The rule for using quotation marks can be summarized as follows:

Direct Quotation = Stated Exactly as Said/Written = Quotation Marks

Paraphrase = Restated in Your Own Words = No Quotation Marks

Diagnostic Exercise

CORRECTED SENTENCES APPEAR ON PAGE 476.

Correct all errors in the following paragraph using the first correction as a model. The number in parentheses at the end of the paragraph indicates how many errors you should find. Count a pair of quotation marks as one error.

Until recently, poor picture quality and a high price tag have prevented consumers from purchasing digital cameras. Industry analyst Kevin Kane recently said, <ins>"The</ins> ~~the~~ next several years will be key in determining what part digital cameras will play in leisure and business budgets.<ins>"</ins> Kane also reported that "digital cameras are now becoming affordable enough for the average consumer." Like PC's, fax machines, and cellular phones, digital cameras first attracted the interest of technology enthusiasts. But recreational photographers like Sanjei Rohan of Spokane, Washington, just appreciate the convenience. As a rock climber, I have seen some amazing landscapes, he says. I take pictures, download them to my computer, and e-mail them to my cousins in Nebraska, where they have fewer rocks to climb. "Industry analysts predict a sharp growth in consumer enthusiasm." (4)

Lesson 25

66   99

Fixing This Problem in Your Writing

Understanding Direct Quotations and Paraphrases

The key to avoiding problems with quotation marks is knowing the difference between a direct quotation and a paraphrase (or indirect quotation). A good way to recognize a paraphrase is the use of the introductory word *that*. While the use of *that* in paraphrases is not always necessary, it helps distinguish them from direct quotations. If you use *that* to begin all your paraphrases, you will have an easier time knowing how to punctuate your writing.

> **THAT PARAPHRASE TIP**   Always use *that* to begin a paraphrase (indirect quotation). Do not use quotation marks.

Let's look at some examples of *that* signaling a paraphrase:

> Little Red Riding Hood thought <u>that</u> she would visit her granny that day.

> Little Red Riding Hood told him <u>that</u> it was none of his business.

Punctuating Direct Quotations and Paraphrases

Understanding the differences between direct quotations and paraphrases makes it easier to use them correctly. This section explains the punctuation rules for each type of quotation.

As you write, you will often find passages that you want to repeat word-for-word in your own writing. When you directly quote other people's material, you must use quotation marks at the beginning and end of the quotation. Use the following tip to decide how to punctuate direct quotations.

> **DIRECT QUOTATION PUNCTUATION TIP**   If the material you are quoting is at least one complete sentence, the quoted material must be preceded by a comma and begin with a capital letter. If the quotation is less than a complete sentence and is incorporated into the body of the sentence, then you do not use a comma or a capital letter.

In the following examples, the quoted material is at least one complete sentence, so the quotation must begin with a capital letter and be preceded by a comma:

Complete Sentence Quotation: Little Red Riding Hood said, "I think I will visit my granny today."

> *Complete Sentence Quotation:*   Little Red Riding Hood told the Wicked Wolf, "Mind your own business."

In the following examples, the quotation is less than a complete sentence and is incorporated into the body of the surrounding sentence, so we do not use a comma or a capital letter:

> *Partial Sentence Quotation:*   The Wicked Wolf couldn't help laughing at his "sweet old lady costume."

> *Partial Sentence Quotation:*   Little Red Riding Hood hated having to do "a good deed every day."

If you have chosen to paraphrase someone, do not use quotation marks, even if the material being paraphrased is a complete sentence. As you learned earlier in this lesson, paraphrases are typically introduced by the word *that*. Here are three examples:

> *Paraphrase:*   Little Red Riding Hood thought <u>that</u> she would visit her granny that day.

> *Paraphrase:*   The Wicked Wolf decided <u>that</u> he would follow the strange girl.

> *Paraphrase:*   Little Red Riding Hood told him <u>that</u> it was none of his business.

✳ *Putting It All Together*

Identify Errors in Using Quotation Marks with Direct Quotations and Paraphrases

_____ Use the *That* Paraphrase Tip to help you determine whether something is a direct quotation or a paraphrase (indirect quotation).

Correct Errors in Using Quotation Marks with Direct Quotations and Paraphrases

_____ When you quote someone word-for-word (a direct quotation), the material must be identified by quotation marks.

_____ In direct quotation, use a comma and a capital letter if the quoted material is at least one complete sentence.

_____ In direct quotation, do not use a comma and a capital letter if the quoted material is less than a complete sentence and is incorporated into the surrounding sentence.   →

> _____ In a paraphrase (indirect quotation) use *that* to introduce the paraphrased material. Do not use quotation marks around material that you have paraphrased.

Sentence Practice 1

CORRECTED SENTENCES APPEAR ON PAGE 476.

First, use each of the following statements as a direct quotation in a sentence of your own (additional information is in brackets). Second, turn the direct quotation into a paraphrase starting with *that*.

Example:
                    Thomas Paine once wrote, "These
          ~~These~~ are the times that try men's souls. *"*
                 ^   ^

          [Thomas Paine, writing about the need to fight the British in 1776]

Paraphrase: *Thomas Paine believed that circumstances in his day tested people's convictions.*

1. I want to seize fate by the throat. [Composer Ludwig van Beethoven, in a letter he wrote in 1801]

2. From where the sun now stands, I will fight no more forever. [Chief Joseph, speaking to his Nez Percé tribe]

3. The covers of this book are too far apart. [Ambrose Bierce, in a review of another writer's book]

4. I beheld the wretch — the miserable monster whom I had created. [Mary Wollstonecraft Shelley, in her 1818 novel, *Frankenstein*]

5. Talk low, talk slow, and don't say too much. [John Wayne, giving advice on acting]

 For more practice using quotation marks, go to **Exercise Central** at bedfordstmartins.com/commonsense

Lesson 25

" "

Sentence Practice 2

CORRECTED SENTENCES APPEAR ON PAGE 476.

First, use each of the following statements as a direct quotation in a sentence of your own (additional information is in brackets). Second, turn the direct quotation into a paraphrase starting with *that*.

Example:

The poet Robert Frost once remarked, "The
~~The~~ brain is a wonderful organ. It starts working the
moment you get up and does not stop until you get into
the office. *"* [Poet Robert Frost]

Paraphrase: *The poet Robert Frost said sarcastically that the brain, though functioning constantly, seems to shut down when a person gets to work.*

1. The reason I'm going ahead with this attempt now is because I just cannot wait any longer to impress you. [Letter by John Hinckley to actress Jodie Foster, on the day he shot President Reagan]

2. The trouble with some women is they get all excited about nothing, and then they marry him. [Cher, singer and actress]

3. My life had its beginning in the midst of the most miserable, desolate, and discouraging surroundings. [Former slave Booker T. Washington, writing in 1901 about the effects of slavery]

4. When I'm good, I'm very good, but when I'm bad, I'm better. [Actress Mae West, in the movie *I'm No Angel*]

5. I see one-third of a nation ill-housed, ill-clad, ill-nourished. [Franklin Roosevelt, referring to the Great Depression in 1937]

Lesson 25

" "

Sentence Practice 3

Combine the following sentences by turning the direct quote in the second sentence into a paraphrase in the first sentence, replacing *IT*.

Example: Simple Simon said IT. "I met a pie-man going to the fair."

Answer: *Simple Simon said that he met a pie-man going to the fair.*

1. Sharon said IT. "I have to leave soon."

2. The coaches said IT. "We are pleased with the team's performance."

3. Dominique said IT. "This book is the best I have ever read."

4. Mark Twain supposedly said IT. "Everybody talks about the weather, but nobody does anything about it."

5. Cal said IT. "The sky is falling!"

6. Right before he died, President Franklin Roosevelt said IT. "I have a terrific headache."

7. The last words of actor Humphrey Bogart were IT. "I should never have switched from scotch to martinis."

8. My father called and asked IT. "Did you remember to pay your tuition this semester?"

9. The mayor said IT. "This year, the city will have to hire a dozen more firefighters."

10. My biology teacher said IT. "A bat's leg bones are so tiny that no bat is able to use its legs to walk."

Lesson 25

" "

Editing Practice 1

CORRECTED SENTENCES APPEAR ON PAGE 477.

Correct all errors involving quotation marks in the following paragraph using the first correction as a model. The number in parentheses at the end of the paragraph indicates how many errors you should find. Count a pair of quotation marks as one error.

                          that she

My mother told me ~~that, "She~~ believed every marriage was a

compromise." For example, my brother Pete has had a lot of trouble quit-

ting smoking. He likes to quote Mark Twain, who said "quitting

smoking is easy. I've done it dozens of times." After my brother got married, his wife told him that "he could not keep smoking inside the house." She wants him to quit, but she knows how hard it will be for him to do it. She told me that "her uncle, who had been a heavy smoker, had died from lung disease." Naturally, she is very concerned about Pete. Last night, Pete told us I am going to try nicotine patches. We all hope that they will work. (4)

Editing Practice 2

CORRECTED SENTENCES APPEAR ON PAGE 477.

Correct all errors involving quotation marks in the following paragraph using the first correction as a model. The number in parentheses at the end of the paragraph indicates how many errors you should find. Count a pair of quotation marks as one error.

Many traditional sayings emphasize the virtues of saving things. My mother always said *, "Waste* ~~waste~~ not, want not. *"* That may be true, but my wife and I have some real differences on saving things. At least once a week my wife asks me honey, do you really want to keep THIS? It doesn't make much difference what the THIS is, but my answer will probably be the same sure I do. I think that every marriage is doomed to have one person who is a saver and one person who is a thrower-away. The saver in me is always saying but I might need that someday. My wife's response is sure, but you will never find it in all the junk you have accumulated. Of course, I would never actually say that to my wife. (4)

Lesson 25

" "

Editing Practice 3

Correct all errors involving quotation marks in the following paragraph using the first correction as a model. The number in parentheses at the end of the paragraph indicates how many errors you should find. Count a pair of quotation marks as one error.

We have all heard the old saying ~~you~~ *, "You* are what you eat. *"* I don't know
if that is true or not, but I do know that there is lots of disagreement about
what we should eat. My wife has recently become a carb-counter. Last
week, she announced I am going to lose 15 pounds by Christmas. I said
that's terrific, dear, but how are you going to do it? She said that "she
would go on a low-carb diet." The problem is that I am a near vegetarian.
I told her maybe I am wrong, but you are going to end up eating a lot
of meat. She agreed that that was probably the case and said that, "we
were going to have to change our grocery shopping and eating habits."
I replied I think we may end up eating at buffets so we can both get what
we want. (6)

Lesson 25

" "

Applying What You Know

On a separate piece of paper, write a short essay about something you and someone close to you disagree about. Include several conversations that employ direct quotation and paraphrase. Exchange essays with a partner, and check to see that your partner has correctly punctuated the direct quotes and has set off paraphrases with the word *that*.

The Bottom Line	As we said in this lesson, "Be sure to use quotation marks in direct quotations."

LESSON 26

Quotation Marks with Other Punctuation

Error: ✗ Edgar Allan Poe wrote "The Raven", "Annabel Lee", and "The Bells".

Correction: Edgar Allan Poe wrote "The Raven‚" ⁄ "Annabel Lee‚" ⁄ and "The Bells‚" ⁄

Error: ✗ Bjorg asked, "Do you want to play tennis"?

Correction: Bjorg asked, "Do you want to play tennis?" ⁄

What's the Problem?

American punctuation style has a number of rules that govern where periods, commas, colons, semicolons, question marks, and exclamation points should go when they are used together with quotation marks. Some of the conventions make sense, but others seem arbitrary. It might help you remember the conventions if you think of them as the "Rule of Two." *Two* punctuation marks (periods and commas) go inside the quotation marks, *two* other marks (colons and semicolons) go outside, and *two* others (question marks and exclamation points) can go either place depending on the meaning of the sentence.

- **Two Go Inside**

    Period: "I know what you mean."

    Comma: The band played "Satin Doll," "Take the A Train," and "Misty."

- **Two Go Outside**

    Semicolon: I didn't like "Satin Doll"; the tempo was too slow.

Colon:	All three horn players soloed during "Misty": the trumpeter, the trombonist, and the saxophonist.

- **Two Can Go Either Place, Depending on Meaning**

Question Mark (Inside):	She asked me, "Do you like jazz?"
Question Mark (Outside):	What didn't you like about "Satin Doll"?
Exclamation Point (Inside):	Someone yelled, "Encore!"
Exclamation Point (Outside):	I want to hear "Autumn Leaves"!

Now you should be able to see what went wrong in the two example sentences. In Example 1, the commas are outside the quotation marks, where they should never be. In Example 2, the question mark is in the wrong place. What is being quoted (*"Do you want to play tennis"*) is a question. Therefore, the question mark should go *inside* the quotation marks along with the rest of the question.

Diagnostic Exercise

CORRECTED SENTENCES APPEAR ON PAGE 477.

Correct all errors in the following paragraph using the first correction as a model. The number in parentheses at the end of the paragraph indicates how many errors you should find.

Lesson 26

" "

Yesterday, my literature teacher asked, "Who can name three poems written by African ~~Americans"?~~ *Americans?"* I was able to come up with "Incident," which was written by Countee Cullen. Herman, the guy who sits next to me, named Langston Hughes's "Harlem". I started to bring up "Letter from Birmingham Jail;" however, I quickly recalled that that is an *essay* by Martin Luther King Jr. Then, somebody in the back row mentioned Hughes's "Same in Blues", and somebody else remembered Richard Wright's "Between the World and Me". Our teacher seemed glad that it didn't take very long for us to answer. I don't know about any of the other students, but in my high school English classes, we studied quite a few African American poets. (4)

Fixing This Problem in Your Writing

Knowing where to place periods, commas, semicolons, and colons with quotation marks is simply a matter of memorizing the "Rule of Two": periods and commas go *inside* the quotation marks; semicolons and colons go *outside* the quotation marks. So far, so good.

However, the placement of question marks and exclamation points is more complicated because their placement depends on the meaning of the sentence. The following tip will help you decide where to put question marks and exclamation points used with quotations.

> **UNQUOTE TIP**   Take whatever is inside the quotation marks out of the sentence and out of the quotation marks. Now, how would you punctuate this new sentence? If you would use a question mark or an exclamation point, then this same punctuation belongs *inside* the closing quotation mark in the original sentence.

Let's apply this tip to Example 2, taking what is inside the quotation marks out of the sentence and out of quotation marks:

Example 2:   ✗ Bjorg asked, "Do you want to play tennis"?

Tip applied: Do you want to play tennis?

As you can see, the quoted material, *Do you want to play tennis*, is a question, so we correct the sentence by placing the question mark inside the closing quotation mark as follows:

Correction: Bjorg asked, "Do you want to play tennis?"

Here is an example in which the question mark belongs outside the quotation mark:

Example: ✗ Have you read Edgar Allan Poe's poem "The Raven?"

Tip applied: The Raven

> *The Raven* is not a question, so the question mark belongs outside the closing quotation mark.

Correction: Have you read Edgar Allan Poe's poem "The Raven"?

Here is an especially tricky case in which the quoted material is a question, but, in addition, the whole sentence is also a question:

Example: Who said, "May we leave early"

Does the question mark belong inside or outside the quotation marks? The Unquote Tip works even here. Because *May we leave early* is a question, the question mark belongs inside the closing quotation mark:

Tip applied: May we leave early?

Correction: Who said, "May we leave early?"

Keep in mind this one final point. Only one closing punctuation mark (period, question mark, or exclamation point) can ever appear after the last word in a sentence. In other words, you can't have one closing punctuation mark inside the quotation mark and another one outside.

Error: ✗ Who said, "May we leave early?"?

Correction: Who said, "May we leave early?"

✳ *Putting It All Together*

Identify Errors in Using Quotation Marks with Other Punctuation

_____ Any time you use quotation marks, check to see whether you have used other punctuation marks correctly.

Correct Errors in Using Quotation Marks with Other Punctuation

_____ Place periods and commas *inside* quotation marks.

_____ Place semicolons and colons *outside* quotation marks.

_____ For question marks and exclamation points, use the Unquote Tip to determine whether the material inside the quotation marks needs a question mark or an exclamation point. If it does, then the quotation mark or exclamation point goes *inside* the quotation mark. Otherwise, the quotation mark or exclamation point goes *outside* the quotation mark.

Sentence Practice 1

CORRECTED SENTENCES APPEAR ON PAGE 477.

For each sentence, take the material that is inside quotation marks out of quotation marks. Using the Unquote Tip, correct any sentence that has punctuation errors. Write *OK* if the sentence is correct.

Lesson 26

" "

Letter from Birmingham Jail

Example: Who wrote "Letter from Birmingham Jail?"?

1. Grace asked, "When will we get our tests back"?

2. The title of my paper is "Can There Be Peace in the Middle East?"

3. The platoon leader yelled at the top of her lungs, "Move it!"

4. The title of the first chapter is "Where Do We Go Next"?

5. Charlene responded, "Why are you following me"?

 For more practice using quotation marks, go to **Exercise Central** at **bedfordstmartins.com/commonsense**

Sentence Practice 2

CORRECTED SENTENCES APPEAR ON PAGE 477.

For each sentence, take the material that is inside quotation marks out of quotation marks. Using the Unquote Tip, correct any sentence that has punctuation errors. Write *OK* if the sentence is correct.

Example: Can you tell me the meaning of the word

alliteration

"alliteration?"?

1. Did she say, "The store opens at noon?"

2. Didn't W. H. Auden write "The Unknown Citizen"?

3. Who wrote the song entitled, "Are You Lonesome Tonight?"

4. A panicked man yelled, "Don't push that button"!

5. Will you tell me who asked, "Will you leave?"

Sentence Practice 3

Combine the following sentences by using the title or quotation in the second sentence in place of *IT* in the first sentence.

Example: They danced to IT. "Isn't She Lovely?"

Answer: *They danced to "Isn't She Lovely?"*

1.   The choir sang IT. "Amazing Grace"

2.   She shouted IT. "Look out for that train!"

3.   Wendy asked IT. "Are we there yet?"

4.   The teacher asked IT. "Are you sick?"

5.   Marta yelled IT. "Look out for that tree!"

Editing Practice 1

CORRECTED SENTENCES APPEAR ON PAGE 477.

Correct all errors in the following passage using the first correction as a model. The number in parentheses at the end of the passage indicates how many errors you should find.

My girlfriend sleepily asked, "Why are you calling me so late?"⁊ It

was 2:00 A.M., and I apparently had awakened her.

"Sorry," I muttered, realizing the time. "I've been studying all night

and needed a break". This apparently wasn't the right answer.

She yelled, "I was sound asleep"! After another moment, she added,

"Do you think I stayed up just in case you needed to call someone"?

"Well, I guess this is a bad time to call," I meekly suggested. "I'll

let you go back to sleep". She hung up before I could say anything else.

I decided that cramming all night before a test was a bad idea for several

reasons. (4)

Editing Practice 2

Correct all errors in the following paragraph using the first correction as a model. The number in parentheses at the end of the paragraph indicates how many errors you should find.

Many conflicts have given rise to what might be called "war songs." / Each war, it seems, becomes the subject of popular music. World War I, for example, had its protest songs, such as "I Didn't Raise My Boy to Be a Soldier". This song captured many Americans' desire to stay out of the war. Once the United States entered the war, though, many songs served to rally the troops and the general public. One of the most famous is "Over There". All good American parents and "sweethearts," according to this song, should be proud and eager to send their loved ones to fight in the war. George M. Cohan received a Congressional Medal of Honor for composing this immensely popular song. In Irving Berlin's "Oh, How I Hate to Get Up in the Morning", however, the singer is less enthusiastic about fighting in the trenches, taking a lighthearted view of military life but still celebrating victory. (3)

Applying What You Know

On a separate piece of paper, write a conversation between you and a friend in which you discuss a movie that you have seen recently. After you have finished writing, check to see whether you have used punctuation marks correctly with all of the quotes you have included.

Lesson 26

66   99

The Bottom Line	Remember this: "Periods and commas always go inside quotation marks. Colons and semicolons always go outside quotation marks."

Semicolons

EXAMPLE 1	*Semicolon Used Instead of Colon*
Error:	✗ Li brought the drinks; lemonade, cola, and iced tea.
Correction:	Li brought the drinks:̸ lemonade, cola, and iced tea.

EXAMPLE 2	*Semicolon Used Instead of Comma*
Error:	✗ Unfortunately, he forgot water; which was what most people wanted.
Correction:	Unfortunately, he forgot water,̸ which was what most people wanted.

What's the Problem?

A **semicolon** is easier to use than you might think; however, a misused semi-colon can be particularly distracting. Sometimes, writers confuse semicolons with colons (as in Example 1) and incorrectly use a semicolon to introduce a list. (See Lesson 28 on correctly using colons to begin lists.) Other times, semicolons are mistakenly used when a comma is needed (as in Example 2).

Many people don't understand the function of a semicolon. The main use of a semicolon is to separate two related **independent clauses**, groups of words that could be separated by a period to form two complete sentences. For example:

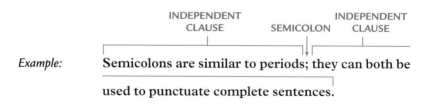

	INDEPENDENT CLAUSE	SEMICOLON	INDEPENDENT CLAUSE
Example:	Semicolons are similar to periods; they can both be used to punctuate complete sentences.		

Diagnostic Exercise

CORRECTED SENTENCES APPEAR ON PAGE 478.

Correct all errors using the first correction as a model. The number in parentheses at the end of the paragraph indicates how many errors you should find.

In the early 1900's, "pulp" magazines were extremely popular. These magazines were named for the cheap pulp paper they were printed on. They contained various types of stories; adventures, detective stories, romance tales, and Western stories. One of the most successful pulp publishers was Street and Smith; this firm sold millions of magazines. Most old issues; however, have been destroyed or lost. Higher quality magazines were printed on glossy paper; which gave them the nickname "slicks." The terms "pulp" and "slicks" are still used today to distinguish simple action-oriented fiction from the more sophisticated writing that might appear in more upscale magazines such as the following; *Cosmopolitan, Esquire,* and *Harper's.* (4)

Lesson 27

;

Fixing This Problem in Your Writing

The following tip can help you determine whether you have correctly used a semicolon to join two independent clauses.

> **IMAGINARY PERIOD TIP** Can you replace the semicolon with a period? If there is a complete sentence on both sides of the imaginary period, the semicolon is correct.

Let's apply this tip to a correct example:

Example: Even baby giraffes are tall; their average height is six feet.

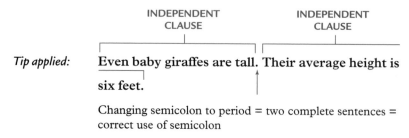

Tip applied: Even baby giraffes are tall. Their average height is six feet.

Changing semicolon to period = two complete sentences = correct use of semicolon

In contrast, the Imaginary Period Tip reveals that Example 1 is an error because what comes after the new period is a **fragment**. (See Lesson 1 on fragments.) *Lemonade, cola, and iced tea* cannot stand alone as a sentence, so there is an error in Example 1:

Example 1:   ✗ Li brought the drinks; lemonade, cola, and iced tea.

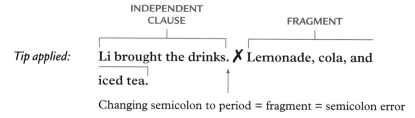

Tip applied: Li brought the drinks. ✗ Lemonade, cola, and iced tea.

Changing semicolon to period = fragment = semicolon error

If you know the rule for using colons (see Lesson 28), it is easy to correct Example 1:

Lesson 27

Correction: Li brought the drinks :/lemonade, cola, and iced tea.

Do not change a semicolon to a colon unless you understand the rules for colons. If you are unsure, reword the original sentence so it has a structure you know how to punctuate. For instance, another correction of Example 1 is *Li brought lemonade, cola, and iced tea.*

The Imaginary Period Tip also reveals the error in Example 2. As usual, it is the second part of the example that becomes a fragment when we apply the Imaginary Period Tip.

Example 2:   ✗ Unfortunately, he forgot water; which was what most people wanted.

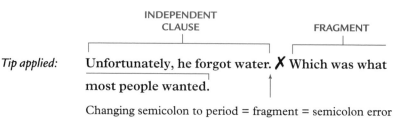

Tip applied: Unfortunately, he forgot water. ✗ Which was what most people wanted.

Changing semicolon to period = fragment = semicolon error

To correct the error, use a comma instead of a semicolon.

Correction: Unfortunately, he forgot water,/ which was what most
people wanted.

Avoid combining just any two ideas with a semicolon; join ideas that are
very closely connected. Semicolons are typically used to show the following
kinds of relationships.

- **Cause-and-effect** relation between two ideas:

  The attic had not been cleaned in years; it smelled of dust and mold.

- **Generalization-and-example** relation between two ideas:

  Telephone solicitors always call at dinnertime; last night, we were
  interrupted twice during our meal.

- **Statement-and-comment** relation between two ideas:

  My wife considers *The Three Stooges* to be utterly moronic; I still
  think they are pretty funny.

In addition, semicolons are often used with **transitional terms** (words like
however, thus, nevertheless, therefore) to help the reader see how the idea in the
second part of the sentence relates to the idea in the first part. When using
a transitional term right after a semicolon, put a comma after the term. (See
Lesson 16 on transitional terms.)

✳ *Putting It All Together*

Identify Semicolon Errors in Your Writing

____ The majority of semicolons are used to join two independent
clauses that are closely related. To confirm that you have correctly
used a semicolon in this way, pretend to replace the semicolon
with a period. If this imaginary period produces two complete
sentences, the semicolon is correct.

____ If you are left with a fragment on either side of the imaginary
period, the semicolon is incorrect.

Correct Semicolon Errors in Your Writing

____ You can usually fix semicolon errors by replacing the semicolon
with a colon or a comma. If you are not sure which replacement is
correct, reword the original sentence so it is a more familiar type
of sentence for you to punctuate.

Lesson 27

;

Sentence Practice 1

CORRECTED SENTENCES APPEAR ON PAGE 478.

Using the Imaginary Period Tip, examine the part of the sentence before the semicolon and the part after the semicolon. If one part can stand alone as a complete sentence, write *OK* above it. If the other part cannot stand alone as a complete sentence, write *X* above it. If either part cannot stand alone, correct the semicolon error.

> *Example:* David wanted to borrow my book; the one about home improvement.
>
>   OK   X
> *Tip applied:* David wanted to borrow my book. The one about home improvement.
>
> *Answer:* David wanted to borrow my book; the one about home improvement.

1. Next week, we will have a major test; one that will be difficult.

2. Delaware's nickname is First State; it was the first state to ratify the Constitution.

3. My car is too loud; I think it needs a new muffler.

4. Allyson and I went to the same high school; Pine Tree High School.

5. Ken brought several items; napkins, glasses, and forks.

For more practice using semicolons, go to **Exercise Central** at **bedfordstmartins.com/commonsense**

Sentence Practice 2

CORRECTED SENTENCES APPEAR ON PAGE 478.

Using the Imaginary Period Tip, examine the part of the sentence before the semicolon and the part after the semicolon. If one part can stand alone as a complete sentence, write *OK* above it. If the other part cannot stand alone as a complete sentence, write *X* above it. If either part cannot stand alone, correct the semicolon error.

Lesson 27

;

Example:	I hate three things; soggy pancakes, runny eggs, and burnt toast.

                               OK   X

Tip applied:	I hate three things. Soggy pancakes, runny eggs, and burnt toast.
Answer:	I hate three things;̸ soggy pancakes, runny eggs, and burnt toast.

1. Her truck failed to start; because the battery was dead.

2. I read an article about Ralph Bunche; the first African American to win the Nobel Peace Prize.

3. Annie ordered a parfait; a dessert made of ice cream, fruit, and syrup.

4. Actor Spencer Tracy was asked to play the Penguin on the TV show *Batman*; he declined when he was told he could not kill Batman.

5. I need to go to the store; which is only about one mile away.

Sentence Practice 3

Combine the two ideas in each of the following items using a semicolon where appropriate. (A semicolon is not appropriate in all cases.)

Example:	Najib's sister called for him. As usual, he was not around.
Answer:	*Najib's sister called for him; as usual, he was not around.*

1. Sara hated the movie. It was too violent for her.

2. I live in Daphne. Which is a small town near Mobile, Alabama.

3. The song "I'd Like to Teach the World to Sing" originated as a Coca-Cola ad. The song was a Top 10 hit in 1972.

4. Pineapples are associated with Hawaii. They originated, however, in South America.

Lesson 27

;

5. Blue M&M candies replaced tan ones in 1995. Because blue was voted the overwhelming favorite in a contest.

6. A fire alarm went off during a test in my geology class. Consequently, the instructor said we would finish the test next week.

7. The longest boxing match occurred in 1893. It lasted over seven hours.

8. Electric eels are not eels at all. They are a type of knifefish.

9. One of the most popular toppings for pizza in Australia is eggs. In China, the top favorites include mussels and clams.

10. This computer needs more memory. It has not been updated in four years.

Editing Practice 1

CORRECTED SENTENCES APPEAR ON PAGE 478.

Correct all errors in the following paragraphs using the first correction as a model. The number in parentheses at the end of each paragraph indicates how many errors you should find.

Lesson 27

Langston Hughes is one of the best-known African American poets;, his fame having begun in 1915, when he was thirteen. At that time, he was elected poet of his graduating class; an unusual selection not merely because he was one of only two African American students in his class but because he had never written any poems. Hughes explained that nobody else in the class had written any poetry either. His classmates elected him; however, because they assumed that poetry requires rhythm and that he must have rhythm because of his ethnicity. (2)

Even though such reasoning had an element of stereotyping, Hughes was inspired; and wrote a graduation poem that the teachers and students enthusiastically received. He went on to publish many types of writing;

poems, plays, short stories, children's books, histories, and song lyrics, just to name a few. (2)

Editing Practice 2

CORRECTED SENTENCES APPEAR ON PAGE 478.

Correct all errors in the following paragraph using the first correction as a model. The number in parentheses at the end of the paragraph indicates how many errors you should find.

Something needs to change at my apartment/ because I cannot cope with the mess any longer. Six months ago, it seemed like living with two high school friends would be great; we liked hanging around each other and shared the same interests. What I did not fully understand was that they were (and are) slobs. One likes cooking; which I think is a great hobby. It's not so great, however, when he doesn't clean up the mess that he makes. My other roommate leaves clothes all over the house; even in our one bathroom. One time, I counted what seemed like half of his entire wardrobe on the bathroom floor; four pairs of jeans, three pairs of dress pants, ten T-shirts, and five dress shirts. Neither of my roommates is bothered by the messiness of our apartment; they seem to thrive in such conditions. I am not a fanatic about cleanliness; however, I cannot stand it when people seem to expect other people to clean up after the mess they make. (3)

Editing Practice 3

Correct all errors in the following paragraphs using the first correction as a model. The number in parentheses at the end of each paragraph indicates how many errors you should find.

Our basketball team has a new coach this year/, Carl McFarlane. The previous coach was offered a position at Utah State University; after they made an offer he could not refuse. Fans here were disappointed when the old coach left, but Coach McFarlane has proven to be a popular choice. He had eight winning seasons in a row when coaching at the University of Georgia; in addition, his teams were usually ranked in the top twenty. (1)

There was some controversy about his salary; Coach McFarlane earns more than anyone else on the university payroll. He also receives several opportunities for bonuses; especially if his team wins the conference title. At first, I thought he was overpaid, but I have changed my thinking. For one thing; sixty percent of his salary comes from money donated to the athletic program. Contrary to what some people think, no funds are taken from academics to pay the coach's salary. A record number of season tickets have already been sold; maybe that indicates the school will be able to recoup some of the money spent on Coach McFarlane's salary. (2)

Lesson 27

;

Applying What You Know

Write a paragraph or two describing a sports team you like or dislike (or a paragraph explaining why you do not have a favorite sports team). Do not use semicolons just yet. Trade your draft with a partner. In your partner's draft, look for two instances when you could use a semicolon to combine ideas that are very closely connected and worth emphasizing. (Add a transitional term after the semicolon, if you wish.) See if your partner agrees with your choices or has other ideas about where semicolons could best be used.

| The Bottom Line | What comes *before* a semicolon should be able to stand alone; what comes *afterward* should also be able to stand alone. |

LESSON 28

Colons

EXAMPLE 1

Error:　　　　✗ Liliana bought: milk, cereal, and sugar.

Correction:　　Liliana bought̸ milk, cereal, and sugar.

EXAMPLE 2

Error:　　　　✗ For our trip, be sure to bring items such as: books, clothes, and lots of money.

Correction:　　For our trip, be sure to bring items such as̸ books, clothes, and lots of money.

What's the Problem?

A **colon** has several functions. One is to introduce a quotation. Another common but often misunderstood function of the colon is to introduce *certain types* of lists. This lesson focuses on colons used with lists because they account for most writers' errors with colons.

A colon is used to introduce a list that is *not* needed for the sentence to be grammatically correct. In the following example, the colon is used correctly because the sentence would be complete even if you left out the list following the colon:

COMPLETE SENTENCE

Example:　　At the theater, I met three friends: Jose, Tyrone, and Mark.

> The part before the colon is a complete sentence, so the colon is OK.

A colon *cannot* introduce a list if the list is needed for the sentence to be complete. For instance, the lists in Examples 1 and 2 are needed for the sentence to be complete. Leaving them out would create **fragments** (see Lesson 1 on fragments). Therefore, these lists should *not* be introduced by a colon.

One reason why this error occurs is that many people mistakenly associate colons with *any* type of list. But remember, you should use a colon only when you could delete the list and still have a grammatical sentence.

Diagnostic Exercise

CORRECTED SENTENCES APPEAR ON PAGE 478.

Correct all errors in the following paragraph using the first correction as a model. The number in parentheses at the end of the paragraph indicates how many errors you should find.

My roommate, who is shopping for a new car, looked at several types, including/ Fords, Nissans, and Mazdas. She knew which features she wanted: automatic transmission, cruise control, and leather seats. However, she quickly discovered that such features were not within her budget. To get the best deal for her money, I suggested that she consult sources such as: her mechanic or *Consumer Reports* magazine. She did some research, but she seemed disappointed because there was no clear choice. She finally narrowed her choices to: a Ford Taurus and a Nissan Sentra. She hasn't gotten much further than that. (2)

Fixing This Problem in Your Writing

Here is a tip that can help you determine whether a colon is correctly used with a list.

> **IMAGINARY PERIOD TIP** If you replace the colon with a period, would the part *before* the period be a *complete* sentence? If so, the colon is probably correct.

Why does this tip work? It reveals whether the list is a necessary part of a grammatical sentence. If the list is necessary, *do not* use a colon:

Grammatically complete sentence + Colon = **Correct**

Fragment + Colon = **Incorrect**

The Imaginary Period Tip reveals that the colon is incorrect in Example 1 because *Liliana bought* is not a complete sentence.

Example 1:   ✗ Liliana bought: milk, cereal, and sugar.

FRAGMENT   More words needed here

Tip applied: ✗ Liliana bought.

Fragment + Colon = Incorrect

Correction: Liliana bought/ milk, cereal, and sugar.

Delete the colon to correct the sentence.

When we apply the Imaginary Period Tip to Example 2, we see that what comes before the colon again cannot stand alone as a grammatical sentence (words are obviously missing):

Example 2:   ✗ For our trip, be sure to bring items such as: books, clothes, and lots of money.

FRAGMENT   More words needed here

Tip applied: ✗ For our trip, be sure to bring items such as.

Fragment + Colon = Incorrect

Correction: For our trip, be sure to bring items such as/ books, clothes, and lots of money.

Lesson 28

When you see an error like this, the correction is usually simple: delete the colon. Rarely, in fact, is any punctuation needed at all.

Now let's see how the Imaginary Period Tip can confirm that a colon is used correctly:

Example: Chris is taking two science courses: Physics 101 and Biology 210.

COMPLETE SENTENCE

Tip applied: Chris is taking two science courses.

Grammatically complete sentence + Colon = Correct

In fact, leaving out the colon in the above example would be an error. Most students, however, create colon errors by using them too often, rather than not often enough.

✳ *More Examples*

Lists with Colons

My roommate has two pets: an iguana and a poodle.

We found three items under the couch: a candy bar, my reading glasses, and a beer bottle.

Lists without Colons

Simón Bolivar liberated five South American countries, including Bolivia, Colombia, and Peru.

For this course, you need to bring a calculator, graph paper, two textbooks, and several erasers.

✳ *Putting It All Together*

Identify Colon Errors

____ Each time you use a colon to introduce a list, see whether what comes *before* the colon could stand alone as a complete, grammatical sentence.

Correct Colon Errors

____ If what comes before the colon *cannot* stand alone, you should not use a colon to introduce the list.

____ If what comes before the colon *can* stand alone, you can use a colon to introduce the list.

Lesson 28

⠇

Sentence Practice 1

CORRECTED SENTENCES APPEAR ON PAGE 479.

Determine whether the colon is correct by applying the Imaginary Period Tip. Write *OK* above colons that are used correctly. Correct any colons that are used incorrectly.

Example:　　To mend these pants, I will need: scissors, thread, a needle, and gratitude.

Tip applied:　　To mend these pants, I will need.

Correction: To mend these pants, I will need̸ scissors, thread, a needle, and gratitude.

1. Many farmers in this area grow: cotton, grain, and turnips.

2. Kamilah and Doug saved enough money to travel throughout: Denmark, Germany, and Belgium.

3. My college will not offer several courses I need, such as: English 100 and Math 201.

4. We will need to buy: a textbook, gloves, and a dissecting kit.

5. This summer, I saw three species of harmless sharks: the whale shark, lemon shark, and nurse shark.

 For more practice using colons, go to Exercise Central at **bedfordstmartins.com/commonsense**

Sentence Practice 2

CORRECTED SENTENCES APPEAR ON PAGE 479.

Lesson 28

Determine whether the colon is correct by applying the Imaginary Period Tip. Write *OK* above colons that are used correctly. Correct any colons that are used incorrectly.

Example: The subjects I like to read about are: Chinese history, dog breeding, and finance.

Tip applied: *The subjects I like to read about are.*

Correction: The subjects I like to read about are̸ Chinese history, dog breeding, and finance.

1. Some famous people had dyslexia, such as: Leonardo da Vinci, Winston Churchill, Albert Einstein, and George Patton.

2. Remember to buy everything we need to clean the apartment: soap, sponges, and a mop.

3. Native Americans added many words to English: *totem, tomahawk, hickory, raccoon,* and other common terms.

4. Many languages have contributed to English, especially: French, Latin, and German.

5. New words in English arise from many sources, including: gang culture, popular music, and the computer industry.

Sentence Practice 3

Combine the sentences by using a colon.

> *Example:*   **The ice cream came in three flavors. The flavors were chocolate, strawberry, and vanilla.**
>
> *Answer:*   *The ice cream came in three flavors: chocolate, strawberry, and vanilla.*

1. The movies you must view are as follows. The movies are *The Patriot, Gone with the Wind,* and *The Texas Chainsaw Massacre.*

2. Our football team has three plays. These three plays are punt, pass, and pray.

3. There are two things you must remember. These two things are call me when you arrive, and bring me back a gift.

4. We close the store for three holidays only. The holidays are Thanksgiving, Christmas, and New Year's Day.

5. I encourage you to take two classes this summer. These two classes are Biology 226 and History 102.

Lesson 28

Editing Practice 1

CORRECTED SENTENCES APPEAR ON PAGE 479.

Correct all errors in the following paragraphs using the first correction as a model. The number in parentheses at the end of each paragraph indicates how many errors you should find.

My college sponsors various trips for students, including/ rafting, skiing, and hiking trips. This fall, I am going on one of the hiking trips. There is a fee involved, but it is still an affordable trip. I have to supply my own: water container, snacks, and backpack. However, the school provides several things: water, lunch, first-aid kits, and even insect repellent. Some items I definitely plan to leave at home are: my cell phone, MP3 player, and credit cards. (2)

I wanted a few of my friends to come, such as: my roommate, his brother, and two guys who work with me at the grocery store. They declined. I myself love to go on long walks. Last year, I hiked in several places: northern Alabama, southern Kentucky, and along the coastline in Georgia. Sure, hiking can be a little tedious at times, and you have to be fit to walk several hours a day. However, the rewards include: getting away from the noise of the city, strengthening your leg muscles, and spending time with people who also love hiking. Compared to other hobbies and activities, it's also pretty cheap. (2)

Lesson 28

:

Editing Practice 2

Correct all errors in the following paragraph using the first correction as a model. The number in parentheses at the end of the paragraph indicates how many errors you should find.

Before he became a politician, Arnold Schwarzenegger starred in major films such as/ *The Terminator*, *True Lies*, and *Predator*. Several of his movies were not only hits but could be interpreted as thought-provoking reflections of our society and greatest fears, especially fears dealing with: technology, the unknown, and governmental control.

In *The Terminator*, for instance, we see glimpses of a world devastated by our own technology. Some of his movies are not so thought provoking. These lesser works include: *Hercules in New York*, *Conan the Destroyer*, and *Batman and Robin*. Understandably, few critics give serious consideration to his best-known comedies: *Kindergarten Cop*, *Jingle All the Way*, and *Twins*. Still, Schwarzenegger was in a number of films that proved to be more than mere "action flicks." He has since retired from movies, except for providing voiceovers in animated films such as: *Cars* and *Crood Awakening*. But just maybe he will be back. (3)

Applying What You Know

Colons have various functions. See what sorts of colons you find in a magazine article or newspaper. For your next class meeting, bring examples of at least three uses of a colon. Be ready to explain to the class the function of each example—what the colon is doing in the sentence.

Lesson 28 :	The Bottom Line	When using a colon to introduce a list, remember these steps: imagine replacing the colon with a period and see whether what comes before this period is a complete sentence.

Capitalization

EXAMPLE 1	*Capitalization Needed*

Error: ✗ My english teacher asked us to read stories by Flannery O'Connor and other writers from the south.

Correction: My ~~english~~ teacher asked us to read stories by
           English

Flannery O'Connor and other writers from the ~~south~~.
           South

EXAMPLE 2	*Unnecessary Capitalization*

Error: ✗ How hard were your Math classes in High School?

Correction: How hard were your ~~Math~~ classes in ~~High School~~?
        math   *high school*

What's the Problem?

Some words (**proper nouns** and **proper adjectives**) should be capitalized to show they are the "official" names or nicknames of specific persons, places, things, or events. In addition, many words are capitalized because they are derived from official names. In Example 1, *English* must be capitalized because it is derived from the name of a country (England). Also, *South* should be capitalized since people widely recognize it as the name of a specific region.

More general words are not capitalized. In Example 2, *math* is a **common noun** that should *not* be capitalized because it is a general term for a type of class. Similarly, *high school* is a general term, *not* the name of a specific school. Compare these common nouns with the proper nouns *Calculus I* and *Lewis and Clark High School*.

Capitalization is not an issue in speech, so the rules can be difficult to learn. Compounding the problem is the fact that capitalization "rules" are not always consistent. For instance, many words are capitalized or not capitalized depending on how they are used in a sentence (compare *My uncle is here* with *I saw Uncle Brett there*). You must be careful because errors in capitalization can confuse readers by sending the wrong message about whether a word is the specific name of somebody (or something) or whether the word is merely a general description.

Diagnostic Exercise

CORRECTED SENTENCES APPEAR ON PAGE 479.

Correct all errors in the following paragraph using the first correction as a model. The number in parentheses at the end of the paragraph indicates how many errors you should find.

                      community college

My sister is attending a ~~Community College~~ in Kansas City, and

we've been comparing our courses. Her spanish class is much different

from mine because hers includes discussion of hispanic cultures. Her

teacher, professor Gonzales, believes students are more interested in

learning a language when they appreciate the culture connected with

that language. (3)

Lesson 29

cap

Fixing This Problem in Your Writing

Because some capitalization guidelines vary according to the profession or field of study you are in, always consult the handbook, style guide, or dictionary suggested by your teacher or readers for capitalization guidelines. The following are a few tips that are valid no matter what class, profession, or reader you might have.

> **PERSON TIP** Capitalize a person's title or a family term when (1) it is followed by a proper name or (2) it is used in *place* of the person's name.

A person's title would be something like *Senator, Associate Dean,* or *General.* A family term might be *Uncle* or *Mother.* These words are not always capitalized — just when they are used before a proper name or as if they were the person's name. To determine the correct capitalization of these words, you have to see how they are used in the sentence, as in the following correct example:

No cap: *Not* used in place of a person's real name or followed by a name

Tip applied: Is <u>Mother</u> ready to meet the <u>detective</u> and <u>Professor</u> Xavier?

Cap: Used in place of person's real name   Cap: Followed by a name

Here is another way to think of the Person Tip: if you can replace the person's title or family term with a first name, you need to capitalize the title or family term. Below we have replaced the titles and family terms in the previous example with proper names to see whether the words should be capitalized:

Replacement does *not* work, so *detective* is *not* a proper noun.

Juanita   ✗ *Sally*   *Chuck*

Tip applied: Is ~~Mother~~ ready to meet the ~~detective~~ and ~~Professor~~ Xavier?

Replacement works, so both *Mother* and *Professor* are proper nouns needing caps.

You would not say *the Sally*, so *detective* cannot be replaced by a real name. Consequently, *detective* is not a proper noun and should not be capitalized in this sentence.

> **GROUP TIP** Capitalize any term that a group of people accept as describing their culture, language, nationality, religion, or ethnic background.

> **PLACE TIP** Capitalize any name you could find on a map or that is widely recognized as a *distinct* place or region. Do not capitalize general directions or general locations.

Lesson 29

cap

Some place names that might be capitalized include *Rocky Mountains*, *Pacific Ocean*, *New England*, *Dixie*, and the *West*. If you merely told a person to *head west* or *drive to the ocean*, these terms would not be capitalized since they are just general directions.

Often, the decision to capitalize depends on whether your readers consider a word to be a specific name. Many Texans would capitalize *East Texas* because they know it is a specific area, but most readers from other parts of the country would not recognize this as a distinct region—just a vague reference (hence, *east Texas* for them).

Example 1 illustrates these two tips:

Group Tip: *English* is derived from the name of a group of people, so it needs a cap.

Example 1:   ✗ My <u>english</u> teacher asked us to read stories by Flannery O'Connor and other writers from the <u>south</u>.

Place Tip: *South* is the name of a specific region, so it needs a cap.

                   English

Correction: My ~~english~~ teacher asked us to read stories by Flannery O'Connor and other writers from the
              South
              ~~south.~~

SCHOOL TIP   Capitalize the official name of a specific school or course. Do *not* capitalize general references to a school, course, or field of study.

Many writers err by always capitalizing schools, subjects, and informal names of courses. However, only specific and formal names should be capitalized, as in the following examples:

Proper Nouns: **Math 101, Department of History, BA in Communication Studies, Kilgore Community College, English Composition II, Pine Tree High School**

Common Nouns: math class, history, a communications degree, the community college, my composition course, high school

Let's apply the School Tip to Example 2:

Example 2:   ✗ How hard were your <u>Math</u> classes in <u>High School</u>?

School Tip: *Math* and *high school* are both general references, not specific titles, so no caps are needed.

                            math   *high school*

Correction: How hard were your ~~Math~~ classes in ~~High School~~?

Lesson 29

cap

✳ *More Examples*

Person Terms

Are you against the bill, **G**overnor? **P**ress **S**ecretary **J**ones said you were.

I asked **D**ad not to call me at work, and so did **A**unt **T**ammie.

The **g**overnor would not answer; her **p**ress secretary stopped talking, too.

My **d**ad can be nosey at times, as my **a**unt often points out.

Group Terms

Most of the **N**ew **E**nglanders I met on my trip were **B**oston **R**ed **S**ox fans.

Yesterday, members of the **E**nglish **H**onors **O**rganization read five poems written by **A**frican **A**mericans.

Some **r**eligious **g**roups boycotted the convention.

The **c**lub will also discuss poetry by other **e**thnic **m**inorities.

Place Terms

I am visiting the **G**rand **C**anyon this summer.

The **W**est is identified with rugged individualism.

The **c**anyon is huge.

We traveled **w**est all the way to **S**an **F**rancisco.

School Terms

I hope to take **H**istory 110 this fall and obtain my **BA** in History by next spring.

My neighbor teaches **O**ceanography **I** at **G**ulfport **H**igh **S**chool.

I am a **h**istory major working on a **b**achelor's **d**egree.

The **h**igh **s**chool I went to did not have any courses in **o**ceanography.

Lesson 29

cap

✳ *Putting It All Together*

Identify Capitalization Errors in Your Writing

_____ Proofread your writing for references to individuals, groups, schools, courses, subjects, and places.

Correct Capitalization Errors in Your Writing

_____ Capitalize proper nouns and proper adjectives — official names and titles of specific people, cultures, and locations. Do not capitalize general references.

_____ Use the four tips in this lesson to help you decide whether terms are proper nouns or adjectives that require capitalization. The tips can be summarized as follows:

Capitalize	*Example*
Family Term + Name	**U**ncle **M**arty called.
Family Term Used as a Name	Did **M**other arrive?
Title + Name	Is **D**octor **C**hang in?
Title Used as a Name	I am here, **S**enator.
Name Accepted by Group	She is a **B**aptist.
Name Found on Map	**G**ulf of **M**exico
Recognized Name of Region	**P**acific **N**orthwest
Name of Specific School	**M**artin **L**uther **K**ing **H**igh **S**chool
Name of Specific Course	**M**ath 110; **A**dvanced **A**lgebra
Name of Specific Degree	**A**ssociate's **D**egree in **L**iberal **A**rts

Lesson 29

cap

Sentence Practice 1

CORRECTED SENTENCES APPEAR ON PAGE 479.

If the underlined word is correct in terms of capitalization, write *OK* over it. Correct any error, and write a brief explanation of why the word should or shouldn't be capitalized by referring to the four tips.

	General	*OK*	*OK*

Example: Yes, ~~general~~, your <u>uncle</u> called from <u>Boston</u> today.

Tip applied: *Person Tip: "General" is a title that could be replaced by a name.*

1. My <u>father</u> has a job teaching <u>Biology</u> in eastern <u>Delaware</u>.

2. Theodore Roosevelt was once <u>governor</u> of <u>New York</u>.

3. Much of the <u>southwestern</u> United States was once <u>Mexican</u> territory.

4. Students write in almost every class at this <u>University</u>, even <u>Physical Education</u> courses.

5. Tenskwatawa was a <u>native american</u> leader who encouraged his people to give up alcohol along with <u>european</u> clothing and tools.

 For more practice using capitalization, go to **Exercise Central** at **bedfordstmartins.com/commonsense**

Sentence Practice 2

CORRECTED SENTENCES APPEAR ON PAGE 479.

If the underlined word is correct in terms of capitalization, write *OK* over it. Correct any error, and write a brief explanation of why the word should or shouldn't be capitalized by referring to the four tips.

	geology
Example:	I have to take my ~~Geology~~ class again.
Tip applied:	*School Tip: The term geology is not the name of a specific class (the word "my" in front indicates a general term).*

Lesson 29

cap

1. In the 1860's, Montana's present <u>Capital</u>, <u>Helena</u>, was named <u>Last Chance Gulch</u>.

2. The <u>university president</u> spoke at <u>graduation</u> this year.

3. Did you say that <u>aunt</u> Iva is arriving today?

4. The <u>rhone river</u> and the <u>rhine river</u> both rise out of the <u>Alps</u> of <u>Switzerland</u>.

5. My <u>Grandmother</u> believes she can meet with the <u>Pope</u> during our visit to <u>Rome</u>.

Sentence Practice 3

Replace the italicized word in the sentence with the words or word groups in the second line, capitalizing as necessary.

Example: They interviewed *her*.

Governor Whitman / the governor of washington

Answer: They interviewed Governor Whitman, the governor of Washington.

1.   She telephoned *her* yesterday.

Ms. Perkins / my supervisor

2.   I will graduate from *it* next year.

fairview community college

3.   Sam learned a great deal from *it*.

accounting 101 / his first business class

4.   *They* got married quite young.

her mother and father

5.   She is a member of *it*.

the nez percé / a local tribe

6.   I took *them* as soon as I could.

history 101 / and the introductory business course

7.   We stopped off *there*.

at rocky mountain national park over the holidays

8.   We saw *them* when we went to California.

my sister and her husband fred

Lesson 29

cap

9. We go to church *there*.

   at the greek orthodox church in dallas

10. I got a call from *him*.

    albert / my mother's cousin

Editing Practice 1

CORRECTED SENTENCES APPEAR ON PAGE 479.

Correct all errors in the following paragraphs using the first correction as a model. The number in parentheses at the end of each paragraph indicates how many errors you should find.

New Orleans
Last fall we stayed in ~~new orleans~~ for a week. We flew from newark

in new jersey. Our trip got off to a bad start because our flight was delayed

for two hours because of thunderstorms over the appalachians. We stayed

in the french quarter, the oldest part of town. It and the lovely old garden

district were not damaged by katrina, the terrible hurricane that did so

much damage to the entire gulf coast. We really enjoyed our stay. The

local businesses need all the support they can get. It was a pleasant change

to be in a city that was truly grateful to see tourists. We should all support

that lovely city in any way we can. (7)

Terrible as it was, we need to bear in mind how much worse the

loss of life could have been if not for very accurate forecasting from the

national hurricane center and the national weather service. For example,

compare katrina with the similar hurricane that struck galveston in 1900.

That storm killed 8,000 people because there was no ability at the time

to monitor off-shore weather. The storm came on shore without any

Lesson 29

cap

warning at all, killing nearly everyone living along that part of texas where the storm hit. (5)

Editing Practice 2

Correct all errors in the following paragraph using the first correction as a model. The number in parentheses at the end of the paragraph indicates how many errors you should find.

college

All of us when we first start ~~College~~ or University struggle with the decision of what to major in. Some people have a very clear idea of what profession they want to enter from the very moment they start school, and so they know exactly what to major in. That certainly was not the case with me. I didn't have a clue what I wanted to do after I got my Bachelor's Degree. As a result I kind of floundered around changing from one Program to another. Some majors in the Humanities, like History, English, or Philosophy, give people a really good, well-rounded education that makes them able to deal with complicated ideas and write well. The problem, of course, is that these programs do not lead directly to any career path. For example, one of my classmates got a rhodes scholarship, one of the most prestigious academic awards in the world, and ended up scooping twenty-nine flavors of ice cream when he got back from oxford. In the long run, however, people with good humanistic educations do very well—better, in fact, than people with more immediately useful degrees like Accounting and Finance. People with only narrow professional educations tend to stall out at mid-career. By the way, my friend with the Scholarship ended up being a highly successful Lawyer, but there is no denying that he had a hard time for a while after he graduated. (12)

Lesson 29

cap

Write a paragraph describing the three most helpful courses you have taken in college or high school, and indicate why these might help you as you work toward a particular major or profession. Use the four tips we have discussed (especially the School Tip) to make sure you have capitalized words correctly.

The Bottom Line	According to rules of formal English, "official" names, titles, and nicknames are capitalized.

Lesson 29

cap

UNIT EIGHT: Using Other Punctuation and Capitalizing Words

Punctuation marks and capitalization form an important part of standard written English. The following chart sums up the tips that will help you avoid five problems writers encounter in using punctuation marks and capitalization.

TIP(S)	QUICK FIX AND EXAMPLE
Lesson 25. Quotation Marks with Direct Quotations and Paraphrases	
The *That* Paraphrase Tip (p. 252) helps you distinguish between a direct quotation and a paraphrase. The Direct Quotation Punctuation Tip (p. 252) tells you how to use commas and capital letters with direct quotes.	Direct quotations require quotation marks. Paraphrases are often introduced by *that* and should never use quotation marks. *Error:* ✗ Sharon said that "she was truly sorry." *Correction:* Sharon said that ⁒she was truly sorry.⁒
Lesson 26. Quotation Marks with Other Punctuation	
The Unquote Tip (p. 261) helps you determine whether quotation marks and exclamation points should go inside or outside closing quotation marks.	Periods and commas always go inside quotation marks. Semicolons and colons always go outside quotation marks. Question marks and exclamation points go *inside* if they are part of the quotation and *outside* if they are part of the entire surrounding sentence. *Error:* ✗ Tim said, "You need to leave". *Correction:* Tim said, "You need to leave‸."
Lesson 27. Semicolons	
The Imaginary Period Tip (p. 267) helps you determine whether a semicolon is correctly joining two independent clauses.	If replacing a semicolon with an imaginary period results in a fragment on either side, the semicolon is incorrect. Try replacing it with a colon or a comma. *Error:* ✗ My parents walked into my dorm room; not even bothering to knock first. *Correction:* My parents walked into my dorm room‸, not even bothering to knock first.

Lesson 28. Colons	
The Imaginary Period Tip (p. 276) helps you make sure that a colon is correctly used to introduce a list.	If what comes before a colon and list *cannot* stand alone as a sentence, the colon is incorrect and should be deleted. *Error:* ✗ My roommate enjoys: jogging, swimming, and playing video games. *Correction:* My roommate enjoys⁄ jogging, swimming, and playing video games.
Lesson 29. Capitalization	
The Person Tip (p. 284), Group Tip (p. 285), Place Tip (p. 285), and School Tip (p. 286) help you know when to capitalize these types of words.	Capitalize "official" names or nicknames of specific people or places. Capitalize cultural, national, religious, ethnic, or language groups. Also capitalize specific school or course names. *Error:* ✗ My spanish instructor asked us to read a book written by a catholic priest. *Spanish* *Correction:* My ~~spanish~~ instructor asked us to read a book written by a ~~catholic~~ *Catholic* priest.

Unit Eight

review

Review Test

Correct all errors in the following paragraph using the first correction as a model. The number in parentheses at the end of the paragraph indicates how many errors you should find. Treat a pair of quotation marks as one error.

roommate

My ~~Roommate~~ Troy invited me to visit his hometown, College Station, Texas. I had never been to the south before, much less to Texas, over Christmas break. Since I had grown up in new England, the prospect of visiting a new part of the Country was pretty exciting. Troy said that "We would have to drive West for twelve hours to reach College Station; which is in the Central part of the state." College Station is really just a college town, but it also has: cotton, retail, and cattle. (8)

Writing Clear Sentences

Terms That Can Help You Understand How to Write Clear Sentences

If you are not familiar with any of the following terms, look them up in the Guide to Grammar Terminology beginning on page 435.

active	**parallelism**
coordinating conjunction	**passive**
faulty parallelism	**past participle**
gerund	**verb**
helping verb	**voice**
infinitive	

The Nuts and Bolts of Writing Clear Sentences

This unit covers two topics that can make your writing unclear: faulty parallelism and the passive voice.

Lesson 30 shows you how to create parallel sentences. **Parallelism** refers to a series of two or more identical grammatical structures joined by a **coordinating conjunction** (usually *and* or *or*). The most common parallelism errors involve verb forms that either end in *-ing* (**gerunds**) or appear after *to* (**infinitives**). **Faulty parallelism** results when items in a series are not all in the same grammatical form.

Example: ✗ Sylvia likes <u>reading</u> poetry, <u>listening</u> to music, and <u>to collect</u> spiders.

Correction: Sylvia likes reading poetry, listening to music, and ~~to collect~~ *collecting* spiders.

Lesson 31 shows you how to revise passive voice sentences. In most sentences, the subject of the sentence performs the action of the verb. This type of sentence is said to be in the **active voice**. In the **passive voice**, the subject of the sentence does not perform the action; instead, it receives the action of the verb. Although using the passive voice is not incorrect, active voice sentences are clearer and stronger.

Example (Passive Voice): The new parking rule was criticized by the students.

Correction (Active Voice): The new parking rule. ~~was criticized by the students.~~ *students criticized the*

Parallelism

EXAMPLE 1

Error: ✗ Mickey likes to <u>to bike</u>, <u>swim</u>, and <u>to go</u> on long walks.

Correction 1:   Mickey likes to bike, ^to^ swim, and to go on long walks.

Correction 2:   Mickey likes to bike, swim, and ~~to~~ go on long walks.

EXAMPLE 2

Error: ✗ He also loves <u>eating</u> pizza and to <u>watch</u> reruns of *Baywatch*.

Correction 1:   He also loves eating pizza and ~~to watch~~ ^watching^ reruns of *Baywatch*.

Correction 2:   He also loves ~~eating~~ ^to eat^ pizza and to watch reruns of *Baywatch*.

What's the Problem?

The term **parallelism** refers to a series of two or more grammatical elements of the same type joined by *and* (or sometimes by *or*). For example, the following sentence has parallel verb forms:

> <u>Eat</u>, <u>drink</u>, and <u>be</u> merry.

When one of the elements breaks the pattern set by the other element(s), the resulting error is called **faulty parallelism**. The most common type of faulty parallelism involves the inconsistent use of verb forms. In Example 1, for instance, *to* is used with the first and third verbs (*to bike* and *to go*), but not with the second verb (*swim*).

In Example 2, *eating* is the *-ing* form of the verb *eat*, but the second verb *to watch* is not the *-ing* form. Either one is grammatical by itself:

He also loves <u>eating</u> pizza.

He also loves <u>to watch</u> reruns of *Baywatch*.

However, when they are joined together by the coordinating conjunction *and*, they create an ungrammatical sentence with faulty parallelism.

CORRECTED SENTENCES APPEAR ON PAGE 480.

Correct all errors in the following paragraph using the first correction as a model. The number in parentheses at the end of the paragraph indicates how many errors you should find.

We all go to college for different reasons — to get an education, meet new people, and ~~to~~ gain the skills for a job. The best programs are ones that reach several of these goals at the same time. I like to take courses that interest me and building skills that will lead to a job. For example, it is great to read about something in a class and then applying it in a practical situation. That is why I am doing an internship program. I have the opportunity to get credits, develop professional skills, and to make important contacts. The internship will be worthwhile, even if I have to go to school an extra semester to earn all the credits I need to graduate. (3)

Lesson 30

//

Fixing This Problem in Your Writing

Faulty parallelism happens when we lose track of exactly which elements are being made parallel. Use the following tip to check to see that the parallel elements you use in your writing do not contain faulty parallelisms.

> **THE PARALLELISM STACK TIP**   Whenever you use an **infinitive** (the *to* form of a verb) or a **gerund** (the *-ing* form of a verb) after an *and* or an *or*, arrange the elements that should be parallel in a "parallelism stack." Placing parallel elements in a column makes it easy to see whether these elements have exactly the same form.

Let's apply the Parallelism Stack Tip to the first example:

Example 1:   ✗ Mickey likes <u>to bike</u>, <u>swim</u>, and <u>to go</u> on long walks.

Tip applied: ✗ Mickey likes   <u>to bike</u>
                                     <u>swim</u>, and
                                     <u>to go</u> on long walks.

The Parallelism Stack Tip shows us at a glance where the parallelism derails: the infinitives *to bike* and *to go* are not parallel to the base form *swim*. (Base forms are simply infinitive verbs without the *to*.)

To correct the error in Example 1, we can use *to* with each of the verbs:

Correction 1:   Mickey likes to bike, ^*to*^ swim, and to go on long walks.

When we apply the Parallelism Stack Tip now, we see that the verbs in the sentence are indeed parallel:

Confirmation: Mickey likes   <u>to bike</u>,
                                    <u>to swim</u>, and
                                    <u>to go</u> on long walks.

We can also correct the sentence by using only one initial *to* plus the base form of each verb (without the *to*):

Correction 2:   Mickey likes to bike, swim, and t̶o̶ go on long walks.

When we apply the Parallelism Stack Tip, we again see that the verbs in the sentence are indeed parallel:

Confirmation: Mickey likes to   <u>bike</u>,
                                      <u>swim</u>, and
                                      <u>go</u> on long walks.

Lesson 30

//

Notice that when we use only a single *to*, it is no longer part of the parallelism stack because *to* is not repeated as part of the parallelism. The parallel elements now are just the base forms *bike*, *swim*, and *go*.

Let's apply the Parallelism Stack Tip to Example 2:

Example 2: ✗ He also loves <u>eating</u> pizza and <u>to watch</u> reruns of *Baywatch*.

Tip applied: ✗ He also loves   <u>eating</u> pizza and
             <u>to watch</u> reruns of *Baywatch*.

We can see at a glance that *eating* and *to watch* are not parallel. Here are the parallelism stacks for the three possible corrections. In this first correction, there are two parallel gerunds (*-ing* verbs):

watching

Correction 1: He also loves <u>eating</u> pizza and ~~to watch~~ reruns of
                            ^
     Baywatch.

Confirmation: He also loves   <u>eating</u> pizza and
                   <u>watching</u> reruns of *Baywatch*.

In the second correction, we use two parallel infinitives (*to* verbs):

to eat

Correction 2: He also loves ~~eating~~ pizza and <u>to watch</u> reruns of
                    ^
     Baywatch.

Confirmation: He also loves   <u>to eat</u> pizza and
                   <u>to watch</u> reruns of *Baywatch*.

Finally, we can also correct the error by using just one *to* plus the base form of each verb:

to eat

Correction 3: He also loves ~~eating~~ pizza and ~~to~~ watch reruns of
                   ^
     Baywatch.

Confirmation: He also loves to   <u>eat</u> pizza and
                   <u>watch</u> reruns of *Baywatch*.

As Example 2 illustrates, there are a number of ways to fix faulty parallelism. The main problem is spotting the faulty parallelism to begin with.

Lesson 30

//

✳ Putting It All Together

Identify Faulty Parallelism

_____ Every time you use a coordinating conjunction (*and, or*), use the Parallelism Stack Tip to make sure that the parallel elements are in exactly the same grammatical form on both sides of the *and* or the *or*. Be especially careful with infinitives (verbs with *to*) since they are the most common source of faulty parallelism.

Correct Faulty Parallelism

_____ Rewrite the faulty element to make it match the other elements in the series. Use all gerunds (*-ing* verbs), all infinitives (*to* forms), or a single initial *to* followed by all base forms (verbs without *to*).

Sentence Practice 1

CORRECTED SENTENCES APPEAR ON PAGE 480.

Create parallelism stacks for the parallel elements in the following sentences. Underline all the verbs that are used in forming the parallel structure. Mark with an *X* any nonparallel elements, and rewrite the sentence to correct the faulty parallelism.

> *Example:*   I want to improve my skills, go online, and to surf the Internet.
>
>   *I want*   <u>to improve</u> *my skills,*
>   **X** <u>go</u> *online, and*
>   <u>to surf</u> *the Internet.*
>
>   *to*
> *Correction:*   I want to improve my skills, go online, and to surf the Internet.
>   ^

1. Before leaving, I have to call my mother, write a report, and to pay my bills.

2. College gives us a chance to be away from home and gaining independence.

3. This book will teach you ways to write better, make good grades, and to amuse your friends.

4. A standard formula for speeches is beginning with a joke and to conclude with a summary.

5. Student representatives on committees are required to attend all meetings, take notes, and to report to the student government.

 For more practice using parallelism, go to **Exercise Central** at bedfordstmartins.com/commonsense

---

Sentence Practice 2

CORRECTED SENTENCES APPEAR ON PAGE 480.

Create parallelism stacks for the parallel elements in the following sentences. Underline all the verbs that are used in forming the parallel structure, and rewrite the sentence to correct faulty parallelism errors. Write *OK* above any sentences that do not contain faulty parallelism.

Example:	**It is hard to admit a mistake and starting over again.**
	It is hard *to admit a mistake and* *starting over again.*
Correction:	*admitting* **It is hard to admit a mistake and starting over again.**

Lesson 30

//

1. The porters began sorting the baggage and clearing a space for us to assemble.

2. I have to put the cat out, water the plants, and to leave a house key with a friend.

3. This semester, I started working at home in the mornings and to do my schoolwork later in the afternoons.

4. I do not want you to lose the directions and becoming lost.

5. I remembered filling out the form, handing it to the clerk, and asking her to check it.

Sentence Practice 3

Combine each of the following groups of sentences. Use parallel forms of the verbs in parentheses.

> *Example:* The children are eager (open) their presents.
> The children are eager (play) with their toys.
> The children are eager (show) them off.

> *Answer:* *The children are eager to open their presents, play with their toys, and show them off.*

1. My boss is eager (get) the costs for the new product. My boss is eager (begin) selling it. My boss is eager (see) profits.

2. (Brush) your teeth correctly is important. (Floss) regularly is important. (Visit) a dentist twice a year is important.

3. I cannot stand it when friends (make) complicated plans. I cannot stand it when friends (call) me at the last second. I cannot stand it when friends (expect) me to be ready on time.

4. Texas Slim likes (drink) Lone Star Beer. Texas Slim likes (eat) barbecue. Texas Slim likes (watch) Martha Stewart on TV.

5. You should try (prepare) nutritious meals. You should try (watch) your weight. You should try (get) enough sleep.

Lesson 30

Editing Practice 1

CORRECTED SENTENCES APPEAR ON PAGE 480.

Correct all parallelism errors in the following paragraph using the first correction as a model. The number in parentheses at the end of the paragraph indicates how many errors you should find.

playing

My boyfriend, Matt, loves talking on his cell phone and ~~to play~~ video

games. In fact, he seems to do little else. He spends hours doing both at

the same time. I talk on my cell and play video games sometimes, but I

also like meeting people face to face, going out with friends, and to have a little variation in what I do. Just last weekend, I had an opportunity to participate in a blood drive and going to a baseball game. During that entire time, Matt managed to run up 200 minutes on his cell phone and to complete *Half-Life 2* for the tenth time. This weekend, I plan to watch a movie with our friends, go for a long walk around the park, and to work in my garden. If I can't get him to join me with at least one of these activities, I might have to find someone who is more compatible with my interests. (3)

Editing Practice 2

Correct all parallelism errors in the following paragraph using the first correction as a model. The number in parentheses at the end of the paragraph indicates how many errors you should find.

Ms. Astin, my supervisor, asked me yesterday to stay late, file reports, and ~~to~~ photocopy a dozen spreadsheets. Normally, I would not mind, but my day was already hectic. I hated to start three new assignments and falling even further behind with my regular duties. Arguing with Ms. Astin, however, was pointless. She ordered me to stop my other work, start on her assignments, and to stay in the office until the work was done. On the positive side, I have worked a great deal of overtime lately, so my next paycheck should be larger than usual. I normally enjoy working in our office and to give extra help when needed. I just need a little more notice next time before my boss assigns extra work. (3)

Lesson 30

//

Applying What You Know

On your own paper, write a short essay listing the kinds of skills you think you will need in future jobs. In your writing, try to use several parallel verb forms. When you are finished, switch papers with a partner and use the Putting It All Together checklist on page 302 to make sure that your partner's writing does not contain faulty parallelism.

The Bottom Line	Make verb forms parallel by **using** the Parallelism Stack Tip and **checking** to see that each verb has exactly the same form.

Lesson 30

//

Passive Voice

Error:　　　　✗ A plane <u>was taken</u> to Chicago by our family.

Correction:　　*Our family took a plane to Chicago.*
　　　　　　　~~A plane was taken to Chicago by our family.~~
　　　　　　　　　^

Error:　　　　✗ A report <u>was written</u>.

Correction:　　*Somebody wrote a report.*
　　　　　　　~~A report was written.~~
　　　　　　　　^

What's the Problem?

All action verbs occur in one of two **voices**: the **active** or the **passive**. In an active sentence, the subject performs the action and is therefore the main focus of the sentence. In a passive sentence, however, the sentence is flipped around to focus on what happened *to* something. In other words, the subject of a passive sentence *receives* the action. For example, compare the following sentences:

Active:　　　Arnold <u>kicked</u> the ball.

　　　　　　The subject (*Arnold*) performs the action.

Passive:　　The ball <u>was kicked</u> by Arnold.

　　　　　　The subject (*ball*) receives the action.

Using the passive voice is not a grammatical error. However, the passive voice can lead to a dull style because it does not stress action (see Example 1). Also, it can "hide" the person or thing doing an action. For instance, Example 2 does not indicate *who* wrote the report.

Sometimes people use the passive to be polite. (For example, compare *Mistakes were made* with *You made mistakes*.) However, writers should avoid using the passive voice unless they have a good reason to do so.

Diagnostic Exercise

CORRECTED SENTENCES APPEAR ON PAGE 480.

Change all passive-voice verbs to the active voice using the first correction as a model. The number in parentheses at the end of the paragraph indicates how many errors you should find.

> *Matt's apartment manager called him, wanting*
> ~~Matt was called by his apartment manager, who wanted~~ to know
> ^

why he played his music so loudly. Matt was surprised by the phone call;

he didn't think his music was loud. He apologized, but he said his radio

was playing at only a fourth of its potential volume. Apparently, the man-

ager was satisfied by this response. Matt was told by her that she would

speak with the people who complained. I have heard that they have a

history of complaining. (3)

Fixing This Problem in Your Writing

Identifying the Passive Voice

Lesson 31

To recognize the passive voice in your writing, use the following tip.

pass

> **TO BE + PAST PARTICIPLE TIP** The passive voice follows a consistent formula: a form of the verb *to be* as a helping verb + a past participle form of another verb.

Let's look at some examples:

Subject	*To Be* +	*Past Participle*
The contract	is	signed.
The game	was	played.
The burgers	were	eaten.
The contest	had been	won.

Note that most past participles end in *-ed* (*borrowed, played*). Some irregular verbs, however, form the past participle with *-en* (*eaten, taken, written*), while others form it by changing a vowel (*sing-sung, ring-rung, win-won*).

Using the Active Voice

Once you have identified the passive voice in your writing, test it against its active-voice counterpart to see which is better. Unless there is a good reason to use the passive, you should generally use the active form. To make a passive sentence active, use the following tip.

> **FLIP-FLOP TIP**   Convert passive sentences into active sentences by flip-flopping what comes before and after the passive verb so that the subject of the new sentence performs the action. If nothing comes after the passive verb, then the new subject in the active sentence will usually be *somebody* or *something*.

Here is the Flip-Flop Tip applied to Example 1:

Example 1:   SUBJECT
✗ A plane was taken to Chicago by our family.

Tip applied: NEW SUBJECT
Our family   took   a plane to Chicago.

The subject (*family*) now performs the action (*took*).

Note that the flip-flop requires that you eliminate the helping verb form of *to be* (*was*), changing *was taken* to *took*.

Here is the Flip-Flop Tip applied to Example 2:

Example 2:   SUBJECT
✗ A report was written. [by somebody]

Tip applied: NEW SUBJECT
Somebody wrote a report.

In this revision, we added the subject *Somebody* because the original sentence did not specify who wrote the report.

Lesson 31

pass

✳ *Putting It All Together*

Identify the Passive Voice

____ Use the *To Be* + Past Participle Tip to identify all instances of passive voice in your writing.

Eliminate Instances of Unnecessary Passive Voice

____ Turn passive-voice sentences into active-voice sentences by using the Flip-Flop Tip to make the subject in the new sentence perform the action.

____ Remember to delete the passive helping verb form of *to be* from the new active sentence to make it grammatically correct.

____ Use the active form unless there is a compelling reason to use the passive.

Sentence Practice 1

CORRECTED SENTENCES APPEAR ON PAGE 481.

In each of the following sentences, underline the *to be* verb and the past participle verb that comes after it. Then change the passive sentence into an active one by flip-flopping what comes before and after the verbs you've underlined.

> *The gardener carelessly left a rake in the yard.*
>
> *Example:* A rake <u>was</u> carelessly <u>left</u> in the yard by the gardener.

1. The plants were uprooted by those kids.

2. The children are frightened by your shouting.

3. The television was broken by you.

4. I am hurt by your actions.

5. The story was written by Eudora Welty.

 For more practice using the passive voice, go to **Exercise Central** at bedfordstmartins.com/commonsense

---

Lesson 31

pass

Sentence Practice 2

CORRECTED SENTENCES APPEAR ON PAGE 481.

In each of the following sentences, underline the *to be* verb and the past participle verb that comes after it. Then change the passive sentence into an active one by flip-flopping what comes before and after the verbs you've underlined.

Example:
> *The famous chef Jamie Oliver presented a cooking demonstration.*
>
> A cooking demonstration <u>was presented</u> by the famous chef Jamie Oliver.

1. The meal was quickly eaten by the hungry workers.

2. On Monday, my van was hit by a driver who pulled in front of me.

3. All the rooms were cleaned over the weekend by the custodians.

4. My dancing partner was violently bumped by another dancer.

5. The pesticide was sprayed by the farmers.

Sentence Practice 3

Each item below contains two nouns and a verb. Use the first noun as the subject of an active sentence; then use the second noun as the subject of a passive sentence.

Example: the Senate/the bill
pass

Answer: *Active:*   *The Senate passed the bill.*
Passive: *The bill was passed by the Senate.*

1. our governor/the new law
supported

2. the voters/the results
protested

3. my pet bird/potato chips
likes

Lesson 31

pass

4. the class/the test
   finished

5. our professor/the papers
   graded

Editing Practice 1

CORRECTED SENTENCES APPEAR ON PAGE 481.

Change every passive-voice sentence in the following paragraph to an active-voice sentence using the first correction as a model. The number in parentheses at the end of the paragraph indicates how many errors you should find.

More and more students have chosen urban campuses
~~Urban campuses have been chosen by more and more students~~
                    ^

in the past few years. At my school, like many others, parking and

transportation have become big issues for many students. Riding the bus

is encouraged by the school, but that is not practical for everybody. Only a

few bus routes can be used by riders. In addition, evening classes are taken

by nearly everybody. Bad as the buses are during the day, at night, they

are impossible. Only one route is covered by the night buses. And that

route has only one bus every hour. If the last bus were missed, you would

be stuck for the night in the middle of a nearly deserted campus. This is

not a pretty thought. (5)

Lesson 31

pass

Editing Practice 2

CORRECTED SENTENCES APPEAR ON PAGE 481.

Change every passive-voice sentence in the following paragraph to an active-voice sentence using the first correction as a model. The number in parentheses at the end of the paragraph indicates how many errors you should find.

The student council has proposed a new plan.
~~A new plan has been proposed by the student council.~~ Their idea is
    ^

that several buses could be chartered by the school. These buses would

shuttle between the campus and the central bus station downtown. Nearly

all the bus routes can be accessed by passengers from the central station.

I think this idea would be supported by a lot of students. This plan is being

put forward by the council. A committee is being formed by the council

to see how many students would be interested in this plan. If a reasonable

number of students can be persuaded by us to sign a petition, I think we

can actually pull it off. (6)

Editing Practice 3

Change every passive-voice sentence in the following paragraph to an active-voice sentence using the first correction as a model. The number in parentheses at the end of the paragraph indicates how many errors you should find.

About half of the students actually use buses.
~~Buses are actually used by about half of the students.~~ Cars are
    ^

used by the other half. The problem for these students is parking. Over the

years, several of the larger parking lots have been replaced by classrooms.

We needed the classrooms, but student parking needs were not consid-

ered by the administration. A big part of the problem is that parking is

needed by everybody during the late afternoon. Plenty of parking meters

have been installed by the city, but they are limited to one hour. Even if

a student is taking only one class, one hour is not long enough to get back

to feed the meter. As a result, students are being overwhelmed by parking

tickets. (6)

Lesson 31

pass

Applying What You Know

Examine several paragraphs of roughly even length from a daily newspaper and from a textbook. Count the number of instances of passive voice in the paragraphs. Share your findings with a small group, and discuss whether textbooks or newspapers seem to use the passive voice more often. Why do you think this is the case?

<table>
<tr><td>

The Bottom Line

</td><td>

In active-voice sentences, the **subject performs** the action.

</td></tr>
</table>

Lesson 31

pass

UNIT NINE: Writing Clear Sentences

This unit presented sentence structures that can be misused (in the case of faulty parallelism) or inappropriately used (in the case of passive voice). The following chart sums up tips that will help you avoid two problems writers encounter in creating parallel structures and using the active voice.

TIP(S)	QUICK FIX AND EXAMPLE
Lesson 30. Parallelism	
The Parallelism Stack Tip (p. 300) helps you spot faulty parallelism in your writing.	When using a series of verbs joined by *and* (or sometimes by *or*), use all *-ing* forms, all *to* forms, or a single *to* followed by all base forms. *Error:* ✗ She prefers dancing, working on her computer, and to spend time with friends. *Correction:* She prefers dancing, working on her computer, and ~~to spend~~ *spending* time with friends.
Lesson 31. Passive Voice	
The *To Be* + Past Participle Tip (p. 308) helps you recognize passive-voice sentences. The Flip-Flop Tip (p. 309) helps you convert passive sentences into active ones.	Revise passive-voice sentences by flip-flopping what comes before with what comes after the passive verb, making the subject of the new sentences perform the action. *Passive:* The test was taken three times by me. *Active:* I took the test three times.

Review Test

Correct all errors in the following paragraphs using the first correction as a model. The number in parentheses at the end of each paragraph indicates how many errors you should find.

This summer, I took a bowling class and learned how to select a comfortable ball, ~~to~~ be consistent in my approach, and aim the ball. I have always liked to bowl or watching my friends bowl. Since I had to take a PE course anyway, the requirement was satisfied by a bowling course. Most of my bad habits were corrected by this course. (3)

Some of my worst habits were to vary my approach almost every time I bowled and throwing the ball with all my strength. I was shown by my instructor that I did not need to hurl the ball at the pins. The pins can easily be knocked down by a slower, more controlled release. Amazingly, it takes just a little effort to knock a pin over and starting a chain reaction that can knock them all down. My scores have been greatly improved by my more deliberate approach. (5)

Unit Nine

review

Choosing the Right Article

Terms That Can Help You Understand Articles

If you are not familiar with any of the following terms, look them up in the Guide to Grammar Terminology beginning on page 435.

article	**indefinite article**
common noun	**modifier**
count noun	**noncount noun**
definite article	

The Nuts and Bolts of Choosing the Right Article

One of the most complicated and confusing aspects of English for non-native speakers is the use of **articles**. There are two types of articles, **definite** (*the*) and **indefinite** (*a* and *an*, together with *some*, which behaves like an indefinite article). The choice among these articles—and the additional option of using no article at all—is determined by the nature of the noun the article modifies. This unit will examine how both the form of nouns and the meaning of nouns affect the choice of articles.

There are two main groups of nouns: proper nouns and common nouns. **Proper nouns** name particular people, places, and institutions and are usually capitalized. Most categories of proper nouns do not involve the use of articles. For example:

People:	Ms. Chin, Martin Luther King Jr., Oprah Winfrey
Places:	Chicago, State Street, Niagara Falls, China, Mexico City
Institutions:	General Motors, Apple Computer, Columbia University

However, some proper nouns are used with the definite article *the*. While many such uses do not follow a particular rule, some uses of *the* do. Just for fun, see whether you can figure out the rules for using *the* with certain classes of proper

317

nouns, based on the following examples. (*Hint:* Think about the difference in meaning between the nouns that don't use articles and the ones that use *the*.)
(ANSWERS APPEAR ON PAGE 481.)

No Article	*Used with* **the**
Mt. Everest, Mt. McKinley, Pikes Peak, Mt. Hood, Mt. Washington	the Alps, the Rockies, the Sierra Nevadas, the Andes, the Himalayas
Lake Como, Golden Pond, Lake Ontario, Walden Pond	the Atlantic, the Mediterranean Sea, the Pacific, the Indian Ocean

This unit focuses on the other type of nouns—common nouns. **Common nouns** are not capitalized and are not the names of particular people, places, or institutions. For example, *Ms. Chin* is the name of a particular person, but the common noun *woman* is not. The choice of which article to use with a common noun (or whether to use any article at all) depends on three questions, each of which is discussed in its own lesson.

Lesson 32 helps you to answer the question *What is the form of the noun?* The choice of which article to use depends, in part, on whether the noun is singular or plural and whether it is a count noun or a noncount noun.

> *Example:*   ✗ Our team manager loaded all the equipments onto the bus before the game.

> *Correction:*   Our team manager loaded all the equipment͏̸ onto the bus before the game.

Lesson 33 helps you to answer the question *Does the reader know which specific noun I am referring to?* The choice of which article to use depends, in part, on whether the writer is referring to a specific person, place, or thing that is known to the reader.

> *Example:*   ✗ Let's go to a coffee shop at the corner of Main Street and Maple.

> *Correction:*   Let's go to a̶ coffee shop at the corner of Main Street and Maple.ˆ *the*

Lesson 34 helps you to answer the question *Am I using the noun to make a generalization?* The choice of which article to use depends, in part, on whether the noun is being used to make a generalization—a broad statement or conclusion—about something.

Example: ✗ The nutritionists now believe that eating soybeans
                     may help stop calcium loss and prevent osteoporosis.

                     Nutritionists
Correction: ~~The nutritionists~~ now believe that eating soybeans may
                     ^
                     help stop calcium loss and prevent osteoporosis.

This unit is somewhat different from other units in the book. In the other
units, the lessons are loosely connected. Usually, you can do one lesson in
a unit without doing any other lessons first. In this unit, however, this is not
the case; the three lessons are tightly connected. You should do all three lessons in order. They work together to give you a specific technique called a
decision tree for deciding which article (if any) you should use with a given
common noun. This technique is found in the Unit Ten review.

Unit Ten

overview
ESL

ESL

Incorrect Plurals and Indefinite Articles with Noncount Nouns

EXAMPLE 1	*Noncount Noun Incorrectly Used with Plural Ending*
Error:	✗ There have been many studies about the effect of television <u>violences</u> on children.
Correction:	There have been many studies about the effect of television ~~violences~~ on children. *violence*

EXAMPLE 2	*Noncount Noun Incorrectly Used with Indefinite Article (a/an)*
Error:	✗ A customs agent might ask to see <u>a luggage</u>.
Correction:	A customs agent might ask to see ~~a~~ luggage.

What's the Problem?

A large number of nouns in English cannot be used in the plural (like ✗ *violences* in Example 1). These nouns are called **noncount nouns** because they cannot be counted with number words like *one, two, three*. That is, we cannot say the following:

✗ one violence, two violences, three violences . . .
✗ one luggage, two luggages, three luggages . . .

Another peculiarity of this group of nouns is that they cannot be used with the indefinite article *a* or *an* (like ✗ *a luggage* in Example 2). The article *a/an* comes from the number word *one*; because we cannot say *one luggage*, we also cannot say *a luggage* or *a violence*. (Note that the indefinite article has two forms: *a* before words beginning with a consonant sound and *an* before words beginning with a vowel sound. For example, *a banana* but *an* apple.)

Diagnostic Exercise

CORRECTED SENTENCES APPEAR ON PAGE 481.

Correct all errors in the following paragraph using the first correction as a model. The number in parentheses at the end of the paragraph indicates how many errors you should find.

> *modernization*
> The ~~modernizations~~ of agriculture has meant a huge increase
>   ^
> in just a few crops—wheats and rices for a human consumption, corns
>
> for an animal consumption, and cottons for industrial productions. This
>
> specialization in a few crops is called a *monoculture*. A monoculture has
>
> some disadvantages: it reduces a biodiversity and requires huge amounts
>
> of energies and fertilizer. (11)

Fixing This Problem in Your Writing

Noncount nouns are hard to characterize. Nevertheless, the following tips will help you make good guesses about which nouns are noncountable.

> **GENERAL CATEGORIES TIP**   Most noncount nouns are generic names for categories of things.

For example, the noncount noun *luggage* is a generic or collective term that refers to an entire category of things we carry with us. In contrast, the names of *specific types* of luggage, like *suitcase*, *backpack*, and *briefcase* are all countable:

> one suitcase, two suitcases
> one backpack, two backpacks
> one briefcase, two briefcases

Lesson 32

art
ESL

> **OTHER NONCOUNT CATEGORIES TIP**   Most noncount nouns fall into the following categories: abstractions, academic fields, food, gerunds (words ending in *-ing* used as nouns), languages, liquids and gases, materials, natural phenomena, sports and games, and weather words.

Here are examples of the main categories of noncount nouns:

Abstractions: hope, faith, charity, beauty, luck, knowledge, reliability

Academic fields: anthropology, chemistry, literature, physics

Food: butter, rice, cheese, meat, chicken, salt, sugar

Gerunds (words ending in *-ing* used as nouns): smiling, wishing, walking

Languages: English, Chinese, Spanish, Russian

Liquids and gases: water, coffee, tea, wine, blood, air, oxygen, gasoline

Materials: gold, paper, wood, silk, glass, sand, plastic

Natural phenomena: gravity, electricity, space, matter

Sports and games: tennis, soccer, baseball, chess, poker

Weather words: fog, snow, rain, pollution, wind

Let's see how the two tips can be applied to the example sentences.

Example 1:   ✗ **There have been many studies about the effect of television <u>violences</u> on children.**

Tip applied: violence = abstraction

Correction: **There have been many studies about the effect of**

                violence
television ~~violences~~ on children.
            ^

The Other Noncount Categories Tip helps us identify *violence* as an abstraction; you cannot point to it, touch it, or weigh it. Unless you know otherwise, you should assume that an abstraction is a noncount noun and cannot be made plural.

Lesson 32

art
ESL

Example 2:   ✗ **A customs agent might ask to see <u>a luggage</u>.**

Tip applied: luggage = general category

The General Categories Tip helps us see that *luggage* is a noncount noun because it is a generic category of countable nouns: suitcases, cartons, boxes, backpacks, etc. Because it is a noncount noun, it should not be used with the article *a*:

Correction: **A customs agent might ask to see ~~a~~ luggage.**

✳ *Putting It All Together*

Identify Noncount Noun Errors

_____ Determine which nouns in your writing refer to general categories of things (like *luggage* or *equipment*) or abstract ideas (like *violence* or *knowledge*). Use the Other Noncount Categories Tip to identify other types of noncount nouns in your writing. These words cannot be made plural and cannot be used with *a* or *an*.

Correct Noncount Noun Errors

_____ Edit noncount nouns by removing the plural *-s* ending or removing the indefinite article *a* or *an*.

Sentence Practice 1

CORRECTED SENTENCES APPEAR ON PAGE 481.

In the following sentences, correct all noncount nouns that have been incorrectly used in the plural or with the article *a* or *an*.

Example: They demonstrated their ~~familiarities~~ with
            the topics.
            familiarity

1. We studied the country's system of transportations.

2. The company hoped to improve its productivities.

3. The desks were made out of metals.

4. We helped the campers get their gears out of the trucks.

5. The amount of trade directly affects the prosperities of nations.

Lesson 32

art
ESL

For more practice with noncount nouns, go to **Exercise Central** at
bedfordstmartins.com/commonsense

Sentence Practice 2

CORRECTED SENTENCES APPEAR ON PAGE 482.

In the following sentences, correct all noncount nouns that have been incorrectly used in the plural or with the article *a* or *an*. Also make whatever other changes are necessary for the corrected sentences to be grammatically correct.

> *Example:* Anxiety
> ~~An anxiety~~ about the future is a normal thing.

1. Good plannings gave us good results.

2. During winter we didn't get a sunlight for days.

3. His idea was a complete nonsense.

4. We were not able to get a good information on those topics.

5. News reportings during wartime are always confusing and misleading.

Sentence Practice 3

Below are other nouns that can be used either as noncount or as count nouns, though often with considerably different meanings. Use each noun in two different sentences—once as a noncount noun and once as a plural count noun. Explain the difference in meaning.

> *Example:*   **paper**
> *Answer:*
>   *Noncount:* *The book is printed on very cheap <u>paper</u>. [<u>Paper</u> is a raw material.]*
>   *Count:* *I read two <u>papers</u> this morning. [<u>Papers</u> means "newspapers" or "essays."]*

1. Baseball

2. Coffee

3. Bridge

4. Iron

5. Nickel

Editing Practice 1

CORRECTED SENTENCES APPEAR ON PAGE 482.

Correct all errors involving noncount nouns in the following paragraph using the first correction as a model. The number in parentheses at the end of the paragraph indicates how many errors you should find.

                                                                    people

There is almost nothing more important to ~~peoples~~ than meals and

eatings. Every culture has elaborate rituals connected with foods. After all,

we are all interested in the natures of the food we eat. Every culture has

its own ideas about what a good nutrition is. For example, in some parts

of Asia, food is divided into two groups — "cooling" and "warming." In

Japan, for example, eels are eaten during warm weathers because eels are

believed to help cool the bloods. (6)

Editing Practice 2

Correct all errors involving noncount nouns in the following paragraph using the first correction as a model. Also make whatever other changes are necessary for the corrected sentences to be grammatically correct. The number in parentheses at the end of the paragraph indicates how many errors you should find.

                                                     knowledge is

In the United States, despite what scientific ~~knowledges are~~ telling

us about food and healths, our eating habits are about the worst in the

world. One of the things that strikes most foreign visitors is how much

obesities they see. Researches show that Americans are consuming about

200 calories a day more than they did ten years ago. It is interesting that

while overeatings have increased in the last decade, nearly every other

health factor has shown a great deal of improvement. Americans now

smoke many fewer cigarettes than they used to, and Americans drink

Lesson 32

art
ESL

less alcohols than they used to. Automobile safeties have also improved greatly. Death due to drunk drivings has declined dramatically. Given how health- and safety-conscious we Americans are, it is hard to see why we cannot get our eating problem under control. (7)

Applying What You Know

Examine several paragraphs of a newspaper. How many noncount nouns can you find? Using the list provided in this lesson (on page 322), identify which categories these noncount nouns fall into.

The Bottom Line	**Count nouns** can be made plural, but noncount nouns cannot.

LESSON 33

Using *A/An*, *Some*, and *The*

ESL

EXAMPLE 1	*Definite Article (the) Used Instead of Indefinite Article (a)*

Error: ✗ Masanori had <u>the good idea</u>.

                a

Correction: Masanori had ~~the~~ good idea.

EXAMPLE 2	*Indefinite Article (a) Used Instead of Definite Article (the)*

Error: ✗ Effie stepped into a telephone booth and picked up <u>a phone</u>.

Correction: Effie stepped into a telephone booth and picked

            the

            up ~~a~~ phone.

What's the Problem?

English has two different types of articles used with nouns: **definite** and **indefinite**:

- The **definite article** is always *the*, which is used with all types of **common nouns** (singular and plural, **count** and **noncount**).

- The **indefinite article** is more complicated. The indefinite articles *a* and *an* are used *only* with singular count nouns (*a truck, an apple*). *Some* is used with plural count nouns (*some trucks, some apples*) and all noncount nouns (*some violence, some water*).

The family of articles is represented in this diagram:

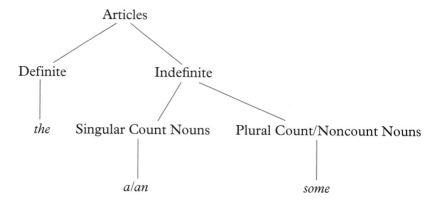

Every time you use a common noun, you must decide which type of article to use. Use the definite article *the* if BOTH of the following statements are true about the noun: (1) you have a specific person, place, thing, or idea in mind, and (2) you can reasonably assume that the reader will know *which* specific noun you mean. Use the indefinite articles *a/an* and *some* when EITHER (1) you do not have a particular person, place, thing, or idea in mind, or (2) you have a particular noun in mind, but you do not assume that the reader can identify *which* one you are talking about.

Diagnostic Exercise

CORRECTED SENTENCES APPEAR ON PAGE 482.

Correct all errors in the following paragraph using the first correction as a model. The number in parentheses at the end of the paragraph indicates how many errors you should find.

Doctors have long known that we need to have iron in our diets.
Recently, however, ~~the~~ new study has revealed that we may be getting too
          ^a
much iron. The human body keeps all an iron it digests. An only way we
lose stored iron in a body is through bleeding. John Murray, the researcher
at the University of Minnesota, discovered that people who live on the
very low iron diet may have the greatly reduced risk of the heart attack.
Another study found that diets high in meat have the strong correlation

with a high risk of heart disease. Apparently, when people have the high

level of iron, excess iron may worsen the effect of cholesterol. (10)

Fixing This Problem in Your Writing

Here are four tips that will help you decide which article to use.

> **PREVIOUS-MENTION TIP** Use the definite article *the* if you have already mentioned the noun.

Suppose Example 1 occurred in the following context:

> Masanori was working on his newest book. ✗ He couldn't think of a title, but then he had <u>the good idea</u>.

Because Masanori's good idea has not been mentioned previously, the sentence should use the indefinite article *a* instead of the definite article *the*:

Tip applied: . . . but then he had ~~the~~ *a* good idea.

Now suppose that this was the next sentence in the example:

> He thought that the idea for the title was promising.

When we apply the Previous-Mention Tip to this sentence, we see that the definite article *the* is correct because the noun *idea* has already been mentioned in the previous sentence.

> **DEFINED-BY-MODIFIERS TIP** Use the definite article *the* if the noun is followed by a word or words that uniquely identify the noun.

Some nouns are followed by *restrictive modifiers*, words that specifically identify the particular noun in question. As a result, the reader can tell which specific noun the writer is referring to, so these nouns require a definite article *even if the noun has not been mentioned previously*. Here are some nouns defined by restrictive modifiers. All of these nouns, even when mentioned for the first time, require the definite article *the*:

DEFINITE
ARTICLE NOUN + RESTRICTIVE MODIFIER

The cat on our porch belongs to a neighbor.

DEFINITE
ARTICLE NOUN + RESTRICTIVE MODIFIER

The cat sitting on the porch belongs to a neighbor.

DEFINITE
ARTICLE NOUN + RESTRICTIVE MODIFIER

The cat that was sitting on the porch belongs to a neighbor.

> **NORMAL-EXPECTATIONS TIP**   Use the definite article *the* if the noun meets our normal expectations about the way things work.

Let's apply this tip to Example 2:

Example 2:   ✗ Effie went into a telephone booth and picked up **a phone.**

Even though the noun *phone* has not been mentioned, the writer should have used the definite article *the* because the reader expects telephone booths to contain phones:

Tip applied: ✗ Effie went into a telephone booth and picked up
                   the
                   ~~a~~ phone.
                   ^

> **UNIQUENESS TIP**   Use the definite article *the* if the noun is unique and everybody would be expected to know about it.

Tip applied: The sun was beginning to rise above the horizon.

Unless you are writing a science-fiction novel, our planet has only one sun and one horizon, and everybody already knows about them. Even though *sun* and *horizon* have not been mentioned before, it would be wrong to use the indefinite article with these two nouns (✗ *A sun was beginning to rise above a horizon*) because it would incorrectly imply that there are multiple suns and multiple horizons.

Lesson 33

art
ESL

✳ *Putting It All Together*

Identify Errors in Using Definite and Indefinite Articles

_____ As you proofread your paper, ask yourself the following questions about the common nouns you are using:

- Have you already mentioned the noun?
- Is the noun followed by a restrictive modifier?

> - Does the noun meet normal expectations about how things work?
> - Is the noun something unique (such as the sun) that everybody already knows about?
>
> ## Correct Errors in Using Definite and Indefinite Articles
>
> ____ If you answer yes to ANY of the questions above, use the definite article *the*.
>
> ____ If you answer no to ALL of the questions above, use the indefinite articles *a/an* or *some*. Use *a/an* with singular count nouns and use *some* with plural count nouns and all noncount nouns.

Sentence Practice 1

CORRECTED SENTENCES APPEAR ON PAGE 482.

The following sentences contain one or more correct uses of the word *the* (underlined). Assume that there is no previous context that these sentences refer to. In each case, indicate which of the four tips in this lesson provides your reason for using the definite article.

> *Example:*   I love my new car, although <u>the</u> brakes are pretty noisy.
>
> *Reason:*   *Normal expectations. We expect cars to have brakes.*

1. We didn't get lost because we could see <u>the</u> North Star.
   Reason:

2. <u>The</u> walnuts you brought have not been shelled.
   Reason:

3. When we got to their house, <u>the</u> lights were all off.
   Reason:

4. Have you heard <u>the</u> rumor about what Harry and Sally did?
   Reason:

5. When people visit a castle, they always want to see <u>the</u> dungeon.
   Reason:

Lesson 33

art
ESL

For more practice using articles, go to **Exercise Central** at **bedfordstmartins.com/commonsense**

Sentence Practice 2

CORRECTED SENTENCES APPEAR ON PAGE 482.

The following sentences contain one or more correct uses of the word *the* (underlined). Assume that there is no previous context that these sentences refer to. In each case, indicate which of the four tips in this lesson provides your reason for using the definite article.

> *Example:*   We saw <u>the</u> movie version of *The Lord of the Rings.*
>
> *Reason:*   *Defined-by-modifiers. The modifying prepositional phrase tells which movie we saw.*

1. If you really liked a movie, you can usually buy <u>the</u> sound track.
    Reason:

2. Before we start on a long hike, we always check <u>the</u> weather.
    Reason:

3. <u>The</u> joke that Louise told was not very funny.
    Reason:

4. A storm far out to sea was making <u>the</u> waves higher than normal.
    Reason:

5. <u>The</u> article that Professor Chou assigned was pretty interesting.
    Reason:

Sentence Practice 3

Fill in the blanks with the correct article: *the* or *a/an.*

Lesson 33

art
ESL

> *Example:*   I took __*a*__ picture of __*the*__ New York skyline.

1. We got _____ city map and found _____ location of _____ restaurant we were going to.

2. I made _____ mistake on _____ first question on _____ exam in chemistry.

3. When they got to _____ airport in Denver, they had to wait _____ hour.

4. There was _____ truck parked in _____ parking lot next to Safeway.

5. After I got home, I went into _____ kitchen and fixed myself _____ sandwich.

Editing Practice 1

CORRECTED SENTENCES APPEAR ON PAGE 482.

Correct all the errors involving definite and indefinite articles in the following paragraph using the first correction as a model. The number in parentheses at the end of the paragraph indicates how many errors you should find.

> *an*
> Like many young people just out of school, I recently moved into ~~the~~
> ^
> apartment. I was on my own for the first time. I rented the unfurnished
> apartment because it was a lot cheaper than getting one already furnished.
> As is normally the case in the United States, an apartment came already
> furnished with the stove and refrigerator. (This is not the case in Europe.
> The friends of mine rented the apartment in Rome for the semester
> abroad program. The unfurnished apartment there did not even have
> the sink, let alone any kitchen appliances.) I decided that a kitchen had
> to be my highest priority. I bought the set of dishes and the pots and pans
> at the big chain store. My parents gave me the old set of kitchen utensils.
> I went to Goodwill and got the really cheap kitchen table and four wobbly
> chairs. With that plus my sleeping bag and air mattress, I was ready to
> move in. (14)

Lesson 33

art
ESL

Editing Practice 2

Correct all the errors involving definite and indefinite articles in the following paragraph using the first correction as a model. The number in parentheses at the end of the paragraph indicates how many errors you should find.

Eventually, of course, I needed a lot more stuff. I could get along

without ~~the~~ _a desk since I could always use a kitchen table for writing. I had

no comfortable place to sit down, so I had to get the living room furniture.

I decided against getting the couch because it would take up too much

space; instead I got the armchairs on sale. I could arrange some armchairs

any way I needed to use them. I thought about buying the TV, but the

new plasma screens are so expensive that I finally decided to just borrow

the unused TV set from my parents. Eventually I would like to get the

real bed, but that will have to wait until I get a few more paychecks. After

seeing what happened to the friends of mine who got into financial trouble

by furnishing their new apartment with credit cards, I decided that if I

couldn't pay cash for furniture, I could get along without it. (9)

Applying What You Know

Photocopy a couple of paragraphs from something you are reading. Go through the copy and cross out every article so that you can no longer tell what the article was. Set the text aside for a while and then see if you can get all the articles right.

	The Bottom Line	Use *the* only when readers will know what **the** noun refers to.

Making Generalizations without Articles

ESL

Error: ✗ The barn is always full of some mice.

Correction: The barn is always full of ~~some~~ mice.

Error: ✗ Our family usually has the fish for dinner on Fridays.

Correction: Our family usually has ~~the~~ fish for dinner on Fridays.

What's the Problem?

Generally speaking, common nouns in English must be preceded by an **article** (*a/an, some,* or *the*) or a **modifier** like a number or a possessive pronoun (*his, her, your, their, our*). However, there is one major exception to this rule: to make a generalization about something, we must use a noun without any articles.

For instance, in Example 1, the writer is not talking about any specific mice. Rather, the writer is making a generalization about the *category* of animals that live in the barn. Therefore, the writer should use *mice* by itself, without any article.

In Example 2, the writer makes a generalization about the family's typical meal on Fridays. Therefore, the writer should have used *fish* by itself, without any article.

Diagnostic Exercise

CORRECTED SENTENCES APPEAR ON PAGE 482.

Correct all errors in the following paragraph using the first correction as a model. The number in parentheses at the end of the paragraph indicates how many errors you should find.

Scientists

~~The scientists~~ have long known that the honeybees are somehow able
                       ^

to tell some other bees where to look for some food. In the 1940's, Karl von

Frisch of the University of Munich discovered that the type of the dance

that the bees make when they return to their beehive is significant. It

seems that the honeybees are able to signal both the direction of the food

that they found and its approximate distance from their hive to the bees

who had remained at the hive. (6)

Fixing This Problem in Your Writing

Anytime you use a **noncount noun** or a plural **count noun**, check to see
whether you are using that noun as part of a generalization. If so, then you
should not use an article.

Following are some tips that will help you recognize the kinds of sentences in which noncount or plural count nouns are being used to make a
generalization and therefore do not require an article in front of them.

> **ADVERB-OF-FREQUENCY TIP** Look for adverbs of frequency such as *always,
> often, generally, frequently,* or *usually.* Adverbs of frequency are often used in
> sentences that describe habitual or repeated actions—typically a sign of a
> generalization.

Notice that both of the example sentences contain adverbs of frequency, a
signal that the sentences are making a generalization about a noun and therefore should not use an article:

Tip applied: The barn is <u>always</u> full of ~~some~~ mice.

Tip applied: Our family <u>usually</u> has ~~the~~ fish for dinner on Fridays.

> **PRESENT TENSE TIP** Sentences used for making generalizations are nor-
> mally written in the present tense.

Writers usually use the present tense to make generalizations, so be especially
sure to check noncount nouns and plural count nouns in sentences that use
the present tense to see whether these nouns are being used to make generalizations. Notice, for instance, that both of the example sentences are in the

present tense. This is a signal that the sentence might be making a generalization about a noun and, therefore, should not use an article with that noun:

Example 1:	The barn <u>is</u> always full of ~~some~~ mice.
Example 2:	Our family usually <u>has</u> ~~the~~ fish for dinner on Fridays.

NO-MODIFIERS TIP A noun used for making a generalization is not usually restricted by any modifiers that follow the noun.

Modifiers after a noun usually restrict the meaning of the noun so that it is not a generalization about a whole category of things. Compare the following two sentences:

No Post-Noun Modifier:	Cheese is very crumbly.
Post-Noun Modifier:	<u>The</u> cheese <u>in the refrigerator</u> is crumbly.

The first sentence is an unrestricted generalization about all cheese; therefore, the noun *cheese* does not use an article. The second sentence is talking only about the cheese that is *in the refrigerator*. Since the writer is referring to a particular piece of cheese (and not making a generalization about all cheeses), the definite article *the* is needed in this sentence.

MOST TIP A noun that can be modified by the word *most* is probably being used to make a generalization.

For example, you can modify the noun *classes* in the following sentence with the word *most* to confirm that you are using *classes* as a generalization:

Example:	Classes are held in the mornings.
Tip applied:	<u>Most</u> classes are held in the mornings.

Classes, therefore, should be used without any article.

Lesson 34

art
ESL

✳ *Putting It All Together*

Identify Errors in Using Articles

_____ When you use a noncount noun or a plural count noun, check to see whether you are using that noun to make a generalization by asking yourself the following questions:

- Are there adverbs of frequency in the sentence?
- Is the sentence in the present tense? →

> ■ Is the noun in question free from following modifiers?
>
> ■ Can you put *most* in front of the noun in question?
>
> ### Correct Errors in Using Articles
>
> ____ If the answer to one or more of the above questions is yes, then it is likely that the noun is being used to make a generalization, and thus no article should be used.

Sentence Practice 1

CORRECTED SENTENCES APPEAR ON PAGE 482.

In the following sentences, underline any noncount nouns and plural count nouns that are used for making generalizations. Cross out any articles incorrectly used with these nouns. Assume that there is no previous context that these sentences refer to.

> *Example:* ~~The~~ <u>sticks and stones</u> may break my bones, but ~~the~~ <u>words</u> will never hurt me. [traditional saying]

1. Most countries tax the cigarettes and the alcohol heavily.

2. During a heavy storm, the streams often are blocked by the leaves and the other trash.

3. Typically, the employers look for the skilled and trained workers.

4. The researchers have found that the American diets contain the excess fats.

5. The detergents work by making the water super wet.

 For more practice using nouns, go to **Exercise Central** at **bedfordstmartins.com/commonsense**

Lesson 34

art ESL

Sentence Practice 2

CORRECTED SENTENCES APPEAR ON PAGE 483.

In the following sentences, underline any noncount nouns and plural count nouns that are used for making generalizations. Cross out any articles incorrectly used with these nouns. Assume that there is no previous context that these sentences refer to.

> *Example:*   ~~The~~ <u>fools</u> and their money are soon parted.
> **[traditional saying]**

1. The substitutions in the recipes often lead to the disasters.

2. The global warming is becoming a common topic in the academic conferences.

3. Increasingly, the tourism is an important source for the national budgets.

4. The classical painting is normally divided into the landscapes, the still lifes, and the portraits.

5. In America, unlike the many countries, you can usually get the prescriptions filled at the grocery stores.

Sentence Practice 3

Combine the following sentences by adding the underlined information in the second sentence to the underlined noun in the first sentence. The added modification restricts the noun so that it is no longer a generalization. Make the necessary changes in articles.

> *Example:*   **<u>Pianos</u> are pretty expensive.**
> **They are <u>used in public performances</u>.**
>
> *Answer:*   *The pianos used in public performances are pretty expensive.*

1. <u>Seniors</u> are excused from class.
   They are <u>in the school play</u>.

2. <u>Clouds</u> were threatening rain.
   They were <u>in the west</u>.

3. <u>Disputes</u> are hard to resolve.
   They were <u>involved in property rights cases</u>.

4. <u>Tea</u> comes from Japan.
   They <u>serve in this restaurant</u>.

Lesson 34

art
ESL

5.   <u>Malls</u> are now too small.
     They were <u>built in the '70's and '80's.</u>

Editing Practice 1

CORRECTED SENTENCES APPEAR ON PAGE 483.

Correct all the errors involving articles in the following paragraph using the first correction as a model. The number in parentheses at the end of the paragraph indicates how many errors you should find.

Deborah Tannen has written extensively about the different conversational styles of ~~the~~ men and women. Males and females use the casual language in quite different ways, especially when the men are talking to men and the women are talking to women. When the groups of men are in a conversation, each speaker tries to control the topic. The most important tool in gaining and keeping the control is the humor. The humor is usually directed at others in the group, often in the form of the teasing. However, the teasing cannot go too far; it cannot be seen as actually insulting. Being able to be teased without getting angry and then responding in kind is a valued skill. The verbal competition among groups of young men is a near cultural universal. (8)

Editing Practice 2

Correct all the errors involving articles in the following paragraph using the first correction as a model. The number in parentheses at the end of the paragraph indicates how many errors you should find.

Young
~~The young~~ women usually behave quite differently. They are very careful about taking the turns. Even in the animated conversations, women are less likely to interrupt than men are. When they do interrupt,

the interruptions that they make are supportive rather than confrontational. For example, interruptions will often provide the examples that
confirm what the speaker is saying. Women are generally very careful to
avoid the confrontations and even the controversial topics. Typically, the
group is careful to make sure that everyone has plenty of the opportunity
to participate. The entire dynamic of their conversation is to build the
group solidarity. (7)

Applying What You Know

On a separate sheet of paper, write a paragraph or two in which you generalize about the differences in male and female language that you have ob-
served. Do you think Dr. Tannen's generalizations are true? (See Editing
Practices 1–2, which discuss Dr. Tannen's theories.) Identify every noncount
noun and plural count noun in your essay. Then trade papers with a partner
and use the Putting It All Together checklist on page 337 to make sure your
partner has not incorrectly used articles with generalizations.

The Bottom Line	**Nouns** that are used to make **generalizations** are not used with **articles**.

Lesson 34

art
ESL

UNIT TEN ESL: Choosing the Right Article

Every time you use a common noun, you must decide whether or not you need to use an article; if you do need to use an article, you must choose which one it should be. Your choice should be governed by four decisions:

- Decision 1: *Generalization?* Is the noun (whether a noncount noun or a plural count noun) being used to make a generalization (see Lesson 34)? If the answer is yes, use *no* article at all. If the answer is no, then you must make the following decision.

- Decision 2: *Known or New?* Is your intended meaning of the noun "known" to the reader or is it "new" (see Lesson 33)? If the intended meaning is known to the reader, use the definite article *the*. If the meaning will be new, use an indefinite article: *a, an,* or *some*. The choice of indefinite article is determined by the next two decisions.

- Decision 3: *Plural or Singular?* If the new noun is plural, then you must use *some*. If the new noun is singular, then you must decide whether it is a count or a noncount noun. That brings you to the final decision.

- Decision 4: *Count or Noncount?* If the singular noun is a count noun, then you must use the indefinite article *a/an*. If the singular noun is a noncount noun, use *some* (see Lesson 32).

Use one or more of these tips to help you make Decision 1:

ADVERB-OF-FREQUENCY TIP Look for adverbs of frequency such as *always, often, generally, frequently,* or *usually*. Adverbs of frequency are often used in sentences that describe habitual or repeated actions — typically a sign of a generalization.

PRESENT TENSE TIP Sentences used for making generalizations are normally written in the present tense.

NO-MODIFIERS TIP A noun used for making a generalization is not usually restricted by any modifiers that follow the noun.

MOST TIP   A noun that can be modified by the word *most* is probably being used to make a generalization.

Use one or more of these tips to help you make Decision 2:

PREVIOUS-MENTION TIP   Use the definite article *the* if you have already mentioned the noun.

DEFINED-BY-MODIFIERS TIP   Use the definite article *the* if the noun is followed by a word or words that uniquely identify the noun.

NORMAL-EXPECTATIONS TIP   Use the definite article *the* if the noun meets our normal expectations about the way things work.

UNIQUENESS TIP   Use the definite article *the* if the noun is unique and everybody would be expected to know about it.

Use these tips to help you make Decisions 3 and 4:

GENERAL CATEGORIES TIP   Most noncount nouns are generic names for categories of things.

OTHER NONCOUNT CATEGORIES TIP   Most noncount nouns fall into the following categories: abstractions, academic fields, food, gerunds (words ending in *-ing* used as nouns), languages, liquids and gases, materials, natural phenomena, sports and games, and weather words.

Unit Ten

review
ESL

Use a decision tree to help you choose the right article

The *decision tree* on the next page maps out a process for choosing the right article for each common noun in your writing. Using this tool, you can proceed step by step from Decision 1 to Decision 4.

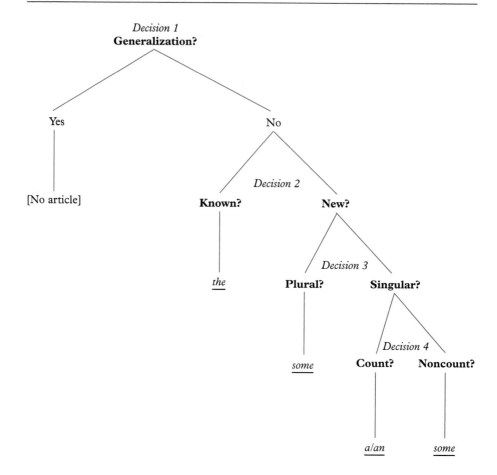

Review Test

The decision tree above shows you how these four sets of decisions flow step by step from Decision 1 to Decision 4. Use the decision tree to edit the following paragraphs for correct use of articles. The number in parentheses at the end of each paragraph indicates how many errors you should find.

Some cellular phones can certainly come in handy in a emergency. If the driver witnesses an accident or is involved in an accident, he or she can call a State Police without having to waste crucial time. In the event of the flat tire or dead battery, a driver can call tow truck without having to walk a mile or two—or more—to a phone. Wireless technology has allowed the family members to reach loved ones in an emergency, even if the person whom they are trying to reach is at the business meeting or a baseball game. (9)

For me, a beauty of having the cell phone is being able to maximize my time. I like having a flexibility to make the important phone calls either when I'm home or as I'm driving home. (4)

Using Verbs Correctly

Terms That Can Help You Understand Verbs

If you are not familiar with any of the following terms, look them up in the Guide to Grammar Terminology beginning on page 435.

adjective	preposition
adverb	prepositional phrase
helping verb	progressive tense
information question	separable two-word verb
inseparable two-word verb	subject
noun clause	two-word verb
object	verb

The Nuts and Bolts of Verbs

ESL

All of the lessons in this unit deal with various aspects of **verb** use that are likely to be troublesome for non-native speakers.

Lesson 35 shows you how to use the **progressive tenses**, which are made with the helping verb *be* (in some form) followed by a verb in the *-ing* form. The progressive tense signals that an action was, is, or will be in progress at some specific moment in time (*Rina is watching TV now*). Some writers do not use the progressive tense when they should, or use it when they shouldn't. Others mistakenly use the progressive tense with certain verbs that do not allow the use of progressive tenses. Here is an example of the first kind of mistake.

Example: Dr. Hernandez can't see you right now. ✗ She talks with another patient.

Correction: Dr. Hernandez can't see you right now. She ~~talks~~ with another patient.
is talking

346

Lesson 36 shows you how to use **two-word verbs**. When a two-word verb (or phrasal verb) is made with an adverb, it is called a **separable two-word verb** because the adverb can be separated from the verb. That is, it can be moved after the object (*Jamie looked up the word* / *Jamie looked the word up*). When the compound is made with a preposition, it is called an **inseparable two-word verb** because the preposition can never be moved away from the verb (*Ben depended on Maria* / ✗ *Ben depended Maria on*). Sometimes writers confuse the two types of two-word verbs and don't move adverbs when they should, or they move prepositions when they shouldn't.

Example: ✗ I didn't know her phone number, so I looked up it.

Correction: I didn't know her phone number, so I ~~looked up it~~. *looked it up*

Lesson 37 shows you how to check for the proper word order in **information questions**. Information questions are questions that begin with words that require a detailed response like *who, where,* and *why* (as opposed to simple questions that can be answered with *yes* or *no*). Sometimes non-native speakers fail to invert the helping verb and the subject word when forming information questions.

Example: ✗ Where you want to go after class?

Correction: Where ~~you want~~ to go after class? *do you want*

Lesson 38 shows you how you can avoid the reverse mistake of inverting the helping verb and the subject, which is appropriate for information questions, when you are creating certain types of **noun clauses**.

Example: ✗ We found out where should we go after class.

Correction: We found out where ~~should we go~~ after class. *we should go*

ESL

The Progressive Tenses

EXAMPLE 1   *Present Tense Used Instead of Progressive Tense*

Error: ✗ I can't talk to you right now. I <u>study</u> for my exams.

Correction: I can't talk to you right now. I ~~study~~ for my exams.
              am studying ^

EXAMPLE 2   *Progressive Tense Used Incorrectly*

Error: ✗ Ms. Higa <u>was owning</u> a house in San Francisco then.

Correction: Ms. Higa ~~was owning~~ a house in San Francisco then.
              owned ^

What's the Problem?

The **progressive tenses** are formed by using some form of the helping verb *be* with a **present participle** (a verb form ending in *-ing*). The progressive tenses are used to indicate continuous activity. There are three forms of progressive verbs:

- The *present progressive tense* uses the helping verb *be* in one of its three present tense forms (*am, are, is*); for example: *I <u>am</u> smiling. They <u>are</u> smiling. She <u>is</u> smiling.*

- The *past progressive tense* uses the helping verb *be* in one of its two past tense forms (*was, were*); for example: *He <u>was</u> smiling. They <u>were</u> smiling.*

- The *future progressive tense* uses *will* with the helping verb *be*; for example: *They <u>will be</u> smiling.*

There are two common types of mistakes in using the progressive tense. The first one is mistakenly using the present tense when the present progressive tense should be used, or vice versa. In Example 1, for instance, the writer incorrectly used the present tense *study* instead of the present progressive tense *am studying*.

The second type of mistake is using any of the progressive tenses with certain verbs that cannot logically take a progressive form because they do not describe an action that occurs over a definite moment of time. We call these verbs *steady-state verbs*. The verb *own* in Example 2 is an example of a steady-state verb that cannot be used in the progressive tense. We'll discuss such steady-state verbs in more detail later in the lesson.

Diagnostic Exercise

CORRECTED SENTENCES APPEAR ON PAGE 483.

Correct all errors in the following paragraph using the first correction as a model. The number in parentheses at the end of the paragraph indicates how many errors you should find.

Every weekday morning at 6 A.M., my alarm ~~is going~~ goes off. By 6:15, the breakfast dishes are on the table, and the coffee brews. I always am getting the children up next. It is very hard for them to get going. On Mondays, they are resembling bears coming out of hibernation. While they take their showers with their eyes still closed, I get everyone's clothes ready. Since the youngest child still is needing a lot of help getting dressed, I usually am spending some extra time with her talking about the day's events. By 7 A.M., we all sit at the table for breakfast. The children are loving pancakes and waffles, but there just isn't time to make them except on weekends. Breakfast goes by quickly, unless somebody is spilling the milk or juice. I am wishing we had more time in the morning, but every morning I am being amazed when I am looking back and realizing that we got it all done again. (13)

Fixing This Problem in Your Writing

To avoid progressive verb mistakes, we first need to understand the basic difference in meaning between the present tense and the present progressive tense.

Lesson 35

vt
ESL

We saw in Lesson 6 that the main function of the present tense in English is to make "timeless" statements or generalizations about events that happen all the time. The present progressive tense is used to talk about what is happening at the exact present moment of time. Compare the following sentences:

Present Tense: I <u>study</u> English every day.

Present Progressive: I <u>am studying</u> English right now.

Both sentences are grammatical, but they mean different things. The present tense sentence is a generalization about the speaker's study habits (he or she studies every day), but it does not tell us what the speaker is actually doing at this moment. For all we know, the speaker is out watching a kung-fu movie with a friend.

The present progressive tense sentence, however, tells us what the speaker is in the process of doing *at the present moment* (he or she is studying English). The sentence tells us nothing about the speaker's study habits. This may be the first and last time that the speaker will ever study English.

As you might guess, the future progressive is used to describe an action that will be in progress at some future point in time, for example:

Future Progressive: I <u>will be working</u> on my paper all next weekend.

Likewise, the past progressive is used to describe an action that was in progress at some past moment of time, for example:

Past Progressive: I <u>was working</u> on my paper when you called.

Here is a tip to help you remember when to use the progressive tenses.

THE PROGRESSIVE TIP   If an action is in progress at some moment of time, use a progressive (*-ing*) form of the verb.

As you saw in Example 2 at the beginning of the lesson, some verbs cannot be used in a progressive form. These *steady-state verbs* are used to describe conditions or states that are unchanging over a long period of time. The unchanging nature of these verbs makes them incompatible with the in-progress, "right now" nature of the progressive tense. For example, compare the following progressive sentences:

Maria **is studying** for the exam.

✗ Maria **is knowing** the answer.

The progressive tense is grammatical in the first sentence, but not in the second. *Studying* is an action that progresses — it starts, goes on for a while, and then ends. The progressive tense correctly conveys this meaning. *Knowing* something, however, is a state of being. It is not an action that occurs over a definite period of time, so it cannot form the progressive tense.

Here is a tip that will help you identify steady-state verbs.

> **STEADY-STATE VERB TIP** Verbs that refer to unchanging, steady-state conditions cannot form the progressive tense. Most steady-state verbs fall into three broad categories: mental activity, emotional condition, and possession.

Here are some examples of steady-state verbs:

- **Mental activity:** *believe, doubt, forget, imagine, know, mean*

- **Emotional condition:** *appreciate, care, dislike, envy, fear, hate, like, love, need, prefer, want*

- **Possession:** *belong, consist of, contain, own, possess*

This list is far from complete. Moreover, some verbs on this list cannot be used with progressive tenses when they have one meaning, but can be used with progressive tenses when they have another meaning. For example, verbs of sense perception cannot be used in the progressive when they describe something:

✗ The soup <u>is tasting</u> too salty.

However, the same verb *can* be used in the progressive when a person physically performs the action of the verb:

The cook <u>is tasting</u> the soup to see if it needs more salt.

The following box shows additional examples of steady-state verbs.

✳ *More Examples*

Mental Activity

Error: ✗ I <u>am thinking</u> that you are right.

Correction: I ~~am thinking~~ that you are right.
                    think

Emotional Condition

Error: ✗ Hiroshi <u>is loving</u> his new job.

Correction: Hiroshi ~~is loving~~ his new job.
                    loves

Possession

Error: ✗ Juan <u>is belonging</u> to the student union.

Correction: Juan <s>is belonging</s> to the student union.
                    belongs
                    ^

✳ *Putting It All Together*

Identify Errors in Using the Progressive Tenses

_____ Check to see whether a verb is describing a continuous, "in-progress" action — an action that progressed, is progressing, or will progress over some particular moment of time.

Correct Errors in Using the Progressive Tenses

_____ If you are describing an action that progressed, is progressing, or will progress over some particular moment of time, use the appropriate progressive tense (form of *be* + a verb ending in *-ing*).

_____ If the verb describes an unchanging condition or state of being, check to see whether the meaning of the verb is a mental activity, emotional condition, or possession. If it does have one of these meanings, then do *not* use the progressive tense.

Sentence Practice 1

CORRECTED SENTENCES APPEAR ON PAGE 483.

The following sentences contain verbs in their dictionary form (underlined). Above each underlined verb, write the correct form of the verb using either the present tense, the past tense, or one of the three progressive tenses, as appropriate.

CORRECTED SENTENCES APPEAR ON PAGE 483.

Example: *was playing*
                I couldn't hear you. The TV <u>play</u> too loudly.

1. Hurry up! The train <u>leave</u> now.

2. I couldn't come to the phone because we <u>eat</u> dinner when you called.

3. Disco <u>be</u> still wildly popular in some places in Europe.

Lesson 35

vt
ESL

4. The book <u>belong</u> to one of my friends.

5. The book <u>be</u> used by one of my friends at the moment.

 For more practice with verb tense, go to **Exercise Central** at **bedfordstmartins.com/commonsense**

Sentence Practice 2

CORRECTED SENTENCES APPEAR ON PAGE 483.

The following sentences contain verbs in their dictionary form (underlined). Above each underlined verb, write the correct form of the verb using either the present tense, the past tense, or one of the three progressive tenses, as appropriate.

Example: During the whole exam, somebody <u>cough</u> his head off.
was coughing

1. By this time next year, I <u>work</u> in New York.

2. As of now, that <u>seem</u> to be the best alternative.

3. My roommate always <u>hate</u> to get up in the morning.

4. She <u>run</u> an errand right now, but she will be back in just a minute.

5. Hi! I <u>return</u> your phone call.

Sentence Practice 3

Combine the following sentences by adding the underlined information in the second sentence to the first sentence. Change the past tense of the first sentence to the appropriate progressive tense.

Example: I flew to Chicago.
It will be <u>this time tomorrow.</u>

Answer: *I will be flying to Chicago this time tomorrow.*

1. I'm sorry. She met with another client.
It is <u>now</u>.

Lesson 35

vt
ESL

2.   She met with another client.
      It was <u>when you called</u>.

3.   We painted the garage.
      We did it <u>when the rain storm hit</u>.

4.   I slept soundly.
      I did it <u>when the alarm went off</u>.

5.   I took my last exam.
      It will happen <u>when you get here</u>.

Editing Practice 1

CORRECTED SENTENCES APPEAR ON PAGE 484.

Correct all errors involving the progressive tenses in the following paragraph using the first correction as a model. The number in parentheses at the end of the paragraph indicates how many errors you should find.

      think

I ~~am thinking~~ that I would go crazy if I tried to write the way
      ^

my husband does. I am spending just as much time on my papers as he

does, but I am writing in a completely different way. I am spending much

of my time thinking through what I am going to say before I ever put a

word down on paper. When I am feeling that I really know what I want

to say, I sit down and write a complete draft. Then I make an outline for

what I have written. Often this outline is showing me where I need to go

back and expand an idea or rearrange something. But, on the whole, I am

not needing to make a lot of changes. My husband is thinking that I am a

lazy writer, but he is wrong. Just because I don't sit at my computer for

hours on end doesn't mean I am not working. (7)

Lesson 35

vt
ESL

Editing Practice 2

Correct all errors involving the progressive tenses in the following paragraphs using the first correction as a model. The number in parentheses at the end of each paragraph indicates how many errors you should find.

compose
Despite the fact that we ~~are composing~~ our papers in totally
^

different ways, we end up at the same point — papers that are needing to be

proofread. We have both learned the hard way that neither one of us is very

good at catching our own mistakes. My husband is an especially bad speller.

He is relying a lot (too much, in my opinion) on his computer's spell-

checker. The spell-checker is wonderful, but it can be a bit of a trap. He is

believing that once he has run the spell-checker, he can forget about spelling

errors. Well, he is wrong. He is having the tendency to make mistakes with

little words. For example, he is often typing *and* for *an* or *as*, *the* for *they*,

and *your* for *you*. The trouble is that the spell-checker doesn't see these little

word substitutions as mistakes, so it is never correcting them. (6)

I tell him it is impossible to read for meaning and read for mechani-

cal errors at the same time. The best way to catch mistakes in grammar,

spelling, and punctuation is to proofread each other's papers. Even then,

we are needing to read very slowly. One trick that is seeming to work is to

proofread backwards. That is, we are starting at the last sentence in each

paragraph. We proofread it. Then we read the next-to-last sentence, and so

on, working our way to the beginning of the paragraph. This is very tedious,

but it seems to work because we are being able to concentrate just on

mechanics without getting distracted by the meaning of the paper. (4)

Lesson 35

vt
ESL

Applying What You Know

On your own paper, write a paragraph or two about your own writing process. Use the Putting It All Together checklist on page 352 to make sure that you have used the present and progressive tenses correctly.

The Bottom Line	The progressive tenses are used for events that **are taking** place at a particular moment of time.

Two-Word Verbs

ESL

[*Note:* See pages 454–456 for a glossary of one hundred commonly used separable two-word verbs.]

EXAMPLE 1

Error: ✗ Roland <u>called up her</u>.

Correction: Roland called ~~up~~ her.
up

EXAMPLE 2

Error: ✗ Misako <u>turned down them</u>.

Correction: Misako turned ~~down~~ them.
down

What's the Problem?

Most **verbs** in English can be combined with an **adverb** or a **preposition** to form a **two-word verb** (also known as *a phrasal verb*). Two-word verbs are very common in English but can pose problems for non-native speakers. One problem is that it is difficult to determine the meaning of a two-word verb based on the meanings of its individual words. Consider the expression *come by*:

How did you <u>come by</u> that picture?

Come by means to "get" or "obtain," but you couldn't know that just by looking at the words *come* and *by*.

Another problem with two-word verbs is a grammatical one. There are two types of two-word verbs: *separable* and *inseparable*:

- **Separable Two-Word Verb = Verb + Adverb**

 VERB   ADVERB
 The prince <u>turned</u> <u>down</u> the king.

 Turned down = rejected

▪ Inseparable Two-Word Verb = Verb + Preposition

VERB   PREPOSITION

The prince <u>turned</u> <u>against</u> the king.

Turned against = became an enemy of

When we use a **separable two-word verb**, the adverb can be separated from the verb (thus the term *separable*) and moved to a position immediately *after* the object. Here is an example:

Before: The prince <u>turned</u> <u>down</u> the king.

After: The prince <u>turned</u> (down) the king.
                [The prince <u>turned</u> the king <u>down</u>.]

When the object is a noun, as in the example above, the two-word verb is correct whether it is separated or not. However, if the object is a **pronoun**, the adverb MUST be moved after the pronoun:

Before: ✗ The prince <u>turned</u> <u>down</u> him.

After: The prince <u>turned</u> (down) him.
                [The prince <u>turned</u> him <u>down</u>.]

When we use an **inseparable two-word verb**, the preposition *cannot* be separated from the verb (thus the term *inseparable*). Here is an example:

Before: The prince <u>turned</u> <u>against</u> the king.

After: ✗ The prince <u>turned</u> (against) the king.
                [✗ The prince <u>turned</u> the king <u>against</u>.]

The problem that non-native speakers face is telling separable and inseparable two-word verbs apart. Later in the lesson we'll offer some tips you can use to help you differentiate between the two.

Lesson 36

vf
ESL

Diagnostic Exercise

CORRECTED SENTENCES APPEAR ON PAGE 484.

Correct all two-word verb errors in the following paragraph using the first correction as a model. The number in parentheses at the end of the paragraph indicates how many errors you should find.

It used to be that making a plane reservation was a simple matter. You found a travel agency and ~~called up it~~ *called it up*. Since the agency didn't work for any airlines, it looked for the best fare and found out it. There was no direct cost to you since the airlines paid the commission; they built in it to the price of your ticket. After the airlines were deregulated, however, this system began to fall apart. Faced with much greater competition, airlines identified commission costs as an unnecessary expense, and they cut down them by reducing the commission they paid agencies. Some airlines, like Southwest, even cut out them entirely. As a result, most travel agencies stopped selling tickets for those airlines. If you want to know about their fares, you must deal with each of the airlines separately. The catch, of course, is that if you call one of them, its representative can talk only about its fares, and you have no way to check out it to see if you have the best bargain. (5)

Fixing This Problem in Your Writing

Here are the ten most common adverbs used in *separable* two-word verbs:

apart	away	down	out	together
around	back	off	over	up

When you see one of these words in a two-word verb, you can be fairly sure that the verb and adverb are separable. The point to keep in mind is that when a separable two-word verb is followed by a *noun*, you have the option of separating the verb and the adverb. However, when the two-word verb is followed by a *pronoun*, then you MUST separate the verb and the adverb.

Look at the following examples of separable two-word verbs. Notice the difference in the position of the adverb when the adverb is followed by a *noun* and when it is followed by a *pronoun*. The first sentence in each pair has a noun object, and the second in each pair has a pronoun object.

SEPARABLE TWO-WORD VERBS

Verb + Adverb	Meaning	Example
take apart	disassemble	We **took apart** the bicycle. We **took** it **apart**.
show around	give a tour to	We **showed around** the visitors. We **showed** them **around**.
throw away	discard	We **threw away** the boxes. We **threw** them **away**.
put back	replace	We **put back** the books. We **put** them **back**.
break down	categorize	We **broke down** the addresses by zip code. We **broke** them **down** by zip code.
call off	cancel	We **called off** the meeting. We **called** it **off**.
find out	discover	We **found out** the truth. We **found** it **out**.
talk over	discuss	We **talked over** the situation. We **talked** it **over**.
keep together	group/bunch	We **kept together** all the loose papers. We **kept** them **together**.
hang up	disconnect	We **hung up** the phone. We **hung** it **up**.

Probably the most useful way to distinguish between *separable* and *inseparable* two-word verbs is to see if the word following the two-word verb can be used in a **prepositional phrase**. If it can, it is a preposition and can't be separated from the verb it is next to. Use the following tip to determine whether the second word in a two-word verb is a preposition.

Lesson 36

vf
ESL

THE MOVIES TIP   If the second word in a two-word verb can be used to form a prepositional phrase with *the movies*, it is a preposition and, thus, inseparable from the verb. If it does not work with *the movies*, it is an adverb and, thus, separable from the verb.

Let's apply *The Movies* Tip to the first example:

 Example 1: ✗ Roland <u>called</u> <u>up</u> her.

 Tip applied: ✗ <u>up</u> the movies

Because *up the movies* does not make sense, we know that *up* is not a preposition. Thus, *up* is an adverb and is separable from the verb. Because the object in this sentence is a pronoun (*her*), *up* MUST be separated from the verb:

           up
 Correction: Roland called ~~up~~ her.
            ^

Now let's apply *The Movies* Tip to the second example sentence:

 Example 2: ✗ Misako <u>turned</u> <u>down</u> them.

 Tip applied: ✗ <u>down</u> the movies

Once again, when we apply *The Movies* Tip we see that *down the movies* does not make sense, so we know that *down* is not a preposition. Thus, *down* is an adverb and MUST be moved *after* the object since the object is a pronoun:

            down
 Correction: Misako turned ~~down~~ them.
             ^

Here is an example with an inseparable two-word verb:

 Example: We <u>stopped at</u> a fast-food restaurant for lunch.

 Tip applied: <u>at</u> the movies

Since *at* makes sense with *the movies* as an object, we can reasonably predict that *stop at* is an inseparable two-word verb. If we replaced the noun phrase *a fast-food restaurant* with the pronoun *it*, we would not move the preposition:

 Example: We <u>stopped at</u> it for lunch.

  Two additional words — *in* and *on* — are commonly used in two-word verbs, either as adverbs in separable two-word verbs or as prepositions in inseparable two-word verbs. Here are some examples.

IN AND *ON* AS ADVERBS (SEPARABLE)

Verb + Adverb	*Meaning*	*Example*
turn in	submit	We **turned in** our papers. We **turned** them **in**.
turn on	activate	We **turned on** the radio. We **turned** it **on**.

IN AND *ON* AS PREPOSITIONS (INSEPARABLE)

Verb + Adverb	Meaning	Example
look into	investigate	The FBI will **look into** the bombing.
		The FBI will **look into** it.
call on	visit	We **called on** some friends.
		We **called on** them.

Unfortunately, *The Movies* Tip does not help with two-word verbs that use *in* or *on* since these words can be either adverbs or prepositions. By listening to native speakers use these words and by using them in your own speaking and writing, you will soon learn the correct uses of two-word verbs with *in* and *on*.

✳ *Putting It All Together*

Identify Two-Word Verb Errors

_____ Use *The Movies* Tip to help distinguish between separable (verb + adverb) and inseparable (verb + preposition) two-word verbs.

Correct Two-Word Verb Errors

_____ If a separable two-word verb is followed by an object noun, you have the option of placing the adverb before or after the noun.

_____ If a separable two-word verb is followed by an object pronoun, you *must* move the adverb to follow the pronoun.

_____ Inseparable two-word verbs must *never* be separated by nouns or pronouns.

Sentence Practice 1

CORRECTED SENTENCES APPEAR ON PAGE 484.

Correct the errors in the underlined two-word verbs. If the sentence is correct as is, write *OK* above it. Use *The Movies* Tip to confirm your answer.

Lesson 36

vf
ESL

Example: I took my books to the desk to ~~check out them~~.

         check them out

Confirmation: *out the movies (adverb = separable)*

1. She emphasized the point to <u>get across it</u>.

2. The children <u>argued about it</u>.

3. I promised to <u>pay back them</u>.

4. The news <u>cheered up them</u> enormously.

5. We promised to <u>bring back them</u> as soon as we could.

 For more practice using two-word verbs, go to **Exercise Central** at **bedfordstmartins.com/commonsense**

Sentence Practice 2

CORRECTED SENTENCES APPEAR ON PAGE 484.

Correct the errors in the underlined two-word verbs. If the sentence is correct as is, write *OK* above it. Use *The Movies* Tip to confirm your answer.

Example: It never <u>occurred to me</u>.
                                                OK

Confirmation: *to the movies (preposition = inseparable)*

1. Jason really liked her, so he <u>asked out her</u>.

2. I don't believe what he said. I think he just <u>dreamed up it</u>.

3. They are afraid that they <u>let down us</u>.

4. The project didn't get full funding, so we had to <u>scale back it</u>.

5. He was <u>punished it for</u>.

Sentence Practice 3

Replace the underlined objects with an appropriate pronoun. If the pronoun follows a separable two-word verb (verb + adverb), then move the adverb to follow the pronoun. If the pronoun follows an inseparable two-word verb (verb + preposition), do not move it.

Lesson 36

vf
ESL

Example: Round up <u>the usual suspects</u>.

Answer: *Round them up.*

1. I was done, so I put away <u>my books</u>.

2. The flashlight kept slipping from <u>my fingers</u>.

3. I really couldn't figure out <u>the problem</u>.

4. Did you back up <u>your computer file</u>?

5. We were just talking about <u>the assignment</u>.

Editing Practice 1

CORRECTED SENTENCES APPEAR ON PAGE 484.

Correct all errors involving separable two-word verbs in the following paragraph using the first correction as a model. The number in parentheses at the end of the paragraph indicates how many errors you should find.

dash them off

I have two papers due this week, but I can't just ~~dash off them~~
like some people (like my wife, for example). I really have to take my time and plan out them. I need to get a bunch of ideas together and then write down them. Then, I have to work up them into some kind of logical order. Sometimes, when I am trying to work out the relationship of a number of half-formed ideas, I find it helps to copy out them onto 3" × 5" cards. Then I can sort out them in a number of different ways until I get a clear picture of what I am trying to say. Then I put my key ideas into a few short sentences so that I can sum up them simply and clearly. If I can't summarize my ideas for myself, I certainly can't get across them to my readers. (7)

Lesson 36

vf
ESL

Editing Practice 2

Correct all errors involving separable two-word verbs in the following paragraphs using the first correction as a model. The number in parentheses at the end of each paragraph indicates how many errors you should find.

put it away

Ideally, at this point I would like to ~~put away it~~ for a day or two, so

that I could come back and look at my ideas with fresh eyes. Unfortunately,

I never seem to have time to put off it for more than a couple of hours,

at best. Even then, putting aside it for a little while seems to help me

organize my ideas and to lay out them in an effective manner. (3)

The next step is to actually start writing the paper. I think of a good

way to get started, and then I try out it. If I have a good beginning, the

paper almost seems to write itself. If I keep getting stuck, then I know

that I have to go back and think over it again because something is wrong.

Often when I am stuck, I find that I have confused two ideas or have

somehow mixed up them. Writer's block, at least in my case, is usually not

a writing problem but a thinking problem. When I know what I want to

say, it is (relatively) easy to write down it. (4)

Applying What You Know

On a separate piece of paper, write a paragraph or two describing your writing process. What steps do you follow when you write a paper? Try to use several separable and inseparable two-word verbs. When you are done, use the Putting It All Together checklist on page 362 to make sure that your placement of nouns and pronouns with the two-word verbs is correct.

The Bottom Line	Adverbs in separable verb phrases are unique. We can **move** them **around**.

Lesson 36

vf
ESL

ESL

Information Questions

EXAMPLE 1	*Helping Verb in Wrong Place*

Error: ✗ Where we <u>can</u> park?

Correction: Where we ~~can~~ park? *(can inserted before park)*

EXAMPLE 2	*Missing Form of Do Following Question Word*

Error: ✗ What he wants to see?

Correction: What ~~he wants~~ to see? *(does he want inserted)*

What's the Problem?

Information questions begin with *question words*. The most common question words are *who(m)*, *what*, *where*, *why*, *when*, plus the compound question words *how often*, *whose* + noun, and *which* + noun/pronoun. Question words are ALWAYS followed immediately by a verb, and sometimes this verb is a **helping verb**. The following are the seven helping verbs (in their various forms):

be (am, is, are, was, were)

have (have, has, had)

can/could

may/might

must

shall/should

will/would

Helping verbs normally come after the subject of a sentence (*You <u>will</u> order*). In a question, however, the helping verb must come immediately after the question word (and thus *before* the subject). For example, we turn the statement *You will order* into a question by moving the helping verb (*will*) to the spot that directly follows the question word (*What*).

Statement: You <u>will</u> order.

Question: What <u>will</u> you order?

When there is no helping verb available, a form of the verb *do* must be added after the question word. For example, the information question *Where did you go?* is formed by inserting the appropriate form of *do* right after the question word:

Statement: You walked.

Question: Where <u>did</u> you walk?

Sometimes non-native speakers form information questions incorrectly by either (a) failing to move a helping verb to a position right after the information question (as in Example 1: ✗ *Where we <u>can</u> park?*) or (b) failing to insert some form of *do* (*do, does, did*) right after the question word when there is no other helping verb in the sentence (as in Example 2: ✗ *What he wants to see?*). Information questions are especially difficult for non-native speakers because many languages form information questions by merely putting the question word at the front of the sentence without moving the verb around.

Diagnostic Exercise

CORRECTED SENTENCES APPEAR ON PAGE 484.

Correct all errors in the following dialogue using the first correction as a model. The number in parentheses at the end of the dialogue indicates how many errors you should find.

Anna: When ~~your flight leave~~? ^{*does your flight leave*}

Maria: At 6:15. Why are so you worried? We're not going to be late, are we?

Anna: I don't think so, but how long it takes to get to the airport?

Maria: It depends on the traffic. If the roads are crowded, it will take an hour.

Lesson 37

info ?s
ESL

Anna: How soon you will be ready to leave?

Maria: Don't get upset. I'm nearly done packing now. Have you seen my alarm clock?

Anna: I don't know where it is. When you used it last?

Maria: For my interview, two days ago. Here it is in the dresser drawer.

Anna: Where I left the car keys?

Maria: Come on! Now you're the one who is going to make us late. Why we didn't get started sooner? (6)

Fixing This Problem in Your Writing

Correcting information question errors involves two steps: (1) check to see whether there is a verb after the question word, and (2) supply the correct verb if one is missing. The following two tips will help you follow these steps.

QUESTION WORD + VERB TIP   Whenever you ask an information question, check to see that there is a verb after the question word. If the question word is not followed by a verb, you must supply one (see the next tip).

MISSING VERB TIP   If there is no verb following an information question, supply one by either (1) moving a helping verb (some form of *be, have, can/could, may/might, must, shall/should,* or *will/would*) or (2) inserting the appropriate form of *do* if there is no helping verb available to be moved.

When we apply the Question Word + Verb Tip to the two example sentences, we see that both sentences contain errors:

Example 1:   ✗ Where we can park?

Tip applied: ✗ Where _____ we can park?
                                MISSING VERB

Example 2:   ✗ What he wants to see?

Tip applied: ✗ What _____ he wants to see?
                                MISSING VERB

Now let's apply the Missing Verb Tip to the two examples:

Tip applied:	Where we (can) park?

Identify the helping verb *can* and move it to follow the question word.

	can
Correction:	Where we ~~can~~ park?
	^

Tip applied:	✗ What he wants to see?

There is no helping verb to move, so add a form of *do*.

	does he want
Correction:	What ~~he wants~~ to see?
	^

Notice that when we add *does* to the above example, the verb *wants* changes to *want*.

So far, we have looked only at examples in which the helping verb *immediately* follows the question word. Sometimes, the question word will be part of a larger group of words such as *how much time, who else,* or *which one.* In these cases, the helping verb or the form of *do* will not immediately follow the question word (*how* or *who,* in these cases), but will follow the question phrase.

How much time <u>do</u> we have?

Who else <u>is</u> going to the party?

Which one <u>are</u> you wearing?

✳ *More Examples*

Correctly Formed Question	*Incorrectly Formed Question*
Helping Verb Correctly Placed	*Helping Verb Incorrectly Placed*
Whom <u>have</u> they chosen?	✗ Whom they <u>have</u> chosen?
Where <u>should</u> I go?	✗ Where I <u>should</u> go?
When <u>will</u> the meeting start?	✗ When the meeting <u>will</u> start?
Form of Do *Correctly Placed*	*Form of* Do *Missing*
What <u>do</u> they want?	✗ What they want?
Why <u>did</u> they say that?	✗ Why they said that?
Which one <u>does</u> he want?	✗ Which one he wants?

Lesson 37

info ?s
ESL

✳ *Putting It All Together*

Identify Information Question Errors

___ When you write information questions, look at the word immediately following the question word. If it is not a verb, then the information question is probably incorrectly formed.

Correct Information Question Errors

___ To correct the error, you must place a verb after the question word.

___ If the sentence contains a helping verb, move that verb so that it follows the question word.

___ If the sentence does not contain a helping verb, add the appropriate form of the verb *do*, and change the main verb if necessary.

Sentence Practice 1

CORRECTED SENTENCES APPEAR ON PAGE 485.

Correct the information questions by applying the two tips. Remember, if you add *do*, you may need to change the main verb.

> *Example:*   ✗ **When they came here before?**
>
> Question Word + Verb Tip: The question is incorrect because the question word *when* is followed by *they*, which is not a verb.
>
> Missing Verb Tip: Since there is no helping verb already in the sentence, add *do* and change the main verb.
>
>   *did*   *come*
> *Correction:*   **When they ~~came~~ here before?**
>   ^   ^

1. Who you talked to?

2. Where Sara found the books?

3. When we plan to leave?

4. Why they didn't bring their lunches?

5. How soon you can be ready?

Lesson 37

info ?s
ESL

For more practice with information questions, go to **Exercise Central** at
bedfordstmartins.com/commonsense

Sentence Practice 2

CORRECTED SENTENCES APPEAR ON PAGE 485.

Correct the information questions by supplying the proper form of the missing helping verb and making any other necessary changes to the main verb. If the question is already correctly formed, write *OK* above it.

> *Example:*   ✗ Whose car we can use?
>
>   *can*
> *Correction:*   Whose car we ~~can~~ use?
>   ^

1. Why the library closed early last Saturday?

2. Who we should thank for the party?

3. Where you parked the car?

4. Why you not ask?

5. Who knows the answer?

Sentence Practice 3

Turn the following statements into information questions by moving the underlined question word to the beginning of the sentence and making the necessary changes to the verb.

> *Example:*   ✗ The Weather Channel predicted rain <u>when</u>.
>
> *Answer:*   *When did the Weather Channel predict rain?*

1. The chicken crossed the road <u>why</u>.

2. The mechanic changes the oil <u>how often</u>.

3. You wanted to see <u>who(m)</u>.

4. They picked <u>which one</u>.

5. They can't come <u>why</u>.

Lesson 37

info ?s
ESL

Editing Practice 1

CORRECTED SENTENCES APPEAR ON PAGE 485.

Correct all errors involving information questions in the following dialogue using the first correction as a model. The number in parentheses at the end of the dialogue indicates how many errors you should find.

       will

Anna: What you ~~will~~ do when you get back home?
      ^

Maria: The usual things. Why you want to know?

Anna: No reason. I'm just asking.

Maria: I think that I will spend most of my time catching up on my writing assignments.

Anna: What you have to work on?

Maria: I have to write a paper for my linguistics class.

Anna: What it is about?

Maria: How children acquire language.

Anna: Who you are going to see?

Maria: Nobody. Why you keep asking?

Anna: I called home last night.

Maria: Oh, who you talked to?

Anna: I talked to Aunt Josie. Guess what she said?

Maria: I don't know. Anyway, why I should care what she said?

Anna: She said Roberto is coming over for dinner. (7)

Editing Practice 2

Correct all errors involving information questions in the following dialogue using the first correction as a model. The number in parentheses at the end of the dialogue indicates how many errors you should find.

       is

Maria: What time it ~~is~~?
       ^

Anna: Why you not tell me about Roberto?

Maria: It's no big deal.

Anna: Oh, then why you are keeping it a big secret?

Maria: It is not a secret. Aunt Josie just asked him over, that's all.

Anna: Uh-huh. When he is coming over?

Maria: I don't know. Maybe Wednesday night.

Anna: Who else Aunt Josie invited over?

Maria: How I should know? Maybe nobody else.

Anna: Uh-huh.

Maria: Look. It's time to go.

Anna: Why you are so anxious to change the subject?

Maria: Why you not mind your own business?

Anna: Because your business is much more interesting! (7)

Applying What You Know

On a separate piece of paper, work with a partner to write a short dialogue about two friends asking each other about their plans for the weekend. Use as many information questions as possible. Use the Putting It All Together checklist on page 370 to make sure that your questions are formed correctly.

The Bottom Line	Where **should** the helping verb go in information questions?

Lesson 37

info ?s
ESL

Word Order in Noun Clauses

EXAMPLE 1

Error: ✗ I know where <u>can</u> you get it.

Correction: I know where ~~can~~ ^{*can*} you get it.

EXAMPLE 2

Error: ✗ What <u>does</u> he want is anybody's guess.

Correction: What ~~does~~ he ~~want~~ ^{*wants*} is anybody's guess.

What's the Problem?

A **noun clause** is a group of words that, like a noun, can function as a subject, object of a verb, or object of a preposition. Here is an example of a noun clause in each of these roles:

Subject:	<u>What they said</u> is none of your business.
Object of a Verb:	We know <u>how you feel about it.</u>
Object of a Preposition:	I asked them about <u>where we could eat.</u>

As you can see from these examples, noun clauses usually begin with one of the following words: *who, what, when, where, why, how, which* + noun, or *whose* + noun/pronoun. Sometimes non-native speakers (and occasionally native speakers too) mistakenly use a helping verb or a form of *do* immediately after the introductory word as they would in an **information question** (see Lesson 37). This is what happened in the two example sentences above.

In Example 1, the helping verb *can* is incorrectly placed right after the introductory word *where*:

Example 1: ✗ I know where <u>can</u> you get it.

In Example 2, *does* is incorrectly inserted after the introductory word *what*:

Example 2:   ✗ What <u>does</u> he want is anybody's guess.

The cause of this problem is easy to identify. As we saw in Lesson 37, we create information questions by moving the helping verb from its normal place between the subject and the main verb to a new position right after the question word. Or, we add some form of *do* after the question word. Because information questions are more common than noun clauses, non-native speakers often mistakenly apply this Question Word + Helping Verb or Question Word + *Do* pattern of information questions to noun clauses. In noun clauses, however, this word order is incorrect:

QUESTION WORD + HELPING VERB

Question (Correct):   <u>Where</u> <u>could</u> we go?

Noun Clause (Incorrect):   ✗ I wondered <u>where</u> <u>could</u> we go.

Since the sentence with a noun clause is not a question, the Question Word + Helping Verb word order is incorrect. We must put the helping verb *could* back in its normal place between the subject and the main verb:

could

Corrected Noun Clause: I wondered where ~~could~~ we go.
                                         ^

Diagnostic Exercise

CORRECTED SENTENCES APPEAR ON PAGE 485.

Correct all noun clause errors in the following paragraph using the first correction as a model. The number in parentheses at the end of the paragraph indicates how many errors you should find.

is

Many non-Americans ask why ~~is~~ the American court system so
                                                                    ^

cumbersome. To understand that, you need to know something about

where did it come from and how did it evolve. Until the Revolutionary

War, the American legal system was exactly what was the British legal

system. Despite the many advantages of the British legal system, colonial

Americans felt that the British had used the powers of the government to

Lesson 38

w.o.
ESL

override the rights of individual citizens. This deep distrust of the ability of the government to use its power fairly explains why is the American system so heavily weighted in favor of the defendant. Often court cases in the United States are fought on the ground of what is admissible government evidence. (5)

Fixing This Problem in Your Writing

The key to using correct word order in noun clauses is to avoid the habit of automatically including a helping verb or some form of *do* immediately after such introductory words as *who, what, when, where,* and the like. These introductory words function in two completely different ways:

- If you are asking an information question, a helping verb or an added form of *do* belongs right after the question word.

- If you are *not* asking an information question, then the word group is a noun clause. In noun clauses, a helping verb or an added form of *do* should *not* come right after the introductory word.

Use the following tip to determine whether your sentence actually contains an information question.

> **QUESTION MARK TIP**   Any time you use *who, what, when, where, why, how, which* + noun, or *whose* + noun/pronoun, ask yourself whether it makes sense to punctuate the sentence with a question mark. If you can, the sentence is an information question, and the Question Word + Helping Verb or Question Word + *Do* word order is correct. If you cannot use a question mark, then you are dealing with a noun clause and may need to move the helping verb to its normal position or delete the added *do*.

Here is the Question Mark Tip applied to an example:

> *Tip applied:*   Where can I get the bus?

Since this is a valid information question, we know that the Question Word + Helping Verb order (*Where can*) is correct.

Now here is the Question Mark Tip applied to Example 1:

> *Example 1:*   ✗ I know where can you get it.

> *Tip applied:*   ✗ I know where can you get it?

Since the question makes no sense, we know that this example is not a valid information question. Instead, it contains a noun clause, which we must restore to its normal statement form. In this case, we move the helping verb *can* to its normal position between the subject and the main verb of the noun clause.

Correction: I know where ~~can~~ ^{can} you get it.

Now let's look at Example 2:

Example 2: ✗ What does he want is anybody's guess.

Tip applied: What does he want is anybody's guess<u>?</u>

Again, the question makes no sense, so we know that we cannot use the Question Word + *Do* word order. To restore the noun clause to its normal statement form, we delete *does*. (Note that when you delete a form of *do*, you must make sure the main verb is in the appropriate form.)

Correction: What ~~does~~ he ~~want~~ ^{wants} is anybody's guess.

The Question Mark Tip is an easy way to remind yourself that every time you use introductory words like *who(m)*, *what*, *why*, or *how*, you should make sure you don't use the inverted information question word order in noun clauses.

✳ *Putting It All Together*

Identify Noun Clause Errors

_____ Whenever you use introductory words such as *who(m)*, *what*, *when*, *where*, *why*, *how*, *which* + noun, and *whose* + noun/pronoun, check to see whether you have really asked an information question by seeing whether a question mark is appropriate.

_____ If the resulting question does not make sense, then you have not asked a real information question in your sentence. Instead, the sentence contains a noun clause, and you should not use the Question Word + Helping Verb or Question Word + *Do* word order. →

Lesson 38

W.O.
ESL

> ### Correct Noun Clause Errors
>
> ____ If the noun clause contains a helping verb right after the subject, move that verb back to its normal place between the subject and the main verb.
>
> ____ If the noun clause has an added *do* (in any form) right after the subject, delete it and make the appropriate change in the main verb of the noun clause.

Sentence Practice 1

CORRECTED SENTENCES APPEAR ON PAGE 485.

All of the following sentences contain incorrectly formed noun clauses. First underline the noun clauses, and then restore the noun clauses to their proper forms.

where they went

Example: I found out ~~where did they go~~.

1.   I realized what did I need to do.

2.   We couldn't agree on which movie did we want to see.

3.   They asked us when did the plane leave.

4.   Why is that a wrong answer seemed obvious to the whole class.

5.   How do you dress tells a lot about you.

 For more practice with word order, go to **Exercise Central** at
bedfordstmartins.com/commonsense

Lesson 38

w.o.

ESL

Sentence Practice 2

CORRECTED SENTENCES APPEAR ON PAGE 485.

Apply the Question Mark Tip to the following unpunctuated sentences. If the tip shows that a sentence is not a valid information question, underline the noun clauses and make the necessary corrections. If the tip shows that a sentence is a valid information question, write *OK* above it.

Example: They guessed what was the right answer

Question Mark Tip: ✗ They guessed <u>what was the right answer</u>?

                                                            was
Correction: They guessed what ~~was~~ the right answer.
                                                            ^

1. It depends on how did you feel about it

2. How can I be of help to you

3. You can leave what don't you like

4. We were surprised at how late was it

5. What did they do was very important to all of us

Sentence Practice 3

Turn the following information questions into noun clauses, and insert them in place of the *IT* in the statements after the questions.

    Example: Where did you go? Tell me IT.

    Answer: *Tell me where you went.*

1. Why were you late? I wondered IT.

2. What did the sign say? I couldn't make out IT.

3. How did Hermione do it? Henry finally figured out IT.

4. Who is the guilty party? It is up to the court to determine IT.

5. Where did we go wrong? IT is obvious to us now.

Lesson 38

Editing Practice 1

CORRECTED SENTENCES APPEAR ON PAGE 485.

W.O.
ESL

Correct all errors involving noun clauses in the following paragraph using the first correction as a model. The number in parentheses at the end of the paragraph indicates how many errors you should find.

One of the many big changes in ~~how can we teach writing~~ has
how we can teach writing
been to look at writing as a topic in its own right. For more than a decade
now, there has been substantial research on how do students learn to
write and what is the difference between the way good and poor writers go
about the process of writing. Perhaps the most helpful finding is that good
writers go through a definite two-step process. What do they write first is
an exploration of the topic. Often it starts as a crude draft that wouldn't
make much sense to anybody but the writer. But apparently it is how are
we able to think through what do we want to say. It is really important
to get to the point where can the writer boil down the key ideas in a few
sentences. This first step in the cycle results in a draft that has all the key
ideas worked out. The second step in the cycle is a semifinal draft that is
very sensitive to how will the paper make sense to the audience. Here is
where is an outline critical to make sure the paper will make sense to the
reader. (8)

Editing Practice 2

Correct all errors involving noun clauses in the following paragraph using
the first correction as a model. The number in parentheses at the end of the
paragraph indicates how many errors you should find.

One of the problems that students in writing classes have is that
who they are
they never know ~~who are they~~ writing to. In other words, they never have
a real subject or a real audience to write for. If you have no real subject,
how can you tell how well have you written about it? The response to this
concern has been another big change in how do we teach writing called

Lesson 38

W.O.
ESL

"writing across the curriculum." The key idea is that writing should also be taught outside the English classroom. For example, students in a history class are asked to write a paper imagining what was it like to live in a different time. Science classes are natural places for writing across the curriculum because nearly all steps in the scientific process lend themselves to writing. For example, students can write what did they observe in an experiment and what did they conclude from the experiment. An effective use of writing in math classes is asking students to explain how did they arrive at their answers. (6)

Applying What You Know

On a separate piece of paper, write a short essay about how you were taught writing. What were the most important things you learned in class? What things did you have to learn on your own? Use the Putting It All Together checklist on page 377 to make sure that you have formed noun clauses correctly.

The Bottom Line	You should know **how noun clauses are different** from information questions.

Lesson 38

W.O.
ESL

UNIT ELEVEN ESL: Using Verbs Correctly

This unit presented various aspects of verb use that non-native speakers find particularly troublesome. The following chart sums up the tips that will help you avoid these problems.

TIP(S)	QUICK FIX AND EXAMPLE
Lesson 35. The Progressive Tenses	
The Progressive Tip (p. 350) helps you know when to use the progressive tense. The Steady-State Verb Tip (p. 351) reminds you which verbs cannot form the progressive tense.	Use the progressive tense for verbs that describe actions in progress at some point in time, not for verbs that describe mental activities, emotional conditions, or possession. *Error:* Could you be a little more quiet? ✗ I talk on the telephone. *Correction:* Could you be a little more quiet? *am talking* I ~~talk~~ on the telephone.
Lesson 36. Two-Word Verbs	
The Movies Tip (p. 360) helps you distinguish between separable and inseparable two-word verbs.	If a separable two-word verb is followed by a noun, you *can* separate the verb (*take out the trash* / *take the trash out*); if it is followed by a pronoun, you must separate the verb (*take it out*). *Error:* ✗ We fought it about all evening. *fought about it* *Correction:* We ~~fought it about~~ all evening.
Lesson 37. Information Questions	
The Question Word + Verb Tip (p. 368) and the Missing Verb Tip (p. 368) help you follow the correct word order when forming an information question.	If a question word is not followed by a helping verb or some form of *do*, move the helping verb there (if there is one) or add the appropriate form of *do*. *Error:* ✗ How much time it will take? *will* *Correction:* How much time it ~~will~~ take?

Lesson 38. Word Order in Noun Clauses	
The Question Mark Tip (p. 376) helps you determine whether a sentence is an information question or a statement that includes a noun clause.	In noun clauses, do *not* place the helping verb immediately after the word that introduces the clause (*who, what, when,* and so on). Instead, the helping verb must go in its normal place between the subject and the main verb. *Error:* **✗** I know how difficult will it be for you to do that. *will* *Correction:* I know how difficult ~~will~~ it be for you to do that. ^

Review Test

Correct the verb errors in the following paragraphs using the first correction as a model. The number in parentheses at the end of each paragraph indicates how many errors you should find.

                    quickly learn

When people visit Venice they ~~are quickly learning~~ about how many
                    ^

problems does the modern city face. The most publicized problem is

flooding. Several times every year, the water is rising to flood parts of the

city in several feet of water. Even the famous Piazza San Marco must be

closed because water covers up it. The flooding is caused by a variety of

factors. What most people think is the main cause? You get a different

answer from nearly every expert you are asking. What do many people

believe is that the canals no longer drain properly because people have

filled in them. As a result, rainwater and the water from rivers flowing

into the top of the lagoon are blocked; the islands have dammed up

them. (8)

    Another problem that everybody is recognizing is that parts

of the city are simply sinking into the lagoon under their own weight.

Unit Eleven

*review
ESL*

For example, consider the Piazza San Marco. In this square are two absolutely enormous stone buildings: the Basilica of San Marco, one of the most amazing churches in the world, and the Ducal Palace. How many hundreds of thousands of tons you think they each weigh? When you look closely at the Ducal Palace, you will notice something odd about the proportions of the stone columns on the ground floor. They are too short. It looks like something has worn down them. In fact, just the opposite is the case. Over the centuries the palace has sunk about five feet, and the ground has been filled them around. What do you see in paintings of the Ducal Palace made 200 years ago is that the columns are noticeably taller than they are today. (5)

UNIT TWELVE
A Commonsense Writing Guide

Though we focus primarily on grammar and usage in this book, we do not want to suggest that you should focus *only* on grammar and usage. So this final unit offers a concise guide to reading and writing.

Here are two points you should know before you start.

- This unit emphasizes an often overlooked fact: teachers have expectations that affect what student writers should do. A writer's situation always affects his or her choices, and teachers are a normal part of a student writer's situation.

- This section offers no formulas for writing. Instead, we encourage you to develop questions to ask yourself, your teacher, or anyone giving you feedback about your writing. Asking yourself critical questions throughout your writing process is one of the most important steps you can take toward improving your writing.

What Readers Look For

Since writing is meant to be read, begin by thinking about what readers typically expect. Though definitions of "good writing" differ from culture to culture, the chart on the next page presents five *basic standards* that readers in the United States use to evaluate writing. Keep in mind that you might have to adjust these standards based on your own specific situation, audience, and assignment.

The remainder of this unit offers strategies you can use so your papers reflect these five standards. Because the main part of this book focuses on style and mechanics, this unit concentrates on purpose, support, and organization.

✳ *Basic Standards for Evaluating Writing*

Purpose: Readers expect a paper to be focused, based on a clear and appropriate purpose. A focused paper

- stays on one subject
- makes a specific point about this subject
- considers its audience
- is narrow enough to fulfill its purpose within the assignment's page-length requirements

Support: Readers expect a paper to contain enough supporting detail to fulfill its purpose. A well-supported paper

- gives readers a clear understanding of the paper's subject matter
- explains or proves the paper's one main point with details, examples, and evidence
- offers in-depth thinking, not just obvious or superficial generalizations

Organization: Readers expect a paper to have a sense of order. This typically means that

- the paper has an introduction, a body, and a conclusion
- each paragraph has one major point
- paragraphs are arranged so they clearly build on one another
- individual sentences flow from one to another

Style: Readers expect writers to use words and sentence patterns that suit their purpose and topic. For most college papers, style means that

- the writing is *either* formal *or* informal, depending on the paper's purpose
- sentences should not be too choppy or too awkward
- writers choose the words that most clearly and precisely convey ideas to a particular audience

Mechanics: Readers expect that writers follow the conventions and rules of standard English. This expectation means that writers should carefully consider the guidelines given in the first part of this book (Units One through Eleven).

Unit Twelve

overview

What Writers Do

Reading and writing: What is the connection? Reading is more closely connected to writing than you might assume. Both writing and reading involve processes—evolving steps you go through to understand and create information. Reading as well as writing depends on your situation. For example, you do not read a physics textbook the same way you read an e-mail from a friend. Nor do you follow the same steps to create a grocery list as you would a research paper. Writing depends on reading (and vice versa), and both are shaped by specific processes and situations. Thus, the next four lessons discuss how to read and write more effectively by considering certain situations, especially those common in higher education, and processes. You already know how to read and write, but these lessons will help you read and write better in college.

This unit begins with a discussion of reading because many (perhaps most) writing assignments in college are closely connected with reading material that you are either assigned or that you must find yourself. Even if your reading skills are strong, we encourage you to study Lesson 39 so you will better understand concepts of and tips for reading that also relate to writing.

What is a *writing process*? At one time or another, most of us have written a paper in one sitting. Sometimes, the result was acceptable or even good; other times, the paper didn't reflect our best thinking. For most people, their "best thinking" isn't what comes off the top of their heads. Rather, it is the result of a process. Using a *process* in writing means coming up with good ideas, developing plans, trying out your best ideas, making improvements, and sharing ideas with readers. There is no one right way to proceed, and the route can even be messy. It would be convenient if there were a formula, but the truth is that each writer, situation, purpose, and audience requires a unique approach. You can, however, think about three general stages.

Planning $\longrightarrow$ Drafting $\longrightarrow$ Revising

Writing is not always a neat step-by-step process. When you revise a paragraph to make it descriptive, for instance, you might also do more planning. Keep in mind as well that writing is not just drafting. You need to plan, write, rewrite, and make improvements. You can consider editing as the final stage, using the other parts of this book to guide you.

What is a *writing situation*? Your exact writing process will depend on your situation. A writer's situation is a combination of everything that

Unit Twelve

overview

directly affects a given piece of writing. Here are the basic elements: assignment, purpose, readers (audience), deadline, tools for writing, and physical environment. Your writing situation will change with every assignment. For example, some assignments may require research. Others may require that you consider a community or a corporate (rather than an academic) audience. Some writing assignments begin and end in the classroom during an exam. Others may be long-term and require several trips to the library or computer lab. How you prepare to write is affected by your overall writing situation.

Reading

Writing depends on reading. At the very least, you yourself read everything you write, and your teacher and classmates frequently read your writing as well. One way to improve your writing ability is to read, read, read.

There is one other reason why you need to consider the connections between reading and writing. Many college teachers base their writing assignments on something they will ask you to read—such as a textbook, novel, journal article, or item from the Internet. College requires you to read a range of items—from textbooks to literature to government documents (just to name a few). There are also different ways to write about these diverse reading selections. Thus, this lesson offers *general* strategies for reading and writing about what you read. Later lessons focus more on the actual process of writing and more specific types of college assignments.

Types of Assignments

College teachers often make writing assignments such as the following, although they might call these assignments by different names:

- **Objective Summary.** This is a brief description of what a reading selection covers—its most important ideas. Your own opinions about the selection and its topic are kept out as much as possible.

- **Evaluative Summary.** This also is a brief description of what an author covers in a reading selection, but you are allowed to offer more of your own opinions and reflections about the selection or the topic.

- **Critique (or Review).** This is not always brief, nor is your specific purpose to summarize. Instead, your purpose is to evaluate a reading selection. Your paper would describe the selection's strengths or weaknesses (or both) and then provide reasons to support your evaluation. The goal is to convince your readers that your evaluation is valid and reasonable.

- **Reflection.** Like a critique, the purpose is not to summarize. Compared to a critique, a reflection is less formal and does not focus on convincing readers. The reflection is a more personal response that makes a connection between you and what the author writes. For instance, you might discuss what you learned from the reading selection or how it relates to your own experiences.

- **Explanation (or Analysis).** This assignment is most often used when the reading selection is a work of fiction or literature—such as a poem, short story, or novel. Your purpose is to offer an explanation about the meaning of the reading selection. This type of writing is particularly broad, covering many specific forms. One common form involves answering a particular question about the author's work; this question could be one you develop or one the teacher assigns. Another common form is describing the overall point or theme of a work of literature.

- **Research Paper.** Although many teachers avoid this particular name, the so-called research paper requires you to use books, magazines, newspapers, or the Internet to find out how much has been written on a topic. Then, you select the best sources and use them to support your own point or position. Some papers might use two or three sources, while others might require a dozen or more.

Lesson 40 describes how you must determine your general purpose in writing a paper. When writing about something you've read, you will usually find that this purpose fits into one of the above categories.

> **COMMONSENSE TIP**   Do not overlook this first step of identifying the purpose of the assignment. Many students seem to think that all "writing about reading" assignments are the same, but it is a crucial mistake to write, for example, a reflective essay when the teacher expects a research paper.

Understanding What You Read

No matter what the assignment is, you need to read something well if you are to write about it. College students face challenging, complex reading selections, and while just skimming or casually reading an article or book will work well enough in some situations, college requires you to have a better understanding of what you read. Keep in mind that "reading" something does not simply mean being able to sound out the words. Reading means *understanding* what is written. Here are four practical suggestions for helping you read (and understand) more effectively.

Lesson 39

read

Tip #1: Do not worry about reading quickly.   Many people think they are poor readers because they do not read quickly, and such an attitude typically lowers their confidence (and, thus, their ability to read well). In truth, many of your professors read slowly, taking time to consider fully what they are reading. Many people "read" quickly but are unable to understand the material, so have they really read it at all?

Certainly, there are occasions when time is essential, and college students usually feel a shortage of time. Avoid thinking that every situation calls for a quick reading. Indeed, reading too quickly can eventually take more time if it results in such a poor understanding that you are unable to write. In sum, find time—ample time—to devote to reading.

Tip #2: Preview what you are going to read.   Research has shown that if you have an idea of what is coming up next in a reading selection, you will better understand what you read. Take a few moments or more to look through the reading material for these "signposts" that indicate what is coming up next in the reading selection:

- An introductory paragraph in which the author indicates his or her purpose

- Information indicating where and when the selection originally appeared (knowing this information can provide useful background for what you are about to read)

- Preface (an overview or description of the reading selection)

- Headings and subheadings (these often indicate what the author considers to be important topics)

- Visual cues, such as pictures, diagrams, and lists

- Words or phrases that are emphasized (boldface, underlining, italics, capitalization)

- A conclusion or summary

- Review or discussion questions at the end (these often tell you what you should know after finishing, so look for the answers *as* you read)

Tip #3: Don't skip the introduction; don't focus just on the ending.   Some authors recognize that readers need to understand what is coming up next in a reading selection. Consequently, authors often explicitly provide a preview in the introduction of, say, a particular chapter. Avoid the temptation to skip this preview, even if it seems dull. The author is basically doing the readers' work for them by providing a preview, and the author's own preview of what is important in the selection is, indeed, likely to be important.

In contrast, some readers assume that the summary or conclusion is basically all they need to know, and they skim (or skip) everything else.

Lesson 39

read

Even the best-written summary is just a *general* description of an author's ideas, and many college teachers—realizing what the conclusion does not cover—want students to understand the important details, not just the simple basics.

Tip #4: Use writing to reinforce your reading.   Researchers who study reading and writing have found that people who write *as* they read (or soon afterward) better understand what they read. Here are a few strategies to try:

- **Highlighting.** This technique is "writing" in the sense that you produce markings to indicate a type of meaning (even if you are just emphasizing somebody else's ideas). Highlighting not only helps you identify important portions of a text, but also keeps you more active during the reading process, making you more alert and receptive.

  Many students, however, rely on just this one simple strategy. Although helpful, it can be a bit superficial in terms of engaging the reader in understanding, interpreting, and critiquing a text. Other strategies, such as those below, require more work but usually result in a better understanding.

- **Note taking.** For many students, one of the most useful strategies is taking notes while they read—brief comments, questions, definitions, explanations, or evaluations. Use notes to clarify what you read or help you identify problematic portions. Notes can even make connections to what the teacher or others have said (especially if there is disagreement). Such notes can be put in the margin (if it's your book), on cards, on paper, or on the computer.

> **COMMONSENSE TIP**   Many students buy used textbooks in which another student has written notes or highlighted. Do *not* assume the previous owner of the book was accurate or logical in terms of his or her highlighting or note taking! In addition, relying on somebody else's markings or notes does little to increase your own active involvement in the act of reading.

- **Summarizing.** A study conducted several years ago found that students in a psychology course received better test scores when they wrote summaries of chapters assigned from their psychology textbook. Even if you are not required to write an objective summary (a type of writing described earlier in this lesson), writing a brief, straightforward summary will help you understand whatever you summarize. In doing

Lesson 39

read

so, you will likely reread the selection, which alone helps you better understand the material.

Be selective about what you summarize. This strategy can be a time-consuming way to improve your comprehension of what you read, and you cannot use it for every reading situation. If it is not practical to write a summary, at least consider an oral summary—summarizing aloud, perhaps in a study group.

■ **Rereading and Reviewing.** As you read, you will naturally find yourself not truly understanding some parts. Whether your attention is drifting or whether you just don't follow what the author is writing, don't continue until you have reread the troublesome sentence, passage, or page.

What happens if rereading does not help? In such cases, it is best to backtrack to earlier portions that might have set up the troublesome portion of the text. If that does not help, *then* you should proceed in hopes that the subsequent sections will clarify the author's message.

Many people consider their reading done when they reach the last words of a text. In some situations, though, the act of reading—of really understanding the text—has only begun at that point. Making sense of a reading selection means understanding, evaluating, and questioning the material, and these acts can best be done *after* an initial reading of the text. Reviewing might mean, in fact, rereading some or all of the reading selection, or it might mean taking notes or highlighting significant portions. The important point to remember is that reading often means taking time to reflect on what you read—time to absorb, critique, and reconsider the message.

✳ *Critical Questions for Reading*

You might be confused about what you should do to "reflect" on something you read. Reflection is a highly individualistic activity that depends on what you read, why you are reading it, and who you are. However, we wish to end this lesson by noting questions you can use to help you understand, evaluate, and write about a reading selection.

Topic and Purpose

■ What does the author's purpose seem to be? What is his or her thesis, claim, or position?

■ Do you agree with the author's major point? Do you think most people would? →

Lesson 39

read

Relevance

- Can you think of something current or historical that is relevant to the major topic of this passage?
- How does this reading selection relate to your life? That is, is it relevant to your past, present, or future?
- What about other people — is the selection relevant to most people? For whom is it not?
- Is there something else you have read (or heard or seen) that supports or contradicts this reading selection?

Support

- What does the selection fail to include even though it is related to the topic, and was it reasonable for the author to leave out this material?
- If the reading selection involves a story, consider the characters, setting, and actions. How do all or any of these contribute to a particular interpretation of the story?
- Find two or three sentences you found memorable, insightful, or interesting. Why are these notable or important to you?
- If the author is making an argument or recommendation, what would be the results if society were to accept it? What is needed to turn the author's ideas into something concrete and useful?

Organization

- Consider how the reading selection is organized — what comes first and last, and how it can otherwise be divided into different sections. How well does the author's arrangement work?
- Is the introduction successful in pulling the reader in? Does the conclusion merely summarize, or does it make a more important point?

Style and Tone

- Consider the author's word choice and the way he or she puts sentences together. Are these effective choices?
- What sort of person does the author appear to be? Consider the author's tone, his or her word choice, and the types of reasons or information provided to readers.
- Could some people find the reading selection offensive at times?
- No matter whether you agree or disagree with the author, why do you respect or not respect the way he or she writes?

Lesson 39

read

For additional questions, consider the questions found in Lesson 40 dealing with purpose and standards. Although intended for writers, those questions are also relevant to reading.

Above all, do not merely accept what another person has put down in writing. College readers should not only understand a reading selection, but also question and evaluate it.

Applying What You Know

Find a brief article from a magazine or Web site. Bring it to class and be ready to discuss the article in terms of any of the questions listed in the Critical Questions for Reading. End your discussion by stating why you did or did not enjoy reading this particular article.

Planning

Whether you are assigned an in-class essay or a long-term research project, start by determining your purpose. Determining your purpose means more than completing the sentence, "What I want to do in this paper is . . ." It also involves answering these questions:

- What effect do I want to have on readers?

- What do I want to get out of this paper—besides a good grade?

- How will my paper reflect the task that the teacher assigned?

- What does the teacher want me to learn from doing this task?

Working your way through questions like these can be overwhelming, so we suggest first thinking about purpose in two ways: Your *general purpose* is the basic goal of the paper according to the assignment. Your *specific purpose* is the general purpose plus your narrowed topic and the point you want to make.

Determine Your General Purpose

Your first step in the planning stage is determining your general purpose—what you are required to do with the subject or topic.

> **COMMONSENSE TIP** Don't assume that your paper meets the assignment simply because it is "on topic." In this early stage of writing, many people mistakenly place more emphasis on staying on the topic than on making sure they understand the general purpose of the assignment.

Rarely will teachers say simply, "Write a paper on the pyramids." Although some teachers will assign just a subject, most teachers have additional expectations about what you should do with this subject. Most college writing has one of three general purposes: to express yourself, to inform readers, or to persuade readers.

- **Expressing Yourself.** The goal is to express your personal reactions and feelings. The emphasis is on you and your individual response to a subject. A personal narrative, a paper describing an event in your life of special significance, is a common type of expressive writing assignment. For a paper on the pyramids, your teacher might ask the following: What relevance does this story about a woman's trip to see the pyramids have to your life?

- **Informing Readers.** The goal is to explain or describe something in a clear, accurate, thorough way. Usually you should try to be objective and keep your personal feelings out of the assignment. Like a reporter, you are focusing on the subject and on providing information that would be new to readers. For example, you might be asked to write a paper that explains the origins of the pyramids.

- **Persuading Readers.** The goal is to convince readers to accept your claim or position. In most of the persuasive writing you do in college, you should concentrate on logic, not emotions. The desired effect of persuasion is to convince readers to agree with you. A persuasive assignment might ask the following: Should the pyramids be preserved? Take a stand.

COMMONSENSE TIP If you believe your teacher has given you a wide-open assignment, you might be able to pick any subject or general purpose, but double-check to see if the paper can *really* do anything you want. Usually teachers (like most readers) have some expectations about a written assignment.

Suppose your teacher has assigned a paper that asks you to summarize the plot of a novel. This paper is likely to have an informative purpose. But suppose your paper winds up describing how you personally reacted to the book (expression), or it argues that the main character is a horrible person (persuasion). Your paper might fail because it does not achieve the general purpose your teacher assigned—to inform.

BUT WHAT HAPPENS IF . . . ?

"I still cannot determine what my general purpose should be." Your best approach might be to ask the teacher. You will want to avoid putting it this way, though: "What do you want in this paper?" That is too general and may suggest that you just want a formula. Ask a specific question: for instance, "Is the general purpose to express myself, to provide information, or to support a claim?"

"But asking the teacher isn't practical, and I really, really don't know what the general purpose is!" You might consult someone else in the class, but if all

Lesson 40

plan

else fails, we suggest you assume that the general purpose is to persuade. Persuasion is one of the most common types of writing in college.

"The assignment allows me to write almost anything I want." Again, be sure to confirm this interpretation, preferably by trying out a sample approach with the teacher to see if there are restrictions. Even if there are none, do not assume that your paper can wander from one purpose to another. Having a wide-open assignment does not give you license to say everything; it gives you the added responsibility of determining a clear purpose.

Determine Your Specific Purpose

The second part of determining your purpose is adding your own narrowed topic, which leads to your *specific purpose*. In other words, your specific purpose is your own particular approach to the general assignment—your paper's focus.

The following chart will help you see the difference between an assignment's general purpose and a writer's specific purpose.

If Your General Purpose Is . . .	Your Specific Purpose Might Be . . .
To express your feelings about a holiday or celebration	To express your discomfort with school-sponsored celebrations of Halloween
To inform others about a holiday or celebration	To inform others about the ancient origins of Halloween
To make an argument about a holiday or celebration	To argue that Halloween should not be celebrated in public schools

Understand Your Audience

When you are narrowing your subject and purpose, you should consider your audience. Are you writing for just your teacher, a larger public, or a specific group? Once you make this determination, there are many additional questions to ask. We suggest you start with the following:

■ What should I assume readers already know about the subject?

■ What information would readers consider new, necessary, and insightful?

- Will they care about the subject and have strong opinions about it?
- Will they resist any of my ideas?

Suppose your nursing instructor asks you to present a proposal for improving response time in a hospital emergency room and tells you that your audience is a group of local hospital administrators. Your *general purpose* will be to persuade your readers, and your *specific purpose* will be to argue for your idea about how to solve the problem. In planning, you would keep in mind that administrators often think of the hospital's bottom-line financial situation first, so solutions that require an increase in staff without an increase in revenue will meet with resistance. If, on the other hand, your audience is fellow nurses committed to quality care, you may have to work harder to propose that ER staff spend less time with each patient. What's certain is that your proposal will be strengthened by careful consideration of your audience's point of view.

> COMMONSENSE TIP It can be frustrating to second-guess an audience's views, especially if it is one you find intimidating. However, at least consider an audience's general level of expertise and attitude about your subject. If it is distracting to try to define your audience exactly, wait until later. But determine at least a *basic* idea of how your audience might react to what you have to say.

Connecting Purpose and Audience

Let's consider another student's planning choices. The first assignment in Stephanie's writing class was to explain why she chose to go to college. Her initial impulse was to list several general reasons explaining why most people go to college; however, Stephanie decided to consider her writing situation more carefully. First, she took out the assignment sheet (often called a *prompt*) and highlighted the words that indicated the purpose of the paper (general or specific purpose) and the audience.

> *Write an **explanation** of **why** you decided to attend college. This **information** will help **me understand** you better as both a **person** and a **writer**. Keep your response to one paragraph of 250 to 300 words, and bring it to our next class meeting.*

Obviously, the teacher would be the audience for this paper (the word *me* emphasized this fact). The words *explanation, information,* and *understand* made it clear to Stephanie that the general purpose of this short paper would be to inform—to tell this teacher something new and useful. Stephanie's specific purpose seemed merely to explain why she went to college. As straightforward

Lesson 40

plan

as this prompt seemed, the more Stephanie thought about it, the more she questioned her plan of listing several reasons why most people attend college. She thought about two planning issues more carefully: her specific purpose and how her audience might react to various options.

Stephanie correctly assumed her teacher would not be really informed if all Stephanie did was briefly cover a number of reasons why most people go to college. First, this teacher had probably heard the same general reasons already, and it is difficult to inform someone in such a position by providing only basic, commonplace explanations. In addition, Stephanie saw that the prompt indicated that the teacher wanted to know the students better as *individuals*, so Stephanie had to think about reasons why *she* in particular went to college—not why people in general go.

Thus, Stephanie's first major decision during the planning stage was to approach her explanation in a way that would not be generic or ordinary, for she indeed had her own special experiences that influenced her choice of attending college. After reflecting on these experiences, she developed a more specific purpose that she eventually turned into the first sentence of her paragraph. Below is a draft, with this "purpose sentence" underlined.

> *Like many people, I decided to go to college because I want job opportunities, but I am also here because I want to avoid the problems my brothers now face.* In some ways, I am like other students you have encountered. I am in college because a college degree will give me the skills employers want. What I hope you will understand about me, however, is that I am also in college because I have seen people close to me jump into major responsibilities right after high school, and I have seen how college can often take a backseat to other things. My two brothers, Carl and Tom, had all sorts of plans about what they would do with a college degree, but they postponed these so they could marry and have full-time jobs. I know people are able to go back to college in situations such as theirs, but Carl and Tom are now so caught up with their jobs and families that they do not know when, if ever, they will return to college. Are they happy? I think so. Will a college degree guarantee happiness? I know it does not. However, I decided to go to college before taking on major responsibilities and to make sure I have the opportunity to find out if college is for me. It is still early to tell, but I am glad I can take time to determine what I want to do in life.

Everything in this paragraph goes back to a unique specific purpose that arose when Stephanie gave time to making plans based around both purpose and audience. Later, we will discuss in detail why writers revise drafts, but it isn't too early to stress that writers must consider how to alter their plans. Stephanie worried that her teacher might find the paragraph *too* personal or

Lesson 40

plan

might assume Stephanie was making massive generalizations about the chances of older adults going to college. Stephanie decided she would stay with her true feelings since these did indeed account for why she chose college, but she decided to delete the last sentence of her draft and add the following:

> *Perhaps my brothers can find out one day if college would make them happier, for I see many older, married students at this college. However, I decided to find out now if college is for me, rather than waiting for "one day" that might never happen.*

In sum, this student started to do what many writers do when first given an assignment: write about the first ideas that come to mind, and cover each idea very quickly. Only after considering a purpose that her audience might appreciate more did this particular student begin writing a paragraph that avoids these common problems.

Explore Your Subject and Develop Support

For your paper to be effective, you must narrow your topic to something you can manage within the boundaries of the assignment. For example, a three- to five-page essay would hardly cover the broad subject of *nutrition*. But if you spend some time exploring aspects of the topic that most interest you and are appropriate to your purpose and your audience, you might come up with a narrower, more manageable subject like *the importance of folic acid in a pregnant woman's diet*. Here are two prewriting strategies to help you narrow your subject and decide what you might use as supporting information.

The idea behind these prewriting strategies is to narrow a topic and explore ideas without worrying about correct spelling or grammar at this early stage. If English is not your first language, you may find it easier to free-write or cluster in your native language.

ESL

Freewriting. This technique is helpful for people whose thinking is often spontaneous and creative (which would include most of us some of the time). Here are some guidelines:

- **Start writing** on the assigned subject or task without worrying about where you are headed. Just do a "mind spill," spontaneously writing whatever comes to mind about the subject and/or your purpose.

- **Write quickly** and legibly, but avoid thinking too long about what you should say next. Just keep pen or fingers moving. Do not worry

Lesson 40

plan

about spelling, grammar, wording, or anything that slows your thinking. You are writing to generate ideas for yourself, not for others.

- **Keep writing** whatever comes to mind. There is no magic time limit, but write long enough so that new ideas develop and the words come more easily.

- **Ask questions** if you are running into "writer's block." Don't talk yourself into believing you have nothing to say. If all else fails, explain why you think you have nothing to say, or answer one of these questions: "How has this subject affected me personally?" or "Why has it never mattered?"

- **Reflect** on what you have written after you are done. Reread your freewriting and look for something that interests you or your readers. Circle these parts.

Clustering.   Instead of sentences, use words and brief phrases to explore a subject. Clustering has a visual aspect that appeals to many writers. Here are the basic steps:

- **Write down your subject** in the middle of a blank page. Circle it.

- **Start branching** off this central idea. That is, write down related words that come to mind. Circle each new idea. Draw lines to connect related ideas.

- **Continue branching** as related ideas cross your mind. Don't expect that every idea will have the same number of branches. Your point is to explore ideas, not to draw a tidy diagram.

- **Develop several layers** for at least a couple of topics. If you don't have many layers, you could wind up with ordinary, rather superficial ideas.

- **Reflect** on what you have written after you are done. Then examine the connections you have made and continue to draw lines between groups of ideas. Doing so allows you to consider how ideas support one another.

The next page shows a cluster for an assignment on ways to enhance safety. One writer, as part of his planning, decided that he needed to narrow the broad topic of "safety" to something more focused and manageable. Notice that this writer developed some ideas more than others.

Think about what clustering does. You come up with not only a more specific subject, but also major ideas to bring in to your writing. If this writer decided to write on "road rage," the cluster diagram offers supporting ideas, such as "ways to control temper" and "relaxation techniques."

Lesson 40

plan

COMMONSENSE TIP Use these planning techniques whenever you need to develop ideas. In this section, we focus on clustering and other techniques to help you narrow your subject and come up with major ideas, but you can use these techniques earlier in the process to choose a subject and determine your audience and purpose. These techniques also help you to find and group supporting ideas.

Write a Thesis Sentence

Once you have explored possible topics and purposes, you should write an initial thesis sentence. This sentence expresses the point you want to make in your paper. It may change as you think more about your assignment, but

Lesson 40

plan

it helps to have a *working thesis* at this point. In most college writing, a thesis sentence has these characteristics:

- It states the writer's single main point.
- It is clear and specific.
- It is placed in the opening paragraph (generally, it is the first or last sentence).
- It prepares readers for the rest of the paper.

Here are some sample thesis sentences based on the general and specific purposes described on page 398.

Thesis Sentence for Expressive Writing
Halloween might seem a casual, fun holiday for some, but for me it was offensive and uncomfortable when I felt forced to celebrate it in school.

Thesis Sentence for Informative Writing
If you think Halloween is just a "kids' night," you might be surprised to know that this holiday has ancient religious origins.

Thesis Sentence for Persuasive Writing
Halloween should not be celebrated in public schools.

> **COMMONSENSE TIP** See pages 410–11 for a list of different types of topic sentences that indicate the purpose of a single paragraph. Read through these categories to get an idea of the various ways to create a thesis sentence.

ESL In some cultures, writers avoid making points directly. In English, however, readers appreciate writing that has a clear, direct point. Start by drafting a thesis sentence. You can revise it to make it more straightforward later.

Plan Your Paper's Organization

Once you have some idea about what you want to say, consider how to organize, or arrange, these ideas. Sometimes, deciding how to arrange ideas helps writers come up with a better purpose or better support, so be willing to make changes.

Think of your paper as needing these distinct parts:

Lesson 40

1. an **introduction:** a way to announce your subject, draw your readers' attention and interest, and indicate your specific purpose and main point

plan

2. a **body:** the section in which you provide major ideas and supporting ideas to achieve your purpose
3. a **conclusion:** the place where your readers feel a sense of completion

The first step of planning your paper's organization is to remind yourself of your purpose.

> **COMMONSENSE TIP** If you are still not sure how to word your thesis sentence, try to phrase it in the most direct way possible: "In this paper, my primary purpose is to . . ." Later, you can revise this sentence to be less formulaic.

The next step is to answer this question: *Does the teacher expect a particular type of organization?* You must determine how much flexibility you have in organizing your paper. Look at the assignment's wording, ask classmates, ask your teacher, or reread any material covered in class about organization. Teachers often expect writers to use a particular organizing structure. Sometimes, they are direct about this expectation by using certain "tip off" words: *arrange, develop, form, format, method of development, mode, order, organize, pattern, scheme, shape,* or *structure.*

Your writing instructor may name the type of writing you are to do (such as a business letter, a lab report, or a book review) and expect you to use the organization associated with this type of writing. Most common assignments, however, require you to organize your writing in whatever way best suits your purpose, audience, and subject. In a personal narrative, you might present events in chronological (time) order. In an informative essay, you might explain a process by proceeding through the steps in the process. Finally, you might develop a persuasive essay by presenting your ideas in order of importance, from strong to strongest. No matter what the assignment, you can think further about your organization by writing an informal outline.

Write an Informal Outline. Think of an outline as a *tentative plan* for arranging your ideas. Some students remember being told to write an outline with so many formal *dos* and *don'ts*, they have forgotten its real purpose. We suggest you develop an outline that is more than rough notes, but not so formal that it distracts you from your writing process. That is, develop an outline that would be clear to someone else (especially if you want feedback), but avoid becoming frustrated by questions such as "Do I indent three or five spaces?" or "Do I use a Roman numeral here?" Even if you are given formal rules to follow, it is more manageable to start with an informal outline that focuses on ideas, not technical details. You can revise it later.

Lesson 40

plan

Write an informal outline that indicates the following:

- your thesis statement (the point of your paper)
- your major support
- some minor ideas that support the major ones

An outline should also reflect the type of organization that readers expect or the type you have selected.

Here is an outline of one writer's effort to persuade her company's benefits manager to endorse a tuition reimbursement program for employees. The assignment did not specify a type of organization, so the writer decided to give background information, anticipate any opposition, and then base the major body paragraphs on the reasons supporting her thesis.

Thesis: As part of the general employee benefits package, the company should provide tuition reimbursement.

Introduction

—Discuss the company's history of poor employee retention.

—Discuss recent news about the value of adult education.

—State thesis.

Body

(Anticipate possible opposition) A tuition reimbursement program is unnecessary.

—Tuition reimbursement is too expensive.

—The company's training department sufficiently meets the needs of the company.

(Major support point) A tuition reimbursement fund is not wasted money.

—Tuition reimbursement offsets the costs of advertising for, recruiting, and training new employees.

—Tuition reimbursement as part of a comprehensive benefits package attracts quality job candidates and retains good employees.

(Major support point) Tuition reimbursement builds employee confidence and job satisfaction.

—This kind of program helps employees to build job-relevant skills.

—Increased job satisfaction means a decrease in employee turnover.

(Major support point) Tuition reimbursement programs enhance a company's internal training function.

—*Employee education is strengthened by a team approach; company train-ers still assess employees' needs and then inform employees about local schools and programs that meet those needs.*

—*The company's internal training staff is free from repeated new-employee training; staff can focus on developing more customized programs.*

Conclusion

—*Summarize benefits of thesis.*

— *Emphasize that a tuition reimbursement program can help the company fulfill its mission: to develop quality products and honor quality employees.*

COMMONSENSE TIP Use question marks, bullets, indentation, or num-bered lists to remind you where you have questions or to indicate which ideas are more important than others. The appearance of an outline can help you see how ideas connect. Don't obsess over making your outline look neat and orderly, though.

BUT WHAT HAPPENS IF . . . ?

"I don't know how many paragraphs I should have—especially in the middle part of my paper." There is no magic number of paragraphs a paper needs, but you should consider any number indicated in the assignment, the length requirements of the paper, and how much you need to say to achieve your specific purpose. Unless the assignment calls for a very short paper, you need more than one paragraph in the body. At the same time, be careful not to have too many. For example, more than ten paragraphs in a three-page paper may mean that your paragraphs are too short to be clear, convincing, or interesting.

"I can sketch out major ideas, but I don't know what to put under them." You may find it helpful to do more freewriting or clustering (see pages 401–403). Then you could add more to your outline.

✱ *Critical Questions for Planning*

Write down your general purpose, specific purpose, and possible audience. Next, answer the set of questions that best relates to your general purpose.

If your assignment is . . .	*Answer these questions . . .*
Expressive	What could you say about your own experiences with this subject that would also matter to your readers? →

Lesson 40

plan

		Do you have personal experiences with this subject that are so unusual that your readers would be intrigued?
		What strong feelings do you have about this subject? Can you write about them in a way that your readers will understand these feelings?
Informative		What questions might your readers already have about this subject?
		What do they need to know to be fully informed?
		If readers are somehow going to use this information in their lives, what should they know?
Persuasive		What controversies already exist in regard to your subject?
		How would you defend your position against specific objections raised by readers?
		What additional information or evidence could you provide that would change their minds?

Applying What You Know

In college and the workforce, you cannot always pick what you will write about, but often you can find a way to work in a subject you know well or enjoy. Make a list of five topics, controversies, or things you know well or enjoy. Share these in a small-group discussion, and explain why you listed them. Your teacher will likely want to know what topics the class finds intriguing, so be prepared to share these with the entire class.

Lesson 40

plan

LESSON 41

Drafting

As you begin to draft, you should have a clear plan for your paper based on the following checklist. If there is an item on this list that you have not considered, you may want to do some more planning.

____ I have determined the assignment's *general purpose:* expressive, informative, or persuasive.

____ I have determined my *specific purpose:* what I specifically want to express, inform readers about, or persuade them to believe (my narrowed topic).

____ I have considered my *audience* and have an idea of who will (or should) read my paper, their background in the subject, and their attitude toward it.

____ I have written a working *thesis sentence:* a clear and specific statement of the point of my paper.

____ I have developed major *support* for my specific purpose: the main explanations, information, evidence, or events that will help me make my overall point.

____ I have written an *organizational plan:* the way I will arrange at least the major ideas.

Now you should write a draft, modifying your plan or discarding it if necessary. The key to successful drafting is *flexibility*. We suggest you start with a basic introduction that includes your specific purpose and thesis statement, and prepares your reader for the rest of your paper, and then proceed by drafting according to your informal outline.

> **COMMONSENSE TIP** Don't spend a huge amount of time on the introduction while you are drafting. If drafting the paper causes you to modify your specific purpose and thesis, you'll need to revise the introduction anyway.

Pay most attention to presenting the point of your paper (purpose), to developing your ideas (support), and to connecting these ideas to each other (organization). Pay less attention to stylistic and mechanical matters covered in the first part of this book. You can address these matters in the revision stage.

Write Topic Sentences and Paragraphs

Let's start by drafting paragraphs. Keep in mind that each paragraph should include just one main topic. If your paragraph "rambles" or covers too many topics, you run the risk of confusing your readers.

One way writers help readers is by using topic sentences. A topic sentence is usually a one-sentence statement that indicates the purpose, subject, or point of a paragraph. It might help you to think of the topic sentence as the controlling idea for a paragraph. Just as a thesis sentence presents the controlling idea for a paper, a topic sentence presents the controlling idea for each paragraph in the body of your paper. Sometimes, in fact, you might be assigned to write just a paragraph, not an entire essay. In this case, your topic sentence becomes your contract with your readers. (See page 412 for guidelines on completing the single-paragraph assignment.)

There is no law requiring that the topic sentence should be the first sentence of a paragraph, but we suggest you start each paragraph in the body of your paper with a topic sentence because an introductory topic sentence gives you something to refer to while developing the paragraph, reminding you of the point. You can always alter your use of topic sentences later. Also, topic sentences help readers identify your major ideas.

> **COMMONSENSE TIP** One exception to the important role of topic sentences is narration, telling a story (often called a "personal narrative"). When relating an experience, you might not use topic sentences often, though you would still divide the story into paragraphs. Instead of using topic sentences, you would rely on chronological order (telling events as they happened) and careful transitions.

Topic sentences vary in how they convey the main idea of a paragraph. Try various approaches. If you use a question for every topic sentence in a paper, for example, your readers could find your paper predictable and boring.

COMMON TYPES OF TOPIC SENTENCES

The Direct Approach explicitly announces the purpose of the paragraph.

Lesson 41

draft

In this paragraph, I will explain why the school would lose money with a football team.

The purpose of this paragraph is to define a few important terms.

The Question indicates the paragraph's purpose by posing a question it will answer.

Why should we debate this issue anyway?

Where does lava come from?

The Nutshell states the major idea—not the purpose—of the paragraph, usually in just one sentence. (This is probably the most common type of topic sentence in college writing.)

A second reason for impeaching the governor is that she received illegal contributions.

Before long, I realized my aunt was sick.

Addressing the Reader anticipates what readers might be wondering about or doubting. The paragraph provides a response.

You might be wondering why it is necessary to build a new stadium.

My opponents would reasonably question my statistics, but the figures are accurate.

Connecting to the Previous Paragraph makes a clear link with the preceding ideas.

In contrast, however, the African swallow flies at a much faster rate.

After you complete the third step, proceed to the next: applying the varnish.

Let me offer one example of this concept.

The Alert calls special attention to a point the paragraph will cover. Readers should understand the importance of the paragraph.

It would be a mistake to assume that students do not care about racism.

If our leaders do not change this law, there will be a terrible price to pay.

Nothing will ever make me forget what I felt when I heard about Juan's death.

With a topic sentence to guide you as well as your readers, you can now provide the details needed to clarify, support, or expand the paragraph's point.

Lesson 41

draft

> **COMMONSENSE TIP** Be careful about being too direct when you write a topic sentence. Although useful for complex or highly formal papers, it often strikes readers as dull and contrived. However, the direct approach can be useful in a draft to clarify what you should focus on. You could revise it later into something less direct.

Strategies for Writing a Single-Paragraph Assignment

Suppose your assignment is to write a single paragraph. Fortunately, almost everything covered in this writing guide applies to writing paragraphs. When planning, drafting, and revising a paragraph, you still have to consider basic standards for effective writing (like those outlined on page 386). Here is a checklist for completing the single-paragraph assignment.

✳ *Checklist: Writing a Paragraph*

_____ Determine your purpose. See page 396.

- Determine the general purpose of the assignment (to express, to inform, or to persuade).
- Determine your specific purpose.

_____ Consider your audience. See page 398.

- Ask yourself questions about your readers' knowledge of and attitudes about your subject.

_____ Use a prewriting strategy (freewriting, clustering) to narrow your subject. See page 401.

_____ Write a topic sentence that states the main point of your paragraph. See page 403.

_____ Based on what you considered while prewriting, choose the details, examples, and evidence that best support your topic sentence. See page 404.

_____ Consider how you will organize these supporting ideas so that they clearly build on one another. See pages 404–407.

- Arrange these ideas in a brief informal outline of your paragraph.
- Plan a paragraph that is clearly structured. See page 410. In college writing, a paragraph often has the following parts:

  a *topic sentence* that states the main point of your

Lesson 41

draft

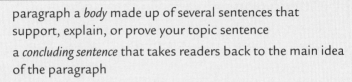

paragraph a *body* made up of several sentences that support, explain, or prove your topic sentence

a *concluding sentence* that takes readers back to the main idea of the paragraph

____ Write a draft of your paragraph based on your planning. See page 409.

____ Revise your paragraph. Consider what steps you might take to improve it. See page 420.

- Ask your teacher and other students for their feedback.

- Ask yourself revision questions based on your purpose.

- Ask yourself revision questions based on the five basic standards.

____ Edit your paragraph by eliminating errors in grammar, punctuation, mechanics, and word use. Follow specific guidelines given in Units One through Eleven of this book.

Consider how the following paragraph, written as part of an economics exam, reflects some of the steps in the checklist on page 412.

Example Assignment:　*Explain the difference between a country's gross national product (GNP) and its gross domestic product (GDP).*

EXAMPLE PARAGRAPH RESPONSE

Though they are both important indicators of a country's economic well-being, GNP and GDP are not the same. The GNP is the total market value of all goods and services produced by a country's labor force and capital anywhere in the world. For example, the market value of clothing produced and sold by The Gap, regardless of store and factory location, would figure into the United States' GNP. The GNP would include profits earned from Canadian and European stores, as well as from stores in places like Boston, Atlanta, and Los Angeles. The GDP, on the other hand, is the total market value of goods and services produced by a country's labor force and capital within a country's borders. Profits earned by The Gap in places other than the United States would not count toward the country's GDP. Each of these figures is a separate but equally valuable way to measure a country's economic health.

As the topic sentence indicates, the paragraph will focus on differences between GNP and GDP, and every sentence afterward explains at least one of these two concepts. Because this is a complex paragraph with technical information, the paragraph ends by reminding us of the overall point.

Lesson 41

draft

Put More Support into Paragraphs

Drafting involves arranging and developing the major ideas you sketched out in your outline. You should present each major idea in a paragraph. Then, within each paragraph, you have to provide additional details and support for the major idea. Avoid simply rewording your topic sentence; support it by adding new information, evidence, or ideas in each paragraph. To do this, ask yourself questions based on your purpose and audience.

GENERAL PURPOSE: *TO EXPRESS*

- If my subject involves an experience, what details can I include to bring this experience to life? How do I make clear to my audience how this experience affected me?

- If I am writing about a more abstract subject (such as something I read or a feeling I have about an idea), what details should I include to describe this subject and, more important, my personal reaction to it?

GENERAL PURPOSE: *TO INFORM*

- Considering limits on the paper's length, what should I tell my audience about the subject? What details, examples, or explanations will they need?

- Have I defined important terms, especially those that have a special meaning?

- To help readers understand the subject, can I compare it to something more familiar? Have I fully described the parts or functions of my subject?

- What information could I add that would be new to readers?

GENERAL PURPOSE: *TO PERSUADE*

- What are the major reasons why readers should accept the claim I am making?

- To prove my point, can I draw on what other writers have said?

- Can I give real or hypothetical examples to support my argument?

- If readers have doubts about my facts, can I convince them that my information is accurate?

- Have I carefully considered any objections or criticisms my readers might raise?

Lesson 41

draft

> **COMMONSENSE TIP** If your paragraph becomes too long, divide it into two or more paragraphs. You should avoid having more than one purpose or point in a single paragraph, but you certainly can have two or more paragraphs that deal with a similar idea in different ways.

One Student's Draft

To better understand your choices as you write, take a look at one student's draft. Daniel was given the following assignment:

Take a position on a controversy that involves some form of recreation or sport. Convince readers to accept your position. Use your own ideas and experiences, rather than drawing on outside research.

Daniel adapted the processes described in this lesson but did not follow a formula. Here are the basic steps of the drafting process and how he went through them.

Step 1: Determine the general purpose of the assignment.

Three words in the assignment were especially important for Daniel: *controversy, convince,* and *position.* These words made it clear the teacher wanted a persuasive essay. Thus, Daniel knew he was not supposed to merely write about his opinion. He realized the real goal was to write an essay that would compel readers to agree with him on a controversial subject. From the wording of the assignment, he also knew he had to write about a specific type of recreation or sport. Daniel immediately thought of two sports he knew and enjoyed: hunting and water skiing. He liked water skiing the most but knew hunting was a much more controversial topic that would lend itself to an argumentative essay.

Step 2: Consider how the audience might affect the essay.

The teacher's assignment did not say much about the audience for the paper, except that writers would need to convince them. For a brief time, Daniel considered writing the paper for fellow hunters. But why write an argument to people who already agreed with him? He thus assumed he would aim his argument at people who disliked hunting or who did not consider it a true sport. He knew they might never become hunters no matter how well he wrote, but he could attempt to persuade them to respect hunting as a sport.

Step 3: Narrow the topic to determine a specific purpose.

Daniel freewrote for five minutes and discovered how many types of hunting (and hunters) there were—all the way from shark hunting to hunting with

Lesson 41

draft

a bow and arrow. He focused on the type he knew best: deer hunting. He decided to defend the sport against criticisms he had heard from friends and acquaintances.

Step 4: Consider possible support and develop an informal outline.

Daniel recalled all the complaints he had heard about hunting and wasn't certain what his exact thesis would be. He decided that, for this draft, he would use a broad thesis sentence and revise it later if need be. Once he had that matter settled, he decided on the major points he most wanted to bring up, based on the arguments he had heard before about why deer hunting is "wrong." He listed all the arguments (for and against) that he had encountered. Then, he made an outline that covered some of these points—the ones he considered the most persuasive. Here is his outline:

> *Thesis statement: In this paper, I will argue why deer hunting is a true sport.*
>
> *Introduction:*
>
> * *Give personal experience about some people's misconceptions about hunting.*
> * *Indicate my position (my thesis statement).*
> * *(Separate paragraph?) Explain what I mean by "hunting" and "sport."*
>
> *Reason #1:*
>
> * *Deer hunting is a true sport because*
>   * *—it is competitive because the deer has its own advantages in the contest*
>   * *—it takes special skills*
>
> *Conclusion:*
>
> * *Point out my experience with enjoying people and wildlife through hunting.*

Step 5: Write a draft.

With this basic plan, Daniel began writing. He was worried about how many paragraphs he should have but decided the goal for draft one was just to write down his major ideas. He knew he could revise the essay later for any organizational problems.

Before you read Daniel's draft, consider the basic guidelines below for writing an argument. We tailored the basic standards from page 386 to cover this particular type of writing. Consider how these guidelines might have helped Daniel as he drafted—as well as helped him consider what to change once he completed a draft.

GUIDELINES FOR WRITING AN ARGUMENT

Purpose: The thesis must be controversial. That is, someone must disagree with it if the claim is truly argumentative.

Support: You usually can't cover every possible reason for and against your thesis. Focus on the reasons that would be most likely to convince most people who disagree with your position.

Organization: There is no rule about where to put your most important reason. What is essential is that you avoid the temptation to list a bunch of reasons—especially in just one paragraph. Focus each paragraph on thoroughly explaining one major reason that supports your thesis.

Style: Your goal is to make your readers accept your claim. Therefore, avoid a rude or confrontational tone. You rarely win over an audience by insulting them.

Mechanics: Right or not, many people will judge your argument by how well you follow conventions of formal English. Mechanical errors can affect your overall credibility. However, the revising stage will allow you to correct any such problems. For now, focus on getting your best ideas onto paper.

Here is Daniel's draft. He adhered to his informal outline for the most part, but then changed his mind about a few things (such as the conclusion). How well does this draft reflect the guidelines listed above? Remember: this is a work in progress, and the writer has time to revise. (Daniel's revision is not included in this lesson. You will have the opportunity to revise his draft in Lesson 42.)

DANIEL'S FIRST DRAFT

Deer Hunting as a True Sport

Not long ago, a girl I work with asked me what I was doing over the weekend, and I told her I was going deer hunting. She immediately said, "Why do you want to murder deer? What challenge is there in blasting harmless animals with a high-powered rifle?" She became upset and walked away before I could even explain why I enjoy this sport. My friend might never read this paper, but I want to explain to others why deer hunting is a true sport.

First, I should explain what I mean by "sport" and "hunting." I know all too well that some people say they're going deer hunting when all they do is camp out, get drunk, and drive through the woods trying to shoot deer. I don't consider that hunting. True hunting involves a serious attempt to carefully find your prey and then kill the deer with one accurate shot.

Lesson 41

draft

The word "sport" refers to any recreational activity where mental and physical talent is needed to achieve a difficult goal, and hunting meets this definition.

Hunting deer requires a good deal of talent if the hunter is to compete against a deer. You might think the unarmed deer has no advantages in this contest. However, the truth is that the deer has natural defenses that give it the advantage. Deer move silently if they move at all. Many learn to stay hidden in thick bushes during deer season. When they do come out, they are well camouflaged and hard to detect. Another advantage the deer has is its speed. These are not stupid animals. They seem to know when they are being hunted, and the slightest sound can make them bolt away so fast that even an expert sharpshooter would miss. They usually travel in a herd and use special signs to warn each other. If a deer hears something suspicious, it will raise its tail as a warning to others. If one deer hears or sees you, then in seconds they will all know. Their sense of smell, sight, and hearing are superb, so it is not common for you to be in their presence long without their knowing it.

A hunter has to be skilled to compete against this adversary. Successful hunters have to wait patiently while remaining still and quiet in a spot where they suspect the deer might come. Not just anyone can pick out fresh deer trails or remain out of sight, especially at 6:00 in the morning when the temperature is below freezing.

Another talent the hunter needs is the ability to shoot well. I myself have had to shoot a deer from one hundred yards away. Even with a scope, it can be a difficult shot because you do not want to merely wound the deer. A steady hand and patience are just as important as having good eyesight or a high-powered scope.

Many people will never give deer hunting a try. I understand it is not a sport for everyone. But too many people criticize deer hunters without really understanding the sport. I might not have persuaded you to become a hunter, but I hope to have proven that deer hunting is not a mindless activity that pits a human against a helpless opponent.

✳ *Critical Questions for Drafting*

Whether you are writing a single paragraph or an essay, these questions can assist you, especially toward the end of the drafting stage.

Purpose and Audience

- Have you changed your mind about your topic since you began your draft? If so, start thinking about the changes your draft will need in order to be consistent.

- Now that you have examined your topic more carefully, who is the best audience for this draft? If you have changed your mind about your audience, you might also need to reconsider some of what you have written thus far.

Support

- What ideas need clarification? Adding details is one of the important parts of the drafting stage. Add too much detail rather than too little. Later, you can decide what to delete, if anything.

- What claims need more support or proof? If you are trying to persuade readers, you cannot just express yourself. You must convince them. Consider their possible objections and respond to them.

Organization

- Does each paragraph focus on one main idea? It's very common for paragraphs to ramble a bit while the writer explores ideas. You can fix such problems later, but at least be aware that some paragraphs might need to be tightened and revised for coherence.

- Is there an introduction and conclusion to your essay? During the drafting stage, these sections are often far from complete, but you need to recognize these potential problems so you can address them later.

Applying What You Know

Once you have completed a draft of an essay, make an outline that effectively summarizes its major points. If you cannot do so, the draft will likely need to be revised later for organization.

Lesson 41

draft

Revising

If your deadline allows, put your draft aside and return later to revise it. You might make small changes here and there as you draft, but don't consider your writing complete simply because you have put your ideas onto paper. Now it is time to consider how to improve your draft. You will get the most out of this stage of writing if you understand one of the most often-overlooked principles of writing.

> **COMMONSENSE TIP** Revision is *more* than looking for problems with individual words and sentences. It means looking for ways to improve your overall purpose, support, and organization. You revise your paper to make it clearer and stronger.

Too often, writers look only at individual sentences and words when they revise. These are important, of course; that is why we wrote this book. However, a grammatically correct paper can be useless if it lacks ideas or is unorganized. This lesson will help you revise your paper.

Ask Questions as You Revise

Many writers are confused about what to revise. As one student put it, "If I knew what had to be revised, I would have done it when I drafted the paper!" But even experienced writers cannot keep track of all the questions they could ask themselves as they write that would improve their paper. Revising, therefore, means looking for opportunities for improvement that perhaps did not occur to you in the midst of putting ideas into words, sentences, and paragraphs.

In college, you are usually writing not just for yourself but for others, so it is useful to obtain feedback from at least one other person. It might be helpful to write down specific questions for this person to consider. Developing a habit of asking yourself such questions will also help you understand what to revise when feedback isn't practical. Here are two sets of questions to ask of your draft:

Questions based on your *general purpose*.

Questions based on *basic standards* that apply to most college writing.

These overlap, but each set of questions presents a different way of thinking about revision. Tailor these to fit your own specific purpose and situation.

Ask Questions about *General Purpose.*   We began this writing guide by telling you to start your writing process by determining your purpose. You should also make a habit of rethinking your purpose at the revision stage. Here are some more questions to ask yourself as you revise.

GENERAL PURPOSE: *TO EXPRESS*

- What is the point of my story? Is that point clear?
- Does this paper give an account of how I really feel?
- What details could I add to help show how I feel or think about my subject?
- Have I brought my subject to life for my readers?
- Are the events in my narrative arranged in an order that makes sense for my purpose and audience?

GENERAL PURPOSE: *TO INFORM*

- What is the point of my paper? Is that point clear?
- What information have I left out? Would readers expect me to cover this material?
- Have I told my readers something that is new or not widely known? Have I provided enough examples or explanations?
- Have I gone beyond the "basic idea" and given my readers a deeper understanding of the subject?
- Can I add more facts, details, or examples, perhaps based on research?
- Are my details and examples arranged in an order that makes sense for my purpose and audience?

GENERAL PURPOSE: *TO PERSUADE*

- What is the point of my paper? Is that point clear?
- Is my claim really arguable? Did I mistakenly word it in a way that nobody could disagree with?
- Where is my strongest support? How can I make it stronger? Where is my weakest support? Should I keep it? If I keep it, how can I strengthen it?

- What criticisms will I face from readers with an opposing viewpoint? What can I do to gain their support?

- Do my supporting ideas follow each other in an order that makes the most sense for my purpose and audience?

Some of these questions are similar to those you asked when you developed paragraphs and topic sentences (pages 403, 410). It is not unusual for writers to ask themselves similar questions from the beginning to the end of the writing process. After all, if you had to ask completely new questions, you might end up writing a new paper.

Ask Questions Based on *Basic Standards*.   Another way to approach revision is to think about how readers evaluate writing. Practically everything we have discussed so far goes back to the basic standards for good writing that we presented in the Overview: purpose, support, organization, style, and mechanics (see page 386). If readers indeed use these criteria to evaluate writing, then one way to revise is to ask yourself questions about these criteria. Consider how these questions might be tailored to suit both your general and your specific purposes.

BASIC STANDARD: *PURPOSE*

- Is my specific purpose clear?

- Does my thesis control the paper? Do my topic sentences help my paragraphs show, explain, or prove my thesis?

- Have I delivered on my thesis? That is, did I do everything it indicated I would do? If not, should I continue to narrow my specific purpose?

- Or, if my paper does not deliver on my thesis, should I add more to my paper so that it does everything I indicated I would do?

COMMONSENSE TIP   While you were planning and drafting, your thesis sentence was something to start you off, but at this stage, think of it as a contract. In one sense you are promising readers that your paper will achieve whatever purpose you have indicated in your thesis sentence. Make sure the wording is exactly what it should be to match your paper.

BASIC STANDARD: *SUPPORT*

Lesson 42

rev

- Where can I add more details, examples, or facts so readers will understand my point? On the other hand, should I delete some specifics because they do not clearly support my point?

- Do I give the most support to the paragraphs that are most important for my purpose?

- In each paragraph, what would my readers possibly disagree with? What could I delete, add, or change to make my argument more convincing?

- Is my support too general or vague as a whole or within paragraphs? What can I do to be more specific?

- Are my details, examples, and evidence too common or obvious?

BASIC STANDARD: *ORGANIZATION*

- Do I have an introduction that alerts readers to my specific purpose and my thesis?

- Does each paragraph revolve around one point?

- Do my paragraphs build on each other? Does each have a clear connection to the one before and after it? If not, can I rearrange paragraphs, add words or sentences to clarify connections, or delete paragraphs that do not fit?

- Within paragraphs, does each sentence relate to the one before and after it?

- Does the conclusion merely summarize? If so, what else could I do to give a sense of closure?

COMMONSENSE TIP To help you clarify the connections between sentences, consider using transitional words and phrases like these:

also	for example	in fact
as a matter of fact	for instance	in short
as a result	furthermore	indeed
as I said earlier	however	nevertheless
consequently	in addition	next
finally	in brief	therefore
first	in comparison	to sum up

Be careful not to overuse these terms; use them only when they express a true relationship. (See Lesson 16 for guidance in punctuating transitional terms.)

BASIC STANDARD: *STYLE*

- Considering my audience and my purpose, is my paper too formal? Too informal? Do I use too much slang? Too many stuffy words? Do I seem too "chummy" or relaxed with readers? Too impersonal?

Lesson 42

rev

- Can I combine sentences for more variety? What sentences seem too choppy or too awkward?

- What clearer or more precise words could I use?

BASIC STANDARD: *MECHANICS*

- Have I followed the guidelines in Units One through Eleven of this book?

You must decide how to answer these questions. We wish we could give the answers as easily as we pose the questions, but your own opinions and writing situation will determine how you will respond. Here is an example of one student's revision process.

Using Questions

Consider how one student, Maria, asked a few questions to help revise a short paper. Here is the assignment:

> *Write a paragraph (about 250 words) that explains your position about a controversy in a town or city you know well. This is a brief argument, so focus on important reasons.*

After freewriting, Maria chose a problem involving her hometown of Marshall, Texas: whether to have a curfew for minors. Maria realized that she needed to take a stance and decided she was against the proposed curfew. Thus, she developed a thesis sentence that would serve as a topic sentence for her paragraph: *"Marshall should not have a curfew for minors."* Using clustering, she considered several reasons supporting her position. (These prewriting and drafting techniques are discussed in the previous two lessons.) Maria then wrote the following draft.

> *Marshall should not have a curfew for minors. First, it's not fair to have a curfew for just minors. Second, how can it be enforced? There are not enough police officers working at night to help with real crimes. Third, a curfew punishes all teenagers just because a few have caused trouble lately after midnight. Finally, the real troublemakers are going to cause trouble no matter what the curfew is. How would a curfew cut down, for instance, on teenagers who sell illegal drugs? This proposed curfew is completely illogical and will not accomplish anything.*

This paragraph was far shorter than what the teacher required. Maria was not sure how to revise the paragraph to make it longer, for the paragraph seemed to express her feelings on the topic. To help her not only with the length but also with detecting other problems, Maria looked at the questions dealing with her general purpose.

She considered the assignment again and noticed several important terms from the prompt: "your position," "controversy," "argument," and "important reasons." She realized that her general purpose was not just to express her opinion but to *convince* readers to accept her position. This perspective led Maria to consider one set of questions especially important for persuasive writing:

Where is my strongest support, and how can I make it even stronger?

Where is my weakest support, and should I keep it? If so, how can I make it strong?

Maria's first draft was, unfortunately, a "shotgun" approach. She tossed in as many reasons as she could without concentrating on any of them, hoping that at least one reason would work. She also did not make her reasons strong from a reader's perspective. Maria realized she had merely given a list of reasons without really trying to convince people. To improve this draft as well as to make it meet the word requirement, she decided to focus on what she thought to be the two most convincing reasons: the first and third reasons from the draft.

Maria was not sure how to make these reasons stronger, so she next considered questions dealing with basic standards. Rather than answering all these questions, she focused on the ones dealing with support, since these are designed to help writers add and improve reasons that strengthen their claims. She thought two in particular would help her add useful support:

Where can I add more details, examples, or facts so readers will understand my point?

What would my readers disagree with?

After considering these questions, Maria realized she did not have a single specific example (or any sort of specifics at all) in her draft. Nor had she considered why people might disagree with any of her reasons. The two questions above helped her realize she would be clearer and more convincing if her paragraph would (1) give concrete, realistic details and (2) explain why her reasons are valid despite potential criticism from some readers.

She used her hometown newspaper to provide her with specifics. To deal with potential criticisms, she talked with a friend who supported the idea of a curfew. Her revised paragraph focused on doing a good job with two reasons, rather than superficially covering four vague reasons.

Lesson 42

rev

Marshall should not have a curfew for minors. First, it is not fair to have a curfew for just minors. I examined the Marshall newspaper for the last three days. There were sixteen crimes described in the paper, and the reporters gave ages for suspects in twelve of the crimes. Only four of the twelve suspects were minors, and only two of these crimes occurred late at night. If the curfew is designed to cut down on crime, should it not be applied to the people who actually commit the most crimes? I do not believe there is enough evidence to prove that minors commit the majority of crimes, so they should not be singled out. In addition, a curfew punishes all teenagers just because a few have caused trouble after midnight. Some people might say that a curfew is not a real punishment at all. They say that minors could stay at home for entertainment, go to a friend's home, or be accompanied by an adult after the curfew. However, keeping people from enjoying themselves in public is a punishment. Some movies, for example, end after the curfew, and many people like to enjoy a late-night meal at a restaurant after seeing a show or dancing. Furthermore, not all parents are willing or able to hang out with their children at night. Forbidding people to enjoy a harmless but enjoyable activity is a punishment, and it is an unfair punishment because teenagers who do not break the law should not suffer simply because a few teenagers are guilty.

The more Maria thought about specific information and how people might respond to her reasons, the more she realized she could add to even this much longer paragraph. Thus, she added two final sentences not only to give a sense of closure to the paragraph but also to let people know that even more could be said.

The idea of a curfew is complex and controversial. I have covered only two reasons, but many issues need to be considered before Marshall adopts a curfew.

BUT WHAT HAPPENS IF . . . ?

"I now see a need to revise but am not sure how." Suppose you see a problem with your logic in one paragraph. We suggest you go back to the prewriting techniques suggested earlier (see page 401) — or to whatever critical thinking strategies you use to come up with ideas or solve a problem. Don't underestimate the value of using the *basic standards* on page 386 as your own personal revision checklist, though.

"I'm not sure if my revision made the paper any better." We have to be truthful: there are times when revisions hurt rather than help. If you are unsure, it is time to have someone read your draft and give you an honest reaction. Try to get feedback from at least two people.

Lesson 42

rev

COMMONSENSE TIP When you ask for help, avoid explaining the reason behind a revision, or at least wait until your reader has finished reading and responding. Otherwise, you are basically saying, "Here's why I did this. Tell me I'm right."

"My paper is a total mess. I'm not sure where to start revising." Don't overlook this option: maybe your draft has done the job of helping you explore ideas. Now put it away and start over. This is undoubtedly the hardest thing a writer can do, admit that a draft isn't working. Many people, in fact, cannot bring themselves to start over. But consider it as an option.

COMMONSENSE TIP One last time before you're ready to turn in the assignment, look back at the wording the teacher used in giving the assignment. Too many students get so caught up in their writing process, they overlook specific requirements.

The bottom line? Writing is a process that is never 100 percent complete. There is no such thing as a perfect draft. If you go about your writing believing that the goal is perfection, you might get discouraged. Instead, think of it this way: the goal is to produce writing that is *as effective as you can make it*, given your deadline.

✳ *Critical Questions for Revising*

Lesson 42 has focused on questions you should ask yourself while revising. It's nearly impossible to remember them all, so we end this lesson by noting what we believe are the most important questions you should ask as you revise your writing.

Purpose and Audience

- What is the overall purpose of your draft?
- Where might readers think that you have drifted away from this purpose?
- Does your draft fulfill all your teacher's requirements? (Check the written assignment, if one was given to you.)

Support

- What details can you add to help readers fully understand what your draft is saying? →

Lesson 42

rev

- What additional logic or evidence can you add to persuade readers to accept anything you have said that might be debatable?

Organization

- What is the purpose of each paragraph? Do paragraphs ramble, or is there a controlling idea that will be clear to your readers?

- Have you made the connections between sentences clear?

Style, Grammar, and Usage

- What words could you change to make more clear or more specific?

- Are there any sentences that seem too long or awkward?

- Do you have any doubts about particular punctuation choices you made? (Look at your use of commas and apostrophes in particular.)

Applying What You Know

Reread Daniel's draft presented at the end of Lesson 41. Use the questions listed above to describe at least five specific changes you think Daniel should consider. Make sure at least a couple go beyond merely changing particular words or punctuation marks.

APPENDIX A

Brief Documentation Guide

In college, it is particularly important that student writers indicate when they are using words or ideas taken from somebody else. Students must let readers know which words or ideas were borrowed and where they originally appeared. This process is known as documentation — properly and clearly indicating the use of other people's words and ideas that are not the writer's own. Improper or incomplete documentation is plagiarism, a serious offense normally considered a form of cheating or fraud.

When writers document sources, they must follow very specific rules for citing the research materials they use. This brief guide provides the basic rules of what is called the MLA system of documentation, which is the most common system for composition courses. This guide is not intended to cover all possible types of sources you might use, just the most common ones. For more information on correctly using other people's ideas, see Lesson 25 (Quotation Marks with Direct Quotations and Paraphrases), or go to *Research and Documentation Online* at dianahacker.com/resdoc.

MLA Format for In-Text Citations

You should provide an in-text citation every time you quote from, paraphrase, or summarize an outside source. Your citation, which usually includes both source and page number, should appear next to the sentences in your paper that refer to the source information. Follow the models below for correct examples of in-text citations.

ONE AUTHOR

"Every day, around thirty-four new food products alone are introduced. The dizzying array of new items reflects a micro-splitting of problems to create more 'must-have' new solutions" (Hammerslough 14).

Hammerslough points out that "[e]very day, around thirty-four new food products alone are introduced. The dizzying array of new items reflects a microsplitting of problems to create more 'must-have' new solutions" (14).

TWO OR THREE AUTHORS

More than 90 percent of the hazardous waste produced in the United States comes from seven major industries, all energy-intensive (Romm and Curtis 70).

FOUR OR MORE AUTHORS

Boys tend to get called on in the classroom more often than girls (Oesterling et al. 243).

CORPORATE AUTHOR OR GOVERNMENT PUBLICATION

Physical activity has been shown to protect against certain forms of cancer "either by balancing caloric intake with energy expenditure or by other mechanisms" (American Cancer Society 43).

UNKNOWN AUTHOR

According to a recent study, drivers are 42 percent more likely to get into an accident if they are using a wireless phone while driving ("Driving Dangerously" 32).

BIBLE

Consider the words of Solomon: "If your enemies are hungry, give them bread to eat; and if they are thirsty, give them water to drink" (*New Revised Standard Bible*, Prov. 25.21).

SOURCE WITHOUT PAGE NUMBERS

"There is no definitive correlation between benign breast tumors and breast cancer" (Pratt).

INDIRECT SOURCES

In discussing the baby mania trend, *Time* writers claimed, "Career women are opting for pregnancy and they are doing it in style" (qtd. in Faludi 106).

MLA Format for a List of Works Cited

At the end of your paper, you must provide a list of the sources from which you quoted, paraphrased, or summarized. Put the entire list in alphabetical order using the author's last name first and the title as it appears on the title page of the source. If your source has no author, alphabetize it by the first main word of the title. Double-space your works cited page. Begin each entry at the left margin and indent the subsequent lines five spaces.

Books

ONE AUTHOR

Hammerslough, Jane. *Dematerializing: Taming the Power of Possessions.*
Cambridge: Perseus, 2001. Print.

TWO OR THREE AUTHORS

Douglas, Susan J., and Meredith W. Michaels. *The Mommy Myth: The
Idealization of Motherhood and How It Has Undermined Women.* New
York: Free Press, 2004. Print.

FOUR OR MORE AUTHORS

Foster, Hal, et al. *Art Since 1900.* New York: Thames, 2005. Print.

UNKNOWN AUTHOR

National Geographic Atlas of the World. 8th ed. Washington, DC:
National Geographic, 2004. Print.

EDITOR OR COMPILER

Byrne, Patrick H., ed. *Dialogue Between Science and Religion.*
Scranton: U of Scranton P, 2005. Print.

EDITOR AND AUTHOR

Ellison, Ralph. *Living with Music: Ralph Ellison's Jazz Writings.*
Ed. Robert G. O'Meally. New York: Modern, 2002. Print.

EDITION NUMBERS

Honderich, Ted, ed. *The Oxford Companion to Philosophy.* 2nd ed.
Oxford: Oxford UP, 2005. Print.

ANTHOLOGY

Singer, Peter, and Renata Singer, eds. *The Moral of the Story: An
Anthology of Ethics Through Literature.* Oxford: Blackwell, 2005. Print.

A WORK IN AN ANTHOLOGY

Roberts, Deborah. "Unmasking Step-Motherhood." *Rise Up Singing:
Black Women Writers on Motherhood.* Ed. Cecelie S. Berry. New
York: Doubleday, 2004. 127–32. Print.

SIGNED ARTICLE IN A REFERENCE BOOK

Cheney, Ralph Holt. "Coffee." *Collier's Encyclopedia.* 2004 ed. Print.

UNSIGNED ARTICLE IN A REFERENCE BOOK

"Sonata." *The American Heritage Dictionary of the English Language.* 4th ed. 2000. Print.

Periodicals

ARTICLE IN A MONTHLY MAGAZINE

Douthat, Ross. "The God Vote: The Significance of the Religion Gap." *Atlantic Monthly* Sept. 2004: 52–53. Print.

ARTICLE IN A WEEKLY MAGAZINE

Corliss, Richard. "Should We All Be Vegetarians?" *Time* 15 July 2002: 48–56. Print.

ARTICLE IN A NEWSPAPER

Winter, Greg. "Governors Seek Rise in High School Standards." *New York Times* 23 Feb. 2005: A17. Print.

UNKNOWN AUTHOR

"Consumer Confidence Suffers Sharper Fall than Expected." Associated Press. *New York Times* 31 July 2002: C6. Print.

EDITORIAL

"Terry Schiavo's Affliction." Editorial. *Boston Globe* 5 Apr. 2005: A14. Print.

LETTER TO THE EDITOR

Levy, Ronald. "Distorted View of Israel." Letter. *Boston Globe* 1 Aug. 2002: A18. Print.

ARTICLE IN A JOURNAL

Ryan, Katy. "Revolutionary Suicide in Toni Morrison's Fiction." *African American Review* 34.3 (2000): 389–412. Print.

Electronic Sources

PROFESSIONAL SITE: ENTIRE WEB SITE

National Council of Teachers of English. *National Council of Teachers of English.* NCTE, 2010. Web. 5 Mar. 2010.

PROFESSIONAL SITE: SPECIFIC PAGE

National Council of Teachers of English. "Mission Statement." *National Council of Teachers of English.* NCTE, 2010. Web. 11 Mar. 2010.

"Disability Services Online." *Stephen F. Austin State University*. SFASU, 2008. Web. 8 June 2008.

PERSONAL WEB SITE

Kilbourne, Jean. Home page. Jean Kilbourne, 9 Sept. 2007. Web. 10 Nov. 2007.

ARTICLE FROM AN ONLINE MAGAZINE OR NEWSPAPER

Greenwald, Glenn. "The Art of Neoconservative Innuendo." *Salon.com*. Salon Media Group, 20 Sept. 2007. Web. 22 Sept. 2007.

ONLINE BOOK

Burroughs, Edgar Rice. *The Mad King*. New York: Ace, 1914. *Electronic Text Center, University of Virginia Library*. Web. 14 Feb. 2008.

ARTICLE FROM AN ONLINE DATABASE

Kim, Sharon. "Edith Wharton and Epiphany." *Journal of Modern Literature* 29.3 (2006): 150-75. *General OneFile*. Web. 17 Sept. 2008.

Rice, Raymond J. "Cannibalism and the Act of Revenge in Tudor-Stuart Drama." *Studies in English Literature, 1500–1900* 44.2 (2004): 297-317. *Expanded Academic ASAP*. Web. 9 Jan. 2008.

E-MAIL MESSAGE

Balbert, Peter. "Re: The Hemingway Hero." Message to the author. 15 Mar. 2005. E-mail.

POSTING TO AN ONLINE DISCUSSION

Ponterio, Bob. "Re: European Constitution." *Foreign Language Teaching Forum*. University at Buffalo, 7 Apr. 2005. Web. 9 Apr. 2008.

CD-ROM

"Potemkin." *The Oxford English Dictionary*. 2nd ed. Oxford: Oxford UP, 2000. CD-ROM.

Other Sources

ADVERTISEMENT

Nike. Advertisement. *Vogue* Nov. 2001: 94–95. Print.

RADIO OR TELEVISION INTERVIEW

Dole, Bob. Interview by Terry Gross. *Fresh Air*. Natl. Public Radio. WBUR, Boston. 12 Apr. 2005. Radio.

PAMPHLET

Administrative Office of the United States Courts. *Bankruptcy Basics.* Washington: GPO, 2006. Print.

FILM OR DVD

Black Hawk Down. Dir. Ridley Scott. Perf. Josh Hartnett, Ewan McGregor, Tom Sizemore, and Sam Shepard. Columbia, 2001. DVD.

SOUND RECORDING

Palmer, Keke. "The Game Song." *So Uncool.* Atlantic, 2007. CD.

TELEVISION OR RADIO PROGRAM

Lawrence of Arabia: The Battle for the Arab World. PBS. WSRE, Pensacola, FL. 20 Sept. 2007. Television.

PUBLISHED INTERVIEW

Gould, Stephen Jay. "Life's Work: Questions for Stephen Jay Gould." *New York Times Magazine* 2 June 2002: 18. Print.

APPENDIX B

Guide to Grammar Terminology

This guide is an alphabetical listing of all the grammar terms used in this book. Each term is defined with an example. For some grammar terms, there are also helpful hints and suggestions. Anytime you encounter a grammar term you are unsure about, look it up in this guide.

> **NOTE** Examples of the term being defined are in ***bold italic*** type. References to important related terms are <u>underlined</u>. Ungrammatical phrases or sentences are indicated by an **✗**.

Active The term *active* or *active voice* refers to sentences in which the subject plays the role of the actor, or the "doer" of the action, as opposed to <u>passive</u> sentences, in which the subject is the person or thing *receiving* the action of the verb. For example, in the active sentence ***Sandy saw Pat***, the subject *Sandy* is doing the seeing, whereas in the passive sentence ***Pat was seen by Sandy***, *Pat* is the person being seen. Also see <u>passive</u>.

Adjective Adjectives play two different roles: (1) they modify the nouns that they precede (*a **large** tree*); or (2) after certain verbs like *be, seem,* and *become,* adjectives describe the subject of the sentence. For example, in the sentence *The tree is **green***, the adjective *green* describes the subject *tree*. Also see <u>article</u> and <u>proper adjective</u>.

Adjective clause An adjective clause (also called a <u>relative clause</u>) always modifies the noun it follows. In the sentence *The tree **that we planted** is getting leaves*, the adjective clause *that we planted* modifies the noun *tree*. An adjective clause begins with a <u>relative pronoun</u> (*that* in the example sentence is a relative pronoun). There are two types of adjective clauses. Depending on the relation of the adjective clause to the noun it modifies, the clause is either an <u>essential adjective clause</u> or a <u>nonessential adjective clause</u>.

Adverb An adverb modifies a verb (*walked **briskly***), an adjective (***pretty** tall*), another adverb (***very** badly*), or a sentence (***Truthfully***, *I do not know the answer*). Adverbs that modify verbs give *when, where, why, how,* or *to what degree* information. Such adverbs normally occur at the end of a sentence but can usually be

435

moved to the beginning; for example: *I got a ticket* **yesterday. Yesterday**, *I got a ticket*. An <u>adverb prepositional phrase</u> or an <u>adverb clause</u> also modifies a verb and may move to the beginning of the sentence.

Adverb clause   An adverb clause modifies a verb, giving *when, where, why,* or *how* information. Adverb clauses are easily moved to the beginning of the <u>independent clause</u> from their normal position after the main clause; for example: *I was at the office* **when you called. When you called,** *I was at the office.*

Agreement   Some words in a sentence are so closely related that the form of one determines the form of another. When such words are correctly chosen in relation to one another, they are in *agreement*. A <u>pronoun</u> should agree with its <u>antecedent</u> in terms of gender and number (*The* **boy** *ate* **his** *food*), and a subject should agree with its verb in terms of number (**He was** *hungry*). Also see <u>subject-verb agreement</u>.

Antecedent   See <u>pronoun antecedent</u>.

Appositive   An appositive is a noun (or a noun and its modifiers) that renames (further identifies) a preceding noun. For example, in *My English teacher,* **Ms. Rodriguez,** *also teaches Spanish, Ms. Rodriguez* is an appositive that renames (further identifies) the noun *teacher.* Usually, two commas set off the appositive from the rest of the sentence, as in the example here.

Article   Articles are a special kind of <u>adjective</u> that come before all other types of adjectives. For example, in the phrase ***the*** *tall trees*, the article *the* must come before the adjective *tall*; that is, we cannot say ✗ *tall the trees*. There are two types of articles: <u>definite</u> (*the*) and <u>indefinite</u> (*a* and *an*).

Clause   A clause contains at least one subject and one verb. A clause that stands alone as a complete thought is called an <u>independent clause</u> or a *main clause*. All sentences must contain at least one main clause. For types of clauses that cannot stand alone, see <u>dependent clause</u>.

Colon   The colon (:) is frequently used to introduce lists. The part of the sentence before the colon should be able to stand alone as an <u>independent clause</u>, for example, ***These are the three most common flavors of ice cream: vanilla, chocolate, and strawberry***. Do not break up an independent clause with a colon. A common error is adding a colon after the verb, for example, ✗ *The three most common flavors of ice cream are: vanilla, chocolate, and strawberry.*

Comma splice   A comma splice is the incorrect use of a comma to join two sentences or two <u>independent clauses</u> (✗ ***Angela answered the phone, she was the only person in the office***). Also see <u>fused sentence</u> and <u>run-on sentence</u>.

Common noun   A common noun refers to categories of people, places, things, and ideas, in contrast to a <u>proper noun</u>, which names particular individual people or places. For example, ***reporter*** is a common noun, but *Lois Lane* is a proper noun. Common nouns can be identified by their use of the <u>definite article</u> *the*. For example, *replace* and *replacement* are related words, but you can tell that **replacement** is a common noun because you can say *the replacement*. *Replace* is not a common noun because you cannot say ✗ *the replace*.

Complement A complement is a <u>noun</u>, <u>pronoun</u>, or <u>adjective</u> required by a verb to make a valid sentence. For example, in the sentence *Scrooge became* **rich**, the adjective *rich* is the complement of the verb *became*. If the complement is omitted, the sentence is no longer valid: ✗ *Scrooge became*. In traditional grammar, the complement must refer back to and describe the subject. In our example sentence, *rich* describes the subject, *Scrooge*.

Complete sentence A complete sentence is an <u>independent clause</u> that can be correctly punctuated with a terminal punctuation mark, such as a period, a question mark, or an exclamation point. The opposite of a complete sentence is a <u>fragment</u>, which is only part of a sentence and which cannot be punctuated correctly with a terminal punctuation mark.

Compound A compound consists of two or more grammatical units of the same type joined by *and* or another <u>coordinating conjunction</u>. For example, in the sentence *Donald is* **rich** *and* **famous**, *rich* and *famous* are compound adjectives. For more examples, see <u>compound predicate</u>, <u>compound sentence</u>, and <u>compound subject</u>.

Compound sentence When two or more sentences (<u>independent clauses</u>) are combined into one, the result is a compound sentence. A compound sentence is usually created by inserting a <u>coordinating conjunction</u> between the two "former" sentences, as in *I left the party early,* **but** *Angie refused to leave*.

Compound subject Compound subjects are two (or more) <u>subjects</u> joined by a <u>coordinating conjunction</u>. For example, the sentence **My next-door neighbor** *and* **I** *usually carpool to work*, contains two subjects (*my next-door neighbor* and *I*) joined by the coordinating conjunction *and*.

Compound verb Compound verbs are two verbs (more accurately, two <u>predicates</u>) joined by a <u>coordinating conjunction</u>. For example, in the sentence *Batman* **went** *to his bat cave and* **called** *his mother*, the verbs *went* and *called* are compound verbs joined by the coordinating conjunction *and*.

Conjunction The term *conjunction* means "join together." Conjunctions are words that join grammatical elements together. There are two types of conjunctions: (1) <u>coordinating conjunctions</u>—words like **and, but**, and **or**; and (2) subordinating conjunctions—words like **when, since, because**, and **if**, which begin adverb clauses.

Conjunctive adverb See <u>transitional term</u>.

Contraction A contraction is the shortened form of a word that results from leaving out some letters or sounds. In writing, the missing letters in contractions are indicated by an apostrophe ('); for example, *I'll* is the contracted form of *I will*. This use of the apostrophe in contractions is different from its use to indicate possession; see possessive apostrophe.

Coordinating conjunction A coordinating conjunction joins grammatical units of the same type, creating a compound. There are seven coordinating conjunctions, which can be remembered by the acronym *FANBOYS:* **for, and, nor, but, or, yet, so**.

Count noun A count noun is a common noun that can be counted: **one cat/ two cats**. Nouns that have irregular plural forms — such as **one child/two children, one goose/two geese**, and **one deer/two deer** — are also count nouns. For nouns that cannot be counted, see noncount noun.

Dangling modifier A dangling modifier is a noun modifier (usually a participial phrase) that does not actually modify the noun it is intended to modify. The modifier is said to be "dangling" because the noun it is supposed to modify is not in the sentence. For example, in the sentence **Based on the evidence,** *the jury acquitted the defendant,* the phrase *based on the evidence* is a dangling modifier because it does not really modify *jury*. (You cannot say that *the jury was based on the evidence*.) Also see misplaced modifier.

Definite article The definite article is *the*, which can be used either with a singular or with a plural common noun. Use the definite article when referring to a specific object or thing that is also known to the reader or listener. For example, in the sentence *Please hand me* **the** *cup,* you can assume that the speaker is referring to a specific cup that the reader or hearer can also identify. When not referring to anything specific, or when referring to something that is *not* known to the listener, use an indefinite article: *a* or *an*.

Dependent clause A dependent clause is a clause that cannot be used as a complete sentence by itself, as opposed to an independent clause, which can stand alone. There are three types of dependent clauses: (1) an adjective clause modifies a noun (*I read the book* **that you recommended**); (2) an adverb clause modifies a verb (*I was in the shower* **when the telephone rang**); and (3) a noun clause plays the role of subject or object (**What you see** *is* **what you get**). A dependent clause is also called a subordinate clause.

Direct object Direct object is the technical term for an object required by a verb. For example, in the sentence *Donald bought a new* **toupee**, the noun *toupee* is the direct object of the verb *bought*. The verb *buy* requires a direct object — when you buy, you have to buy SOMETHING.

Direct quotation A direct quotation uses quotation marks (" ") to show the reader that the words inside the marks are *exactly* what the person said or wrote; for example: *Tina said,* **"I know where we can buy tickets."** The opposite of a direct quotation is an indirect quotation, which does not use quotation marks, as in the following sentence: *Tina said that she knew where they could buy tickets.*

Elliptical adverb clause An elliptical adverb is a reduced form of an <u>adverb</u> <u>clause</u> from which the subject has been deleted and the verb changed to a <u>par-</u> <u>ticiple</u> form. For example, in the adverb clause beginning the sentence *When* *I looked for my hat*, *I found my gloves* can be reduced to an elliptical adverb clause: *When looking for my hat*, *I found my gloves.*

Essential adjective clause Every <u>adjective clause</u> (also called a *relative clause*) modifies a noun, but different types of adjective clauses are related to the nouns they modify in different ways. Essential adjective clauses (also called *restrictive* adjective clauses) narrow or limit the meaning of the nouns they modify. For example, in the sentence *All the students **who miss the test** will fail the course*, the adjective clause *who miss the test* limits or defines the meaning of the noun *students*: the students threatened with failure are only those who miss the test. Essential adjective clauses are never set off with commas. An adjective clause that does not limit or define the meaning of the noun it modifies is called a <u>non-</u> <u>essential adjective clause.</u>

Faulty parallelism The term *faulty parallelism* refers to a series of two or more grammatical elements in which not all the elements are in the same grammatical form. For example, the sentence ✗ *Senator Blather is **loud, pompous**, a fraud, and **talks too much*** presents a series of four elements, but there is faulty parallelism because the first two elements (*loud* and *pompous*) are adjectives; the third element (*fraud*) is a noun; and the fourth element (*talks too much*) is a verb phrase.

Fragment A fragment is part of a sentence that is punctuated as though it were a <u>complete sentence</u>. Typically, fragments are pieces cut off from the preceding sentence; for example: *The computer lost my paper.* ✗ ***Which I had worked on*** ***all night***. One way to recognize a fragment is to test it with the *I Realize* Tip. You can put the words *I realize* in front of most complete sentences and make a new grammatical sentence. However, when you put *I realize* in front of a fragment, the result will not make sense.

Fused sentence A fused sentence is a type of <u>run-on sentence</u> in which two complete sentences (or independent clauses) are joined together without any mark of punctuation. ✗ ***My brother caught a cold he has been out of school*** ***for a week*** is an example of a fused sentence because it consists of two complete sentences (*My brother caught a cold* and *He has been out of school for a week*) that are joined without proper punctuation. A <u>comma splice</u> is a similar type of error that incorrectly joins complete sentences with a comma.

Gender Certain third-person personal pronouns are marked for gender: *she*, *her*, and *hers* refer to females; *he, him,* and *his* refer to males. The third-person plural pronouns *they* and *them* are not marked for gender; that is, these pronouns can refer to males, females, or both. *They* and *them* are sometimes called "gender-neutral" or "gender-exclusive" pronouns. The third-person singular pronoun *it* refers to things that do not have gender, such as concrete objects and abstractions; so do the third-person plural pronouns *they, them,* and *their*.

Gerund A gerund is the *-ing* form of a verb (the <u>present participle</u>) that is used as a noun. For example, in the sentence *I like **taking** the bus to work*, *taking* is the gerund. The term *gerund* can also be used to refer to the *-ing* verb together with all the words that go with it (in what is technically called a *gerund phrase*). In the example sentence, the whole phrase ***taking the bus to work*** is a gerund phrase.

Helping verb When two or more verbs are used together in a string, the last verb in the sequence is called the <u>main verb</u>. All the other verbs that come before the main verb are called *helping verbs*. For example, in the sentence *We **should have been** tuning our instruments*, the last verb (*tuning*) is the main verb, and all the preceding verbs (*should have been*) are the helping verbs. The first helping verb in the sequence is the only verb that agrees with the subject. The most important helping verbs are ***be*** and ***have*** (in all their different forms), plus ***can, could, may, might, must, shall, should, will***, and ***would***.

Indefinite article Indefinite articles appear in two forms, depending on the initial sound of the following word: *a* is used before words beginning with a consonant sound (***a** yellow banana*), and *an* is used before words beginning with a vowel sound (***an** old banana*). Use an indefinite article when mentioning something the reader or listener does not already know about; after that point, use the definite article *the*. For example: *I bought **an** Apple computer. The computer has **a** built-in modem. The modem is connected to my telephone line.*

Independent clause An independent clause (also called a *main clause*) can always stand alone as a <u>complete sentence</u>. Every sentence must contain at least one independent clause.

Indirect quotation An indirect quotation is a <u>paraphrase</u> of the writer's or speaker's actual, verbatim words. For example, if Mr. Lopez said, "*We are going to Florida tomorrow*," the indirect quotation might be the following: *He said **that he and his family were going to Florida the next day***. One of the distinctive features of indirect quotation is the use of *that* before the paraphrase of the writer's or speaker's words. Also notice that, unlike <u>direct quotation</u>, an indirect quotation uses no quotation marks.

Infinitive An infinitive is the form of a <u>verb</u> as it appears in the dictionary. For example, the infinitive form of *is, am, was*, and *were* is ***be***. Like the *-ing* <u>present participle</u> form of verbs (<u>gerunds</u>), infinitives are often used as nouns. When serving as nouns, infinitives almost always are used with *to*; for example, *I like **to eat** pizza with my fingers*. As with gerunds, the term *infinitive* can also be used more broadly to include both the infinitive and the words that go with it (together called an *infinitive phrase*). In this broader sense, the infinitive in the example sentence is ***to eat pizza with my fingers***.

Information question Information questions are phrases that begin with a question word, for example, *who, what, where, why, when, how often, whose* + noun, and *which* + noun or pronoun. An information question usually also contains a helping verb and a form of the verb *do*. For example, in "***Where did** Liu go*," the verb *did* (the past tense of *do*) has been added after the question word *where*. The question word *where* seeks further specific information.

Inseparable two-word verb A <u>two-word verb</u> is a type of compound verb. When the compound is formed from a verb and a preposition, it is called an inseparable two-word verb because the preposition can never be moved away or "separated" from the verb. For example, in the sentence *The prince **turned against** the king*, the preposition *against* can never be moved away from the verb: ✗ *The prince **turned** the king **against***. However, when the two-word verb is formed with an adverb, the adverb can be moved away from the verb. A two-word verb of this type is called a <u>separable two-word verb</u>.

Introductory element An introductory element is any kind of word, phrase, or clause that has been placed at the beginning of a sentence rather than in its expected position in the middle or at the end of the sentence. Introductory elements are usually set off from the rest of the sentence by a comma (especially if the introductory element is a phrase or a clause), for example, ***Feeling a little down**, Scrooge left the party early*.

Linking verb Linking verbs are a class of verbs that can be followed by adjectives. For example, in the sentence *Jason **is** funny*, the verb *is* is a linking verb followed by the adjective *funny*. Linking verbs are not used to express action. Instead, linking verbs describe their subjects. In the example sentence, the adjective *funny* describes *Jason*.

Main clause See <u>independent clause</u>.

Main verb The main verb is the last verb in a string of verbs. All the verbs that precede the main verb are <u>helping verbs</u>. For example, in the sentence *Cinderella must have **eaten** all the chili dogs*, the main verb is *eaten*. The other two verbs (*must* and *have*) are helping verbs.

Mass noun See <u>noncount noun</u>.

Misplaced adverb A misplaced adverb is an adverb that does not actually modify the word that it is next to; it really modifies a word elsewhere in the sentence. For example, in the sentence *We **barely** packed enough clothes for the trip*, the adverb *barely* does not really modify *packed*. Either we packed or we didn't. The adverb *barely* really modifies *enough clothes*. Also see <u>squinting adverb</u>.

Modifier Modifiers are words that describe or give additional information about other words in a sentence. <u>Adjectives</u>, <u>participles</u>, and <u>adjective clauses</u> modify nouns. <u>Adverbs</u> and <u>adverb clauses</u> modify verbs, adverbs, adjectives, or whole sentences.

Noncount noun A noncount noun (also called a <u>mass noun</u>) is a <u>common noun</u> that cannot be used in the plural or with number words (✗ *one homework/* ✗ *two homeworks;* ✗ *one dirt/* ✗ *two dirts*). A noun that can be used in the plural and with number words is called a <u>count noun</u>.

Nonessential adjective clause Every <u>adjective clause</u> (also called a *relative clause*) modifies a noun, but different types of adjective clauses have different relations with the nouns they modify. Nonessential adjective clauses (also called *nonrestrictive* adjective clauses) do not narrow or limit the meaning of the nouns they modify. Like <u>appositives</u>, nonessential clauses rename the nouns they modify, and, like appositives, they are set off with commas. For example, in the sentence *My mother,* **who was born in Tonga**, *came to the United States as a child*, the relative clause *who was born in Tonga* is nonessential because it does not narrow or define the meaning of *my mother*. My mother is still my mother no matter where she was born. A clause that defines or limits the meaning of the noun it modifies is called an <u>essential adjective clause</u>.

Nonrestrictive adjective clause See <u>nonessential adjective clause</u>.

Noun Nouns are names of people, places, things, and ideas. A noun that refers to categories (**teacher, city**) is a <u>common noun</u>; a noun that refers to actual individual persons or places (**Mr. Smith, Chicago**) is a <u>proper noun</u>. See also <u>count noun</u> and <u>noncount noun</u>.

Noun clause A noun clause is a group of words that work together to function as a noun, as in **Whether you go or not** *is up to you*. If you look at the noun clause by itself, you will always find a word acting like a subject and a word serving as its verb. In the example above, *you* is acting like a subject, and *go* is its verb.

Object When a noun or a pronoun follows certain verbs or any preposition, it is called an *object*. For example, in the sentence *Kermit kissed* **Miss Piggy**, the object of the verb *kissed* is *Miss Piggy*. Most pronouns have distinct object forms. Thus, to replace *Miss Piggy* with a pronoun in the example sentence, we would have to use the object form *her* rather than the subject form *she: Kermit kissed* **her**. <u>Prepositional phrases</u> consist of prepositions and their objects. For example, in the prepositional phrase *on the* **ladder**, the object of the preposition *on* is the noun *ladder*.

Parallelism The term *parallelism* refers to a series of two or more elements of the same grammatical type, usually joined by a coordinating conjunction. For example, in the sentence *I love* **to eat, to drink**, *and* **to dance** *the polka*, there are three parallel forms — all infinitives: *to eat, to drink*, and *to dance*. Failure to express parallel elements in the same grammatical form is called <u>faulty parallelism</u>.

Paraphrase To *paraphrase* means to rephrase something in a different grammatical form or with different wording while keeping the meaning of the original. For example, the passive sentence *I was given a present by Mary* is a paraphrase of the corresponding active sentence *Mary gave me a present*. Paraphrase is common in <u>indirect quotation</u>.

Participial phrase A participial phrase contains either a present or a past <u>participle</u>. Participial phrases modify nouns. For example, in the sentence *The workers* **repairing the roof** *found water damage*, *repairing the roof* is a present participial phrase modifying the noun *workers*. In the sentence *The workers **injured in the accident** sued the company, injured in the accident* is a past participial phrase modifying the noun *workers*.

Participle Participles are verb forms. There are two types of participles: (1) present participles (the *-ing* form of verbs such as *seeing, doing,* and *having*); and (2) past participles (for example, *seen, done,* and *had*). Both types of participles can be used as verbs (following certain helping verbs). For example, in the sentence *Michio is **watching** the movie,* the word *watching* is in the present participle form. In the sentence *Michio has **watched** the movie,* the word *watched* is in the past participle form.

Both present participles and past participles can also be used as adjectives. For example, in the saying *A **watched** pot never boils,* the past participle *watched* functions as an adjective modifying the noun *pot*.

Passive The term *passive* or *passive voice* describes sentences in which the subject is not the "doer" of the action but instead *receives* the action of the verb. For example, in the passive sentence *Sandy **was seen** by Pat,* the subject *Sandy* is not the person doing the seeing but instead is the person being seen. The passive voice can always be recognized by a unique sequence of verbs: the helping verb *be* (in some form) followed by a past participle verb form. In the example above, *was* is the past tense form of *be,* and *seen* is the past participle form of *see.* Sentences that are not in the passive voice are said to be in the active voice.

Past participle Past participle verb forms are used in the perfect tenses after the helping verb *have* (as in *Thelma has **seen** that movie*) or after the helping verb *be* in passive sentences (*That movie was **seen** by Thelma*). The past participle form of most verbs ends in *-ed*—as do most past tense forms of most verbs. How, then, can we tell a past participle from a past tense? The difference is that the past participle form of a verb always follows a helping verb. For example, in the sentence *Liam has **loved** the movies, loved* is a past participle because it follows the helping verb *has.* In the sentence *Liam **loved** the movies,* however, *loved* is a past tense verb because it does *not* follow a helping verb. Past participles can also be used as adjectives (*The car **seen** in that commercial belongs to my uncle*).

Past perfect tense See perfect tenses.

Past tense The past tense is used to describe an action that took place at some past time; for example, *Carlos **borrowed** my car last night.* For regular verbs, the past tense form ends in *-ed.* However, there are a large number of irregular verbs that form their past tense in different ways. The most unusual past tense is found in the verb *be,* which has two past tense forms: *was* in the singular and *were* in the plural.

Perfect tenses The perfect tenses refer to action that takes place over a period of time or is frequently repeated. There are three perfect tenses: (1) present perfect (*Niles **has seen** Daphne twice this week*); (2) past perfect (*Niles **had seen** Daphne two times last week*); and (3) future perfect (*Niles **will have seen** Daphne* *twice by Friday*). Notice that all the perfect tenses use *have* (in some form) as a <u>helping verb</u>, followed by a verb in the <u>past participle</u> form (*seen*, in all these examples).

Personal pronoun   There are three sets of personal pronouns: (1) first-person pronouns refer to the speaker (***I, me, mine; we, us, ours***); (2) second-person pronouns refer to the hearer (***you, yours***); and (3) third-person pronouns refer to another person or thing (***he, him, his, she, her, hers, it, its; they, them, theirs***). A personal pronoun can also be categorized by the role it plays in a sentence: <u>subject</u> (*I, we, you, he, she, it, they*) or <u>object</u> (*me, us, you, him, her, them*).

Phrase   In grammatical terminology, a *phrase* is a group of related words that act as a single part of speech. The most common type is the <u>prepositional phrase</u>. For example, in the sentence *Kermit kissed Miss Piggy* **on the balcony**, the prepositional phrase is *on the balcony*, here acting as an adverb.

Plural   Referring to more than one. Plural nouns are usually formed by adding *-s* to the singular form of the noun. Also see <u>agreement</u>; <u>subject-verb agreement</u>.

Possessive apostrophe   Possessive nouns (***John's*** *book*) and possessive indefinite pronouns (***one's*** *ideas*, ***somebody's*** *book*, ***anybody's*** *guess*) are spelled with an apostrophe (') to show that the *-s* added at the end of the word is a "possessive *-s*," as opposed to a "plural *-s*." When an *-s* at the end of a word is both possessive *and* plural, the apostrophe goes after the *-s* (*The* ***girls'*** *dresses*). This use of the apostrophe to indicate possession is different from its use to indicate a <u>contraction</u>.

Predicate   The predicate is everything in a sentence that is NOT part of the <u>subject</u>. The predicate is thus the <u>verb</u> portion of the sentence — the verb together with everything the verb controls — <u>objects</u>, <u>complements</u>, and all species of optional and obligatory <u>adverbs</u>. For example, in the sentence *Prince Charming* **was beginning to put on a little weight**, everything except the subject *Prince Charming* is part of the predicate.

Preposition   Prepositions are words such as ***on, by, with, of, in, from, between***, and ***to***. A preposition is used with a following noun or pronoun <u>object</u> to make a <u>prepositional phrase</u>.

Prepositional phrase   A prepositional phrase is a phrase consisting of a preposition and its object; for example: *on the beach, at noon, by Shakespeare*. Prepositional phrases function as adverbs or adjectives. For example, in the sentence *I got a message* **at my office**, the prepositional phrase *at my office* functions as an adverb telling where I got the message. In the sentence *The chair* **at my office** *is not very comfortable*, the prepositional phrase *at my office* is an adjective modifying *chair*.

Present participle   Present participle verb forms are used in the <u>progressive tenses</u> after the <u>helping verb</u> *be*, in some form. For example, in the sentence *Pranav and Liu were* **practicing** *their duets*, *were* is a form of the helping verb *be,* and *practicing* is in the present participle form. The present participle form is completely regular because it always ends in *-ing*; for example: *doing, being, seeing, helping.* Present participles can also be used as adjectives (*The car **turning** at the signal is a Buick*) or as nouns (***Seeing** is **believing***).

Present perfect tense See perfect tenses.

Present tense Despite its name, the most common use of the present tense is not to describe present time but, rather, to make timeless generalizations (*The earth **is** round*) or to describe habitual, repeated actions (*I always **shop** on Saturdays*).

Present tense verb forms have an added *-s* when the subject is a third-person singular pronoun (*he, she,* or *it*) or when the subject is a noun that can be replaced with a third-person pronoun. See subject-verb agreement.

Progressive tenses Progressive tenses are used to refer to actions that are ongoing at the time of the sentence—as opposed to the present tense, which is essentially timeless. The term *progressive* refers to three related verb constructions that employ *be* (in some form) as a helping verb. If *be* is in the present tense (*am, is, are*), then the construction is called the *present progressive*; for example: *The president **is visiting** Peru now.* If *be* is in the past tense (*was, were*), then the construction is called the *past progressive*; for example: *The president **was visiting** Peru last week.* If *be* is used in the future (*will be*), then the construction is called the *future progressive;* for example: *The president **will be visiting** Peru next week.*

Pronoun A pronoun can replace a noun either as a subject or as an object. Among the many different types of pronouns, the most important is the personal pronoun. Also discussed in this book is the relative pronoun, which is the kind that begins an adjective clause. Also see gender, pronoun antecedent, and vague pronoun.

Pronoun antecedent Many pronouns refer back to a person or persons or to a thing or things mentioned earlier in the sentence or even in a previous sentence. For example, in the sentences *My **aunts** live next door. **They** are my mother's sisters*, the antecedent of the pronoun *they* is *aunts.* When a pronoun might refer to more than one antecedent, it is said to exhibit "ambiguous pronoun reference." For example, in the sentence *Aunt Sadie asked Mother where **her** keys were*, the pronoun *her* is ambiguous because it might refer either to Aunt Sadie or to Mother. A pronoun that has no real antecedent is called a vague pronoun. For example, in the sentence ***They** shouldn't allow smoking in restaurants*, the pronoun *they* is vague because it does not have any actual antecedent — it does not refer to any identified individuals.

Pronoun-antecedent agreement See agreement.

Proper adjective A proper adjective is derived from a proper noun. For example, the adjective *Jamaican* in ***Jamaican** coffee* is the adjective form of the proper noun *Jamaica.* Proper adjectives are always capitalized.

Proper noun Proper nouns are the names of specific individual persons, titles, or places. Proper nouns are always capitalized; for example: ***Queen Elizabeth, Michael Jordan, New York Times, Vancouver***. When a noun refers to a category rather than to a specific individual, it is called a common noun.

Quotation There are two types of quotation: (1) direct quotation, which uses quotation marks to report exactly what someone said, with word-for-word accuracy; and (2) indirect quotation, which paraphrases what a person said without using the writer's or speaker's exact words. Indirect quotations are not set within quotation marks.

Relative clause See adjective clause.

Relative pronoun A relative pronoun begins an adjective clause. The relative pronouns are *who, whom, whose, which,* and *that.* Relative pronouns must refer to the noun in the independent clause that the adjective clause modifies. For example, in the sentence *I got an offer **that** I can't refuse,* the relative pronoun *that* refers to *offer.* The relative pronouns *who, whom,* and *whose* are used to refer to people. For example, in the sentence *He is a man **whom** you can rely on,* the relative pronoun *whom* refers to *man.* Using *that* to refer to people is incorrect in formal writing; for example: ✗ *He is a man **that** you can rely on.*

Restrictive adjective clause See essential adjective clause.

Run-on sentence A run-on sentence consists of two or more sentences (independent clauses) that are joined together without adequate punctuation. Joining two sentences together with only a comma is called a comma splice (✗ ***My grandmother lived in Mexico when she was a girl, she moved to Texas when she was nineteen***). Joining two sentences together with no punctuation at all is called a fused sentence (✗ ***Kelsey's party is this weekend I bet she's looking forward to it***).

Semicolon The semicolon (;) is used in place of a period to join two closely related independent clauses, for example, ***A water main in the building had burst; the floors were covered with water.***

Sentence A sentence consists of at least one independent clause (with or without an accompanying dependent clause) that is punctuated with a period, an exclamation point, or a question mark.

Separable two-word verb A two-word verb is a type of compound verb. When such a compound is formed from a verb and an adverb, it is called a separable two-word verb because the adverb can be moved away or "separated" from the verb. For example, in the sentence *I **called up** my parents,* the adverb *up* can be separated from the verb by moving it after the object: *I **called** my parents **up**.* However, when the two-word verb is formed with a preposition, the preposition can never be moved away from the verb. A two-word verb of this type is called an inseparable two-word verb.

Sexist language Language that stereotypes, demeans, or unfairly excludes men or women is referred to as sexist language. One of the most common forms is the sexist or gender-exclusive use of pronouns. In this example, notice how it appears that only men vote: *Everybody should vote for **his** favorite candidate for governor.*

Singular Referring to one. Also see <u>agreement</u>; <u>subject-verb agreement</u>.

Squinting adverb A squinting adverb is an adverb incorrectly placed so that the adverb can modify either what comes before the adverb or what follows the adverb. Either interpretation is correct; the problem is that the reader cannot tell which one the writer intended. For example, in the following sentence, *A friend whom I e-mail **frequently** has computer viruses, frequently* can modify either *e-mail* or *has*. Also see <u>misplaced adverb</u>.

Subject The subject of a sentence is the doer of the action or what the sentence is about. The term *subject* has two slightly different meanings: (1) the *simple subject* is the noun or pronoun that is the doer or the topic of the sentence, and (2) the *complete subject* is the simple subject together with all its modifiers. For example, in the sentence *The **book** on the shelf belongs to my cousin*, the simple subject is *book*, and the complete subject is *the book on the shelf*.

Subject-verb agreement This term refers to the matching of the number of a present tense verb (or a present tense <u>helping verb</u> if there is more than one verb) with the number of the subject of that verb. Following are three examples with different subjects: (1) *Aunt Sadie **lives** in Denver.* (2) *My aunts **live** in Denver.* (3) *Aunt Sadie and Uncle Albert **live** in Denver.*

If the subject is a third-person singular <u>personal pronoun</u> (*he, she, it*) or if the subject is a noun that can be replaced by a third-person singular personal pronoun (as is the case with *Aunt Sadie* in example 1), then it is necessary to add an *-s* (called the *third-person singular -s*) to the present tense verb.

If the subject *cannot* be replaced by a third-person singular pronoun (as is the case in examples 2 and 3), do *not* add the third-person singular *-s* to the present tense.

Only the verb *be* has past tense forms that change to agree with the subject: *was* is used with first-person singular and third-person singular subjects (*I **was** in Denver; Aunt Sadie **was** in Denver*); and *were* is used with all other subjects (*My aunts **were** in Denver*).

Subordinate clause See <u>dependent clause</u>.

Subordinating conjunction A *subordinating conjunction* (such as **when**, **since**, **because**, or **if**) begins a <u>dependent clause</u>.

Tense The term *tense* is used in two quite different ways. (1) It can refer to the *time* in which the action of the sentence takes place: present time, past time, and future time. (2) Usually in this book, however, the term is used in a narrower, more technical sense to mean just the *form* of the verb. In this limited sense, the term refers either to the <u>present tense</u> form of a verb (**see** and **sees**, for example) or to its <u>past tense</u> form (**saw**). There is no separate future tense form in English; we can talk about future time by using the <u>helping verb</u> *will*.

Tense shifting Tense shifting occurs in a piece of writing when the author shifts from one tense to another—usually from past tense to present tense or vice versa. For example, in the sentence *We **ate** at the restaurant that **is** on the pier*, the first verb (*ate*) is in the past tense, while the second verb (*is*) is in the present tense. In this particular sentence, the shifting from past tense to present tense is appropriate; sometimes, however, writers confuse readers by incorrectly shifting tenses when there is no reason to do so.

Transitional term A *transitional term* shows how the meaning of a second sentence is related to the meaning of the first sentence. For example, in the pair of sentences *I had planned to leave at noon. **However**, my flight was delayed*, the transitional term *however* signals to the reader that the second sentence will contradict the first sentence in some way. Some other transitional terms are ***nevertheless, moreover***, and ***therefore***.

Two-word verb Two-word verbs are <u>compounds</u> (often with idiomatic meanings) formed from a verb plus either a preposition or an adverb. When the compound contains a preposition, the compound is called an <u>inseparable two-word verb</u> because the preposition can never be separated from the verb. When the compound contains an adverb, the adverb can be moved away from the verb; these compounds are called <u>separable two-word verbs</u>. Two-word verbs are also called *phrasal verbs*.

Vague pronoun A pronoun must have an <u>antecedent</u> to make its meaning clear. A *vague pronoun* is one that does not seem to refer to anything or anyone in particular. For example, in the sentence ***They** should do something about these terrible roads*, the pronoun *they* is a vague pronoun because it could refer to anybody — the highway department, the police, the government.

Verb A *verb* tells about an action in a sentence (*Alfy **sneezed***) or describes the subject of the sentence (*Alfy **seemed** angry*). Only verbs can change form to show <u>tense</u>. That is, only verbs have <u>present tense</u> and <u>past tense</u> forms. A simple test to see whether a word is a verb is to see whether you can change it into a past tense by adding *-ed* to it.

Voice *Voice* is a technical term in grammar that refers to the relation of the subject of a sentence to the verb. If the subject is the "doer" of the action of the verb, as in the sentence ***Keisha wrecked** the car*, then the sentence is said to be in the <u>active</u> voice. However, if the subject is the recipient of the action of the verb, as in the sentence *The **car was wrecked** by Keisha*, then the sentence is said to be in the <u>passive</u> voice.

APPENDIX C

Glossary of Commonly Confused Words

Writers sometimes confuse certain words because some words sound alike but are spelled differently. Even a computer spell-checker will not catch these problem words because they are not misspelled. For example, *breaks* in the following sentence is incorrect:

✗ My car's **breaks** are squealing.

But a spell-check program would not suggest the correct usage

My car's **brakes** are squealing.

because it doesn't "see" the error in meaning.

Below is a list of words that are often confused with one another. (Some of these words have several meanings, but we have given only the most common usage.) Use this list of easily confused words to help you edit your writing. If you are unsure about a word that doesn't appear here, consult a dictionary.

Word	Definition	Example
accept	to approve	I **accept** your offer.
except	excluding	I kept all the receipts **except** that one.
advice	a suggestion	Can you give me investment **advice**?
advise	to recommend	I **advise** you not to go there.
affect	to influence or alter	The medication didn't **affect** Lydia at all.
effect	a result	One **effect** of this drug is drowsiness.
aisle	the space between rows	The groom fell down in the **aisle**.
isle	an island	Gilligan was bored with the **isle**.
already	previously	I have **already** eaten lunch.
all ready	completely prepared	Jan is **all ready** for the test, but I'm not.
altogether	thoroughly or generally	She was not **altogether** ready for college.
all together	in a group	The holiday brought us **all together**.
brake	a device for stopping or to stop	The **brakes** in this car are awful.
break	to destroy or divide into pieces	If you **break** the window, you'll have to pay to replace it.

Word	Definition	Example
breath	an inhalation or exhalation	Take a deep **breath** before diving.
breathe	to inhale or exhale	I can't **breathe** in a sauna.
capital	a city recognized as the home of a government	The **capital** of Texas is Austin.
capitol	the building where lawmakers meet	The **capitol** building is huge.
choose	to select	Our group will **choose** topics tomorrow.
chose	past tense of *choose*	She **chose** to make up the test.
complement	to go well with	This wine **complements** the chicken.
compliment	to praise	He **complimented** my leadership skills.
dessert	a tasty sweet	For **dessert**, we had key lime pie.
desert	a dry area	You'll need water to cross that **desert**.
device	a mechanism	This **device** will help you start a car.
devise	to arrange	Ira **devised** this meeting between us.
its	possessive form of *it*	My hamster ate all **its** food.
it's	contraction for *it is*	**It's** going to rain today, so be prepared.
later	subsequently	We ate too much. **Later**, we felt sick.
latter	the last thing mentioned	There is turkey and ham in the refrigerator. I prefer the **latter**.
lead	a metallic element	They used **lead** paint on these windows.
led	past tense of *lead*	The guide **led** us through the canyon.
loose	not snug	Your pants are **loose** in the rear.
lose	to misplace; to fail to win	Did you **lose** the race?
maybe	perhaps	**Maybe** I'll get a raise next month.
may be	might possibly be	The project **may be** ready next week.
passed	past tense of *pass*	I **passed** her on the way to school.
past	previous time	In the **past**, I owned an IBM typewriter.
personal	private	A lot of my e-mail is **personal**.
personnel	staff	All store **personnel** should wear name tags.
principal	head of a school; most important	Report to the **principal's** office. The **principal** reason is cost.
principle	a basic truth	What **principles** would you fight for?
quiet	little or no sound	It was **quiet** in the library.
quite	very	Marc looked **quite** handsome in that suit.
set	to put	**Set** the glasses on the table, please.
sit	to be seated	The teacher wants us to **sit** in groups.
than	as compared to	My dog is smarter **than** my cat.
then	next	Fix this car. **Then** fix that car.

Word	Definition	Example
their	possessive of *they*	The players lost **their** final game.
there	adverb indicating place	Put the printer **there** for now.
they're	a contraction for *they are*	**They're** meeting us after work.
to	a preposition	Russell went **to** his algebra class.
too	very or also	He was **too** tired to work, **too**.
two	the number 2	Shannon wrote **two** papers this week.
weak	not strong	Tomás felt **weak** after the game.
week	seven days	I need a **week** off from work.
weather	the state of the atmosphere	Today's **weather** will be stormy.
whether	if	**Whether** you go or not is your decision.
whose	possessive of *who*	**Whose** turn is it now?
who's	contraction for *who is*	**Who's** ready to leave?
your	possessive of *you*	**Your** car is a mess.
you're	contraction for *you are*	If **you're** hungry, let's get lunch.

APPENDIX D

Glossary of Commonly Misspelled Words

Even in this age of automated spell-checkers, misspellings account for some of the most common, most distracting mistakes that appear in writing. One way to improve your spelling is to avoid completely relying on a spell-checker. Use this tool, but don't always trust it. As you know, spell-checkers are awful at detecting misspellings when you confuse two words, such as writing *there* when you meant *their*. Another problem with spell-checkers is you cannot always use them, such as when taking a test.

Writing and reading improve your spelling ability, but it also helps to study the correct spelling of words you misspell. Some spellings are challenging for many people, such as the words listed in this appendix and in Appendix C. Research indicates the best way to study the correct spelling of words like these is to do something active while you study, rather than just reading the words and thinking about the way they are spelled.

Here is a more active way to learn the spelling of challenging words. Say each letter aloud as you read the word. Try this at least two or three times. Then, put the correct spelling aside and try slowly to spell the word aloud, letter by letter. After that, write down what you believe to be the correct spelling, and then consult your list or book to make sure you are correct. Repeat this procedure until spelling the word becomes automatic and routine.

It can also help to prioritize the spellings you study. Focus on the troublemakers. Again, be sure to look at Appendix C for a list of commonly confused words. These account for the majority of misspellings overlooked by students using a spell-checker.

While there is little agreement about the "top ten" most common misspellings, here is a short list of frequently misspelled words in college writing (excluding the "confused words" misspellings covered in Appendix C).

Common Misspellings in College Writing

a lot (two words, not one)	definite	misspelling
absence	disappoint	parallel
disappoint	February	perceive

professor	roommate	sophomore
receive	separate	writing

The previous list is a starting place for practicing your spelling, but focus on words that are challenging for you in particular. Not sure? Here is a longer list of words that are difficult to spell.

Fifty More Words That Are Frequently Misspelled

apologize	foreign	potato
arctic	grammar	privilege
arithmetic	handkerchief	probably
athlete	harass	rebellion
becoming	height	recommend
beginning	heroes	referring
believe	interest(ing)	restaurant
building	laboratory	rhythm
bureau(crat)	leisure	sandwich
calendar	maintenance	secretary
changeable	marriage	through
coming	mischievous	truly
commitment	mother	until
develop	necessary	villain
embarrass(ment)	occasion	Wednesday
existence	occurrence	yield
familiar	pastime	

APPENDIX E

Glossary of Common Two-Word Verbs

The following is an alphabetical list of one hundred common two-word verbs.

Each of the verbs on this list is a *separable* two-word verb (verb + adverb construction). Remember that if the sentence includes an object *noun*, the adverb can be placed either before or after the noun. In other words, the noun can separate the two parts of the verb. Both of these examples are correct:

Carly **turned down** the offer.

Carly **turned** the offer **down**.

However, when the object following the adverb is a *pronoun*, the adverb must be placed after the pronoun. In this case, the pronoun must separate the two parts of the verb.

✗ Carly **turned down** it.

Carly **turned** it **down**.

To learn more about how to identify and correct problems with two-word verbs, see Lesson 36. You may also want to consult the *Longman Phrasal Verbs Dictionary* (2001), the most complete listing of two-word verbs and their meanings.

Two-Word Verb	*Meaning*	*Example*
ask out	ask for a date	He wanted to **ask** her **out**.
ask over	invite to one's home	We **asked** them **over** for coffee.
back up	support	They **backed** our proposal **up**.
beat out	defeat, overcome	Our plan **beat out** theirs.
blow up	destroy	The bomb **blew** the building **up**.
break down	disassemble, analyze	This chart **breaks** the costs **down**.
break in	train, start	They **broke in** the new staff.
break off	discontinue, stop	We **broke off** the discussions.
bring around	convince	We'll **bring** the others **around** in time.
bring back	return	She **brought** the books **back**.
bring off	succeed in doing	They **brought** the party **off**.

Two-Word Verb	Meaning	Example
bring up	mention, propose	I'll **bring** the issue **up** to my boss.
brush off	ignore, dismiss	He **brushed** their complaints **off**.
buy out	purchase	We want to **buy** the company **out**.
call off	cancel	They **called off** the meeting.
call up	telephone	Her boss **called** her **up**.
carry away	overcome objections	His idea **carried** them **away**.
carry out	do, follow	Be sure to **carry** the orders **out**.
check out	investigate	We plan to **check** the offers **out**.
check over	test for accuracy	They **checked** the bills **over**.
cost out	price	They **cost out** the bid.
cover up	hide	They **covered up** the crime.
crack up	make someone laugh	His stories **crack** me **up**.
do in	kill, destroy	His mistakes finally **did** him **in**.
do over	repeat	I have to **do** my paper **over** again.
drag out	make longer	The boss will **drag** the meeting **out**.
dream up	create, imagine	They **dreamed** the whole thing **up**.
drop off	deliver, leave	I **dropped** the kids **off** at school.
figure out	discover	It's easy to **figure** the answer **out**.
fill in	explain something	Let's go **fill** the newcomers **in**.
fit in	schedule	I'll **fit** you **in** at one o'clock.
fix up	repair, decorate	They **fixed** the office **up** nicely.
follow up	oversee, pursue	I **followed** the plans **up**.
freeze out	exclude, keep out	We'll **freeze** the competition **out**.
get across	explain successfully	At least they **got** their ideas **across**.
give up	quit using	He **gave** junk food **up**.
hand in	submit	It is time to **hand** my paper **in**.
hang up	cause a delay	The problem really **hung** them **up**.
help out	assist	The tutor really **helped** them **out**.
hold up	restrain, delay	The accident **held** them **up**.
lay off	fire	The firm **laid** the employees **off**.
lay out	present, arrange	She wanted to **lay** the options **out**.
lead on	encourage falsely	The ads **lead** the customers **on**.
leave off	omit	I **left** my name **off** the list.
let down	disappoint	Our failure **let** them **down**.
look up	find information	We **looked** their address **up**.
make up	lie about	They **made** the whole story **up**.
mix up	confuse	Our directions **mixed** them **up**.
pass out	distribute	We **passed** the books **out**.
pass up	decline	I couldn't **pass up** chocolate cake.
pay back	repay a debt	We **paid** our loan **back**.
pay off	bribe	They **paid** the police **off**.
phase out	terminate gradually	We will **phase** the product **out** by 2010.
pick up	make happy	The news really **picked** them **up**.
point out	identify	We **pointed** the changes **out**.

Two-Word Verb	Meaning	Example
polish off	finish	We **polished** the last job **off**.
pull off	succeed in doing	I **pulled** a big surprise **off**.
put back	return	She **put** the book **back** on the shelf.
put off	delay, discourage	We **put off** the decision until later.
put on	deceive, tease	You are **putting** me **on**.
rip off	cheat	The salesman **ripped** us **off**.
run down	criticize	They **ran** the opposition **down**.
scale back	reduce	We needed to **scale back** our plan.
seek out	search for	I **sought** the best deal **out**.
sell out	betray	He **sold** his partner **out**.
set back	delay	The rain **set** the job **back**.
set off	trigger, activate	The noise **set** the alarm **off**.
shake up	scare	The accident **shook** me **up**.
shoot down	reject	My lab group **shot** my ideas **down**.
show off	display boastingly	He **showed** his new car **off**.
shut off	stop	They **shut** the radio **off**.
shut up	silence someone	Sam **shut** his partner **up**.
smooth over	fix temporarily	He will **smooth** the situation **over**.
sound out	test one's opinion	We **sounded** them **out**.
spell out	give all details	She **spelled out** the proposal carefully.
stand up	fail to meet someone	My date **stood** me **up** twice!
straighten out	correct someone	The boss **straightened** us **out**.
string along	deceive	He was **stringing** them **along**.
sum up	summarize	My job is to **sum** the proposal **up**.
take in	deceive, trick	Their scheme really **took** us **in**.
talk over	discuss	I'd like to **talk** the plan **over**.
tear down	destroy, demolish	They **tore** the old house **down**.
tell apart	distinguish	I can't **tell** them **apart**.
think up	invent	We **thought up** a new plan.
throw away	discard	I **threw** the old papers **away**.
throw off	confuse, delay	The announcement **threw** them **off**.
track down	find	We **tracked** the book **down**.
trip up	cause a mistake	Our carelessness **tripped** us **up**.
try out	test, explore	I should **try** the new computer **out**.
tune out	ignore	I can't **tune** the distractions **out**.
turn around	change for the better	They **turned** the company **around**.
turn down	reject	She **turned** our offer **down**.
turn in	submit	I **turned** my assignment **in**.
turn off	cause to lose interest	The bad smell **turned** me **off**.
use up	use until gone	I **used** all my money **up**.
wear down	weaken gradually	Some kids **wear** their parents **down**.
wear out	exhaust	The noise **wore** me **out**.
wipe out	destroy completely	The floods **wiped** the city **out**.
work up	prepare	I **worked** the new draft **up**.
write off	cancel, dismiss	They **wrote** the investment **off**.

Answer Key

LESSON 1: Fragments

Diagnostic Exercise, *page 10*

I wish I could change my worst bad habit, **always** running late. I am always tempted to do just one more thing before heading out the door in the morning. I know I am going to be busy all day, **trying** to balance schoolwork with my job. I have learned that it helps to make a schedule, **which** I really do try to follow. However, I never seem to budget enough time for routine chores **because** I really hate doing things in a sloppy way. As a result, I am always tempted to take an extra minute or two to do things right. The problem is that those few extra minutes quickly add up. Before I know it, I am late, **again**. Another problem is that I don't have enough time built in for unexpected delays, **which** seem to happen with depressing regularity. You wouldn't believe what happened to me this morning. A huge SUV was parked in front of my driveway, **blocking** me for a good fifteen minutes.

Sentence Practice 1, *page 14*

1. The Rockies are actually part of a larger chain, **which** stretches to the Andes in South America. 2. The climate to the east of the Rockies is relatively dry **because** the mountains cut off moist winds from the Pacific. 3. To the west of the Rockies there is another, newer mountain range, **the** Sierra Nevadas. 4. OK 5. To the east of the Rockies are the Great Plains, **the** remains of a gigantic inland sea.

Sentence Practice 2, *page 15*

1. We had to go this winter **because** our miles were going to expire. 2. OK 3. We didn't want to spend half of our vacation on the road, **driving** from Orlando to Key West and back. 4. After all, from Orlando to Key West is a 400-mile trip, **a** full day's journey. 5. We ended up flying to Miami, **which** is much closer to where we wanted to go.

Editing Practice 1, *page 17*

Key West is a great place to visit **for** a lot of reasons. First of all, the physical setting is magnificent, **blue** sky and beautiful ocean views. Being on an island makes you much more aware of the water and the sky. Unlike the often cloudless skies on the Pacific coast, the skies in the keys often have small puffy clouds, **giving** a sense of space and depth to the sky. The color of the water is always changing **because** the coral reefs reflect the continually changing play of sun and cloud. The fact that the ocean around Key West is so shallow and so varied gives the water vibrant colors, **with** dozens of shades of green and blue everywhere you look. The beaches in California are quite drab by comparison **because** they are . . .

Editing Practice 2, *page 18*

It is interesting to compare Key West with a similar ocean-side destination in California, **Santa** Barbara, for instance. Besides being beach destinations, they share another important feature, **a** lengthy Spanish heritage. Key West today doesn't feel Spanish at all, **even** though it (and the rest of Florida) was part of the Spanish empire for nearly three hundred years. There was never any permanent Spanish settlement there **because** there was no source of fresh water on the island. Key West was a temporary home for fishermen and pirates, **a** source of much humor today. Santa Barbara, on the other hand, is overflowing with its Spanish heritage, **especially** in its architecture. Santa Barbara today looks classically Spanish, **with** its white buildings . . .

LESSON 2: Run-ons: Fused Sentences and Comma Splices

Diagnostic Exercise, *page 21*

My friend Miranda is a junior majoring in government, **and** she plans to go to law school. Most law schools accept applicants from all majors, **but** she thinks that majoring in government would help her prepare for law. All law schools do require good grades and a high score on the LSAT. Her grades are high; she has about a 3.8 GPA currently. She works very hard, **and** she studies more than any person I know. She plans to take the LSAT this fall, **and** she will be studying for it on top of everything else. I admire her energy; I'm sure . . .

Sentence Practice 1, *page 25*

1. Colleen called. **She** wants me to help her with her homework. 2. London was the first city to have a population of over one million. **It** reached that milestone in 1811. 3. My son wants to buy a snake, **but** his mother is not happy about the idea. 4. The mascot for Yale is now a bulldog; **its** mascot over a hundred years ago was a cat. 5. Colombia was once considered part of South America, **but** its government decided in 1903 to proclaim Colombia was part of North America.

Sentence Practice 2, *page 25*

1. OK 2. The first home TV set was demonstrated in 1928; **it** measured only 3 inches by 4 inches. 3. The street lights in the city of Hershey, Pennsylvania, look strange. **They** resemble Hershey's chocolate kisses. 4. I liked the early *Harry Potter* books better. **The** later ones got too dark for me. 5. I thought the actors in the *Harry Potter* movies were terrific. **Even** the minor characters were wonderful.

Editing Practice 1, *page 27*

I was late to my first class; my car broke down on the side of the highway. This is the third time this fall that I have had to pull over because of an engine problem, **and** I am not going to suffer through a fourth time. According to a mechanic, the problem has something to do with the fuel injector. I have replaced the fuse, and the mechanic has tried various other methods. Nothing has worked, **so** it does not make sense spending yet more money on something that cannot be fixed. I might need a whole new fuel injector, **so** I am considering buying a new car. The one I have is only six years old, so I hate buying a new one already. It all depends on what I can afford.

Editing Practice 2, *page 28*

At my college, on-campus parking can be extremely difficult, **and** the situation will soon be worse. Currently, the college has eight parking lots for students, **but** two of them hold only about a dozen cars. During the summer, construction will begin on a new library, which we certainly need. The construction will last a year, **and** two parking lots will be closed during the construction phase. When the library opens up next year, only one of the two lots will be reopened; **the** other will have vanished because the library will cover it. Almost everyone believes we need a new library. **It** is too bad . . .

Unit Two

LESSON 3: Nearest-Noun Agreement Errors

Diagnostic Exercise, *page 35*

The beginning of the first public schools in the United States **dates** from the early 1800's. The pressure to create public schools open to children of working-class parents **was** a direct result of the union movements in large cities. In response, state legislatures gave communities the legal right to levy local property taxes to pay for free schools open to the public. By the middle of the nineteenth century, control of the school policies and curriculum **was** in the hands of the state government. As school populations outgrew one-room schoolhouses, the design of school buildings on the East Coast **was** completely changed to accommodate separate rooms for children of different ages. Before this time, all children in a schoolhouse, regardless of age, **were** taught together . . .

Sentence Practice 1, *page 37*

1. The newest schedule for fall classes **is** ready. 2. The federal government's proposal for the pricing of prescription drugs **was** just published in the Federal Register. 3. The problems with his idea about the contest **are** what we expected. 4. In the first place, access to the computers in all campus buildings **requires** a student ID. 5. OK

Sentence Practice 2, *page 38*

1. The characteristics of the early hominid found in Java by an archaeologist **are** still under debate. 2. Uncertainty about the terms of the agreement **has** thrown the issue into the courts. 3. As a result of the election, the public awareness of the many environmental issues surrounding the wetlands **has** been heightened. 4. The motion by the student council president and the two members **was** rejected. 5. Anne told me that one of those MP3 players that can play over five thousand songs **was** sold last week on eBay for just $50.

Editing Practice 1, *page 39*

Owning a pet, even the least demanding of creatures, **is** never easy. Over the years, we have had a number of cats, each of which **has** had a unique personality. Sometimes people seek out cats, and sometimes cats, instinctively knowing the house with the most defenseless owner, **choose** where to live. One of the cats that **falls** into the latter category is a big, yellow tomcat we call Ferdinand. If cats could belong to political parties, Ferdinand would be a pacifist. Absolutely nothing that happens around him **seems** to upset him. For example, every one of the cats that we had before as pets **was** terrified . . .

Editing Practice 2, *page 40*

A researcher who has studied the history of cats **believes** that the ancestor of today's domestic cats **was** a species of small wildcats native to northern Africa and southern Europe. The first evidence of cats being domesticated animals kept by humans **was** found in Egypt. An Egyptian official who oversaw large government grain storehouses **was** apparently the first to use cats to control rats and mice. In fact, in Egypt, the pet cats of an important official **were** considered sacred . . .

LESSON 4: Agreement with *There is* and *There was*

Diagnostic Exercise, *page 43*

Each year there **are** many new movies coming out of Hollywood. Each is designed for a certain segment of the moviegoing audience. There **are** car-crash films aimed at males under thirty. There **are** heart-warming romantic comedies for women over twenty. There **are** even the dreadful "slasher" movies for an audience that it is better not to think about.

Sentence Practice 1, *page 44*

1. There **were** still <u>dozens</u> of presents to wrap. 2. Recently, there **have** been <u>complaints</u> about the noise in the dorms. 3. In the past, there **were** many more independently owned <u>grocery stores</u>. 4. There **are** still five shopping <u>days</u> until Christmas. 5. I didn't like the ending because there **were** too many loose <u>ends</u> that were not tied up.

Sentence Practice 2, *page 45*

1. OK 2. Since it had snowed all night, there **were** only some <u>trucks</u> on the road. 3. There **are** some <u>cookies and pastries</u> to go with the coffee. 4. Fortunately, there **were** a <u>flashlight and</u> some <u>candles</u> in the closet. 5. There **are** <u>lots</u> of things for the kids to do there.

Editing Practice 1, *page 46*

There **are** lots of reasons to visit Spain. First of all, there **are** all those wonderful, long, sunny afternoons. Even though Spain is west of England, Spain uses the same time zone as France and Italy, essentially giving Spain year-round daylight savings time. Moreover, when Spain goes on daylight savings time in the summer with the rest of Europe, there **are** actually two extra hours of daylight in Spain. The extra daylight in the afternoon means that when the stores reopen after the siesta at 6 P.M., there is still plenty of daylight when people are out and about. Most businesses and offices open at 8 or 9 in the morning to take advantage of the fact that there **are** many hours . . .

Editing Practice 2, *page 47*

Another reason to visit Spain is to explore the art and architecture. There **are** some of the world's greatest museums, art galleries, and churches in Spain. In Madrid, there **are** half a dozen great art collections, the most famous being the Prado. The Prado has the world's greatest collection of Spanish paintings: there **are** innumerable paintings by Goya, Velazquez, and El Greco. The enormous wealth Spain acquired from its conquests in the New World allowed Spanish kings to purchase numerous collections of great art masterpieces from the rest of Europe. In the Prado there **are** fantastic collections of Dutch and Flemish paintings. For example, there **are** nearly one hundred paintings by Rubens alone.

LESSON 5: Agreement with Compound Subjects

Diagnostic Exercise, *page 49*

I work in a busy law office. Even though we now have voice mail, answering the phone and writing down messages **take** up a lot of my time. I am also responsible for maintaining the law library, although most of the time I do nothing more glamorous than shelving. The law books and reference material **are** always left scattered around the library, and some of the lawyers even leave their dirty coffee cups on the tables. I used to have a relatively comfortable working area, but the new computer terminal and modem **have** now taken up most of my personal space; that's progress, I guess. Despite all the stress, meeting the needs of clients and keeping track of all the information required in a modern law office **make** it . . .

Sentence Practice 1, *page 51*

1. The <u>milk</u> and the <u>eggs</u> **were** still in the car. 2. The <u>causes</u> and <u>treatments</u> of chronic disease **are** becoming much better understood. 3. You don't have to be a health nut to believe that <u>vegetables</u> and <u>fruit</u> **are** the basis of a good diet. 4. <u>Weekends</u> and <u>holidays</u> **last** forever when you're not busy. 5. The <u>advantages</u> and <u>disadvantages</u> always **seem** to balance out.

Sentence Practice 2, *page 52*

1. A <u>rifle</u> and a <u>shotgun</u> **are** used for very different kinds of hunting. 2. <u>French</u>, <u>Latin</u>, and <u>German</u> **are** the main source of English vocabulary. 3. The <u>heat</u> and <u>humidity</u> **make** it very uncomfortable in the summer. 4. A <u>cup</u> of coffee and a <u>cigarette</u> **don't** make a complete meal. 5. <u>What we see</u> and <u>what we get</u> **are** not always the same thing.

Editing Practice 1, *page 53*

Many stories, plays, and even a famous opera **are** based on the legend of Don Juan. Don Juan's charm and wit supposedly **make** him utterly irresistible to women. The most famous treatment of the Don Juan legend is in Mozart's opera, *Don Giovanni* (*Giovanni* is the Italian form of the Spanish name *Juan*, or *John* in English). Mozart's opera is highly unusual in that comedy and villainy **are** mixed together in almost equal parts. For example, the actions and behavior of the Don constantly **keep** the audience off balance. His charm and bravery **make** him almost a hero at times. However, at other times, his aristocratic arrogance and deliberate cruelty to women **reveal** he is far from a true hero. The delicate seduction of a willing woman and a violent rape **are** all the same to him.

Unit Three

LESSON 6: Present, Past, and Tense Shifting

Diagnostic Exercise, *page 60*

Last summer we took a trip to Provence, a region in the southeast corner of France, which **borders** Italy. The name *Provence* **refers** to the fact that it was the first province created by the ancient Romans outside the Italian peninsula. Today, Provence still **contains** an amazing number of well-preserved Roman ruins. While there **are** a few big towns on the coast, Provence **is** famous for its wild country and beautiful scenery. Provence **is** especially known for its abundance of wildflowers in the spring. These flowers **are** used . . .

Sentence Practice 1, *page 63*

1. Key West **is** the southernmost point in the continental United States. 2. Whenever the weather changes, my joints **start** to ache. 3. We visited one ancient site after another until they all **ran** together. 4. Shakespeare **was** idolized in the nineteenth century. 5. Interstate Highway 405 **goes** around downtown Seattle, allowing drivers to miss the worst of urban traffic.

Sentence Practice 2, *page 63*

1. Telephone marketers always call when we **are** eating. 2. According to the style sheet, scientific papers **are** rarely written in the first person. 3. I always try to return messages before I **leave** the office. 4. She broke her ankle skiing down the trail that **leads** to the ranger cabin. 5. When it rains, it **pours**.

Editing Practice 1, *page 64*

Even though Shakespeare died in 1616, performances of his plays **have** continued without interruption right up to today. I recently **attended** the Oregon Shakespeare Festival in Ashland, Oregon. In planning the performances, the director **had** to make some big decisions about how to stage plays that **are** more than 350 years old. The biggest problem for all directors today **is** whether to present Shakespearian plays in period costume or in more modern dress.

Staging the plays in modern dress **makes** the plays more interesting and often a lot more fun. For example, in a performance of *Henry IV, Part I* at Ashland a few years ago, Falstaff **came** on stage for the first time on a motor scooter with a case of beer strapped on behind. Sometimes, staging plays in different time periods **allows** the director to make political or social comments. An outstanding example of this **is** the 1995 movie version of *Richard III* with Ian McKellen in an imaginary Fascist England in the 1930's. McKellen's performance as an all-powerful, sadistic ruler in an authoritarian state **chills** the . . .

Editing Practice 2, *page 65*

Ashland's Shakespeare Festival **began** almost by accident as an outgrowth of the old Chautauqua circuit. Chautauqua **provided** entertainment to rural America before the days of radio and movies. Chautauqua **was** a mix of popular lecturers, music, and vaudeville acts — something that seems strange today. After the collapse of Chautauqua, Ashland **found** itself with a good-sized summer theater facility. After unsuccessfully trying a variety of entertainments, including boxing matches, the faculty from the local college **decided** to stage a few Shakespearian plays. The plays proved to be so successful that the Oregon Shakespeare Festival **was** born . . .

LESSON 7: The Past and the Perfect Tenses

Diagnostic Exercise, *page 69*

Unfortunately, most people **have been** involved in an automobile accident at some time. I **have been** involved in several, but my luckiest accident was one that never happened. Just after I **had gotten** my driver's license, I borrowed the family car to go to a party. Although it **had been** a very tame party, I left feeling a little hyper and silly. It was night, and there were no street lights nearby. I **had parked** a little distance from the house, so my car was by itself. I got into the car and decided to show off a little bit by throwing the car into reverse and flooring it. I **had gone** about twenty yards backward before I thought to myself that I was doing something pretty dangerous. I slammed on the brakes in a panic. I got out of the car and found that my back bumper was about four inches from a parked car that I **had never seen**. Whenever . . .

Sentence Practice 1, *page 72*

1. We **have had** a test every week this semester. 2. It **rained** last week during the parade. 3. When we returned from vacation, we found that our house **had been** broken into. 4. I **have been** interested in Egyptology for years. 5. After Holmes **had solved** a case, Watson wrote it up for posterity.

Sentence Practice 2, *page 73*

1. He **wrecked** his knee making a tackle on the first play of the game. 2. I **had already noticed** the problem before you told me about it. 3. He **has worked** overtime for the past six months. 4. We had to forfeit the game after we **had used** an ineligible player. 5. It **has snowed** every day since Christmas.

Editing Practice 1, *page 74*

The number of deaths resulting from traffic accidents **has** declined steadily over the past decade. In recent years, researchers **have cited** a number of different reasons: improved safety of vehicles, increased use of seat belts and airbags, and fewer drunk drivers. Automobile manufacturers **had been** reluctant to even talk about safety until the federal government began mandating standards in the 1980's. Over the years, manufacturers **have continued** to resist installing even inexpensive safety features. For example, manufacturers **have been** very slow to produce cars with daytime headlights, even though in recent years many Canadian researchers **have demonstrated** that this no-cost item results in significantly fewer accidents.

Unit Four

LESSON 8: Pronoun Agreement

Some answers in this lesson will vary. Sample answers are shown.

Diagnostic Exercise, *page 81*

Soldiers commit a war crime when they violate norms of acceptable behavior in times of war. Few people want war, but most want their rights and those of others to be respected as much as possible when war occurs. For instance, almost everybody agrees that **prisoners** should have their physical needs attended to and should not be physically or mentally tortured. An officer who orders **his or her** troops . . .

Sentence Practice 1, *page 84*

1. **Doctors** must have insurance covering them against malpractice liability. 2. Everyone must bring **his or her** calculator on Friday. 3. College students have to pick majors that interest **them.** 4. OK 5. Anybody who hasn't turned in **his or her** test should do so now.

Sentence Practice 2, *page 85*

1. Someone parked **a** car in a place where it will be towed. 2. OK 3. OK 4. Did somebody take my pen instead of **his or hers**? 5. OK (*Their* does not rename *nobody*. It renames *Becca and Alyssa*, which is plural and thus agrees with *their*.)

Editing Practice 1, *page 86*

My brother has been collecting certain cards that have been popular in the last few years. **People** might merely collect these cards, or they might actually play games with them. Many years ago, **card collectors** would have likely collected sports cards, but nowadays they . . .

At one time, Pokémon was the most popular card game. The person who created these cards must have made a great deal of money from **his or her** creations. Another Japanese-inspired game is called Yu Gi Oh, and it is still popular. In Yu Gi Oh, a player selects a card from **his or her** hand to play. The opponent likewise picks a card **to** duel with. I thought this was a mindless game until I saw how much math and strategy are involved in the dueling stage. The game is so complex that **new players** learning the game **need** all the help they can get . . .

LESSON 9: Vague Pronouns: *This, That,* and *It*

Some answers in this lesson will vary. Sample answers are shown.

Diagnostic Exercise, *page 90*

"Star Wars" was the name of a military program as well as a movie. **The program** was a large research program calling for military defense in outer space. This **plan** was initiated by President Reagan in the 1980's, and it had the official title of "Strategic Defense Initiative." The public never embraced that **name** as much as . . .

Sentence Practice 1, *page 93*

1. OK; meteorite 2. I knew **this problem** was going to happen! 3. **This number** could change, however. 4. **That development** is not a surprise. 5. A deer poked its head up from the grass where a fawn was resting, and then I saw **the deer** run away.

Sentence Practice 2, *page 94*

1. **Listening to her** took almost an hour of my time. 2. We need a new governor, but **that change** won't happen anytime soon. 3. In the early 1800's, **Cincinnati** was built on

the busy Ohio River. 4. **The car** seemed to want to pass me. 5. World War I was ended by the Versailles Treaty; **this treaty** also led to the formation of the League of Nations.

Editing Practice 1, *page 95*

Some credit card companies are taking advantage of students. **This practice** is becoming increasingly common. I see salespeople from the card companies almost every week on my campus, and **their presence** seems even more common in the spring semester when students are graduating. Most students have little experience with credit companies, and the representatives know **that fact**.

The companies give away T-shirts or candy bars to get students' attention. This gimmick sparks students' interest, and then the salespeople tell students that they are "preapproved" and can get a card immediately. **The gimmick** seems to work because I always see students signing up for these cards. The salespeople often forget a small detail: that little card is going to cost an annual fee plus 21 percent interest on all charges. Most students seem to think **the offer** is still great, but they will change their minds when they see the bills adding up. Believe me, **this trick** happened to me.

Editing Practice 2, *page 96*

My college finally decided to invest in a new system for allowing students to register online without having to come to campus during registration. **The new system** is a good idea. In fact, I am surprised **this technology** has taken so long to implement here. **Online registration** has been used at other colleges in the region. **That fact** is not unusual, . . .

Under the new system, students will be given passwords allowing them to access their student accounts. Initially, **a password** will be automatically assigned to each student, but the password can be changed later. By following the onscreen directions, students can pick and choose which classes they want to take, and **their schedules** can be changed anytime up to the first day of the semester. Students can now pay tuition online as well by using their credit cards. **That payment option** is good, even though . . .

LESSON 10: Choosing the Correct Pronoun Form

Diagnostic Exercise, *page 100*

A friend and **I** visited her cousin Jim, who lives in a cabin he built from scratch. My friend asked Jim if he would mind if **she** and **I** could stay in the cabin with **him** for a few days this summer. He said that was fine if we would work with **him** building a new storeroom he wanted to add onto his cabin. My friend told him that neither **she** nor **I** had any real experience building things. Jim said that it was OK. He would work with **us**. Both my friend and **I** learned how to measure and cut lumber, pound nails, and paint without getting it all over ourselves. Jim was very good natured about the whole thing, even though my friend and **I** were probably more trouble than we were worth.

Sentence Practice 1, *page 103*

1. The pharaoh visited the burial tomb intended for just **him**. 2. Janet and **I** are going out this Friday. 3. OK 4. **She** and the dog were rescued by firefighters. 5. Mom promised to write, and today I received a card from **her**.

Sentence Practice 2, *page 103*

1. Just between you and **me**, we are having an unannounced quiz on Monday. 2. Dwayne and **I** are studying on Sunday. 3. OK 4. If not for **me**, you would not be having a birthday at all today. 5. Elian and **he** left on Thursday for a vacation.

Editing Practice 1, *page 104*

When I was in high school, my father and **I** would build a new house every other summer. My father and mother were both teachers so **they** always had summers off. During the first summer, my father and **I** would pour the foundation and do the framing and roofing. During the school year, a contractor would supervise the plumbing, wiring, and other specialities. The following summer, my father and **I** would finish the interior work. During the next school year, my mother would take charge of all the interior decoration, and then **she** would put the house on the market.

The key to making this scheme work was having the contractor; without **him**, we could never have done it. When we first started building houses, we needed **him** for his expertise. Later on that was not the case. We needed **him** because he could control the subcontractors.

LESSON 11: *Who, Whom,* and *That*

Diagnostic Exercise, *page 108*

An experience that we all have had is working for a bad boss. One boss **whom** we have all had is the petty tyrant, a person **who** loves to find fault with every employee **who** works in the building. It seems like the petty tyrant is more interested in finding employees **whom** he or she can belittle than in getting the job done. Even worse than the petty tyrant is a supervisor **who** is inconsistent. An inconsistent boss is a person **whom** the employees can never trust. A game that this kind of boss loves is playing favorites. One day, this boss is your best buddy; the next day, the boss acts as if he or she doesn't know the name of a person **who** has worked with the company for ten years.

Sentence Practice 1, *page 111*

1. The woman **who** answered the phone was chewing gum loudly. 2. Senator Blather ignored the reporters **who** had been waiting outside. 3. I called the couple **who** had answered the ad. 4. OK 5. A friend **whom** I have known for years loaned me her truck.

Sentence Practice 2, *page 112*

1. OK 2. I want to know the name of the mechanic **who** fixed your car. 3. A guy **whom** I knew in high school sits next to me in my art class. 4. Who was the president **who** succeeded Ronald Reagan? 5. The first person **who** makes fun of my hair color is going to be sorry.

Editing Practice 1, *page 113*

My boss is someone **whom** you might consider strange. I work part-time at a convenience store that is located outside the city. My boss, Ms. McDonald, is someone who wants everything exactly her way. If you ever disagree with her, she tells you to hush and then covers her ears. She is married to a man **who** sells exotic goats for a living, and he occasionally brings them to the store. Last weekend, one goat bit a customer who was buying tomatoes that the goat wanted. Ms. McDonald, **whom** the goat also tried to bite, called the police. By the time they arrived, both the goat and my boss's husband had escaped. The customer **who** was bitten said he would sue the store; Ms. McDonald simply told him to hush and covered her ears. The officers, **who** were all too familiar with her strange behavior, said she could no longer have goats in the store. It's not exactly a funny situation, but she certainly makes my job interesting.

Editing Practice 2, *page 113*

Many Americans, even those **who** are knowledgeable about different cultures, know little about many religions. One example is Buddhism. This religion was founded in India by Siddhartha Gautama, **who** is known as Buddha, and it has over 300 million followers worldwide. Another example is Confucianism. This religion is based on the teachings of Confucius, a Chinese philosopher **who** stressed . . .

Some lesser-known religions were actually founded by people **who** migrated to America. The Amish Mennonites can be traced back to the birth of the Mennonite religion in Switzerland during the 1500's. In 1693, however, the followers of Jacob Ammann broke from other Mennonites, but a great many rejoined the main group in the eighteenth century. The remainder, **who** stayed loyal to Jacob Ammann's views, migrated to Pennsylvania. These are the followers **who** became known . . .

LESSON 12: Eliminating Sexist Pronouns

Some answers in this lesson will vary. Sample answers are shown.

Diagnostic Exercise, *page 117*

My psychology teacher, Ms. Crystal, had each member of the class complete a questionnaire that would help him **or her** choose an appropriate career. I had already decided on a profession, but she said the questionnaire would offer me other options. I've always wanted to be an electrical engineer because I like to design things; **engineers spend** much of **their** time drawing designs and writing specifications. Ms. Crystal said my survey results indicated I should consider being an accountant. She also told me, however, that the survey was just one resource for choosing a career. I agree. **People have** to consider what **they know** better than anyone else: **their** own interests.

Sentence Practice 1, *page 120*

1. **Leaders have** to be responsible to **their** constituents. 2. OK 3. We must hire a secretary **who is** organized and efficient. 4. I prefer a teacher who knows **his or her** subject material but who allows students to solve problems for themselves. 5. **All voters** should cast **their ballots** in the upcoming school bond election.

Sentence Practice 2, *page 121*

1. OK [The writer is referring to a specific neighbor, who apparently is male.] 2. If you ever put your children into day care, meet with the person who will watch your children and see if **he or she** is patient. 3. Has everyone done **the** homework? 4. A writer must choose words carefully. 5. I have never met anyone who brushes **his or her** teeth as often as you!

Editing Practice 1, *page 122*

In American high schools and colleges, **students** can avail **themselves** of a number of free activities open to **them**. This is completely different from European schools where **students have** virtually no extracurricular activities available to **them**. In Europe, **school-aged athletes** must find (and pay for) a private, after-school sports club that **they** can join. When European **students come** to the United States, **they are** astonished at the extracurricular activities routinely available to **them**. Often **exchange students** will single out the extracurricular activities that **they** participated in as the most enjoyable part of **their** experience in the United States. Europeans point out that one reason why test scores for the average American are so low (by international standards) is that the American **students spend** too much of **their** school day in nonacademic activities. Whether or not **American students are** well served by **their** extracurricular experience is obviously a matter of debate.

Unit Five

LESSON 13: Dangling Modifiers

Some answers in this lesson will vary. Sample answers are shown.

Diagnostic Exercise, *page 130*

Studying for hours, **I felt my eyes grow tired**. I walked to the snack bar for a cup of coffee. **When I arrived**, the place was closed. Deciding against walking a mile to another place, **I thought** that maybe I should quit for a while and get some sleep. I returned to my room and tried to decide what to do. **I was torn** between the need to sleep and the need to study. **The** alarm clock went off and made me realize it was time for class. After struggling to stay awake in class, **I decided** to . . .

Sentence Practice 1, *page 133*

1. Lunch realized that it was time to eat = Illogical action. *Correction:* Realizing that it was time to eat, the cafeteria staff served lunch to the hungry students. 2. The sunken wreck hoped there was plenty of air = Illogical action. *Correction:* Hoping there was plenty of air in her tank, the scuba diver explored the sunken wreck a bit longer. 3. Sharon's day saw the wreck = Illogical action. *Correction:* After seeing the wreck, Sharon realized her day was ruined. 4. Somebody was reading my e-mail = Illogical action. *Correction:* While reading my e-mail, I heard somebody knock on the door. 5. Vajra's nose was running up the stairs = Illogical action. *Correction:* Running up the stairs, Vajra fell and broke her nose.

Sentence Practice 2, *page 134*

1. It read the contract = Illogical action. *Correction:* After the business partners read the contract carefully, they decided to wait a few days before both parties would sign. 2. Dark clouds were relaxing = Illogical action. *Correction:* While the tourists were relaxing in the sun, dark clouds suddenly appeared. 3. Ted's tennis racket was enraged = Illogical action. *Correction:* Enraged by his pitiful score, Ted hurled his tennis racket across the court. 4. Ted's bad temper broke the pencil = Illogical action. *Correction:* Breaking the pencil in anger, Ted revealed his bad temper again. 5. Eating supper was feeling hungry = Illogical action. *Correction:* Feeling hungry because I skipped lunch, I realized that eating supper seemed a really good idea.

Editing Practice 1, *page 135*

Last summer I flew from Seattle to New York. Not having flown for a while, **I had an eye-opening experience.** On the positive side, it really is much easier than it used to be to compare rates and schedules. Spending a few minutes (well, quite a few minutes actually) on the computer, **I found the obvious choice.** That's it for the good news. Everything else was downhill from there. Knowing that I needed to get to the airport in plenty of time, **I planned** to get there an hour and a half before departure time. Even then, I very nearly missed my flight. What I hadn't bargained on was how much longer it would take to get through security. Taking off my coat, jacket, and shoes and unpacking my laptop was awkward enough. The real problem was trying to get my shoes back on while juggling all my clothes and my computer. Balancing on one foot and then the other, **I found it** almost impossible to wedge my shoes onto my feet one-handed.

The flight itself was uneventful, though not very pleasant. Seated in the middle seat, **I felt like** the flight lasted forever. One thing that had changed since the last time I have flown was the lack of leg room. Even being of only average height, **I couldn't fit my legs** into the space. I thought that was pretty bad; then the person in front of me reclined his seat to the maximum. The top of his seat was about 12 inches from my face. I quickly discovered that I could not read. Holding my book so close to my face, **I couldn't focus my eyes** on the page . . .

LESSON 14: Misplaced and Squinting Adverbs

Diagnostic Exercise, *page 139*

My brother **today** informed me he would travel to Europe. He plans to go as soon as school is out this summer. A travel agent told him it would cost **only** $400 for a round-trip ticket to London. The agent he spoke with said **enthusiastically** that he should take advantage of this price. My brother asked whether I wanted to go with him, but I have already committed myself to a summer job. He talked for **almost** an hour . . .

Sentence Practice 1, *page 143*

1. OK 2. Hamsters are pregnant for **only** sixteen days. 3. We read **almost** forty short stories in my American literature class. 4. My biology teacher said **yesterday** that there are 138,000 varieties of butterflies and moths. 5. She hit the ball **nearly** out of the park.

Sentence Practice 2, *page 143*

1. OK [Unless "slowly" is referring to the man's pace of reading, in which case "slowly" should be moved before "reading."] 2. **Yesterday,** Iva said she found my keys. 3. He bought that DVD for **only** $6. 4. OK 5. OK

Editing Practice 1, *page 144*

I don't watch a lot of TV. I suppose that I watch **hardly** three programs a week. It's not that I don't like television; the problem is that I never seem to find programs that I really want to watch when I have a little down time. I suppose that if I had TiVo, I would watch more often since I could watch my favorites whenever I wanted to. As it is now, I **quickly** flick through the program guide losing interest. [*Quickly* is a squinting adverb. Correction 1: I **quickly** flick . . . Correction 2: losing interest **quickly**.] Besides, I tell myself, **too often** watching TV is a complete waste of time. [*Too often* is a squinting adverb. Correction 1: I tell myself, **too often** watching TV . . . Correction 2: I tell myself, watching TV **too often** is a complete waste. . . .]

Another problem is that many TV programs **actually** seem to have become serials. [*Actually* is a squinting adverb. Correction 1: programs **actually** seem to have . . . Correction 2: seem to have **actually** become serials. Correction 3: have become **actual** serials.] That is, they have a storyline that continues from week to week. Each new episode builds on what has happened before. I suppose this soap opera-like construction is attractive to the producers since they can build in layers of complicated relations that bring the audience back week after week. The trouble with this approach for casual viewers like me is that tuning into an ongoing program is like starting to read a long book by starting in the middle—I have no idea what is going on. This kind of program accounts for **almost** half the shows on TV today.

Unit Six

LESSON 15: Commas with *And, But, Or,* and Other Coordinating Conjunctions

Diagnostic Exercise, *page 153*

When he reached the Americas, Christopher Columbus believed he had reached the East Indies, so he called the people whom he found *Indians.* That term is still used, but many indigenous people prefer the term *Native Americans.* Some people think of Native Americans as a group, but that is really a mistake because there are vast differences in their cultures and languages. People also tend to think of the tribes from the plains as being typical Native Americans, for those are the tribes most often represented in movies,/ and on TV. The plains tribes hunted buffalo,/ and lived in tepees, but few coastal tribes ever saw a buffalo or a tepee. Instead, coastal tribes hunted whales,/ and lived in wooden homes.

Sentence Practice 1, *page 156*

1. Pig iron is refined in a blast furnace,/ and contains iron along with small amounts of manganese and other minerals. 2. Piero di Cosimo was a Florentine painter,/ and is remembered for his scenes depicting mythology. 3. Tom decided he would walk to class,/ but changed his mind when it started raining. 4. OK 5. The Norman Conquest of England took place in 1066,/ and brought many changes in English life.

22222

Sentence Practice 2, *page 157*

1. OK 2. OK 3. My father bought an old sword in England**,** but the old relic is not worth much. 4. OK 5. Bahir is dropping by my place later**,** so I suppose I should try to clean up a bit.

Editing Practice 1, *page 158*

Writing is a form of visible language**,** but there is a form of writing that is not meant to be seen. Braille is written as a series of dots or bumps**,** so visually impaired people can "read" it with their fingers. It is written as a series of cells**,** and each cell contains dots that can be variously arranged. Each particular arrangement of dots has its own meaning**,** but what the dots represent depends on the style of Braille. There are two forms of Braille: Grade 1**/** and Grade 2. Grade 1 Braille is a system in which the dots represent letters**/** and some very short words. Grade 2 Braille is not a completely different system**,** but it is a shorthand version of Grade 1 that is much harder to read.

Editing Practice 2, *page 159*

The wedding ring has been around for many centuries**,** and its history is more complex than people might think. Ancient Greeks are often credited with inventing this tradition**,** but many historians believe it started with the Egyptians or Hebrews. We do know the first rings were not made of precious metals. Many of the earliest rings were made of iron**/** and did not have a gemstone. The ring was usually placed on the woman's fourth finger**,** for it was believed a nerve behind this finger led directly to the heart. In the United States, the ring is placed on the left hand**,** but it is traditionally placed on the right hand . . .

LESSON 16: Commas with Transitional Terms

Diagnostic Exercise, *page 163*

Many places around the globe have universal appeal. They are**, however,** not necessarily accessible to the general public. An international committee has designated some sites as World Heritage Sites, which are sites having international value and responsibility. In the United States**, for example,** the committee has chosen Yosemite Park and the Statue of Liberty, both of which are part of our national parks system. We tend to take our parks system for granted**; however,** it is really quite unusual. Very few developed countries have extensive public land**; consequently,** their important public sites are little more than individual buildings. The vast size of some national parks in the American West makes them unique**; therefore,** they attract visitors from every country.

Sentence Practice 1, *page 167*

1. Bill said he might be late. <u>Indeed,</u> he was four hours late. 2. Little is known about the Pilgrim ship *Mayflower*; we do <u>know, however,</u> that it weighed about 180 tons. 3. English is the predominant language in the United States. <u>Nevertheless,</u> over three hundred languages are spoken within its borders. 4. none 5. A serious accident has caused major delays. <u>In fact,</u> some commuters have decided to stay home.

Sentence Practice 2, *page 168*

1. Sean Connery is remembered most for his James Bond movies. <u>However,</u> he won an Oscar for a different role in *The Untouchables.* 2. Scott Joplin wrote over sixty musical compositions. He wrote, <u>for instance,</u> an opera entitled *Treemonisha*. 3. none 4. The top position in the British army is field marshal. The top position in its navy, <u>in contrast,</u> is admiral of the fleet. 5. The singer Prince has gone by more than one name. <u>For example,</u> his birth name is Prince Rogers Nelson.

Editing Practice 1, *page 169*

I am facing a difficult decision**; however,** it is one I have to make soon. My family would like me to help with our family business after I graduate from college. My parents own a construction company, and my major is in accounting. **Consequently,** I believe that I would have a lot to offer my parents' company once I finish my degree. I could, **for example,** help them develop more precise estimates for construction projects. My plans seemed so clear and logical at one time.

I enjoy talking with my parents about different accounting methods. **Nevertheless,** I have lately been considering moving to a different part of the country and working in a different type of business. New England would be a great place to live, **for example**. **Additionally,** I am considering working as an accountant for a company that manufactures computer parts. Even though I want the family business to do well, I want to try something very different. My parents have always supported my choices; **still,** I know they will be disappointed if I do not work for them.

LESSON 17: Commas with Adverb Clauses

Diagnostic Exercise, *page 173*

After everybody was asleep Monday night, there was a fire in the dorm next door. Fortunately, a smoke detector went off,/ when smoke got into the staircase. While the fire department was fighting the fire, six rooms were totally destroyed. A friend of mine in another part of the building lost her computer,/ because of the smoke and water damage. If school officials close down the dorm for repairs, she will have to find a new place to stay. I heard they will make a decision today,/ as soon as they get a report from the fire inspectors.

Sentence Practice 1, *page 176*

1. When I visit my parents in New Mexico, I always bring them something from my part of the country. 2. I will go with you,/ after I finish eating. 3. After Omar competed in the third basketball tournament of the season, he was not eager to travel again. 4. Because the test included over a hundred questions, I could not finish it in just fifteen minutes. 5. Stephanie wants to leave,/ because she smells a strange odor in the room.

Sentence Practice 2, *page 177*

1. While we were watching some children playing in the park, Luis and I talked about our own childhoods. 2. Although sharks are normally found in salt water, some freshwater sharks exist in Lake Nicaragua. 3. We need to stop at the next gas station, even though we stopped at one just an hour ago. 4. Because I tend to work forty hours each week, I have to spend most of my weekends studying. 5. Whenever you are ready to leave, I will be happy to go.

Editing Practice 1, *page 178*

Because I am a full-time student, my income is limited. I don't want to borrow money from my family,/ unless no other option is available. Twice, I have used a government loan to pay for my tuition, fees, and books. Without those loans, I would not have been able to attend college. Although I would prefer not to take out any more student loans, I will likely have to do so again.

My part-time job does not pay well,/ since it is a minimum-wage position. Although I can't afford any luxuries, living on this meager income is manageable. In a few years, I will likely be able to improve my standard of living greatly, so my situation is not depressing. When I graduate from college, I should be able to find a job,/ because my field is very much in demand. Until then, I will be able to get by on an occasional student loan.

LESSON 18: Commas with Introductory Elements

Diagnostic Exercise, *page 182*

Last Tuesday, there was a fire in one of the dorms. According to the school newspaper, no one was hurt. When the fire department finally arrived, several rooms were engulfed in flames. A friend of mine had her room filled with smoke. However, her room suffered no major damage. Tomorrow, school officials will tour the dorm and make recommendations. I have heard they plan to move everybody out within the next week.

Sentence Practice 1, *page 185*

1. Although Wally Amos is best known for his brand of cookies, he was also the first African American talent agent for the William Morris Agency. 2. In France, shepherds once carried small sundials as pocket watches. 3. Even though he was best known as an actor, Jimmy Stewart was a brigadier general in the U.S. Air Force Reserve. 4. After eating, our cat likes to nap. 5. Whenever I walk, our dog likes to go with me.

Sentence Practice 2, *page 185*

1. To keep people from sneaking up on him, Wild Bill Hickok placed crumpled newspapers around his bed. 2. Before his career was suddenly ended, Jesse James robbed twelve banks and seven trains. 3. Therefore, he was a successful criminal for a time. 4. Believe it or not, the state "gem" of Washington is petrified wood. 5. When she was in a high school band, singer Dolly Parton played the snare drum.

Editing Practice 1, *page 187*

When I tried to start a student organization on campus last semester, I was surprised by the difficulties and hurdles. I wanted to establish a club for students who enjoy science fiction. After being encouraged by several friends, I contacted the school official who oversees campus organizations. She informed me I would need a faculty sponsor and had to go through an approval process that could take several weeks. Upon reading some twelve pages of forms and directions, I almost gave up. Fortunately, a couple of friends agreed to help me fill out the forms and gather signatures from students interested in the club. However, the work was still not finished. We had to arrange a schedule of events and apply for funding. It took three months before the science fiction club was approved by various committees and school administrators. Now that the club has had three successful meetings, I feel that all the work was worthwhile.

Editing Practice 2, *page 187*

As you might expect, there are heavy physical demands on marathon runners. In addition to the common problem of fatigue, the greatest problem marathon runners have is with their feet. Among all marathon runners, the universal topic of conversation is shoes. Every brand is minutely compared in terms of weight, support, and cost. Because most runners train on asphalt, running shoes wear out amazingly quickly. Replacing an expensive pair of shoes every few months can be pretty costly; nevertheless, every runner has learned that running in worn shoes is asking for foot and ankle problems. Despite the fact that running shoes are tremendously expensive, there is no doubt that they are getting better. The improved design of modern running shoes has eliminated many of the nagging foot and ankle problems that used to plague runners. For most runners, the main issue in shoes is the trade-off between weight and support — the more weight, the more support . . .

LESSON 19: Commas with Adjective Clauses

Diagnostic Exercise, *page 191*

It was strange going back to my high school reunion, which was held this summer. Allison, who was my best friend once, didn't recognize me. I guess she didn't expect to see me bald. I also saw a friend / whom I have stayed in touch with through e-mail but have not seen in years. He told me he moved to Oregon, where he found a job. Since I now live in Idaho, we agreed to get together. After the reunion was over, I had dinner with him and Allison at a restaurant / that we enjoyed . . .

Sentence Practice 1, *page 194*

1. OK [essential] 2. Bo is reading *The Silmarillion*, which was written by J. R. R. Tolkien. [nonessential] 3. OK [essential] 4. This neighborhood cafe, which first opened in 1939, is one of my favorite places to drink coffee. [nonessential] 5. My parents were married in the Middle Eastern country of Yemen, where a wedding feast can last three weeks. [nonessential]

Sentence Practice 2, *page 195*

1. My dentist is from Seattle, which is over 600 miles from here. [nonessential] 2. Queen Latifah, who is best known as a rap artist, has also been a television host and an actress. [nonessential] 3. OK [essential] 4. OK [essential] 5. The only river／that flows north and south of the equator／ is the Congo River, which crosses the equator twice. [essential and nonessential]

Editing Practice 1, *page 196*

I recently purchased a green-cheeked conure, which is a type of small parrot. It is an intelligent bird／that is becoming increasingly popular as an exotic pet. *Pyrrhura molinae,* which is the bird's scientific name, is mostly green. The green-cheeked conure obtains its name from the bright green feathers on its cheeks. It is a very playful and active bird. My father, who generally dislikes all birds, even likes my bird, which I named "Pepper" because she likes to eat raw peppers. Most of the time, Pepper eats a blend of colored pellets that I buy at the pet store. Like many conures, Pepper is capable of mimicking speech but is not a great talker. She mainly whistles and makes a variety of odd noises／that often wake me early in the morning.

Editing Practice 2, *page 197*

I am rooming with Harold Lee, who is very practical. We couldn't afford to spend much for Christmas gifts this year, so we decided to can some vegetables. First, we made a relish／that was primarily composed of tomatoes, onions, and cabbage. The tomatoes, which we bought at the local market, had to be completely green. The jars had to be carefully sterilized, and the directions confused us. Luckily, we received advice from my mom, whom I called in a panic. Once we understood the process better, we went on to asparagus, which . . .

LESSON 20: Commas with Appositives

Diagnostic Exercise, *page 200*

Every summer I visit my Aunt Carol, a vigorous woman of sixty-five. Aunt Carol lives in a small town in Minnesota, a state in the northern part of the American Midwest. Even though I love her, we argue about one thing, coffee. Like many midwesterners, she drinks coffee all day, and her coffee is very weak. The problem is that I am from Seattle, the home of Starbucks. Starbucks, one of the fastest growing companies in the United States, has made espresso into a lifestyle choice. My favorite drink, a double mocha, has the caffeine equivalent of a dozen cups of Aunt Carol's coffee. The first time I made coffee at her house, she had a fit. She not only threw out all the coffee I made, but also made me wash the pot. From then on, she made the coffee, the kind you can see through.

Sentence Practice 1, *page 204*

1. Ian Fleming, the creator of 007, named James Bond after the author of a book about birds. 2. Ian Fleming also wrote *Chitty Chitty Bang Bang*, a children's book. 3. Tim's mother, a registered nurse, thinks I have a virus. 4. Richard, a guy in my geology class, fell asleep during the lecture. 5. Spanish Fort, a town in south Alabama, was the site of one of the last battles of the Civil War.

Sentence Practice 2, *page 204*

1. My roommate, a political science major, plans to run for public office. [specific; non-essential] 2. He has a date this Friday with Janet Spain, the woman who sits next to you in History 101. [specific; nonessential] 3. OK [general; essential] 4. Matthew Henson, an African American, codiscovered the North Pole with Robert Peary in 1909. [specific; non-essential] 5. I had to take Junior, one of my cats, to get his shots. [specific; nonessential]

Editing Practice 1, *page 206*

World War II, one of the best-known wars of all time, was followed a few years later by a conflict that still is not well understood. The Korean War, a conflict between the United Nations and North Korea, was never officially a war. Harry Truman, the U.S. president at the time of the conflict, never . . .

This war caused many problems for the United States, possibly because its status and purpose were not clear. General Douglas MacArthur, the commander of the U.N. forces, was removed from office for insubordination to President Truman, the commander in chief. After the landings at Inchon, a major turning point, the North Koreans . . .

Unit Seven

LESSON 21: Apostrophes in Contractions

Diagnostic Exercise, *page 214*

The student government announced today the election results for representation in the student senate. Almost half the students **didn't** vote at all, and there **weren't** many candidates running. **I'm** not sure why, but apathy was widespread. My guess is that many students **don't** think the senators have much real power, or perhaps the candidates' qualifications and goals were unclear. **It's** clear that students **aren't** enthusiastic . . .

Sentence Practice 1, *page 216*

1. **Let us** get one thing straight. [Let's] 2. It **will not** be a problem. [won't] 3. **I am** afraid that we **were not** ready for the test. [I'm/weren't] 4. **They are** ready for you now. [They're] 5. OK

Sentence Practice 2, *page 217*

1. OK 2. **You are** really in trouble now. [You're] 3. Do you want to come; **we are** going to the early show. [we're] 4. **I have** had enough of you for one day. [I've] 5. **It is** six of one and half a dozen of the other. [It's]

Editing Practice 1, *page 218*

Rice might seem to be a common (and perhaps dull) subject to Americans. However, **it's** such an important part of life in other parts of the world that rice has an honored place in many cultures. **You've** probably long known about the tradition of throwing rice at newlyweds when **they're** leaving a church. But you probably did not know that in India rice is traditionally the first food a bride offers her husband. In Indonesia, tradition has it that a woman **can't** be considered for marriage until she can skillfully prepare rice.

Rice **isn't** associated with just marriage. Even the word itself is special. **I've** been to one region in China where the word for rice is also the word for food. In Japan, the word for cooked rice is also the word for meal. **It's** also common . . .

LESSON 22: Apostrophes Showing Possession

Diagnostic Exercise, *page 221*

Paul Ortega has been one of my **family's** best friends over the years. Although he was born in Mexico, he speaks English like a native because his **father's** employer relocated his family to Arizona when Paul was six. In a few years, **Paul's** English was as good as **anyone's**. Nearly every summer, however, Paul and his sisters went back to Mexico City, where they stayed at a **relative's** house. As a result, he is completely at home in either **country's** culture. He and my father have been business partners for many years. The **company's** success . . .

Sentence Practice 1, *page 225*

1. It's **nobody's** business. 2. I really like that **guitar's** sound. 3. The **ladder's** rungs were covered with paint. 4. **Plato's** dialogues are still an important part of philosophy. 5. The team met to discuss the **tumor's** treatment.

Sentence Practice 2, *page 225*

1. The whole community was opposed to the **bridge's** destruction. 2. Some of **Wagner's** operas are the longest ever written. 3. I hastily scribbled my notes on the **envelope's** back. 4. We were met by the **hospital's** administrator. 5. **Mike's** feelings were hurt by what you said.

Editing Practice 1, *page 227*

You have probably never heard Alfred **Wegener's** name. Wegener was born in Berlin in 1880. He got a PhD in astronomy, but his **life's** work was the new field of meteorology (the study of weather). As a young man, he became interested in ballooning and, for a time, held the **world's** record for altitude. As a balloonist he was well aware of the fact the **wind's** direction and speed on the **earth's** surface did not correspond at all with the **wind's** movement high above the surface. He was the first person to exploit the **balloon's** ability to carry weather instruments high into the atmosphere and to track wind movement at various altitudes. He was one of a group of early researchers who studied a remarkable current of air that circulated around the North Pole. The researchers had discovered what we now call the jet stream. In 1930, he and a colleague disappeared in an expedition to Greenland. His and his **colleague's** frozen bodies were found a year later.

LESSON 23: Other Uses of the Apostrophe

Diagnostic Exercise, *page 231*

This **semester's** schedule is hectic for me. I seem to have only a **moment's** peace before I have to go to work or school. I am working and attending school full time, and I want to do something about all the C's I made last year. I cannot afford to work fewer hours because I lost two **months'** pay over the summer because of an accident. Even a few **minutes'** delay in getting to school or work seems to make me late. Next **semester's** schedule . . .

Sentence Practice 1, *page 233*

1. The attacks of September 11 were this **century's** first major U.S. crisis. [first major U.S. crisis of this century] 2. I don't know if this vacation was worth **two weeks'** wages. [wages of two weeks] 3. That is **tomorrow's** problem. [problem of tomorrow] 4. Rafael bought five **dollars'** worth of fabric. [worth of five dollars] 5. I can do it with just a **minute's** notice. [notice of a minute]

Sentence Practice 2, *page 234*

1. Last **winter's** snowfall was so bad that I missed school five times. [snowfall of last winter] 2. An **hour's** notice is not sufficient. [notice of an hour] 3. I try to keep a **week's** worth of food in the pantry. [worth of a week] 4. You are not giving me a **moment's** peace about that little mistake I made. [peace of a moment] 5. You will need a **month's** pay to afford that wide-screen television. [pay of a month]

Editing Practice 1, *page 235*

Last week, a major hurricane hit the city where I live. Luckily, we had two **days'** notice that Hurricane Candice would almost certainly come our way. Candice was a Category 4 hurricane, which is about as high as they can get. To make matters worse, three other Category 4's have affected our town in the last two years. The force of this one was so bad that its effects are already being called this **year's** biggest local story. I was lucky. The house I am renting suffered no structural damage; a few trees were blown over, and a few roof shingles were blown off. It would cost me a **week's** pay to cover these losses, but I don't have to pay for them since I only rent the house. Despite the horrible weather a week ago, this **week's** weather . . .

LESSON 24: Unnecessary Apostrophes

Diagnostic Exercise, *page 237*

Some old **friends** of mine stopped by my apartment for coffee. My roommate's coffee pot was broken, so I made them some instant coffee. I'm not good at making coffee, but everybody had two **cups** apiece. The coffee was pretty old, yet nobody seemed to care. We talked about our **schedules** . . .

Sentence Practice 1, *page 240*

1. I can't wait to turn my **essays** in. [can't = contraction] 2. We bought some maple **bars** at the store. 3. We finally took out **memberships** in a health club. 4. Please revise the **schedules** as soon as possible. 5. Gary's excuses were the lamest **reasons** I've ever heard. [Gary's = possession; I've = contraction]

Sentence Practice 2, *page 240*

1. I can't believe that **classes** were canceled today. [can't = contraction] 2. The president's remarks certainly raised some **eyebrows** around the table. [president's = possession] 3. OK [everyone's = possession; I'd = contraction] 4. There is an amazing variety of **reds** in his photographs of desert sunsets. 5. Do you want to ask the **Adamses** to give us a ride to Paolo's party this weekend? [Paolo's = possession]

Editing Practice 1, *page 241*

The word *parasite* comes from a Greek word meaning a flunky who does no honest work but depends entirely on **handouts** from wealthy and powerful patrons. In biology, the term was adopted to describe a huge variety of **creatures** that steal their nourishment from hosts, often causing their hosts' death. The behavior of **parasites** strikes all of us as profoundly vicious and ugly. One of the best fictional **depictions** of parasites is in the 1979 science fiction movie *Alien*. In that movie, the crew of a spaceship investigates a clutch of **eggs** left on an otherwise lifeless planet. As one of the crewmen examines an egg, a crablike thing bursts out of the shell and wraps a tail around the crewman's neck. By the next day, the crablike thing has disappeared and the crewman seems normal. Later, the crewman clutches his stomach in terrible pain, and a little knobby-headed alien pierces through his skin and leaps out. The alien has laid an egg in the crewman's guts; the egg has hatched and has been devouring his intestines. This horrible scenario is in fact based on the real behavior of parasitic **wasps** that lay their **eggs** in living caterpillars. As the **eggs** mature, they devour the internal organs of the caterpillar, sparing only the **organs** necessary . . .

Unit Eight

LESSON 25: Quotation Marks with Direct Quotations and Paraphrases
Some answers in this lesson will vary. Sample answers are shown.

Diagnostic Exercise, *page 251*

Until recently, poor picture quality and a high price tag have prevented consumers from purchasing digital cameras. Industry analyst Kevin Kane recently said, **"The** next several years will be key in determining what part digital cameras will play in leisure and business budgets." Kane also reported that /digital cameras are now becoming affordable enough for the average consumer./ Like PC's, fax machines, and cellular phones, digital cameras first attracted the interest of technology enthusiasts. But recreational photographers like Sanjei Rohan of Spokane, Washington, just appreciate the convenience. "As a rock climber, I have seen some amazing landscapes," he says. "I take pictures, download them to my computer, and e-mail them to my cousins in Nebraska, where they have fewer rocks to climb." /Industry analysts predict a sharp growth in consumer enthusiasm./

Sentence Practice 1, *page 254*

1. In a letter written in 1801, Beethoven stated: "I want to seize fate by the throat."
   In a letter written in 1801, Beethoven stated that he wanted to grab fate by its throat.

2. Speaking to the Nez Percé tribe, Chief Joseph said, "From where the sun now stands, I will fight no more forever."
   Speaking to the Nez Percé tribe, Chief Joseph said that he would not fight any longer.

3. In a review of another writer's book, Ambrose Bierce wrote, "The covers of this book are too far apart."
   In a review of another writer's book, Ambrose Bierce indicated that its covers were too far apart.

4. In her novel *Frankenstein*, Mary Wollstonecraft Shelley wrote: "I beheld the wretch — the miserable monster whom I had created."
   In her novel *Frankenstein,* one of Mary Wollstonecraft Shelley's characters said that he saw the miserable monster he had created.

5. John Wayne gave this advice on acting: "Talk low, talk slow, and don't say too much."
   John Wayne said that actors should talk low and slowly without saying too much.

Sentence Practice 2, *page 255*

1. In a letter John Hinckley wrote to an actress on the day he shot President Reagan, Hinckley said, "The reason I'm going ahead with this attempt now is because I just cannot wait any longer to impress you."
   In a letter John Hinckley wrote to an actress on the day he shot President Reagan, Hinckley said that he wanted to impress this actress.

2. Cher once said, "The trouble with some women is they get all excited about nothing, and then they marry him."
   Cher once said that some women's trouble is that they become excited about somebody who is not special and then marry him.

3. In 1901, former slave Booker T. Washington wrote: "My life had its beginning in the midst of the most miserable, desolate, and discouraging surroundings."
   In 1901, former slave Booker T. Washington said that he was brought up in the middle of "miserable, desolate, and discouraging surroundings." [This paraphrase maintains significant wording from the original.]

4. As Mae West said in one movie, "When I'm good, I'm very good, but when I'm bad, I'm better."
   In one movie, Mae West said that she could be good but was even better when she was bad.

5. Franklin Roosevelt once said: "I see one-third of a nation ill-housed, ill-clad, ill-nourished."
   Franklin Roosevelt once said that he saw much of the nation suffering from poverty.

Editing Practice 1, *page 256*

My mother told me **that ⸍she** believed every marriage was a compromise.⸍ For example, my brother Pete has had a lot of trouble quitting smoking. He likes to quote Mark Twain, who said**,** "**Q**uitting smoking is easy. I've done it dozens of times." After my brother got married, his wife told him that ⸍he could not keep smoking inside the house.⸍ She wants him to quit, but she knows how hard it will be for him to do it. She told me that ⸍her uncle, who had been a heavy smoker, had died from lung disease.⸍ Naturally, she is very concerned about Pete. Last night, Pete told us, "I am going to try nicotine patches." . . .

Editing Practice 2, *page 257*

Many traditional sayings emphasize the virtues of saving things. My mother always said**,** "**W**aste not, want not." That may be true, but my wife and I have some real differences on saving things. At least once a week my wife asks me, "**H**oney, do you really want to keep THIS?" It doesn't make much difference what the THIS is, but my answer will probably be the same: "**S**ure I do." I think that every marriage is doomed to have one person who is a saver and one person who is a thrower-away. The saver in me is always saying, "**B**ut I might need that someday." My wife's response is, "**S**ure, but you will never find it in all the junk you have accumulated." . . .

LESSON 26: Quotation Marks with Other Punctuation

Diagnostic Exercise, *page 260*

Yesterday, my literature teacher asked, "Who can name three poems written by African Americans?" I was able to come up with "Incident," which was written by Countee Cullen. Herman, the guy who sits next to me, named Langston Hughes's "Harlem." I started to bring up "Letter from Birmingham Jail"; however, I quickly recalled that that is an *essay* by Martin Luther King Jr. Then, somebody in the back row mentioned Hughes's "Same in Blues," and somebody else remembered Richard Wright's "Between the World and Me." Our . . .

Sentence Practice 1, *page 262*

1. Grace asked, "When will we get our tests back?" 2. OK 3. OK 4. The title of the first chapter is "Where Do We Go Next?" 5. Charlene responded, "Why are you following me?"

Sentence Practice 2, *page 263*

1. Did she say, "The store opens at noon"? 2. OK 3. OK 4. A panicked man yelled, "Don't push that button!" 5. OK

Editing Practice 1, *page 264*

My girlfriend sleepily asked, "Why are you calling me so late?" It was 2:00 A.M., and I apparently had awakened her.

"Sorry," I muttered, realizing the time. "I've been studying all night and needed a break." This apparently wasn't the right answer.

She yelled, "I was sound asleep!" After another moment, she added, "Do you think I stayed up just in case you needed to call someone?"

"Well, I guess this is a bad time to call," I meekly suggested. "I'll let you go back to sleep." She hung up . . .

LESSON 27: Semicolons

Diagnostic Exercise, *page 267*

In the early 1900's, "pulp" magazines were extremely popular. These magazines were named for the cheap pulp paper they were printed on. They contained various types of stories: adventures, detective stories, romance tales, and Western stories. One of the most successful pulp publishers was Street and Smith; this firm sold millions of magazines. Most old issues, however, have been destroyed or lost. Higher quality magazines were printed on glossy paper, which gave them the nickname "slicks." The terms "pulp" and "slicks" are still used today to distinguish simple action-oriented fiction from the more sophisticated writing that might appear in more upscale magazines such as the following: *Cosmopolitan, Esquire,* and *Harper's.*

Sentence Practice 1, *page 270*

1. Next week, we will have a major test, one that will be difficult. 2. OK 3. OK 4. Allyson and I went to the same high school, Pine Tree High School. 5. Ken brought several items: napkins, glasses, and forks.

Sentence Practice 2, *page 270*

1. Her truck failed to start because the battery was dead. 2. I read an article about Ralph Bunche, the first African American to win the Nobel Peace Prize. 3. Annie ordered a parfait, a dessert made of ice cream, fruit, and syrup. 4. OK 5. I need to go to the store, which is only about one mile away.

Editing Practice 1, *page 272*

Langston Hughes is one of the best-known African American poets, his fame having begun in 1915, when he was thirteen. At that time, he was elected poet of his graduating class, an unusual selection not merely because he was one of only two African American students in his class but because he had never written any poems. Hughes explained that nobody else in the class had written any poetry either. His classmates elected him, however, because . . .

Even though such reasoning had an element of stereotyping, Hughes was inspired, and wrote a graduation poem that the teachers and students enthusiastically received. He went on to publish many types of writing: poems, . . .

Editing Practice 2, *page 273*

Something needs to change at my apartment, because I cannot cope with the mess any longer. Six months ago, it seemed like living with two high school friends would be great; we liked hanging around each other and shared the same interests. What I did not fully understand was that they were (and are) slobs. One likes cooking, which I think is a great hobby. It's not so great, however, when he doesn't clean up the mess that he makes. My other roommate leaves clothes all over the house, even in our one bathroom. One time, I counted what seemed like half of his entire wardrobe on the bathroom floor: four pairs of jeans, three pairs of dress pants, ten T-shirts, and five dress shirts . . .

LESSON 28: Colons

Diagnostic Exercise, *page 276*

My roommate, who is shopping for a new car, looked at several types, including, Fords, Nissans, and Mazdas. She knew which features she wanted: automatic transmission, cruise control, and leather seats. However, she quickly discovered that such features were not within her budget. To get the best deal for her money, I suggested that she consult sources such as˒ her mechanic or *Consumer Reports* magazine. She did some research, but she seemed disappointed because there was no clear choice. She finally narrowed her choices to˒ a Ford Taurus . . .

Sentence Practice 1, *page 278*

1. Many farmers in this area grow˒ cotton, grain, and turnips. 2. Kamilah and Doug saved enough money to travel throughout˒ Denmark, Germany, and Belgium. 3. My college will not offer several courses I need, such as˒ English 100 and Math 201. 4. We will need to buy˒ a textbook, gloves, and a dissecting kit. 5. OK

Sentence Practice 2, *page 279*

1. Some famous people had dyslexia, such as˒ Leonardo da Vinci, Winston Churchill, Albert Einstein, and George Patton. 2. OK 3. OK 4. Many languages have contributed to English, especially˒ French, Latin, and German. 5. New words in English arise from many sources, including˒ gang culture, popular music, and the computer industry.

Editing Practice 1, *page 280*

My college sponsors various trips for students, including˒ rafting, skiing, and hiking trips. This fall, I am going on one of the hiking trips. There is a fee involved, but it is still an affordable trip. I have to supply my own˒ water container, snacks, and backpack. However, the school provides several things: water, lunch, first-aid kits, and even insect repellent. Some items I definitely plan to leave at home are˒ my cell phone, MP3 player, and credit cards.

I wanted a few of my friends to come, such as˒ my roommate, his brother, and two guys who work with me at the grocery store. They declined. I myself love to go on long walks. Last year, I hiked in several places: northern Alabama, southern Kentucky, and along the coastline in Georgia. Sure, hiking can be a little tedious at times, and you have to be fit to walk several hours a day. However, the rewards include˒ getting away from the noise of the city . . .

LESSON 29: Capitalization

Diagnostic Exercise, *page 284*

My sister is attending a **community college** in Kansas City, and we've been comparing our courses. Her **Spanish** class is much different from mine because hers includes discussion of **Hispanic** cultures. Her teacher, **Professor** Gonzales, . . .

Sentence Practice 1, *page 288*

1. My father has a job teaching **biology** in eastern Delaware. 2. OK 3. OK 4. Students write in almost every class at this **university,** even **physical education** courses. 5. Tenskwatawa was a **Native American** leader who encouraged his people to give up alcohol along with **European** clothing and tools.

Sentence Practice 2, *page 289*

1. In the 1860's, Montana's present **capital,** Helena, was named Last Chance Gulch. 2. OK 3. Did you say that **Aunt** Iva is arriving today? 4. The **Rhone River** and the **Rhine River** both rise out of the Alps of Switzerland. 5. My **grandmother** believes she can meet with the Pope during our visit to Rome.

Editing Practice 1, *page 291*

Last fall we stayed in **New Orleans** for a week. We flew from **Newark** in **New Jersey.** Our trip got off to a bad start because our flight was delayed for two hours because of thunderstorms over the **Appalachians.** We stayed in the **French Quarter,** the oldest part of town. It and the lovely old **Garden District** were not damaged by **Katrina,** the terrible hurricane that did so much damage to the entire **Gulf Coast** . . .

Terrible as it was, we need to bear in mind how much worse the loss of life could have been if not for very accurate forecasting from the **National Hurricane Center** and the **National Weather Service.** For example, compare **Katrina** with the similar hurricane that struck **Galveston** in 1900. That storm killed 8,000 people because there was no ability at the time to monitor off-shore weather. The storm came on shore without any warning at all, killing nearly everyone living along that part of **Texas** where the storm hit.

Unit Nine

LESSON 30: Parallelism

Some answers in this lesson will vary. Sample answers are shown.

Diagnostic Exercise, *page 299*

We all go to college for different reasons — to get an education, meet new people, and **gain** the skills for a job. The best programs are ones that reach several of these goals at the same time. I like to take courses that interest me and **build** skills that will lead to a job. For example, it is great to read about something in a class and then **apply** it in a practical situation. That is why I am doing an internship program. I have the opportunity to get credits, develop professional skills, and **make** important . . .

Sentence Practice 1, *page 302*

1. Before leaving, I have to call my mother, write a report, and **pay** my bills. 2. College gives us a chance to be away from home and **gain** independence. 3. This book will teach you ways to write better, make good grades, and **amuse** your friends. 4. A standard formula for speeches is **to begin** with a joke and to conclude with a summary. 5. Student representatives on committees are required to attend all meetings, **to** take notes, and to report to the student government.

Sentence Practice 2, *page 303*

1. OK 2. I have to put the cat out, water the plants, and ~~to~~ leave a house key with a friend. 3. This semester, I started working at home in the mornings and **doing** my schoolwork later in the afternoons. 4. I do not want you to lose the directions and **become** lost. 5. OK

Editing Practice 1, *page 304*

My boyfriend, Matt, loves talking on his cell phone and **playing** video games. In fact, he seems to do little else. He spends hours doing both at the same time. I talk on my cell and play video games sometimes, but I also like meeting people face to face, going out with friends, and **having** a little variation in what I do. Just last weekend, I had an opportunity to participate in a blood drive and **go** to a baseball game. During that entire time, Matt managed to run up 200 minutes on his cell phone and to complete *Half-Life 2* for the tenth time. This weekend, I plan to watch a movie with our friends, go for a long walk around the park, and **work** in my garden . . .

LESSON 31: Passive Voice

Diagnostic Exercise, *page 308*

Matt's apartment manager called him, wanting to know why he played his music so loudly. **The phone call surprised Matt;** he didn't think his music was loud. He apologized, but he said his radio was playing at only a fourth of its potential volume. Apparently, **this response satisfied the manager. She told Matt** that . . .

Sentence Practice 1, *page 310*

1. Those kids uprooted the plants. 2. Your shouting frightened the children. 3. You broke the television. 4. Your actions hurt me. 5. Eudora Welty wrote the story.

Sentence Practice 2, *page 311*

1. The hungry workers quickly ate the meal. 2. On Monday, a driver who pulled in front of me hit my van. 3. The custodians cleaned all the rooms over the weekend. 4. Another dancer violently bumped my dancing partner. 5. The farmers sprayed the pesticide.

Editing Practice 1, *page 312*

More and more students have chosen urban campuses in the past few years. At my school, like many others, parking and transportation have become big issues for many students. **The school encourages riding the bus,** but that is not practical for everybody. **Riders can use only** a few bus routes. In addition, **nearly everybody takes evening classes.** Bad as the buses are during the day, at night, they are impossible. **The night buses only cover one route**. And that route has only one bus every hour. **If you missed the last bus,** you would . . .

Editing Practice 2, *page 312*

The student council has proposed a new plan. Their idea is that **the school could charter several buses.** These buses would shuttle between the campus and the central bus station downtown. **Passengers can access nearly all the bus routes** from the central station. I think **a lot of students would support this idea. The council is putting forward this plan. The council is forming a committee** to see how many students would be interested in this plan. **If we can persuade a reasonable number of students** to sign . . .

Unit Ten

OVERVIEW: Articles with Geographic Proper Names, *page 318*

No articles for specific mountains or small bodies of water; use *the* **with** the names of mountain ranges and large bodies of water (such as oceans and seas).

LESSON 32: Incorrect Plurals and Indefinite Articles with Noncount Nouns

Diagnostic Exercise, *page 321*

The **modernization** of agriculture has meant a huge increase in just a few crops — **wheat** and **rice** for a̶ human consumption, **corn** for a̶n̶ animal consumption, and **cotton** for industrial **production**. This specialization in a few crops is called a̶ *monoculture*. A̶ Monoculture has some disadvantages: it reduces a̶ biodiversity and requires huge amounts of **energy** and fertilizer.

Sentence Practice 1, *page 323*

1. We studied the country's system of **transportation**. 2. The company hoped to improve its **productivity**. 3. The desks were made out of **metal**. 4. We helped the campers get their **gear** out of the trucks. 5. The amount of trade directly affects the **prosperity** of nations.

Sentence Practice 2, *page 324*

1. Good **planning** gave us good results. 2. During winter we didn't get a̶ sunlight for days. 3. His idea was a̶ complete nonsense. 4. We were not able to get a̶ good information on those topics. 5. News **reporting** during wartime **is** always confusing and misleading.

Editing Practice 1, *page 325*

There is almost nothing more important to **people** than meals and **eating.** Every culture has elaborate rituals connected with **food.** After all, we are all interested in the **nature** of the food we eat. Every culture has its own ideas about what a̶ good nutrition is. For example, in some parts of Asia, food is divided into two groups—"cooling" and "warming." In Japan, for example, eels are eaten during warm **weather** because eels are believed to help cool the **blood.**

LESSON 33: Using *A/An, Some,* and *The*

Diagnostic Exercise, *page 328*

Doctors have long known that we need to have iron in our diets. Recently, however, **a** new study has revealed that we may be getting too much iron. The human body keeps all **the** iron it digests. **The** only way we lose stored iron in **the** body is through bleeding. John Murray, **a** researcher at the University of Minnesota, discovered that people who live on **a** very low iron diet may have **a** greatly reduced risk of **a** heart attack. Another study found that diets high in meat have **a** strong correlation with a high risk of heart disease. Apparently, when people have **a** high level of iron, **[the]**★ excess iron . . . (★raises error count to 10)

Sentence Practice 1, *page 331*

1. Reason: Uniqueness 2. Reason: Defined-by-modifiers 3. Reason: Normal expectations 4. Reason: Defined-by-modifiers 5. Reason: Normal expectations

Sentence Practice 2, *page 332*

1. Reason: Normal expectations 2. Reason: Uniqueness 3. Reason: Defined-by-modifiers 4. Reason: Normal expectations 5. Reason: Defined-by-modifiers

Editing Practice 1, *page 333*

Like many young people just out of school, I recently moved into **an** apartment. I was on my own for the first time. I rented **an** unfurnished apartment because it was a lot cheaper than getting one already furnished. As is normally the case in the United States, **the** apartment came already furnished with **a** stove and refrigerator. (This is not the case in Europe. **Some** friends of mine rented **an** apartment in Rome for **a** semester abroad program. **An** unfurnished apartment there did not even have **a** sink, let alone any kitchen appliances.) I decided that **the** kitchen had to be my highest priority. I bought **a** set of dishes and **some** pots and pans at **a** big chain store. My parents gave me **an** old set of kitchen utensils. I went to Goodwill and got **a** really cheap kitchen table . . .

LESSON 34: Making Generalizations without Articles

Diagnostic Exercise, *page 335*

T̶h̶e̶ **Scientists** have long known that t̶h̶e̶ honeybees are somehow able to tell s̶o̶m̶e̶ other bees where to look for s̶o̶m̶e̶ food. In the 1940's, Karl von Frisch of the University of Munich discovered that the type of t̶h̶e̶ dance that t̶h̶e̶ bees make when they return to their beehive is significant. It seems that t̶h̶e̶ honeybees . . .

Sentence Practice 1, *page 338*

1. Most countries tax t̶h̶e̶ <u>cigarettes</u> and t̶h̶e̶ <u>alcohol</u> heavily.
2. During a heavy storm, t̶h̶e̶ <u>streams</u> often are blocked by t̶h̶e̶ <u>leaves</u> and t̶h̶e̶ other <u>trash</u>.

3. Typically, ~~the~~ employers look for ~~the~~ skilled and trained workers.
4. ~~The~~ Researchers have found that ~~the~~ American diets contain ~~the~~ excess fats.
5. ~~The~~ Detergents work by making ~~the~~ water super wet.

Sentence Practice 2, *page 338*

1. ~~The~~ Substitutions in ~~the~~ recipes often lead to ~~the~~ disasters.
2. ~~The~~ Global warming is becoming a common topic in ~~the~~ academic conferences.
3. Increasingly, ~~the~~ tourism is an important source for ~~the~~ national budgets.
4. ~~The~~ Classical painting is normally divided into ~~the~~ landscapes, ~~the~~ still lifes, and ~~the~~ portraits.
5. In America, unlike ~~the~~ many countries, you can usually get ~~the~~ prescriptions filled at ~~the~~ grocery stores.

Editing Practice 1, *page 340*

Deborah Tannen has written extensively about the different conversational styles of ~~the~~ men and women. Males and females use ~~the~~ casual language in quite different ways, especially when ~~the~~ men are talking to men and ~~the~~ women are talking to women. When ~~the~~ groups of men are in a conversation, each speaker tries to control the topic. The most important tool in gaining and keeping ~~the~~ control is ~~the~~ humor. The humor is usually directed at others in the group, often in the form of ~~the~~ teasing. However, the teasing cannot go too far; it cannot be seen as actually insulting. Being able to be teased without getting angry and then responding in kind is a valued skill. ~~The~~ Verbal competition among groups of young men is a near cultural universal.

Unit Eleven

LESSON 35: The Progressive Tenses

Diagnostic Exercise, *page 349*

Every weekday morning at 6 A.M., my alarm **goes** off. By 6:15, the breakfast dishes are on the table, and the coffee **is brewing.** I always **get** the children up next. It is very hard for them to get going. On Mondays, they **resemble** bears coming out of hibernation. While they **are taking** their showers with their eyes still closed, I get everyone's clothes ready. Since the youngest child still **needs** a lot of help getting dressed, I usually **spend** some extra time with her talking about the day's events. By 7 A.M., we all **are sitting** at the table for breakfast. The children **love** pancakes and waffles, but there just isn't time to make them except on weekends. Breakfast goes by quickly, unless somebody **spills** the milk or juice. I **wish** we had more time in the morning, but every morning I am **amazed** when I **look** back and **realize** that . . .

Sentence Practice 1, *page 352*

1. Hurry up! The train **is leaving** now. 2. I couldn't come to the phone because we **were eating** dinner when you called. 3. Disco **is** still wildly popular in some places in Europe. 4. The book **belongs** to one of my friends. 5. The book **is being** used by one of my friends at the moment.

Sentence Practice 2, *page 353*

1. By this time next year, I **will be working** in New York. 2. As of now, that **seems** to be the best alternative. 3. My roommate always **hated** to get up in the morning. 4. She **is running** an errand right now, but she will be back in just a minute. 5. Hi! I **am returning** your phone call.

Editing Practice 1, *page 354*

I **think** that I would go crazy if I tried to write the way my husband does. I **spend** just as much time on my papers as he does, but I **write** in a completely different way. I **spend** much of my time thinking through what I am going to say before I ever put a word down on paper. When I **feel** that I really know what I want to say, I sit down and write a complete draft. Then I make an outline for what I have written. Often this outline **shows** me where I need to go back and expand an idea or rearrange something. But, on the whole, I **do not need** to make a lot of changes. My husband **thinks** that . . .

LESSON 36: Two-Word Verbs

Diagnostic Exercise, *page 358*

It used to be that making a plane reservation was a simple matter. You found a travel agency and **called it up.** Since the agency didn't work for any airlines, it looked for the best fare and **found it out.** There was no direct cost to you since the airlines paid the commission; they **built it in** to the price of your ticket. After the airlines were deregulated, however, this system began to fall apart. Faced with much greater competition, airlines identified commission costs as an unnecessary expense, and they **cut them down** by reducing the commission they paid agencies. Some airlines, like Southwest, even **cut them out** entirely. As a result, most travel agencies stopped selling tickets for those airlines. If you want to know about their fares, you must deal with each of the airlines separately. The catch, of course, is that if you call one of them, its representative can talk only about its fares, and you have no way to **check it out** to see if you have the best bargain.

Sentence Practice 1, *page 362*

1. She emphasized the point to **get it across.** 2. OK 3. I promised to **pay them back.** 4. The news **cheered them up** enormously. 5. We promised to **bring them back** as soon as we could.

Sentence Practice 2, *page 363*

1. Jason really liked her, so he **asked her out.** 2. I don't believe what he said. I think he just **dreamed it up.** 3. They are afraid that they **let us down.** 4. The project didn't get full funding, so we had to **scale it back.** 5. He was **punished for it.**

Editing Practice 1, *page 364*

I have two papers due this week, but I can't just **dash them off** like some people (like my wife, for example). I really have to take my time and **plan them out.** I need to get a bunch of ideas together and then **write them down.** Then, I have to **work them up** into some kind of logical order. Sometimes, when I am trying to work out the relationship of a number of half-formed ideas, I find it helps to **copy them out** onto 3" × 5" cards. Then I can **sort them out** in a number of different ways until I get a clear picture of what I am trying to say. Then I put my key ideas into a few short sentences so that I can **sum them up** simply and clearly. If I can't summarize my ideas for myself, I certainly can't **get them across** . . .

LESSON 37: Information Questions

Diagnostic Exercise, *page 367*

ANNA: When **does your flight leave?**
MARIA: At 6:15. Why **are you** so worried? We're not going to be late, are we?
ANNA: I don't think so, but how long **does** it **take** to get to the airport?
MARIA: It depends on the traffic. If the roads are crowded, it will take an hour.
ANNA: How soon **will you** be ready to leave?
MARIA: Don't get upset. I'm nearly done packing now. Have you seen my alarm clock?
ANNA: I don't know where it is. When **did** you **use** it last?

MARIA: For my interview, two days ago. Here it is in the dresser drawer.
ANNA: Where **did I leave** the car keys?
MARIA: Come on! Now you're the one who is going to make us late. Why **didn't we** get started sooner?

Sentence Practice 1, *page 370*

1. Who **did** you **talk** to? 2. Where **did** Sara **find** the books? 3. When **do/did** we plan to leave? 4. Why **didn't** they bring their lunches? 5. How soon **can** you be ready?

Sentence Practice 2, *page 371*

1. Why **did** the library **close** early last Saturday? 2. Who **should** we thank for the party? 3. Where **did** you **park** the car? 4. Why **didn't** you ask? 5. OK

Editing Practice 1, *page 372*

ANNA: What **will** you do when you get back home?
MARIA: The usual things. Why **do** you want to know?
ANNA: No reason. I'm just asking.
MARIA: I think that I will spend most of my time catching up on my writing assignments.
ANNA: What **do** you have to work on?
MARIA: I have to write a paper for my linguistics class.
ANNA: What **is** it about?
MARIA: How children acquire language.
ANNA: Who **are** you going to see?
MARIA: Nobody. Why **do** you keep asking?
ANNA: I called home last night.
MARIA: Oh, who **did** you **talk** to?
ANNA: I talked to Aunt Josie. Guess what she said?
MARIA: I don't know. Anyway, why **should I** . . .

LESSON 38: Word Order in Noun Clauses

Diagnostic Exercise, *page 375*

Many non-Americans ask why the American court system **is** so cumbersome. To understand that, you need to know something about where ~~did~~ it **came** from and how ~~did~~ it **evolved**. Until the Revolutionary War, the American legal system was exactly what the British legal system **was**. Despite the many advantages of the British legal system, colonial Americans felt that the British had used the powers of the government to override the rights of individual citizens. This deep distrust of the ability of the government to use its power fairly explains why the American system **is** so heavily weighted in favor of the defendant. Often court cases in the United States are fought on the ground of what admissible government evidence **is**.

Sentence Practice 1, *page 378*

1. I realized **what I needed to do.** 2. We couldn't agree on **which movie we wanted to see.** 3. They asked us **when the plane left.** 4. **Why that is a wrong answer** seemed obvious to the whole class. 5. **How you dress** tells a lot about you.

Sentence Practice 2, *page 378*

1. It depends on **how you felt about it.** 2. OK 3. You can leave **what you don't like.** 4. We were surprised at **how late it was.** 5. **What they did** was very important to all of us.

Editing Practice 1, *page 379*

One of the many big changes in how we **can** teach writing has been to look at writing as a topic in its own right. For more than a decade now, there has been substantial research on how ~~do~~ students learn to write and what the difference **is** between the way good and poor writers go about the process of writing. Perhaps the most helpful finding is that good writers go through a definite two-step process. What ~~do~~ they write first is an exploration of the topic. Often it starts as a crude draft that wouldn't make much sense to anybody but the writer. But apparently it is how we **are** able to think through what ~~do~~ we want to say. It is really important to get to the point where the writer **can** boil down the key ideas in a few sentences. This first step in the cycle results in a draft that has all the key ideas worked out. The second step in the cycle is a semifinal draft that is very sensitive to how the paper **will** make sense to the audience. Here is where an outline **is** critical . . .

Index

If English is not your first language, you may find the ESL index helpful. (The ESL index follows this main index.)

ESL Index

If English is not your first language, you may have noticed the icon (ESL) as you flipped through this book for the first time. This index offers an alphabetical listing of topics that may be especially challenging for non-native speakers of English.

Correction Symbols

Many instructors use correction symbols to point out grammar, usage, and writing problems. This chart lists common symbols and directs you to the help that you need to revise and edit your writing. The numbers below refer you to specific lessons in this book.

art	article	32, 33, 34
cap	capitalization	29
coord	coordination	15
cs	comma splice (run-on)	2
dm	dangling modifier	13
frag	sentence fragment	1
fs	fused sentence (run-on)	2
mm	misplaced modifier (misplaced and squinting adverb)	14
no ꝟ	unnecessary apostrophe	24
pass	passive voice	31
plan	further planning needed	40
pron agr	pronoun agreement	8
pron case	pronoun case	10, 11
pron ref	pronoun reference	9
revise	further revision needed	42
run-on	run-on	2
sexist pron	sexist pronoun	12
shift	verb tense shift	6
sp	spelling	Appendix D
s-v agr	subject-verb agreement	3, 4, 5
trans	transition	16, 42
ts	topic sentence/thesis statement	40, 41
usage	wrong word	Appendix C
vf	verb form	36
vt	verb tense	6, 7, 35
⌃,	comma	15, 16, 17, 18, 19, 20
//	faulty parallelism	30
:	colon	28
;	semicolon	27
ꝟ	apostrophe	21, 22, 23
" "	quotation marks	25, 26
¶	new paragraph	40, 41
⌃	insert	
___ or ⟋	delete	
⊃⊂	close up space	
⁀	reverse words or letters	